1990
Cycle A

AN ALMANAC OF PARISH LITURGY

SOURCEBOOK

FOR SUNDAYS AND SEASONS

Peter Mazar

Peter Scagnelli
Fred Moleck

LITURGY TRAINING PUBLICATIONS

Liturgy Training Publications
1800 North Hermitage Avenue
Chicago IL 60622-1101
Editorial offices: 312/486-8970
Order phone: 312/486-7008
FAX: 312/489-7094

Printed in the United States of America.

Copy editing by Theresa Pincich.
Editorial assistance by Karen Schonbachler.
Illustrations by Evelyn Grala.
Cover design by Ana M. Stephenson.
Book design by Jane Kremsreiter.
Typesetting by Mark Hollopeter.

ISBN 0-929650-03-4

CONTENTS

46 Lent
Official description ◆ Resources for Lent, Triduum and Eastertime ◆
A sense of the season ◆ Preparing the parish ◆ Words ◆ Vesture
◆ The Mass ◆ Music ◆ The worship environment ◆ Other ritual prayer ◆
Sample prayer texts ◆ Sample bulletin insert for before Lent ◆ A penitential
procession for the First Sunday of Lent

65 Triduum
Official description ◆ A sense of the season ◆ Preparing the parish ◆
Vesture ◆ The worship environment ◆ The paschal fast ◆ Holy Thursday
Evening: The Mass of the Lord's Supper ◆ Good Friday Afternoon:
The Celebration of the Passion of the Lord ◆ Holy Saturday: The Paschal Sabbath
◆ The Easter Vigil: Nightwatch of the Resurrection ◆ Easter Sunday ◆
Sample Triduum schedule ◆ Sample bulletin insert for before the Triduum

95 Eastertime
Official description ◆ A sense of the season ◆ Preparing the parish ◆
Words ◆ Vesture ◆ The Mass ◆ Music ◆ The worship environment ◆
Other ritual prayer ◆ Sample prayer texts ◆ A vigil service for Pentecost Eve

112 Ordinary Time
Official description ◆ Resources for Ordinary Time and for the Lord's
Day ◆ A sense of Ordinary Time ◆ Preparing the parish ◆ Vesture ◆
The Mass ◆ Music ◆ Suggested parish repertory for Ordinary Time ◆
The worship environment ◆ Other ritual prayer ◆ Sample prayer texts
◆ An introduction and outline of the Gospel of Matthew in Ordinary Time

THE CALENDAR

Sourcebook for Sundays and Seasons is put together in the style of an almanac: We bring back much from previous years, updated and enriched. We add new material, which is why the book keeps getting fatter. And—often in response to readers' suggestions—we keep trying to improve the way the varied information in this book is organized.

An almanac is the work of many people in many places over many years. Most immediately, this book has been shaped by four contributors. Peter Scagnelli is a priest of the diocese of Providence, director of the worship office for that diocese, a translator and an author. He has contributed much of the original "layer" of this book and has added a wealth of sample texts, introductions and orders of service—either newly composed or carefully selected and translated from several non-English sacramentaries. Fred Moleck is a musician whose editorial skills are seen in *Worship*, third edition, and whose pastoral work has been done in parishes and diocesan workshops throughout the United States. He has contributed much of the information on music and its place in liturgy. Evelyn Grala is a Chicago artist. Her botanical drawings throughout the calendar are plants that folklore has associated with particular feasts or seasons. Finally, Peter Mazar is the editor at LTP who has brought together these strands and others, woven in much of his own work, and produced a volume that should be a parish treasure for the work of liturgy in 1990.

Great thanks also go to Theresa Pincich and Karen Schonbachler for their tremendous editorial work, as well as to Jane Kremsreiter, Ana Stephenson, Mark Hollopeter and Julianne Clark for the production of this book.

—Gabe Huck

INTRODUCTION

This *Sourcebook* aims at nurturing a realization that there is no present or future without a past. We can look forward only as much as we look back. Our liturgical preparation, creativity and adaptation presume an understanding of the rituals, the material things, the music and the words—the tradition—that have developed throughout our history. Liturgical tradition, however, no matter how sensitively it looks to the past and is handed on to the future, can never replace an equally committed sense of spirituality—of mystical prayer—and a sense of parish—of the people who form the assembly. Good pastoral practice must be rooted in such a sense of tradition and prayer and people.

This book is divided into three sections: Resources, the Seasons and the Calendar:

RESOURCES

In this section we suggest resources for the sacristy library and the home reference shelf. This section also includes a few sources for the many material things used in worship, from incense to icons.

THE SEASONS

Part 2 of this *Sourcebook* deals first with the two great seasons in our year: Advent-Christmastime and Lent-Triduum-Eastertime. Then we discuss the year itself, the "Ordinary Time." These pages contain seasonal bibliographies, lively introductions, music and art notes, a general approach to the Masses and other liturgies during each season. This material gives planners an opportunity to consider an overall approach to a season while at the same time calling attention to the options in our ritual books, especially the sacramentary. There are sample prayer texts—such as the general intercessions—drawn mainly from the current Italian, Spanish and Polish missals, as well as outlines for such special observances as Christmas Eve or the Pentecost Vigil.

THE CALENDAR

The calendar includes information for every day of the year. The thin column consists of dates, days of the week, solemnities, feasts and memorials, the Jewish festivals, the national days and other secular observances, as well as citations of the assigned and optional readings for the Mass of the day with their lectionary numbers. The wide column of the calendar includes points about preparation of the liturgy for specific days.

Two keys to using the calendar are these:

1. Become familiar with "The Seasons"—the general information—before delving into "The Calendar"—the specific information. For example, preparing the Third Sunday of Lent begins by reading over the Lent part of "The Seasons" before reading the entry in "The Calendar" for this Sunday.

2. Work weeks and months ahead. It is too late if you read about Christmas on the Third Sunday of Advent. Read ahead and devise a way to make this calendar mesh with your own, with the liturgy committee's, with the parish's.

Resources: Publications

This resource list was put together by Peter Scagnelli and by the editors at LTP and has been upgraded to include many entries in Austin Fleming's resource list found in *Liturgy 80* (May/June 1989). In the following listings, especially in classifying publications that deal with Sunday worship, it was difficult to decide whether a particular book would fall under the category of "commentaries," "history" or "pastorally oriented works."

Ritual Books

These are the basic texts that should be part of the sacristy library of every Roman Catholic parish.

The Lectionary for Mass. The complete edition (various publishers, first published in 1970) and the Sunday edition remain in use. A new introduction, however, appeared in Latin in 1981 and is published by the Bishops' Committee on the Liturgy. This introduction is a clear statement of the structure and importance of our lectionary. It should be familiar to all who prepare the liturgy.

The Sacramentary, 1985 edition. This has been published by Catholic Book Publishing and by The Liturgical Press. The 1985 edition replaced the 1974 text and is to be used as the currently approved text. Those who prepare liturgy must be "at home" in the sacramentary. Certainly it is a book in need of improvement in many ways. Some of that will come in a new edition being readied for publication in the 1990s. But even as it is, the sacramentary is a rich resource with a great wealth of prayer texts that deserve our attention.

Book of Blessings. Has a vast number of seasonal and occasional blessings in a new format derived from the Latin *De Benedictionibus,* scheduled for publication in autumn of 1989.

Catholic Household Blessings and Prayers (United States Catholic Conference [USCC], 1988). The "ritual book" for the home. On many appropriate occasions throughout the year, be sure to call the parish's attention to relevant parts of this important book and make it readily available in your parish for purchase.

Holy Communion and Worship of the Eucharist outside Mass (1974).

Liturgical Calendar. The Bishops' Committee on the Liturgy publishes a calendar for the U.S.A. complete with the citations of the readings for every day as well as ordo information (e.g., vestment colors, use of the Gloria and Creed). Available from the USCC.

The Liturgy of the Hours (4 volumes). The complete and rather expensive edition. A number of publishers have a one-volume adaptation called *Christian Prayer.* The Daughters of St. Paul offers a companion volume, *The Office of Readings.* The *General Instruction on the Liturgy of the Hours* gives wide flexibility to those who plan and preside at communal celebrations. The basic guideline seems to be: "Whatever you have to do to introduce the people to this form of prayer and get them to do it—especially on Sundays and feast days—*do it!*" Published by LTP, *Morning and Evening Prayer in the Parish* (by Lawrence Mayer, 1985) provides a simple, singable way for people to pray a form of the church's morning and evening offices. Leaders' books and participants' cards are available. *Praise God in Song* is a very useful collection of ecumenical settings for Morning, Evening and Night Prayer published by GIA.

Order of Christian Funerals. A completely revised and pastorally rearranged rite from ICEL replaces the *Rite of Funerals;* it is scheduled for publica-

tion in the autumn of 1989. Study editions will be available in 1990.

Pastoral Care of the Sick: Rites of Anointing and Viaticum (1983). The book is available in a sanctuary-size, hardbound edition for public worship and a plastic-bound pocket size for hospital visits.

Rite of Baptism for Children (1970).

Rite of Christian Initiation of Adults (1988). The RCIA has been mandatory in the U.S.A. since September 1, 1988.

Rite of Marriage (1970).

Rite of Penance (1976).

Liturgical Documents

The Code of Canon Law (Canon Law Society of America) contains a good deal of ecclesial legislation pertaining to the celebration of the liturgy. Pastoral decisions can be enhanced by knowledge of the appropriate canons.

Documents on the Liturgy, 1963–1979: Conciliar, Papal, and Curial Texts (Collegeville: The Liturgical Press, 1982). A fine translation and compilation of everything official. The massive and detailed index makes this a goldmine of information.

The Liturgy Documents (Chicago: LTP, 1985 edition). The most recent (and more accurate) translations of Roman liturgical documents along with documents of the Bishops' Committee on the Liturgy.

Study Editions, Commentaries, Missals

And You Visited Me: Pastoral Care of the Sick by Charles Gusmer (New York: Pueblo Publishing Co., 1984). A blending of history, theology and pastoral insights.

Christian Initiation of Adults: A Commentary is principally authored by Barbara O'Dea (Washington, D.C.: USCC, 1985).

Christians at Prayer edited by John Gallen (Notre Dame: University of Notre Dame Press, 1977).

Commentaries on the Rite of Christian Initiation of Adults edited by James Wilde (Chicago: LTP, 1988).

The Death of a Christian: The Rite of Funerals by Richard Rutherford (New York: Pueblo Publishing Co., 1980).

Disputed Questions in the Liturgy Today by John Huels (Chicago: LTP, 1988).

Liturgical Law: An Introduction by John Huels (Washington, D.C.: The Pastoral Press, 1988).

Liturgy with Style and Grace. The revised edition of Gabe Huck's work from LTP: practical information for every liturgical minister and for those who must train people for ministerial service in the community.

New Liturgy, New Laws by R. Kevin Seasoltz (Collegeville: The Liturgical Press, 1980).

One Table, Many Laws: Essays on Catholic Eucharistic Practice by John Huels (Collegeville: The Liturgical Press, 1986).

Parish Funerals: A Guide to the Order of Christian Funerals by Michael Marchal (Chicago: LTP, 1987).

Reconciled Sinners: Healing Human Brokenness by Bernard Cooke (Mystic, Connecticut: Twenty-third Publications, 1986).

Reconciliation: The Continuing Agenda edited by Robert Kennedy (Collegeville: The Liturgical Press, 1987).

The Reconciling Community: The Rite of Penance by James Dallen (New York: Pueblo Publishing Co., 1986).

The Rites (1976), *The Rites II* (1980), *The Rites IA* (1988). (New York: Pueblo Publishing Co.). A handy compendium of just about every rite of the church (books for study, not for ritual use).

CONTINUED

Saint Andrew Bible Missal (Brooklyn: William J. Hirten Co., 1982). Contains insightful introductions to the liturgical seasons and to the readings as well as attention to Christian initiation. Perhaps the finest English missal available.

Study Text 2: Pastoral Care of the Sick and Dying, revised edition (Washington, D.C.: USCC, 1984).

To Give Thanks and Praise: General Instruction of the Roman Missal with Commentary for Musicians and Priests (1980), and *To Hear and Proclaim: Introduction to the Lectionary for Mass with Commentary for Musicians and Priests* (1983), both by Ralph Keifer (Washington, D.C.: The Pastoral Press). Readable, sensible, for *all* parish ministers.

To Join Together: The Rite of Marriage by Kenneth Stevenson (New York: Pueblo Publishing Co., 1987).

The Word and Eucharist Handbook by Lawrence Johnson (San Jose: Resource Publications, 1986).

On the History, Theology and Spirituality of Liturgy

At That Time: Cycles and Seasons in the Life of a Christian edited by James Wilde (Chicago: LTP, 1989).

Called to Prayer: Liturgical Spirituality Today edited by Lawrence Johnson (Collegeville: The Liturgical Press, 1986).

Christian Worship in East and West by Herman Wegman (New York: Pueblo Publishing Co., 1985).

The Church at Prayer by A. G. Martimort, et al., vol. 1, Principles of the Liturgy; vol. 2, The Eucharist; vol. 3, The Sacraments; vol. 4, The Liturgy and Time (Collegeville: The Liturgical Press, 1986). This comprehensive series is highly recommended.

The Eucharistic Prayers of the Roman Rite by Enrico Mazza (New York: Pueblo Publishing Co., 1986).

The Liturgy of the Hours in East and West by Robert Taft, SJ (Collegeville: The Liturgical Press, 1986). Parts of this book may be intimidating in their detailed scholarship, but most of this book offers profound insights into the heart of the rites of daily prayer.

The Shape of the Liturgy, the classic text by Dom Gregory Dix, has been reprinted and updated by way of notes from Paul Marshall (San Francisco: Harper and Row, 1982).

A Short History of the Western Liturgy by Theodore Klauser (New York: Oxford University Press, 1979).

The Study of the Liturgy by Cheslyn Jones, et al. (New York: Oxford University Press, 1978).

Pastorally Oriented Works for Preparing Liturgy

Celebrating Marriage: Preparing the Wedding Liturgy edited by Paul Covino (Washington, D.C.: The Pastoral Press, 1987).

The Communion Rite at Sunday Mass by Gabe Huck (Chicago: LTP, 1989). A practical and thorough discussion of doing this rite well every Sunday.

Elements of Rite by Aidan Kavanagh (New York: Pueblo Publishing Co., 1982).

Groundwork: Planning Liturgical Seasons by Yvonne Cassa and Joanne Sanders (Chicago: LTP, 1982).

Handbook for Cantors by Diana Kodner Sotak (Chicago: LTP, 1988).

How Not to Say Mass by Dennis C. Smolarski (Mahwah, New Jersey: Paulist Press, 1986).

How to Form a Parish Liturgy Board by Yvonne Cassa and Joanne Sanders (Chicago: LTP, 1987).

CONTINUED

Introducing Dance in Christian Worship coauthored by Ronald Gagne, Thomas Kane and Robert VerEecke (Washington, D.C.: The Pastoral Press, 1984).

Liturgy Made Simple by Mark Searle (Collegeville: The Liturgical Press, 1981).

The Ministers of Music by Lawrence Johnson (Washington, D.C.: The Pastoral Press, 1983).

Persons in Liturgical Celebrations by Lucien Deiss (Schiller Park, Illinois: World Library Publications, 1978).

Parish: A Place for Worship edited by Mark Searle (Collegeville: The Liturgical Press, 1981).

Parish Weddings by Austin Fleming (Chicago: LTP, 1987). How weddings are done in the larger order of parish liturgy.

Preparing for Liturgy by Austin Fleming (Washington, D.C.: The Pastoral Press, 1985).

Story of the Mass by the Canadian Conference of Catholic Bishops (originally published as *National Bulletin on Liturgy,* no. 54, 1976). Available from the Priests of the Sacred Heart, Hales Corners WI 53130, Form 7-2. Traces origins and development of each part of the Mass.

Strong, Loving and Wise: Presiding in Liturgy by Robert Hovda (Collegeville: The Liturgical Press, 1976).

Workbook for Lectors and Gospel Readers (LTP, annual). Each Sunday's readings with background notes and interpretive helps.

Periodicals

Assembly (Notre Dame: Center for Pastoral Liturgy). Five times a year. Each issue explores the tradition and practice of some aspect of the liturgical event in order to help the community and its ministers enter more deeply into the spirit of the liturgy.

Bishops' Committee on the Liturgy Newsletter (Washington, D.C.: USCC). Ten times a year.

Catechumenate: A Journal of Christian Initiation (Chicago: LTP). Six times a year.

Environment and Art Letter (Chicago: LTP). Monthly.

Liturgy (Washington, D.C.: The Liturgical Conference). Quarterly. The Journal of The Liturgical Conference, an ecumenical organization. Each issue explores a single aspect of liturgy, taking in many disciplines and many church traditions. Back issues are available and are excellent resources.

Liturgy 90 (Chicago: LTP). Eight times a year. Features articles on the seasons and sacraments, regular columns on music, environment and art, questions and answers.

Pastoral Music (Washington, D.C.: National Association of Pastoral Musicians). Six times a year. Often several major articles on a single theme together with reviews and announcements. Centers on music but touches on all areas of liturgy.

Worship (Collegeville: The Order of Saint Benedict). Six times a year. Scholarly journal that since 1926 has been the primary support of liturgical renewal throughout the English-speaking world.

For additional lists of resources on preparing the liturgies of the seasons, see page 11 in this Sourcebook *for Advent-Christmastime, and page 46 for Lent-Triduum-Eastertime.*

Canadian Resources

The church in Canada has an established reputation for publishing fine liturgical materials in French and English. These include:

Guidelines for Pastoral Liturgy: Liturgical Calendar. An ordo and so much more! The layout, typography and artwork—not to mention the fine pas-

CONTINUED

torally oriented content—show what can be done with the annual necessity of the ordo. When the sacramentary has exclusive language, there are entries under the appropriate dates with alternative readings to render the texts inclusive. Some of these will be noted in this *Sourcebook*.

Marriage Ritual. In addition to the rite itself, an introduction provides pastoral notes on preparing the liturgy; the appendices provide everything from the blessing of engagements and anniversaries to the old "exhortation before marriage" beloved by so many generations of English-speaking brides and grooms. French-speaking parishes may be interested in the eucharistic prayer for celebrations of marriage.

National Bulletin on Liturgy (Ottawa: National Liturgical Office). Now published four times a year. Each issue explores one topic in detail, often with extensive bibliographies. Many of the "thematic" back issues of this fine journal are still available.

All Canadian publications are available from the Publications Service of the Canadian Conference of Catholic Bishops. Some titles are available on a one-copy-only basis for study purposes.

Ecumenical Resources

Some Byzantine-rite Catholic resources are available from Alleluia Press. Orthodox liturgical books are available from St. Vladimir's Seminary Press (who publish the works of such important liturgical writers as Thomas Hopko, Alexander Schmemann and Kallistos Ware). The small people's participation booklets from the Orthodox Church in America are a valuable resource, especially for the introductions by such writers as Schmemann and Hopko.

Liturgical renewal has been carried out in the Episcopal and Lutheran communions, and this Sourcebook *makes several references to four ecumenical resources in par-*

ticular that contain much material that may be serviceable where options are permitted and that should be in the parish's desk-reference library for liturgy:

The Book of Common Prayer. The Episcopal church's worship book, available from the Church Hymnal Corporation, contains excellent translations of many Roman collects, fine litanies, and a psalter that avoids at least some exclusive language.

The Book of Occasional Services, second edition (1988). A companion volume to *The Book of Common Prayer,* filled with supplementary material for the seasons, pastoral rituals, blessings of persons, etc.

Lesser Feasts and Fasts. Another companion volume to the above with collects for saints' days and helpful biographical material on many of the saints we celebrate in common.

The Lutheran Book of Worship: Ministers' Desk Edition. Available from Augsburg Publishing House or a Fortress bookstore. As the "rubrical guide" of a communion renewing its ritual life, the pastoral notes provide insights on the how and why of celebration as well as a fine collection of texts.

Three ecumenical resources from Pueblo Publishing Company that are useful for all three cycles of the Roman, Episcopal and Lutheran lectionaries are:

Lectionary for the Christian People (1986, 1987, 1988), edited by Gail Ramshaw and Gordon Lathrop, an inclusive-language emendation of the *Revised Standard Version Bible.* The RSV itself is one of the three translations of scriptures approved for liturgical proclamation in Roman Catholic parishes.

Intercessions for the Christian People (1988).

Homilies for the Christian People (1989).

Resources:
Addresses of Publishers

Alleluia Press
Box 103
Allendale NJ 07401-0103

Augsburg Publishing House
Fortress Press
PO Box 1209
Minneapolis MN 55440

Catholic Book Publishing Company
257 West 17th Street
New York NY 10011

Center for Pastoral Liturgy
PO Box 81
Notre Dame IN 46556

Church Hymnal Corporation
800 Second Avenue
New York NY 10017

GIA Publications
7404 South Mason Avenue
Chicago IL 60638

Michael Glazier Inc.
1935 West Fourth Street
Wilmington DE 19805

The Liturgical Conference
1017 12th Street NW
Washington DC 20005

The Liturgical Press
St. John's Abbey
Collegeville MN 56321

Liturgy Training Publications
1800 North Hermitage Avenue
Chicago IL 60622-1101

NALR (North American Liturgy
Resources)
10802 North 23rd Avenue
Phoenix AZ 85029

NPM (National Association of
Pastoral Musicians)
The Pastoral Press
225 Sheridan Street NW
Washington DC 20011

National Catholic Reporter
Publishing Company
Sheed and Ward
115 East Armour Boulevard
Kansas City MO 64141

OCP Publications
5536 NE Hassalo
Portland OR 97213

Oxford University Press
200 Madison Avenue
New York NY 10016

Paulist Press
992 Macarthur Boulevard
Mahwah NJ 07430

Publications Service, Canadian
Conference of Catholic Bishops
90 Parent Avenue
Ottawa, Ontario K1N 7B1, Canada

Pueblo Publishing Company
100 West 32nd Street
New York NY 10001-3210

Resource Publications
160 East Virginia Street, #290
San Jose CA 95112

St. Vladimir's Seminary Press
575 Scarsdale Road
Crestwood NY 10707

Twenty-third Publications
185 Willow Street
PO Box 180
Mystic CT 06355

USCC (United States Catholic
Conference)
3211 Fourth Street, NE
Washington DC 20017-1194

World Library Publications
3815 North Willow Road
Schiller Park IL 60176

Resources: Material Things

A good working relationship with your local church supply stores means not just perusing the catalogs, but calling or visiting and asking a lot of questions of the stores and of the diocesan worship office. Eventually you will be able to learn the best local (and national) suppliers of breads, wines, palms, candles, incense, vesture and vessels. Actually, the word "suppliers" is wrong here; rather, you want to get in touch with craftspeople and artists—and these people may or may not be represented by the local stores. It's never a matter of one-stop shopping. Of course, especially if the parish is building or renovating, a wide range of artists, consultants and craftspeople will be needed. See LTP's *Environment and Art Letter* for introductions to some noteworthy liturgical artisans.

Bread

Ideally, the parish has evolved a ministry of bread baking (see the recipe on page 25) or at least supports this ministry by purchasing breads from a local religious community. Often this purchase supports another ministry, such as work with the deaf. Upgrading the quality of breads to make them more like real food involves a continuing dialogue with the bakers. Flavorful unleavened breads can be purchased from:

Benedictine Convent, Altar Bread Department, Clyde MO 64432.

Santa Rita Abbey, HCR Box 929, Sonoita AZ 85637.

St. Michael Altar Bread distributed by Altar Bread Agency, Meyer-Vogelpohl, 717 Race Street, Cincinnati OH 45202.

Clip Art

Clip art is often used to grace worship folders and parish bulletins. Are you familiar with the "public domain" designs and illustrations in the many books of the Dover Pictorial Archive Series, Dover Publications, Inc., 31 East Second Street, Mineola NY 11501? Also useful are these other books of reproducible art with liturgical themes:

Clip Art for Celebrations and Service by Gertrud Mueller Nelson (Pueblo Publishing Co., 1987).

Clip Art for Feasts and Seasons by Gertrud Mueller Nelson (Pueblo Publishing Co., 1982).

Clip Art for Feasts and Seasons by Helen Siegl (Pueblo Publishing Co., 1984).

Clip Art for the Liturgical Year by Clemens Schmidt (The Liturgical Press, 1988).

Eye Contact with God through Pictures by Ade Bethune (Sheed and Ward, 1986).

Liturgical Art by Meinrad Craighead (Sheed and Ward, 1988).

Fragrances

Whether to add a few drops to punch up the aroma of sacred chrism, or to daub in protected places (to avoid contact with clothing) around the church building on great feasts, oil-based fragrances are part of the olfactory traditions of christening. Flower oils are often found in apothecaries and East Indian grocers.

Holy Transfiguration Monastery, 278 Warren Street, Brookline MA 02146 offers a number of scented oils for liturgical use.

Bethlehem Chrism fragrance is a mixture of flower and herb oils especially suited to Eastertime. Balsam fragrance is better suited to Christmastime. Both are available from:

Maria G. Arctander, 6665 Valley View Boulevard, Las Vegas NV 89118, or may also be ordered through LTP.

Icons

In Orthodox and Eastern Catholic parishes, icons of the great feasts are displayed as nonverbal invitations to celebrate the

CONTINUED

mystery at hand. See Henri J. M. Nouwen's fine book Behold the Beauty of the Lord: Praying with Icons *(Ave Maria Press) for ideas on how your community's personal and communal prayer life could be enhanced by prayerful attentiveness to the power of an icon. If you cannot find a place near you that provides such icons, you might write these places for a catalog:*

Bridge Building Icons, PO Box 1048, Burlington VT 05401. Among the icons available are particularly beautiful icon prints of such modern-day holy people as Mohandas Gandhi, Dorothy Day and Martin Luther King, Jr.

Eastern Christian Supply Company, PO Box 677, Etna CA 96027.

Holy Transfiguration Monastery, 278 Warren Street, Brookline MA 02146.

Monastery Icons, 3500 Coltrane Road, Oklahoma City OK 73121.

St. Vladimir's Seminary Press, 575 Scarsdale Road, Crestwood NY 10707.

Sisters of the Divine Master, 215 South Los Angeles Street, Los Angeles CA 90012; 213/680-9197. They offer a series of 20 splendid prints of Fra Angelico paintings, corresponding to the feasts and seasons of the liturgical year (including fine notes by Adrian Nocent).

Incense

Suppliers of incense are many; however, here are a few that offer a wide range of fragrances so that each season can be celebrated with a characteristic aroma:

Eastern Christian Supply Company, PO Box 677, Etna CA 96027.

Holy Savior Priory, Tower Hill, Pineville SC 29468.

Holy Transfiguration Monastery, 278 Warren Street, Brookline MA 02146.

Monastery Incense, Route 1 Box 75, Geneva NE 68361, (402) 759-4952.

Vessels

The parish would do well to commission an artist to produce its liturgical vessels. Matching sets of communion cups and sizable bread plates are often a need. If possible, the vessels can change with the seasons, employing the many materials suited to our worship, for example, pottery, woods, wicker, pewter, glass, ceramics and precious metals. (Liturgical vessels include not only communion ware, but such things as censers, water buckets, oil containers, ash bowls, pots to hold flowers or baskets to collect lenten alms.) Handsome vessels, most notably in glass, are available from:

Meyer-Vogelpohl, Ray H. Meyer Company, Inc., 717 Race Street, Cincinnati OH 45202.

Vesture

Again, there are an enormous number of vestment makers. Local artists should be tapped if they have developed their craft in the spirit of Environment and Art in Catholic Worship, *paragraphs 93–95, especially these words: "The more these vestments fulfill their function by their color, design and enveloping form, the less they will need the signs, slogans and symbols an unkind history has fastened upon them."*

A few vestment companies that have often done splendid work are:

The Holy Rood Guild, St. Joseph's Abbey, Spencer MA 01562.

Maison Bouvrier, Inc., 391 Hanlan Road, Woodbridge, Ontario, Canada L4L 3T1.

Stadelmaier Nijmegen, Box 1011, 6501 BA, Nijmegen, Holland.

THE SEASONS

ADVENT
★
CHRISTMASTIME

ADVENT

OFFICIAL DESCRIPTION

Advent has a twofold character: as a season to prepare for Christmas when Christ's first coming to us is remembered; as a season when that remembrance directs the mind and heart to await Christ's second coming at the end of time. Advent is thus a period for devout and joyful expectation. (*General Norms for the Liturgical Year and Calendar,* #39)

RESOURCES

The following bibliography is useful for both Advent and Christmastime. These seasons are truly parts of a single season and must be prepared together.

Historical Background

Adam, Adolf. *The Liturgical Year* (New York: Pueblo Publishing Co., 1981).

Cobb, Peter G. "1. The History of the Christian Year," under "The Calendar," *The Study of the Liturgy,* Cheslyn Jones, Geoffrey Wainwright, Edward Yarnold, eds. (New York: Oxford University Press, 1978).

Martimort, A. G., et al. *The Church at Prayer,* vol. 4: *The Liturgy and Time* (Collegeville: The Liturgical Press, 1986, new edition).

Nocent, Adrian, OSB. *The Liturgical Year,* vol. 1 (Collegeville: The Liturgical Press, 1977).

Talley, Thomas J. *The Origins of the Liturgical Year* (New York: Pueblo Publishing Co., 1986).

Liturgical/Preaching Help

Brown, Raymond. *An Adult Christ at Christmas* (Collegeville: The Liturgical Press, 1975, 1977). An excellent condensation of his epic work, *The Birth of the Messiah*.

Hopko, Thomas. *The Winter Pascha* (Crestwood, New York: St. Vladimir's Seminary Press, 1984). Although references are to the Byzantine Nativity observance, there is much material here that will be valuable to Christians of the Western rites.

Lawrence, Emeric, OSB. *Jesus Present and Coming* (Collegeville: The Liturgical Press, 1982). The author consistently sets the scriptural text within the liturgical context in a very readable and concise way.

Merton, Thomas. *Seasons of Celebration* (New York: Farrar, Straus and Giroux, reprinted 1983).

Nocent, Adrian, OSB. *The Liturgical Year,* vol. 1 (Collegeville: The Liturgical Press, 1977) "Advent," 27–94 (biblical and liturgical reflections) and 95–167 (structure and themes). See charts of the weekday readings: Daily Mass/hours congregations will like these. "Christmas," 181–229 (biblical and liturgical reflections) and 230–47 (structure and themes). "Epiphany," 257–301 (biblical and liturgical reflections) and 302–25 (structure and themes).

O'Gorman, Thomas, ed. *An Advent Sourcebook* (Chicago: Liturgy Training Publications, 1988). Texts of all kinds from over the centuries to enliven the many separate moments in Advent and the season's overall development.

Simcoe, Mary Ann, ed. *A Christmas Sourcebook* (Chicago: Liturgy Training Publications, 1984). A treasury of texts from various traditions and churches. Extensive attention to the *comites Christi* and to the days between Christmas and the Baptism of the Lord.

Simcoe, Mary Ann, ed. *Parish Path through Advent and Christmastime* (Chicago: Liturgy Training Publications, 1983). Each chapter looks at one element of liturgy: lectionary, music, environment, etc.

A SENSE OF THE SEASON

In the spirit of the liturgy, Advent arrives gradually throughout the autumn, like leaves falling off a tree until its summer glory becomes, in the words of Shakespeare, "bare ruin'd choirs where late the sweet birds sang." This image is found in the refrains of our prayer: "We have all withered like leaves, and our guilt carries us away like the wind" (Isaiah 64:5).

The despoiling of the world, the frosting of gardens, the slow ebbing of daylight—these are all warnings, as sharp as the prophets, as loud as John the Baptist, badgering us to face injustice, suffering, war. We are called to prepare the royal highway for the Sun of Justice, the Healer and the Comforter, the Prince of Peace.

This gradual arrival of Advent can be felt by the assembly in the way we keep all of autumn, maybe through early American hymns and spirituals with their intense eschatological lyrics, maybe through the deepening of vesture from summer's greens to autumn's browns to winter's grays, maybe through unified parish efforts to put other business aside to explore the "last things," death,

judgment, the reign of God—and even such discomforting matters as the way we bury our dead and the pressing need to shelter the homeless as winter looms.

In a wonderful paradox, Advent also arrives suddenly, without warning, a startling change "in the twinkling of an eye," like a snowfall that transforms the landscape. This image is proclaimed loudly in the gospel warnings of the end of time, a terror made more terrifying by the darkening of the sun and the falling of the stars. That is why the Advent liturgy must somehow slap us in the face and bring us to our senses. It must be seen for what it is: a carefully prescribed countercultural antidote to the syrupy sweet December that advertisers have in store for us—pun intended!

Advent is autumn turning into winter, with its darkness, its cold, the threat of starvation, the threat of death. And here is the paradox: In such a fearful night, the lighting of candles brings great joy. In such a numbing silence, the Spirit and the bride sing "come." For when Advent is past and our Christmas festival arrives, Christ indeed will come as our just judge, as our beloved spouse, as our newborn baby; and we will welcome Christ with lights and with flowers and with greenery held high to drive the cold winter away.

PREPARING THE PARISH

Advent and Christmastime present us with a serious problem: It's easy to fool ourselves into thinking that the commercial merriment that precedes December 25 has something to do with the Christian festival of Christmas. After all, so much of our Christian symbolism, such as lights and evergreens and music, have been usurped by advertisers to sell their wares. Yet we have to stop fooling ourselves: Our secular calendar and our religious calendar are incompatible. To the extent that we observe the days before December 25 with parties, concerts and overindulgence, to that extent we are unable to observe Advent. To the extent that the early weeks of December fill us with anxiety about the most superficial aspects of life, to that extent they leave us too full for our Advent.

This incompatibility of calendars has consequences in liturgy. If the parish school, if the parish hall, if the homes of parishioners—including the rectory—reflect little of Advent's holding back and waiting and sober patience, then our worship during Advent is a sham. What's the point of putting on Advent's vesture, or rehearsing its melodies, or announcing its scriptures if the parish's living of the season remains boxed into an hour of Sunday worship? And if all the tokens of our Christmas celebration get tossed out of our homes with the gift wrap after December 25, we show ourselves to be a people undeserving of the festive season that follows Advent.

Before we even think of preparing the liturgies of Advent and Christmastime—or of any season—we have to prepare the parish. Perhaps we can start by reclaiming our Christian calendar. As a church, we have a job waiting to be done: recognizing the value of living according to our calendar. And until this job is done well, until the calendar we keep at worship becomes a calendar we live by, our worship will be but a shadow of what it can be.

Keeping Advent as Advent: Advent is not a season for parish parties or social gatherings of any kind. That's what Christmastime is for. During Advent we should take a walk through the parish school, the church hall, the gathering

places and meeting rooms. We should read through the parish bulletin. Then we should ask ourselves: Do these places and does this bulletin reflect a community that knows how to keep Advent, that knows how to wait?

Religious education: Be wary of schedules at this season. Jamming too much into Advent is a mistake. Are seasonal take-home materials available, and will they be kept available throughout Advent and Christmastime? These materials should be grounded in solid principles of prayer, theology and liturgy; they should not be over-stuffed with busyness and cutesy activities—a common problem with many "Advent programs." Are the catechists taking advantage of the liturgical year and opening up the meaning of Advent and Christmas with the children? How will we combat the cultural pressure to celebrate Christmas before its time? And, the big question, what's in the works for Christmastime?

Come home for Christmas: How do we help those who have, or who feel they have, obstacles to participating in parish life? What sort of year-round work is done by the parish to bring about reconciliation between Christians and the church, and what needs to be done? Should the liturgy committee or parish council be the catalyst for a "Coming Home for Christmas" mailing campaign to inactive households or for a welcoming ad in the newspaper? No doubt deadlines for such an ad fall in earliest December.

A short Advent and a short Christmastime: This year, because December 24 is the Fourth Sunday of Advent, the Advent season is as short as it can be—22 days. And Christmastime is also as short as it can be—15 days. Like last year, the feast of the Baptism of the Lord—the final day of Christmastime—is kept on the Monday after Epiphany. That means that the entire span of time from the First Sunday of Advent until Epiphany races by in 5 weeks!

Keep in mind that the weeks of Ordinary Time during November are a fitting prelude to Advent, rich with the scriptures of expectation, of promise and of hope. And the weeks of Ordinary Time in January that follow Christmastime are filled with the scriptural images of Epiphany—of births and beginnings, of calling and commissioning, of a great light shining in the darkness. All these weeks of late autumn and of winter can be approached in their relationship to the Advent and Christmas seasons that they surround.

WORDS

Judge between the nations, swords into plowshares, walk in the light, the peace of Jerusalem, wake from sleep, night is far spent, armor of light, coming of the Son of Man, the time you least expect, a shoot shall sprout, a little child, the lion shall eat hay, the root of Jesse, justice shall flower, lessons of patience, reform your lives, prepare the way, grasshoppers and wild honey, the ax is laid to the root, hearts are frightened, the lame leap, the dumb will sing, the Lord protects strangers, be patient, the farmer awaits, the judge stands at the gate, a virgin shall be with child, the race that seeks for him, promised long ago, son of David, have no fear, Emmanuel, God is with us.

VESTURE

Shades of violet and purple; slate, sarum and other deep shades of midnight blue; silvers, whites and grays, the colors of winter. Care should be taken to

ensure that the vesture used in Advent is different from that used during Lent and that this vesture returns year after year. Avoid purple vesture with passion symbols pasted on. In fact, avoid vesture with any sort of stylized, appliqué symbol—a bizarre thing to do to any clothing other than a T-shirt.

THE MASS

Introductory rites have as their specific purpose, according to the *General Instruction of the Roman Missal,* the gathering of the people into a unified community prepared to hear the word of the Lord. Let most of this gathering be done wordlessly. The introductory rites of the reformed liturgy have been recognized from the beginning as problematic, a compromise of several differing viewpoints (cf. Josef Jungmann, *The Mass: An Historical, Theological, and Pastoral Survey* [Collegeville: The Liturgical Press, 1976], 165–71; and Ralph Keifer, "Our Cluttered Vestibule," *Worship,* May 1974, 270–74). Great care is necessary in ordering the opening moments of the eucharist. During Advent, the introductory rites are greatly simplified just by the absence of the Gloria.

The Advent liturgy may begin with the ordinary procession to and reverencing of the altar: The presider and ministers make a profound bow before the altar, the presider goes to the altar and kisses it. As a silent form of blessing, perhaps the Advent wreath could be incensed (after the altar has been) while the entrance psalm or the hymn is sung. However, especially if the Advent wreath is in the gathering place or hanging over the assembly, the liturgy can begin with a call to face the wreath, perhaps with the processional cross and incense underneath the wreath, then the greeting and penitential rite, followed by the incensing of the wreath and people, accompanied by instrumental music leading into the entrance psalm or hymn while the ministers move to their places, then the opening prayer. Another pattern entirely is made possible if all the people gather in another place where the Advent wreath is. (In all these patterns, the wreath is already lit before people gather.) As explained in the notes for the First Sunday of Advent (page 139), the ritual lighting of the wreath is best kept as part of Evening Prayer.

An adapted form of the greeting could include the darkness/light motif:

> Grace, light and peace from God our Father
> and from the Lord Jesus Christ
>   be with you all.

Invocations C2 of the penitential rite (in the sacramentary) are appropriate for the first two Sundays of Advent and can be standard (and chanted?) until December 17. They blend well the three comings we think of during this season— past, present and future. As the focus of the season shifts toward the nearness of Christmas, invocations C3 are used from December 17 to 24. The introductory rites conclude with the opening prayer. The Gloria is omitted until Christmas, thus emphasizing the "special and solemn character" of this ancient hymn of praise (*Music in Catholic Worship,* #66).

There is a key to good liturgy that should be remembered here and in all that follows about seasonal preparation. The order of these entrance rites, which will differ from the order of Ordinary Time but will be consistent through a given season, must be learned *thoroughly* by all the ministers *before the season begins.* This includes the presider, musicians, servers, deacons, ushers and any others

who have some role of service to the assembly during this rite. Even printed instructions won't do: Ministers—all of them—must be assembled for rehearsal. All the timing, all the relationships, all the movements must be worked out with the people involved *going through the movements and with all of the objects in place.* The pace of the rite is important, and it may take a while to get this right. The assembly is not served when hurried instructions are whispered in the moments before the liturgy begins. The ministers must be at home with what they are to do and must work as an ensemble.

Sacred silence: Advent provides an occasion for "house cleaning" in regard to silence. For example, what happens after the "Let us pray" that leads into the opening prayer? How do we help people use these silent times purposefully and well? The presider is primarily responsible for this. The presider should speak the "Let us pray" with urgency and as a true invitation. Every other minister and altar server should know that after those words there is to be stillness, silence and prayer in the sense of gathering ourselves together. There is no stronger sense of community in a room than when such silence can envelop all present. The length of such a silence should not vary greatly from presider to presider. They need to work together on this.

Liturgy of the word: The attention directed toward the brevity and simplicity of the introductory rites warrants attention to how the scripture passages are proclaimed. The introduction to the lectionary suggests a period of quiet settling-in before the readings begin, then silence again after the readings and again after the homily:

> The liturgy of the word must be celebrated in a way that fosters meditation. Clearly, any sort of haste that hinders reflectiveness must be avoided. The dialogue between God and God's people taking place through the Holy Spirit demands short intervals of silence, suited to the assembly, as an opportunity to take the word of God to heart and to prepare a response to it in prayer. (Introduction to the lectionary, #28)

The liturgy of the word concludes with the general intercessions. The back of the sacramentary offers models to inspire local creativity. (Also see samples beginning on page 22.) A lack of understanding of these prayers has led to these intercessions being anything but general. The specific needs of local concern and of current interest ought to be prayed for, but these find their place within, even after, the wider needs of the church, the world and the parish.

Go easy on variety with the intercessions and strive instead to help people hear well and maybe even learn by heart some brief texts that could become their own prayers at home. Rarely, if ever, change the response of the assembly.

Liturgy of the eucharist: The preface prayed during most of the season (up until December 16) is Advent Preface I. Once again, as the Advent season moves toward the birth of Christ (December 17–24), the more urgent and emotion-filled words of Advent Preface II are used.

Thought needs to be given to the choice of a eucharistic prayer during Advent. We have a variety of texts from which to choose: the four standard prayers, the three for Masses with Children, the two for Masses of Reconciliation. *The General Instruction of the Roman Missal* gives brief notes on each prayer (paragraph

322). The fine book, *The Eucharistic Prayers of the Roman Rite,* by Enrico Mazza (New York: Pueblo Publishing Co., 1986) explores the history and theology of the eucharistic prayer and then goes on to reflect in great detail on each of the currently available eucharistic prayers (including those used in Europe).

Many find the second eucharistic prayer for reconciliation a good text to hear proclaimed throughout the Advent season. It is a powerful text when proclaimed well. Its conclusion is a celebration of the gathering of all creation into the messianic banquet.

Concluding rite: Let one Advent blessing be chosen and memorized by presider and deacon for all the Sunday Masses throughout Advent. Solemn Blessing 1 from the sacramentary would be appropriate throughout the season. The *Book of Occasional Services* (Episcopal) has these brief forms:

> *Until December 17:*
> May the Sun of Righteousness shine upon you and scatter the darkness
> from before your path; and may almighty God bless you . . .

> *After December 17:*
> May Christ, who by his incarnation gathered into one
> things earthly and heavenly, fill you with his joy and peace;
> and may almighty God bless you . . .

This dismissal is appropriate throughout Advent:

> Let us go forth in peace to prepare the way of the Lord.

MUSIC

Advent and Christmastime yield some of the richest of the products of Western music making. Handel's *Messiah,* carols, seasonal chant and contemporary music make up a large portion of the music library of any parish that boasts such a library. Because of this embarrassment of riches, a musician may be tempted to do as much as can be done with as many pieces as possible. Two reminders are in order. First, the large assemblies on Sundays and feast days that are for the eucharist are just that: for the eucharist. That means the kinds of music most important are those most important at any eucharist: acclamations, psalms, litanies. These may be tunes that are unique to the Advent and/or Christmas seasons, but they are never placed in the shadow of any other sort of music. The hymns and songs of the seasons have their rather modest place at eucharist. Second, though, remember that even in a short Advent and Christmastime there are many weeks. Not everything need be done at once. And not everything need be done at the eucharist.

Hymns: "Creator of the stars of night" *(Conditor Alme Siderum)* is a lovely chant melody with numerous arrangements by various composers. Gaining ground lately is the strong 16th-century tune "Geneva" with the text "Comfort, comfort, O my people." It provides a remarkable dance rhythm when taken briskly with a moderate detachment in the singers' diction. Several soprano and alto recorders can lend a Renaissance flavor. The tune "Venez, divin messie" with the text "O come, Divine Messiah" is a charming carol of the Advent season and adapts well to children's voices as well as adult assemblies. The carol is printed in *Worship* (GIA) and the *Catholic Book of Worship* (Canada), with the complete French text

in the latter. The others are included in *Worship, Lutheran Book of Worship* and *The Hymnal 1982.*

A complete set of gospel acclamations for Advent Sundays has been prepared by David Haas (OCP, #8732). From the same company is Bernadette Farrell's "Come to set us free" (OCP, #7135). It takes more than one exposure to the Farrell piece to give it the sense of urgency it expresses. By the third Sunday the assembly should be ready to fly with it.

The community of Taizé in France has produced some of the most approachable texts and music the church has seen during the past ten years. "Wait for the Lord" (a round), "Prepare the Way of the Lord" and the "Magnificat" seem to be ubiquitous now.

Psalmody for the season has been set by Marty Haugen with his multiple sets of verses for "Lord, make us turn to you" (GIA, G-2884), "My soul in stillness waits" (GIA, G-2652) and "Lord, come and save us" (GIA, G-3261, *Psalms for the Church Year,* volume 2).

One source that musicians sometimes forget about is the great parousia repertory of African-American spirituals, at home in our assemblies especially during November and during Advent. Paramount is the contemporary spiritual by Andraé Crouch, "Soon and very soon" (in *Songs of Zion,* Abingdon Press, and *Hymnal for Catholic Students, GIA and LTP*), as well as the eschatological "My Lord, what a mourning" (in *Songs of Zion,* etc.). "Sign me up for the Christian Jubilee" is an enormously rousing gospel song for soloist and choir (in GIA's *Lead Me, Guide Me*).

The traditional Advent repertory, of course, is crowned with "O come, O come, Emmanuel," whose text paraphrases the O-antiphons. For most of us, this tune conjures some of the most powerful of seasonal images and sounds. That being said, it must also be said that it need not be used every Sunday. In fact, like the O-Antiphons, it is traditional during Advent's final week.

Perhaps our familiarity with "O come, O come, Emmanuel" points out a problem: Is it the only piece of music the assembly associates with Advent? Changing seasonal repertory from year to year makes it impossible for melodies to sink into our consciousness, and yet there is an obvious need for expanding repertory. It's a balancing act. Getting an assembly to learn a wide range of music involves limiting that range and repeating it from week to week and from year to year. It's the art of knowing when to move on to a new piece and when to bring back an old one. This is one of the marks of maturity in choosing liturgical music: You must believe that next year and the year after that will indeed come and that the music sung this year is groundwork for the music sung next year. Failure to respect this principle is one of the great problems in liturgical music ministry, especially in our work among children.

THE WORSHIP ENVIRONMENT

Creating a sense of winter, using the images of darkness, cold or bleakness, can also be combined with creating a sense of mystery, a winter night's sky, the beauty of mist, of silence, of simplicity. Whether you intend to use fabrics or glass

or bare trees, creating a worship environment should always begin by taking a hike: Get outside and open your eyes. Next, read through the entrance antiphons for the season. These refrains form ancient leitmotifs of Sundays and seasons.

Advent is not a season for evergreens, much less flowers and lights. Yet some parishes, capitulating to the mood of shopping malls, have begun to decorate for Advent by hanging wreaths on their doors and festooning greenery in their worship halls, perhaps with purple ribbons as a nod to Advent, changing to red ribbons come Christmas. Perhaps they reason that as long as there's an Advent wreath, why not include all sorts of greenery. Or perhaps it's a matter of getting the most use out of the money spent on Christmas decorations. Yet garlands and wreaths and evergreens represent the triumphal arrival of Christ and our welcome to the Messiah, not our patient longing for this arrival.

A logistical problem this year: Because the Fourth Sunday of Advent is December 24, there simply isn't time to decorate for Christmas between the morning Advent liturgy and the evening Christmas liturgy. See page 32 for suggestions about how to get around this problem.

The Advent wreath is meant to be a small foretaste of the evergreens of Christmas—and that means not using evergreens anywhere else during Advent except within the wreath. (And if you don't use real evergreens, skip the custom entirely. An Advent wreath with plastic greenery is a poor picture of a symbol, something antagonistic to the honesty that worship demands.)

It is certainly simpler to put the wreath on a table, but that just doesn't do what the wreath should do: It's supposed to hang so that it slowly turns. People should be able to gaze up through it. A suspended wreath is a hole to peek into heaven! That's how the people of central Europe do it (and they invented the custom). If the wreath is suspended, a beautiful ritual action at the beginning of liturgy is to hold a bowl of burning incense underneath so that the smoke curls up through it.

Since an Advent wreath is essentially a home custom, it's wise to help all parish households keep this custom in their homes by teaching people about it during November and having parish artisans show examples. In church the wreath is too dominant a symbol to add to the area around the altar, ambo and chair. It is better located in the vestibule, the gathering area or hanging over the main aisle.

Making a truly huge wreath is easier with a metal or wooden frame—an actual wagon wheel is perfect—onto which is attached evergreen roping. It's a bit of an engineering trick to afix candles to a wreath. Surely there is a parishioner who can weld pipe to the frame in the required diameter. Enormous, professionally made beeswax candles with followers are safe and can be ordered a few months ahead of time from any church supply store. Fat, paraffin pillar candles (the kind available in card shops) look nice for a week but then can drown their wicks or, worse, send a few pints of wax spilling down. Don't fret candle colors or added ribbons; let four beeswax candles in an evergreen wreath communicate their mystery without ornament.

The Marian shrine deserves attention through the season. Perhaps that is where the wreath could hang, or other candles and flowers can be kept nearby. A custom from the Middle Ages dresses Holy Mary in midnight blue as a wise

virgin bearing her lamp awaiting the coming of the bridegroom. An icon or other image of Isaiah or John the Baptist belongs somewhere in church, perhaps near the main doors or the font.

Don't make work for yourself by changing the worship environment from week to week, or from one Advent to the next, for that matter. There may be some subtle development each week, but something like a banner that keeps getting additions each week can come off as a gimmick with too much attention focused on the banner. Remember that the central objects of the liturgy—the word, table, bread and wine—remain central through all our seasons and feasts. That should be clear.

Have you ever considered putting something *outside* the church building, something to announce the Advent season to the neighborhood? Sometimes things that don't work particularly well inside church because of their dominance look great hanging outside—like a banner made with weatherproof fabrics. Again, don't announce Christmas until it is Christmas—inside or out.

OTHER RITUAL PRAYER

The eucharist alone cannot release this season's extraordinary power and pathos. Even though people are busy this time of year, they are hungry for an antidote to the shopping season. Consider ways in which the prayer of this season might be nurtured outside of the Mass.

Evening Prayer (also called evensong and vespers, although we would avoid confusion by settling on a single title for this important liturgy of the church) is becoming more a part of the worshiping community's life in many parishes, especially during these special seasons. So much of Advent's prayer seems to arise within the darkness of a wintry evening. Such a service provides a perfect context for the ritual candle lighting which the Advent wreath invites. Why not schedule Evening Prayer on the memorials of Nicholas (December 6) and Lucy (December 13), both falling on Wednesdays this year, or on the feast of Our Lady of Guadalupe (December 12), and include in a gathering afterward some of the ethnic traditions that surround these days?

Materials should be provided for the assembly to take home for private and household prayer. Such material could include a typed sheet or booklet with weekly Advent prayers and an Advent wreath service (prayerfully composed and aesthetically sensitive), or LTP's little pocket prayerbook, *Keeping Advent and Christmastime,* as well as their annual series of Sunday handouts for Advent and Christmastime, *Welcome, Yule!* (This year, *Welcome, Yule!* also includes a meal prayercard and a special handout with a forthright discussion of the problems of commercialism and the Christian calendar.) LTP also publishes *An Advent Sourcebook,* a wonderful treasury of seasonal lyrics, poetry and prose.

Sample Prayer Texts for Advent

Introductory Rites

GREETING

One of these texts can be chosen and used throughout Advent. While the repetition may become tedious for the presider, this will not be the experience of the assembly. Thoughtful repetition creates ritual.

The Lord, who is coming to save us, be with you all.

Or:

Grace, light and peace from God our Father and the Lord Jesus Christ be with you all.

Or:

The God of hope, who by the working of the Holy Spirit fills us with all joy in believing, be with you all.

INTRODUCTION

If an introduction seems superfluous, the introduction can be combined with the invitation.

First Sunday of Advent:
Advent begins with a summons to watchfulness: The Lord, who came once in humility, our brother in the flesh, will come again in glory, our judge and Lord of all. Even now he stands in our midst, unrecognized and unloved. The church bids us realize the time in which we live, the hour that is at hand, the nearness of our salvation.

Second and Third Sundays of Advent:
Advent challenges us with the prophets' call to prepare the way of the Lord, to make straight the Messiah's paths in our world and in our hearts. Advent comforts us with the joyful expectation that the Lord will act on behalf of all who acknowledge their powerlessness and who long for peace.

Fourth Sunday of Advent:
Advent draws to a close with the church's grateful remembrance of God's dramatic intervention to become Emmanuel, God-with-us, in Jesus, Son of God and Son of David.

INVITATION TO THE PENITENTIAL RITE

First Sunday of Advent:
My brothers and sisters: entering into the season of Advent together at the table of the word and eucharist, let us wake from our slumber, acknowledge our sins, put on the Lord Jesus Christ, and walk in his light.

Second and Third Sundays of Advent:
My brothers and sisters: before the God of all patience, let us acknowledge our sins. From the God of all encouragement, let us seek forgiveness.

Fourth Sunday of Advent:
My brothers and sisters: joyfully acknowledging how deep is God's love for us, how high God's designs for our salvation, let us ask pardon and seek the beauty of God's holy face in Jesus who saves us from our sins.

PENITENTIAL RITE

One set of invocations should be chosen and used (sung?) throughout Advent.

You came into the world to save us: Lord, have mercy. You visit us continually through the grace of the Spirit: Christ, have mercy. You will come one day in glory to judge our deeds: Lord, have mercy.

Or:

You came to visit your people with peace: Lord, have mercy. You came to seek out and save what had been lost: Christ, have mercy. You came to create a new world: Lord, have mercy.

Or:

Lord Jesus, defender of the poor: Lord, have mercy. Christ Jesus, shelter of the powerless: Christ, have mercy. Lord Jesus, hope of sinners: Lord, have mercy.

Introduction to the Readings

"Among the possibilities for further accommodating any individual celebration, it is important to consider the admonitions. . . . These enable the people to be drawn into a fuller understanding of the sacred action, or any of its parts, and lead them into a true spirit of participation. The General Instruction of the Roman Missal *entrusts the more important admonitions to the priest for preparation and use. He may introduce the Mass to the people before the celebration begins, during the liturgy of the word prior to the actual readings and in the eucharistic prayer before the preface; he may also conclude the entire sacred action before the dismissal. . . . In all cases it is well to remember the nature of an admonition, and not make them into a sermon or homily; care should be taken to keep them brief and not too wordy, for otherwise they become tedious." (From the* Circular Letter *of the Congregation for Divine Worship, 1973, n. 14. Quoted in the Appendix to the General Instruction for the Dioceses of the United States of America in the 1985 edition of the sacramentary.)*

First Sunday of Advent:
The flood and the thief in the night: With these disturbing images Christ rouses us to confront our coming salvation, and Paul warns us that even now the day with its light is at hand. But Isaiah places all within Advent's motif of joyful expectancy. The nations are being gathered into unity and peace.

Second Sunday of Advent:
Fiery prophet at the Jordan, John the Baptist's uncompromising challenge is clear: Reform, and let conversion lead to practical deeds of justice. Paul proposes the basic beginning: mutual acceptance of one another lived out in harmony. Thus will Christians begin to usher in the peaceable kingdom envisioned by Isaiah.

Third Sunday of Advent:
John the Baptist's question is with us still: Is Jesus the one? The world seeks dramatic signs, but so often the healings wrought by believers are simple, hidden. Isaiah calls for action. James

counsels patience. Working hands and steady hearts together prepare the way of the Lord.

Fourth Sunday of Advent:
Decisively but quietly, God intervenes. A young girl with child is the sign of salvation given to Ahaz. Centuries later, Joseph embraces the mystery, waiting patiently, trustingly, for its fulfillment. Paul links the incarnation with the paschal mystery: This child's birth will bring the rebirth of creation.

General Intercessions

INVITATION TO PRAYER

Through December 17:
The Lord comes to save us and to establish the kingdom: let us ask God to manifest power and compassion.

After December 17:
The day of salvation is about to dawn: with the whole church, let us give voice to the longings of the human race, especially those who are poor and forgotten.

INTERCESSION FOR THE CHURCH

For the pilgrim church on earth: that it may share with all people the hope that lights its way and that it may awaken in every heart a longing for salvation: let us pray to the Lord.

Or:

For the church throughout the world: that it may bring the spirit of gospel love to all human efforts to unite the world as one family: let us pray to the Lord.

INTERCESSION FOR THE WORLD

For all who govern nations and peoples: that their decisions be based on reverence for the unique dignity of every human person, the dignity that Christ came to reveal: let us pray to the Lord.

Or:

For this world in which so many seek recognition of dignity: that the unique

CONTINUED

gifts and potential of each person be realized for the enrichment of all: let us pray to the Lord.

INTERCESSION FOR VARIOUS NEEDS

For all whose hopes have been dashed by life's difficulties: that our prayer and practical charity may awaken in them a confident will to strive for a better future: let us pray to the Lord.

Or:

For the poor and the oppressed: that their plight be recognized and responded to by an increasingly sensitive society: let us pray to the Lord.

INTERCESSION FOR THE ASSEMBLY

For this assembly: that the Lord's coming may convert us to a life-style in which we value people for who they are and not what they have: let us pray to the Lord.

Or:

For all of us here present: that the Lord who comes as judge of human hearts may banish from our lives behaviors and attitudes that contradict the gospel, so that we may hasten to meet him with free and loving hearts: let us pray to the Lord.

Or the intercession for the assembly may be based on the scriptures of the day:

First Sunday of Advent:
For this eucharistic assembly: that we may hasten the coming of the Lord's reign by lives of peacemaking, integrity and alertness to Christ's presence in others: let us pray to the Lord.

Second Sunday of Advent:
For this community: that our commitment to justice and peace, our mutual acceptance and harmony, may give evidence to others of our conversion to Christ: let us pray to the Lord.

Third Sunday of Advent:
For ourselves: that joy and patience be evident in our lives as we await the Day of the Lord and do our best to hasten it: let us pray to the Lord.

Fourth Sunday of Advent:
For all of us here present: that Mary and Joseph may be our models of trusting faith as we open our lives to the mystery of God's saving love: let us pray to the Lord.

CONCLUDING PRAYER

These concluding prayers for the intercessions were selected from ICEL original opening prayers for Mass based on the scripture readings of the day, © 1983, 1986, 1987, 1988, International Committee on English in the Liturgy, Inc. (ICEL). All rights reserved.

First Sunday of Advent:
Above the clamor of our violence
your Word of truth responds,
O God of majesty and power.
Over nations enshrouded in despair
your justice dawns.

Grant your household
a discerning spirit and a watchful eye
to perceive the hour in which we live.
Hasten the advent of that Day
when the weapons of war shall
    be banished,
our deeds of darkness cast off,
and all your scattered children
    gathered into one.

We ask this through him
    whose coming is certain,
whose Day draws near:
your Son, our Lord Jesus Christ,
who lives and reigns with you
    and the Holy Spirit,
one God, for ever and ever.
—*Copyright © ICEL*

Second Sunday of Advent:
O God, whose will is justice
    for the poor
and peace for the afflicted,
let your herald's urgent voice
pierce our hardened hearts
and announce the dawn
    of your kingdom.

Before the advent of the One
    who baptizes

CONTINUED

with the fire of the Holy Spirit,
let our complacency give way
    to conversion,
oppression to justice,
and conflict to acceptance of one
    another in Christ.

We ask this through him
    whose coming is certain,
whose Day draws near:
your Son, our Lord Jesus Christ,
who lives and reigns with you
    and the Holy Spirit,
one God, for ever and ever.
—*Copyright © ICEL*

Third Sunday of Advent:
God of glory and splendor,
at your touch
    the wilderness blossoms,
broken lives are made whole,
and frightened hearts rejoice
    in new strength.

Open our eyes
    to your hidden presence
and loosen our tongues
    for songs of praise.
To all who long for your Son's return
grant perseverance and patience,
that we may announce in word
    and deed
the Good News of the kingdom.

We ask this through him
    whose coming is certain,
whose Day draws near:
your Son, our Lord Jesus Christ,
who lives and reigns with you
    and the Holy Spirit,
one God, for ever and ever.
—*Copyright © ICEL*

Fourth Sunday of Advent:
In the psalms of David,
in the words of the prophets,
in the dream of Joseph,
your promise is spoken, eternal God,
and takes flesh at last
in the womb of the Virgin.

May Emmanuel find welcome
    in our hearts,
take flesh in our lives, and be
    for all peoples
the welcomed advent of redemption
    and grace.

We ask this through him
    whose coming is certain,
whose Day draws near:
your Son, our Lord Jesus Christ,
who lives and reigns with you
    and the Holy Spirit,
one God, for ever and ever.
—*Copyright © ICEL*

Communion Rite

INTRODUCTION TO
THE LORD'S PRAYER

For the entire season:
Let us pray for the coming of the kingdom as Jesus taught us:

INVITATION TO COMMUNION

Through December 17:
This is the Lamb of God, who takes away the sins of the world, the King who is to come: Happy are those who are called to his supper.

After December 17:
This is the Lamb of God, who takes away the sins of the world, the King who now draws near: Happy are those who are called to his supper.

Concluding Rite

BLESSING

For the entire season:

It would be good to keep the Solemn Blessing of Advent at least through the first three Sundays. If a shorter form is desired, or at Evening Prayer and weekday Masses, the Episcopal Book of Occasional Services *has this alternative:*

May the Sun of Righteousness shine upon you and scatter the darkness from before your path; and may almighty God bless you.

CONTINUED

After December 17 there is this possibility from the same source:

May Christ, who by his Incarnation gathered into one things earthly and heavenly, fill you with his joy and peace; and may almighty God bless you. . . .

DISMISSAL
Through December 17:
Let us go in peace to prepare the way of the Lord.
After December 17:
The Lord is at hand. Let us go in peace to prepare the way of the Lord.

Eucharistic Bread Recipe

From Dennis Krouse, professor of liturgy at the University of San Diego:

1. For 70 communicants, use ⅓ cup whole wheat flour to ⅔ cup unbleached white flour. The mixture of flour should be kept in an airtight container in the freezer and used while cold. (The cold flour helps prevent a separate crust from forming.)

2. Use one cup of the flour mixture to approximately ½ cup of spring water (Perrier is good). The water should be refrigerator cold.

3. Quickly mix the flour and water together with a fork until all the flour is moist. Form dough into a smooth ball. Usually more flour needs to be sprinkled on the surface of the dough to prevent stickiness.

4. Gently flatten the ball of dough into a circular loaf about ½- to ¾-inch thick. If necessary, turn any uneven edges underneath.

5. Place the unscored loaf on a lightly oiled baking sheet. (Use Pam and wipe off the excess.)

6. Place in a preheated oven at 425 degrees.

7. After approximately 12–15 minutes the top crust should have raised slightly. Prick the crust with a toothpick in several places, turn the loaf over and continue to bake about five minutes. (This gives an evenness to the top of the loaf.)

8. Turn the loaf right side up again and continue to bake until the crust is very lightly browned, about 10–15 minutes more for a total of 25–30 minutes. Baking time when using more than 1½ cups of flour needs to be extended.

9. Place the loaf on a rack for cooling. (You may wish to slice the bottom crust off to check for any rawness.)

10. Bread is best when made fresh the day of the liturgy. However, after cooking, it can be tightly wrapped and frozen for later use.

When bread is purchased rather than made locally, search out the suppliers with the product that is most like bread as called for in the General Instruction.

CHRISTMASTIME

OFFICIAL DESCRIPTION

Next to the yearly celebration of the paschal mystery, the church holds most sacred the memorial of Christ's birth and early manifestations. This is the purpose of the Christmas season. (*General Norms for the Liturgical Year and Calendar*, 32)

RESOURCES

Advent and Christmastime must be discussed and prepared as a whole. For resource materials on historical background and liturgical help, see the bibliography beginning on page 11 in this *Sourcebook*.

A SENSE OF THE SEASON

No sooner does the winter sun turn in its course back toward the summertime than we Christians latch onto this tiny sign of hope and make midwinter our second spring. Birth is, after all, a springtime event. How harsh a paradox to celebrate birth when winter is just beginning! Yet "new birth" is our cry: *Noel!* So we banish the long nights with firelight and candles. We defy the winter by festooning summer's green from our rafters. We spread our tables with the abundance of the harvest, all signs of God's graciousness, signs of the bounty of heaven itself. We gather around the sparkling tree of life and declare this place, no matter how humble, to be paradise.

Christmas is *not* Jesus' birthday. It is not an anniversary of something that happened long ago. Christmas is a celebration of the birth of Christ, now, *hodie*, today. That is what the words of the gospel proclaim: This day in David's city a savior has been born to you, the Messiah and Lord (Luke 2:11). And over and over in our carols and prayers and poetry we repeat this *hodie:* "Ox and ass before him bow, for he is in the manger now: Christ is born today! Christ is born today!"

This word "today" is a key to entering into the mystery of Christmastime, for if Christ is born today that means we can see and touch and hold Christ. It also means that we must feed, clothe and protect Christ, now, today. If Christ is alive in our midst, then truly the reign of God has begun, the reign in which the very rocks of the earth cry out for justice and compassion, acclaiming the coming of the Lord. And that is the only intelligent way to interpret the authentic customs and decorations of Christmas—not as signs of a birthday anniversary, but as signs of God's reign, emblems of eternity, of health and wholesomeness and the endless delight of heaven itself.

One of the hallmarks of genuine liturgical celebration is this combination of great comfort and joy with tremendous challenge. No wonder it takes so many days to keep Christmastime! And no wonder we must keep Christmastime by renewing our efforts to clothe the naked, feed the hungry and bring together neighbors and strangers alike to share in *Christes Messe,* the feast of Christ.

Preparing the Parish

Those in the parish with responsibility for worship can't begin to prepare Christmastime without preparing the parish itself through education and outreach. Unless we vigorously address the incompatibility of our Christian calendar with the commercial calendar, we force ourselves into the ridiculous posture of asking people to get caught up in the great merriment of, say, Epiphany, only to go back to homes that have been stripped of celebration a week or two earlier.

A great way to raise the community's consciousness of Christmastime is to offer fine liturgies *and* parish-sponsored celebrations throughout the season. The two work together. A carol-sing and pageant on a Christmastime Saturday evening enables people to come together Sunday morning not as spectators but as participants in the mystery of the season. This consciousness of liturgy does not happen in a parish in one year; it happens over a lifetime. That's why it's critical to maintain a consistency in worship from year to year and continually to renew our efforts in education and enthusiasm.

Any such parish preparation, especially the juggling of schedules, must take place months beforehand. In our culture, even the Advent season is too late to prepare the parish for Christmastime; most households' holiday plans tend to become firm by November. Use the bulletin, parish and school newsletters, adult and children's catechetical sessions—whatever means are available—to encourage people to keep the season in a wholehearted way. The manner in which commercial culture tends to portray families this time of year also tends to exclude the single, the separated and divorced, the childless—so the parish must take pains to include all ways and walks of life. Great sensitivity is required, even in language; for example, perhaps the more inclusive word "household" can be used instead of "family."

The parish should not overburden the month of December. This time of year is hectic enough. Keep in mind that January and February, what we now call Ordinary Time, was for centuries the time of carnival, days to drive the cold winter away with hospitality and good cheer. All the days from Christmas Day until Ash Wednesday are the authentic "holiday season" of our religious tradition—a far more humane approach to winter than the commercial culture's January diets and white sales.

Words

Vindication, dawn, victory, burning torch, new name, glorious crown, espoused, bridegroom, bride, a family record, angel, dream, virgin, conceive, give birth, fulfill, child, Emmanuel, rejoice as at the harvest, burned as fuel for flames, Wonder-Counselor, God-Hero, Father-Forever, Prince of Peace, dominion, judgment, justice, sing to the Lord a new song, all the trees of the forest exult, shepherd, flocks, temperately, justly, devoutly, the appearing of the glory, first-born son, swaddling clothes, manger, glad tidings, pondered in her heart, goodwill, all the ends of the earth, in times past, the final age, today I have

begotten you, in the beginning, the light shines on, the Word became flesh, love following upon love, the designated time, heir, the name Jesus, rise up in splendor, radiant, star, lavished, justified, caravans, gold, frankincense, myrrh, the wealth of nations, homage, flee to Egypt, here is my servant, Jordan, the sky opened, beloved, favor, dove, baptism, on the third day, wedding, wine, the Lamb of God who takes away the sin of the world.

VESTURE

For liturgical vesture: white, gold, but also any festive tapestry patterns (liturgical rubrics encourage the community's "best array" to be used on solemnities, whether this array happens to be all white or not). For some of the saints' days: various shades of red for martyrdom; for Mary, white with some shades of blue. Certainly if the parish has a special Christmas set, this should be worn on every day of the season.

In general, the white vesture used during Christmastime looks better in many situations if it is snow white—rather than off white, eggshell or ecru—especially if the parish uses evergreens and red poinsettias to decorate for the season. If your parish is considering acquiring a Christmas set of vesture, compare the fabrics and trims to the aesthetic demands of the often rather dominant Christmastime decorations.

THE MASS

The first step in planning Christmastime is to look back to Advent. Remember, Advent and Christmastime, for all their distinctions, are approached as a whole. The second step is to recognize that although each of these great feasts— Christmas Day, Holy Family, Mary Mother of God, Epiphany—has its singular emphasis (which centers on the magnificent readings of each), the Masses of Christmastime should have a unity: how they look, how they sound, how they smell. Like every season, that unity should leap from year to year, getting stronger each year after evaluating the previous year's efforts. And Christmastime should keep increasing day by day in splendor, beginning in the silent night of Christmas and bursting forth from the very stars by Epiphany.

Introductory rites: The ceremony of the Christmastime introductory rites should exude the richness of the season: the festive music, the procession, the deep bow the ministers offer in front of the altar, the incensing, the invocations of the penitential rite, the singing of the Gloria. As special care is needed for the brief, simple introductory rites of Advent, so another kind of care must be given to the ordering of those rites during Christmastime. Do not let the richness of these opening moments turn into a hodgepodge of nice effects.

In every entrance rite, remember that it is about the *assembly* entering into its liturgy, not about the presider and ministers entering into the sanctuary. The latter *may* be one of the things that happens, but without avail if these rites have not brought all the people *together* into their deed of word and eucharist.

Christmastime brings many special guests and visitors to the parish. Even the parish regulars sometimes come expecting more of a "show" than a liturgy. Take care to spend the necessary time to welcome guests and invite participation. This usually means clearly announcing what sort of participation materials are

WELCOME, YULE!
ADVENT AND CHRISTMASTIME 1989–1990

Use Welcome, Yule! in your parish

★ To bring Christian meaning to the many traditions of the season

★ As a gift to families, shut-ins, patients and inmates

★ For prayer and discussion in the catechumenate, bible study, religious education and parish renewal groups

★ As a decorative reminder of all that these seasons bring

Your supply of Welcome, Yule! will be shipped to arrive before the First Sunday of Advent, December 3, 1989. It will be wrapped in multiples of 100 copies of each handout ready to be given to each household as folks leave church on Sundays or for ministers to take or send to those who cannot be present. A Poster and a "How to Use" book with additional suggestions for use will be included with each order.

How much does it cost?

Welcome, Yule! is available in bulk. For example, if you order 500 copies you get 5 packages of an informative introduction to the season, 5 packages of 100 handouts for each of the six Sundays, 5 packages of 100 prayer leaflets, and a **double order** of special handouts for Christmas to take care of extra attendance. (Sorry, we cannot provide packages of less than 100 or fill orders for individual Sundays.) The price is $45 per 100. An Individual Packet containing one of each handout, a poster and a "How to Use" book is available for $5.00.

Order now from:
Liturgy Training Publications
1800 North Hermitage Avenue
Chicago IL 60622-1101
Phone: **312/486-7008**
FAX: **312/486-7094**
To inquire about orders or payments, call 312/486-4779

Order bulk quantities of **both** Welcome, Yule! and Paschal Mission **at the same time** and save 15% off the total cost. See LTP catalog (page 14) for details.

See page 14 in LTP's 1989 catalog for special coupon

ORDER FORM: Welcome, Yule! 1989-1990

Please send _____ **Welcome, Yule!** for _____ families.

Please send _____ **Individual Packet(s)** (one of each handout) at $5.00 each.

Please send _____ **Welcome Yule!** posters at $1.00 each.

$ _____ Total amount of order.

_____ U.S. funds

If your order is under $20, add $2.00 for shipping and handling, and include payment.

Bill to _____ Account # _____

Street address _____
_____ (We ship UPS. Give street address. No PO boxes.)

City, State, Zip _____

Phone _____ Date ordered ___/___/___

If additional instructions are needed, please attach separate sheet.
Keep a copy of your order for future reference.

227

PASCHAL MISSION 1990
LENT • TRIDUUM • EASTERTIME

Series runs from February 25, 1990 to June 3, 1990.

What is it?

PASCHAL MISSION lets Lent and Easter be a full fifty days. The series begins on the Sunday before Ash Wednesday with a handout that invites all to enter Lent seriously and joyfully. Then every Sunday through Lent and Easter and all the way to Pentecost has a handsome leaflet with a calendar; reflections and seasonal activities for home and community.

How is it used?

PASCHAL MISSION is used year after year by parishes across the country to intensify and support the quarter of the year that is Lent and Eastertime. PASCHAL MISSION is handed out to parishioners as they leave church each Sunday. It is carried to the hospitalized and shut-ins. Schools, religious education classes, parish study groups, the catechumenate, meetings of ministers and committees use it for prayer and discussion. Families use it in the home for prayer and reflection. A poster and a "How to Use" booklet will be included in your order.

How much is it?

PASCHAL MISSION is available by the set (18 different handouts) in lots of 100. The cost is about 5¢ per family each Sunday—less than a handout you would print yourself. The price is $80 per 100.

An Individual Packet containing one of each handout is available for $5.00.

PASCHAL MISSION for 1990 will be available
for shipment December 1, 1989.

ORDER FORM: Paschal Mission, 1990

Please send _____ hundred copies of **PASCHAL MISSION 1990** for _____ families.

Please send _____ **Individual Packet(s)** (one of each handout) at $5.00 each.

Please send _____ **PASCHAL MISSION 1990** posters at $1.00 each.

□ Payment enclosed. (I have added $2.00 for order under $20. LTP pays normal shipping charges for delivery in continental US on prepaid orders $20 and over.)

□ Bill me. (Shipping and handling will be added. Minimum order: $20.)

$ _____ Total amount of order.

_____ U.S. funds

Order early!

Bill to _____ Account # _____

Street address _____
_____ (We ship UPS. Give street address. No PO boxes.)

City, State, Zip _____

Phone _____ Date ordered ___/___/___

If additional instructions are needed, please attach separate sheet.
Keep a copy of your order for future reference.

227

WELCOME, YULE!

ADVENT AND CHRISTMASTIME 1989–1990

An annual series of beautiful handouts to bring home the seasons of Advent and Christmastime in your parish. Plan now to provide your parish families with these handouts for the coming Advent/Christmas season.

What's in Welcome, Yule?

★ Reflections on the comfort and joy of the Sunday scriptures

★ Blessing prayers for wreath, food, lights, tree, crèche, home and new year

★ A weekly calendar of ideas about the Christian traditions of the season

★ Beautiful illustrations to spark the imagination

How many different handouts?

Nine! An introduction to the season and its observance. A leaflet for each of the Sundays of Advent and Christmastime. Prayercards to place on the dinner table. We even include **a double order** of the Christmas leaflet so you can give something special to the many people who attend this day.

Use the other side to order Welcome, Yule! from Liturgy Training Publications.

Liturgy Training Publications
1800 North Hermitage Avenue
Chicago IL 60622-1101

Place
Postage
Here

PASCHAL MISSION 1990

LENT • TRIDUUM • EASTERTIME

PASCHAL MISSION is an annual series of 18 bulletin inserts/wrap-arounds for each week from the Sunday before Ash Wednesday through Pentecost.

Each week you will find:

◆ Delightful art that brings the stories and spirit of the seasons into the home

◆ Meditations on the Sunday scripture readings

◆ Questions that invite discussion and reflection

◆ A calendar for customs and ideas for keeping Lent and Eastertime

Prayercards for home use during the week are included.

PASCHAL MISSION is for:

◆ Parishes that want Lent to be a strong time of initiation and renewal leading to the Easter Triduum

◆ Parishes that want help in welcoming catechumens

◆ Parishes that want Eastertime to be a season of enthusiastic celebration that lasts until Pentecost

◆ All parishioners each Sunday and for small groups as well: renewal programs, prayer groups, Bible study groups and gatherings of catechumens and sponsors

☎ **Phone Orders Welcome: 312/486-7008**
📠 **or FAX: 312/486-7094**

Use this card to order PASCHAL MISSION 1990

Liturgy Training Publications
1800 North Hermitage Avenue
Chicago IL 60622-1101

Place
Postage
Here

used, on what page certain songs may be found, how we go to communion in this church, and other particulars. Fashion a participation aid that is simple and readily usable even by the stranger.

Invocations C3 of the penitential rite are suited to the season. The Gloria should be strong and perhaps sung in a way not used the rest of the year (see the suggestions for the Gloria under "Music"). Keep the opening rites inviting for everyone's participation and don't change too much from Christmas to Epiphany.

Liturgy of the word: The strong opening rites insist on a very strong liturgy of the word. Training lectors—especially in the rush of these days—obviously requires much sensitivity and careful work beforehand. But ask: Which is more important, the flowers or the scriptures? Set priorities. The Christmastime scriptures just about ask to be chanted: So much of Isaiah and John are lyrical poetry. The Word made flesh is a sung word, according to etymologists. The Greek and Hebrew meanings of *Logos* and *Dabar* ("word") imply chanted proclamation, not ordinary speech or written words. Do not forget about sacred silence during this season. The rich jubilation of these days is not incompatible with moments of silence. The good practices of silence begun during Advent should continue now through Christmas and beyond.

Choose a set of general intercessions to be used throughout Christmastime, with one or two variable petitions befitting the emphasis of each day within the season. See the suggestions beginning on page 35.

Liturgy of the eucharist: Notice that there are several proper prefaces to consider for particular days during the season (Mary Mother of God, Epiphany, Baptism of the Lord); on the other feasts, memorials and weekdays of the season, including Christmas Day itself, one of the three general Christmas prefaces may be used.

Concluding rites: On Christmas and New Year's, the good wishes of the parish staff to the community can be spoken after the prayer and before the final blessing. The concluding rite can include a blessing of the New Year and distribution of parish calendars on December 31 or January 1, and the blessing and distribution of chalk, Jordan water and incense on Epiphany. Texts for the solemn blessing during the Christmas season will be found in the sacramentary: #2 for Christmas Day and Holy Family, #3 for New Year's (but #10 might be a better choice as it echoes the first reading, or #15 for feasts of Mary), #4 for Epiphany. See notes on inclusive language in these blessings in "The Calendar."

MUSIC

The scope of the Twelve Days of Christmas with the great spectrum of feasts it contains gives clear evidence that the musician has many opportunities to continue the Christmas festival for nearly two weeks. Church musicians are swamped with an overabundance of musical pieces that number in the thousands and span centuries.

Gloria in excelsis: Like any other season, Christmastime has its own repertory that distinguishes it. Many parishes sustain the high from the Christmas Eve

and Day liturgies by using the Gloria as a processional hymn. Two Glorias that incorporate the "Gloria in excelsis Deo" refrain from the carol, "Angels we have heard on high," are Dan Laginya's "Christmas Gloria" (GIA, G-2971) and Richard Proulx's "Gloria for Christmastime" (GIA, G-3085). The Gloria in Perla Moré's *Misa Cubana* (Instituto Pastoral del Sureste—*Cantemos al Señor*) exhibits great charm with the alternating duple and triple meters. It lends itself to children's voices. Peter Jones's "Glory to God" (OCP, #7148) is festive with the brass and organ. The trumpet line before the refrain telegraphs clearly to the assembly that "it's your turn."

Psalmody: Richard Proulx's setting of the Christmas Mass at Midnight psalm, "Today is born our savior" (GIA, G-2538), requires a skilled cantor as does Howard Hughes's setting of the same antiphon and psalm (G-2026). The inner voice of Hughes's accompaniment works well with a French horn playing the tri-tone countermelody. It's worth the hassle of transposing the part since it provides a good foil to the 6/8 melody. Bear in mind that Psalm 98, "Sing to the Lord a new song," is the common psalm for Christmastime, suitable for any gathering during the season. There are a score of fine arrangements.

Carols during the preparation of the table and gifts, carols during the communion procession, carols during the recessional, carols before Mass—anytime one can find an appropriate space assures the assembly of their role in carrying on this folk tradition of "people music" at Christmastime. For many of the folks, "Adeste Fideles/O come, all ye faithful" and "Silent Night" are part of the *stirpes ecclesiae,* and it would be inhospitable not to include them in the parish's Christmas music program as often as good taste permits.

Choral music abounds. From Handel's *Messiah* to John Rutter's arrangements, choirs of various shapes and sizes do not want for sufficient material. Central and Eastern Europeans as well as Central and South Americans and Filipinos enjoy an immense treasury of carols, often under-represented in many familiar collections. Yet there are hundreds of choral arrangements of these ethnic gems. A brand new one by Neal Campbell is based on the Polish carol *Wzłobie leży*, "Infant Holy" (Salisbury Press, 909). It captures the lovely intimacy of the Polish tune. With similar simplicity is C. Gabarain's "Un niño se te acercó" *(Cantemos al Señor).* Another Spanish carol for Epiphany, "Ya viene la vieja" (G. Schirmer, 10200), is given an exquisite setting by Alice Parker and Robert Shaw. New life can be breathed into some of the choral chestnuts by their use at the beginning of the Sunday liturgy. "Wolcom Yole" from Benjamin Britten's *Ceremony of Carols* makes an arresting fanfare as it lists the feasts of Christmastime. "There is no ros of such vertu" from the same work is appropriate for January 1.

Choirs have no trouble celebrating, and Christmas provides many occasions for concerts, caroling parties, shut-in visits and the like. Another way of marking the season is staging the Christmas pageant with the underage Mary and Joseph and with the corps of third-grade angels on the front steps of the church. Harkening back to the colorful miracle and mystery plays of the medieval church, the site and the season are just right for such a dramatization.

A portable setting of the Christmas gospel (Luke 2:1–14) by the seventeenth-century composer Martin Mayer is found in volume 3 of the *Morning Star Choir*

Book (Concordia, 97-4972). It is portable in the sense that the performing forces are modest ones—the evangelist is sung by an alto or a baritone; a tenor or soprano is assigned to the angel's part, a two-part vocal ensemble sings the "Glory to God," and the continuo could be played easily by a portable keyboard, but without the rhythm devices. Two instruments in C have parts that act as ritornellos where action could happen. A dramatic telling of the hope of Christmas is Tom Conry's *Christmas Proclamation* (OCP, #8778) based on Genesis, Matthew and Luke. The singer tells a story in near-ritual language that climaxes with an intense litany of "be here among us," that demands movement, instruments (Orff) and the waving of banners, a fitting culmination to the Twelve Days of Christmas.

THE WORSHIP ENVIRONMENT

Certain scriptural phrases from chapters 60—66 of Isaiah have been the springboard for customary Christmas decorations: silver and gold, cypress and pine, the sun and the moon, leafy wreaths and jeweled diadems, springing plants, green trees, burning torches, harvest bounty, crimson apparel, an abundance of animals surrounding a child, a nursling at its mother's breast.

It's interesting that at Christmas we turn to ethnic traditions so readily in music, in ritual, in home customs—but when it comes to decorative elements we more than likely turn to commercial "tradition," sometimes resulting in worship environments that mimic shopping malls. Certainly the appreciation of appropriate dimensions and Christmas's emphasis on the lavishness of God mean that there will be a tendency to *appear* to imitate the displays in malls. But we ought also to be including many intimate folkarts in worship—such as Filipino or Moravian paper stars, Lithuanian and Polish straw ornaments, Mexican and Guatemalan woodcarvings, as well as the glorious combinations of fruits, greens and flowers so popular in Italy and the American South. As Epiphany makes abundantly clear, all the world has a place around the Christmas table.

A warning: Christmas deserves a lavish splash of colors, greens and lights to show our exuberant joy, to reflect the utter graciousness of God. But that can't translate into a stage setting. There's a simple solution. When you imagine Christmas decorations, imagine them outside of the immediate vicinity of the altar, ambo and presidential chair. How will you decorate the assembly's space?

Another warning: Will the Christmas decorations be in scale with decorations planned for Eastertime? Or will they say that Christmas, not Easter, is the more important festival? Garlands, lights, banners and flowers are all traditional at Easter too, although we have done a poor job of using them then. As an example, pine and holly are customary at Christmas; but yew, boxwood and pussywillows are customary at Easter. Both are signs of eternal life and victory.

The crèche: The Bethlehem scene, like the Advent wreath and Christmas tree, is a home custom that somehow got adopted into the worship place. The past ten years or so have seen more and more crèches being set up either in front of the altar or the ambo—always a mistake. A traditional scene requires lots of space and lots of details. It is too dominant a focal point to compete with the chair, altar or ambo; it belongs, like any church statuary, in its own shrine, preferably out of

the direct line of sight of the people when they gather for liturgy. And that's really a very satisfying place to put the crèche—a place to visit before or after worship—so that folks can make a "pilgrimage" to Bethlehem.

Within an out-of-the-way place, parish artisans can construct the crèche with great creativity: with lots of animals, birds nestled in branches of trees, flowers poking up through the straw, arrangements of dried grasses and herbs in great bundles, a galaxy of stars and planets hung from overhead. Take your cue from traditional Bethlehem scenes, the Latin American *nacimiento,* the Italian *presepio,* the Pennsylvania Dutch *putz.* A crèche is no place for a tidy arrangement of a few statues. Rather, it is a representation of paradise; every blessed thing in the universe—ourselves included—gathers around God in adoration.

When do you decorate for Christmas? The Fourth Sunday of Advent is also the day before Christmas Day. Surely our liturgical tradition demands that this final Advent liturgy take place in an Advent worship environment. And just as surely the evening or midnight Christmas Eve liturgy demands the great surprise and delight of the Christmastime worship environment. Unless your parish can muster forces willing to exhaust themselves throughout the afternoon of December 24, it will be necessary to plan carefully just what of the Christmas decorations are executed before December 24's morning liturgies and what happens afterward.

You could decorate leisurely throughout the previous week, then veil most everything in dropcloths for Saturday evening and Sunday morning—or is that bizarre? Seasons of preparation are not incompatible with the likes of ladders, scaffolding and coverings. You could set up the heavy, dark elements—like trees, garlanding, wreaths, the crèche—*before* the Fourth Sunday, and then add the colorful, easily moved elements—like ornaments, flowers, bows and the statues—*after* the Sunday morning Mass. Unfortunately, if this is done, the wonderful scent of conifers will be part of the environment of this Fourth Sunday of Advent instead of being one of the olfactory surprises of Christmas. A way to liven up this aroma for Christmas is to daub Balsam fragrance (see "Resources" in this book) around the church. (Yes, there are people who are allergic to evergreens.) Any decorative elements that are both heavy *and* colorful, like bright fabric hangings, might be put in place beforehand—always a time-consuming task—and then pinned up or hidden behind something (such as any Advent hangings) until Sunday afternoon.

OTHER RITUAL PRAYER

If you've been keeping the liturgy of the hours during Advent, don't stop during Christmastime. Embellish Morning and Evening Prayer with caroling and hospitality. Publicize it well.

Lessons and carols: The liturgical form of a traditional service of lessons and carols is actually a vigil service, properly held before any major festival; and Christmastime is full of festival days. There is of course an "Advent lessons and carols" held as a vigil before the First Sunday of Advent, rich with the scriptures and music of Advent, not Christmas. Likewise, there are patterns for Easter and Pentecost vigils in this format. But these services are not concerts, which is what so often happens to them on both sides of the Atlantic.

Unless you regularly use the word "lessons" in place of what a Roman Catholic usually calls "readings," you really shouldn't be hosting anything called "lessons and carols." Granted, it's a catchy title, but we have enough liturgy to work with in the form of Morning and Evening Prayer, eucharist and the other sacraments. And let's not forget the vigil, in which all the repertory of a lessons and carols service can shine, with the addition of psalmody and perhaps a *lucernarium*.

A New Year's watchnight service: Some Catholic parishes have begun a New Year vigil ("watchnight") coupled with festivity. They've borrowed the idea from certain Protestant churches as a chance to praise God for the blessings of the old year and to ask God for blessings in the new. While at first this might sound like a fine idea, any gathering of Christians during these days of Christmas must continue and not stand apart from all that Christmas means. A vigil for the New Year that ignores Christmastime is, at heart, alien to our liturgical tradition.

Perhaps some genuine creativity is needed here, for it would be a mistake to think that New Year's was altogether secular, with no relationship to Christmas. Christmastime itself wraps around January 1. It's more than coincidence that December 25 is eight days (itself a sign of eternity) from the Kalends of January, "janus" meaning the "gateway." The traditional Twelve Days (December 26– January 6) were a way of interpreting this turning of the year, a way of proclaiming that the coming of Christ opens the gate that separates time from eternity. The center point in these Twelve Days is New Year's midnight.

The Episcopal *Book of Occasional Services* offers "A Service for New Year's Eve" that can be amended to include carols as well as the Roman readings and prayers for January 1, concluding with plenty of merry noisemaking and a party at midnight. Any vigil for the New Year can take its cue from the lovely Lutheran carol "From heaven above": "Glory to God in highest heav'n / Who unto us the Son has giv'n. / With angels sing in pious mirth: / A glad new year to all the earth!"

Sample Prayer Texts for Christmastime

Introductory Rites

GREETING

For the entire season:
The peace and love of God our Father, manifested in Christ who was born for our salvation, be with you all.

INTRODUCTION

If an introduction seems superfluous, the introduction can be combined with the invitation.

Christmas:
We have gathered together on this joyful morning, in communion with believers in Christ everywhere in the world, to celebrate the birth of our Lord. To all who are assembled to keep the solemnity of this day, the angel announces the Good News proclaimed to the shepherds: "Today is born for us a Savior: the Messiah, the Lord!"

Holy Family:
On this Sunday of Christmastime, the church celebrates the Word-made-flesh by contemplating the life he shared with Mary and Joseph: a holy, and human, family.

Mary, Mother of God:
On the octave of Christmas, at the dawn of a new year, we continue to celebrate the mystery of the Word made flesh. In setting before us the person of Mary, whose faith and trust were essential to the mystery of our salvation, the church wishes us to see this woman as image of the church and model of believers.

Epiphany of the Lord:
Today's splendid solemnity brings to fulfillment our celebration of the Word made flesh. "Epiphany" means "appearance" or "manifestation." In the magi led to Christ by the guidance of a star, we are to see "our forerunners in calling and in faith," and to rejoice with them in the beginnings of our hope and enlightenment.

INVITATION TO THE PENITENTIAL RITE

In these shining days of our Christmas festival, as we prepare to celebrate the mystery of God with us, let us turn to the Lord and ask God's mercy.

PENITENTIAL RITE

For the entire season:
The penitential rite would be omitted at the Christmas Eve and Midnight Masses if a vigil, proclamation and/or blessing preceded.

Lord Jesus, you are mighty God and Prince of peace: Lord, have mercy. Lord Jesus, you are Son of God and Son of Mary: Christ, have mercy. Lord Jesus, you are Word made flesh and splendor of the Father: Lord, have mercy.

Or:

Eternal Word, through whom all things were made: Lord, have mercy. True Light, you have come into the world and yet the world has not received you: Christ, have mercy. Son of God made flesh, you have pitched your tent among us: Lord, have mercy.

Or:

King of Peace and Holy One of God: Lord, have mercy. Radiant Light, putting to flight all darkness: Christ, have mercy. Model and image of the human person reborn and made new: Lord, have mercy.

Introduction to the Readings

Christmas Vigil:
This lovely night's scriptures are part of our celebration of the wedding of heaven and earth in the mystery of the incarnation: Isaiah sings of Jerusalem, as the "Espoused of the Lord." Paul presents Jesus as the fruit of this

CONTINUED

marriage. Matthew traces the child's human descent even as he proclaims God's miraculous intervention.

Christmas Midnight:
In the beauty of Christmas midnight, the scriptures evoke images of Christ's paschal mystery, the mystery of Easter. Isaiah sings of divine judgment and the victory of justice. Paul exults in our redemption through Christ's sacrifice. Even Luke's timeless gospel foreshadows a future rejection by the world and acceptance by the lowly and marginal.

Christmas Dawn:
The scriptures of Christmas dawn echo the sunrise of salvation. Isaiah calls us "a city not forsaken." Paul announces the amazing grace of our unmerited salvation. And we are invited to take our places before the manger with the little and lowly who alone can welcome the child in simplicity of heart.

Christmas Day:
The scriptures proclaim the beauty of the day of salvation that forever dawns over the mountains of a weary world. The comforting embrace of God which the prophets longed for has brought us closer to the heart of God than any prophecy could have foretold. In Jesus the eternal Word has become flesh in our world of time.

Holy Family:
The word proclaims the ideal of family life but does not spare us the mystery that accompanies reality. Surely Jesus lived the wisdom of the Hebrew Scriptures but did not enjoy the "long life" they spoke of. The way of mutual respect and forgiveness mapped out by Paul is fraught with heartache as well as joy. And even the holy family is victim of the misunderstanding and hostility of others.

Mary, Mother of God:
The first scripture proclaimed in the new year invokes the name of the Lord in blessing over the assembly. Paul celebrates the woman's central and irreplaceable role in our status as adopted children of God, while Luke presents her as the model of all who in wonder and faith welcome into their lives the mystery of salvation.

Epiphany of the Lord:
Splendor and light, radiance and glory are words that leap up from the pages of this feast's scriptures. What pagans search for in the wisdom of human reasoning and what believers seek in the pages of revelation converge to find fulfillment in the person of Jesus and the Good News he proclaims of God's reconciling love.

General Intercessions

INVITATION TO PRAYER

Christmas, Holy Family and
Mary, Mother of God:
Jesus, born at Bethlehem of the Virgin Mary, is Emmanuel, God-with-us: Let us join in prayer with all who believe and hope in the salvation the Lord has wrought.

On Epiphany and the Baptism
of the Lord:
In Christ, God's own Son, who took our flesh upon himself, let us approach the Most High in the spirit of sons and daughters.

INTERCESSION FOR THE CHURCH

The "For . . ." or "That . . ." format should be used consistently throughout a given set of intercessions.

For the holy church of God: that it may manifest within itself and show forth to the world our unity as a true family, where all are loved, supported and forgiven: let us pray to the Lord.

Or:

That the church may reflect the Lord's poverty and spirit of service, announcing to all that God's holy reign is indeed among us: let us pray to the Lord.

CONTINUED

INTERCESSION FOR THE WORLD

For all who hold political responsibility in the world: that they may work together to build a true and just peace that heals the wounded and safeguards the dignity of human life: let us pray to the Lord.

Or:

That all peoples of the earth may reject violence and war, and pledge their resources and energies to the building up of peace and solidarity within the human family: let us pray to the Lord.

INTERCESSION FOR THOSE IN NEED

For innocent victims of violence, the persecuted, marginal and oppressed: that their human rights be recognized and that all may honor in them the image of God's own Son who became a human being for our sake: let us pray to the Lord.

Or:

That the God of justice hear the cries of the oppressed and cause the dawning of a liberation in which all acknowledge the human dignity of every person: let us pray to the Lord.

INTERCESSION FOR THE ASSEMBLY

For this eucharistic community: that we may welcome the grace of this holy season by proclaiming with our lives our faith in the Christ who lives in our midst and whom we serve in others: let us pray to the Lord.

Or:

That we may experience in this season and throughout the new year a deepening of the Lord's peace at home, in school, in our daily work, and in all areas of our lives: let us pray to the Lord.

Or the intercession for the assembly may be based on the scriptures of the day:

Christmas Eve or Day:
For the homeless: that helping hands and loving hearts provide them with a welcome worthy of the Lord who lives within them: let us pray to the Lord.

Holy Family:
For a deepening of peace in households where love is strong, and for the healing of hearts wounded by discord and misunderstanding: let us pray to the Lord.

Mary, Mother of God:
For women everywhere: that the image of Mary, strong woman of faith, gentle mother of peace, be an inspiration and challenge to reflection and action: let us pray to the Lord.

Epiphany of the Lord:
For the nations of the world, torn by dissension within, kept apart by hostility, that the light of Christ's love may draw us together as one human family: let us pray to the Lord.

CONCLUDING PRAYER

These concluding prayers for the intercessions were selected from ICEL original opening prayers for Mass based on the scripture readings of the day, © 1983, 1986, 1987, 1988, International Committee on English in the Liturgy, Inc. (ICEL). All rights reserved.

Any day in Christmastime:
God Most High,
your only Son embraced the
   weakness of flesh,
that we might have power
   to become your children;
your eternal Word chose a dwelling
   among us,
that we might live in your presence.

With grace upon grace,
reveal in our lives
the share of his fullness
   we have all received;
and let us see the glory which he has
with you and the Holy Spirit
as God, for ever and ever.
—*Copyright © ICEL*

Christmas Vigil:
Unwearied is your love for us,
God of Abraham, Isaac, and Jacob,
and steadfast is your covenant.

CONTINUED

But wonderful beyond words,
  God of Mary and Joseph,
the gift of Emmanuel, our Savior.

Count us among the people
  in whom you delight;
and from this night's marriage
  of heaven and earth
draw all generations into the
  embrace of your love.

We ask this through your
  only-begotten Son,
who lives and reigns with you
  and the Holy Spirit,
one God, for ever and ever.
—*Copyright* © ICEL

Christmas Midnight:
Good and gracious God,
on this holy night you gave us
  your Son,
Lord of the universe,
  wrapped in swaddling clothes,
Savior of all, lying in a manger.

On this holy night
draw us into the mystery of your love.
Grant us a voice with the
  heavenly host
that we may sing your glory on high,
and give us a place
  among the shepherds
that we may find the one
  for whom we have waited,
Jesus Christ, the Messiah and Lord,
who lives and reigns with you
  and the Holy Spirit,
one God, for ever and ever.
—*Copyright* © ICEL

Christmas Dawn:
On this day, O God,
your loving kindness shines forth
  from the face of a child.
On this day
your saving compassion dawns,
for the birth of your Son
  in human flesh
has made us heirs of eternal life.

Fill us with wonder on this holy day:
let what we have seen and heard
  find a place in our hearts,
and let our lives proclaim
  what you have revealed.

We ask this through
  our Lord Jesus Christ, your Son,
who lives and reigns with you
  and the Holy Spirit,
one God, for ever and ever.
—*Copyright* © ICEL

Christmas Day:
We praise you, gracious God,
for glad tidings of peace
and good news of great joy:
your Word has become flesh
and made his dwelling among us.

By this gift of enduring love
  and truth
transfigure our lives;
and reveal to all the world
the Light no darkness can
  extinguish:
your Son, our Lord Jesus Christ,
who lives and reigns with you
  and the Holy Spirit,
one God, for ever and ever.
—*Copyright* © ICEL

Holy Family:
God our Creator,
guardian of our homes
  and source of all blessings,
your Son, begotten before the dawn
  of creation,
entered the human family
and was entrusted to the care
  of Mary and Joseph.

Confirm in us a reverence
for the gift and mystery of life,
so that parents and children,
like the holy family of Nazareth,
may cherish one another and be
  heartened by your love.

We ask this through Emmanuel,
your Son, our Lord Jesus Christ,
who lives and reigns with you
  and the Holy Spirit,
one God, for ever and ever.
—*Copyright* © ICEL

Mary, Mother of God:
Most high God,
you come near to us this
  Christmas season
in a child born of the woman, Mary.

CONTINUED

In the midst of darkness,
  she gave birth to light.
In the midst of silence,
  she brought forth the Word.

Grant that, like her,
we may ponder these things
  in our hearts
and recognize in her child
  the God who saves,
Jesus, your Son,
living and reigning with you
  and the Holy Spirit,
one God, for ever and ever.
—*Copyright © ICEL*

Epiphany of the Lord:
We have seen the star of your glory
rising in splendor,
Lord God of the nations.
The radiance of your
  Word-made-flesh
pierces the darkness that covers
  the earth
and signals the dawn of justice
  and peace.

May his brightness illumine our lives
and beckon all nations to walk
  in your light.

We ask this through Emmanuel,
your Son, our Lord Jesus Christ,
who lives and reigns with you
  and the Holy Spirit,
one God, for ever and ever.
—*Copyright © ICEL*

Baptism of the Lord:
God of the covenant,
you anointed your beloved Son
with the power of the Holy Spirit
to be light for the nations
and release for captives.

May we who have been born again
  of water and the Spirit,
proclaim with our lips the good news
  of his peace
and manifest in our lives the victory
  of his justice.

We ask this through the Son in whom
  you delight,

Jesus Christ, our Lord,
who lives and reigns with you
  and the Holy Spirit,
one God, for ever and ever.
—*Copyright © ICEL*

Communion Rite

INTRODUCTION TO
THE LORD'S PRAYER

For the entire season:
Jesus taught us to call God our Father,
and so we have the courage to say:

Or:

The Son of God became a child of earth
that we might become children of God;
with thankful praise we cry out:

PRAYER FOR PEACE

For the entire season:
Lord Jesus Christ, on the night of your
birth the choirs of angels announced
peace to God's people on earth: Look
not on our sins, but on the faith of your
church. . . .

INVITATION TO COMMUNION

For the entire season:
This is the Lamb of God, who takes
away the sins of the world: Emmanuel,
God-with-us. (*Or on Holy Family and
Mary, Mother of God:* Son of God and
Son of Mary) (*Or on Epiphany/Bap-
tism of the Lord:* the eternal Son of
God, manifested now to all nations)
Happy are those who are called to his
supper.

Concluding Rite

BLESSING

The Episcopal Church's Book of Occasional
Services *provides a version of the Christmas Solemn Blessing that avoids exclusive
language. Here is an attempt to combine the
best of this version with the Italian and
Spanish versions:*

May the God of infinite goodness,
whose Son by his birth scattered

CONTINUED

earth's darkness and by his glorious incarnation made radiant this holy night (day), dispel from your lives the darkness of sin and brighten your hearts with the light of grace.

May God, who sent angels to proclaim to shepherds the good news and glad tidings of our Savior's birth, fill you with joy and make you heralds of the gospel.

May God, who in the Word made flesh joined heaven to earth and earth to heaven, give you peace and good will, and welcome you one day among the citizens of heaven.

May almighty God bless you. . . .

The Book of Occasional Services *has this interesting variation on the Solemn Blessing for Epiphany, incorporating (as does the antiphon at Mary's canticle for Evening Prayer II) the three manifestations associated with this solemnity:*

May almighty God, who led the magi by the shining of a star to find Christ, the Light from Light, lead you also in your pilgrimage to find the Lord.

May God, who sent the Holy Spirit to rest upon the Only-begotten One at his baptism in the Jordan River, pour out that Spirit on you who have come through the waters of new birth.

May God, by the power that turned water into wine at the wedding feast at Cana, transform your lives and make glad your hearts.

May almighty God bless you. . . .

Dismissal

For the entire season:
As witnesses of God's glory and messengers of God's peace, let us go forth in joy and gladness to love and serve the Lord.

A Vigil Service for Christmas Eve

The following might be used as a Christmas Vigil service, as a prelude to the Vigil Mass, or as a prelude to the Midnight Mass. It has been adapted in part from the Ambrosian rite of Milan. Note that its structure is patterned after the liturgy of the word of the Easter Vigil. Perhaps any pre-Midnight Mass choir concert might be worked into this format:

Entrance Procession and Greeting

During the entrance procession the invitatory from the liturgy of the hours may be sung ("Christ is born for us; come let us adore him") or another suitable antiphon or carol. The priest kisses the altar and may incense it, then goes to the chair. This greeting from the new Spanish Order of Mass may be used:

The peace and love of God our Father, revealed to us in Christ, born for our salvation, be with you all.

The priest may introduce the vigil in these or similar words:

In this vigil on this holy night we celebrate the dawn of our salvation in the incarnation of our Lord Jesus Christ, the Father's only-begotten Son, born for us of the Virgin Mary. With gratitude let us recall his humanity and the life he shared with the children of the earth, praying that the power of his divinity may enable us to answer his call to forgiveness and life.

Candle lighting

A simple lucernarium *involves the lighting of a single candle or perhaps candles throughout the church, or even a candle-decked fir tree. This rite is accompanied by the thanksgiving for light, as in* Praise God in Song *(GIA).*

Psalmody or Liturgy of the Word

Either the psalmody from the Office of Readings (see Volume I, *Liturgy of the Hours, 400–403) or this series of readings may follow:*

READING ONE

Genesis 15:1–10, 17–18 (descendants are promised to Abraham). Sung psalm or carol, then the collect:

O God, in the human nature of your Son, you have given us the origin and fulfillment of our relationship with you. Keep us faithful to this gift we have received, for our every hope of salvation is in him, who lives and reigns for ever and ever.

READING TWO

Samuel 1:7c–18 (Hannah asks the Lord for a child). Sung psalm or carol, then the collect:

Merciful God, with the birth of your only-begotten Son according to the flesh and by his death on the cross, you have brought to completion the salvation of your people. Grant us, your servants, a firm faith in this wondrous plan of love, that we might arrive safely at the fulfillment of your glorious promises under the guidance and by the grace of Christ your Son, who lives and reigns for ever and ever.

READING THREE

Isaiah 7:1–17 (the virgin will bear Emmanuel). Sung psalm or carol, then the collect:

Listen, O our Redeemer, to the voice of supplication of all of us who celebrate this joyful night. On this night, to save us and bring us immortality, your heavenly and eternal life entered into and renewed our human nature: Bring us on the final day to your heavenly feast, where you live and reign for ever and ever.

READING FOUR

Judges 13:2–9a (the angel of the Lord announces the birth of a child to a barren woman). Sung psalm or carol, then the collect:

In the mystery of your only-begotten Son's birth among us, you have helped us to understand, O God our Father, your wondrous kindness and your desire to save us. Help us respond to such generosity and live with a heart-felt resolution to love always as your children, doing good to all. We ask this through Christ our Lord.

PATRISTIC READING

From the Sermon by Saint Leo the Great, found in the Liturgy of the Hours. *This marvelous reading is a classic Christmas text that deserves to be proclaimed this holy night.*

Proclamation of the Birth of Christ

On page 42 of this Sourcebook.

Blessing of the crèche

From the Book of Blessings.

Gloria

No greeting or penitential rite.

Opening Prayer of Mass

The liturgy continues as usual with the readings and with the psalm from Mass.

The Epiphany Blessing of Incense, Water and Chalk

The old Roman Ritual provided an Epiphany blessing of incense, water and chalk in church to be distributed and taken home. With some adaptation, the custom might well be preserved. At home, the current year and the initials of the legendary names of the Magi are marked above the doorway with blessed chalk:

   19 + C + M + B + 90

while the presiding member of the household prays:

May all who come to our home
   this year
rejoice to find Christ living among us;
and may we seek and serve,
   in everyone we meet,
Jesus who is Lord for ever and ever.

The C-M-B are the initials of the legendary names of the magi, Caspar, Melchior and Balthasar. Another explanation of C-M-B is: Christus mansionem benedicat, "May Christ bless this dwelling place." Incense is burned during a festive meal, and the rooms of the home may be sprinkled with water, a sign of the River Jordan.

Here is a new blessing of the chalk, water and incense to be prayed at home or in the church. It is based on thoughts from the old:

Blessed are you,
Lord God of all creation:
by the guidance of a star you led the
   magi to your child,
and by the light of faith you bring us
   to know Christ as Lord,
   the Messiah you have sent.

Bless us as we burn this incense, a
   sign of the fragrance of prayerful
   lives offered up before you;

bless us as we use this chalk to mark
   our doors in your honor;
bless us as we sprinkle our homes
   with this water,
sign of the Lord Jesus' baptism
   in the River Jordan.

May the homes where these things
   are used in faith
be dwelling places of goodness,
   humility, self-control,
   mutual respect for one another,
   hospitality toward strangers,
   and loving obedience to your word.
We ask this through Christ our Lord.

This prayer could be included in the bulletin or wrapped inside the parish calendar to provide a link between liturgical prayer and communal prayer in the "domestic church." Catholic Household Blessings and Prayers *contains a blessing of the home and household on the Epiphany—be sure to call everyone's attention to this blessing. The new* Book of Blessings *has an order for the blessing of homes especially appropriate for pastoral visits at this season (and for the Easter season, too).*

A bit of advice: Attractive water holders are easy to come by and inexpensive if you purchase pint food containers from a restaurant supply store or even your local deli. If you order them in advance, most supermarkets can get them for you without any writing on them. Chalk in quantity can be bought from stationers or school supply stores. Incense can be burned in the home without charcoal simply by heating it in any metal container on the stove.

PROCLAMATION OF THE BIRTH OF CHRIST

The twenty-fifth day of December. In the five thousand and ninety-ninth year of the creation of the world, from the time when God in the beginning created the heavens and the earth; the two thousand, nine hundred and fifty-seventh year after the flood; the two thousand and fifteenth year from the birth of Abraham; the one thousand, five hundred and tenth year from Moses and the going forth of the people of Israel from Egypt; the one thousand and thirty-second year from David's being anointed king; in the sixty-fifth week according to the prophecy of Daniel; in the one hundred and ninety-fourth Olympiad; the seven hundred and fifty-second year from the foundation of the city of Rome; the forty-second year of the

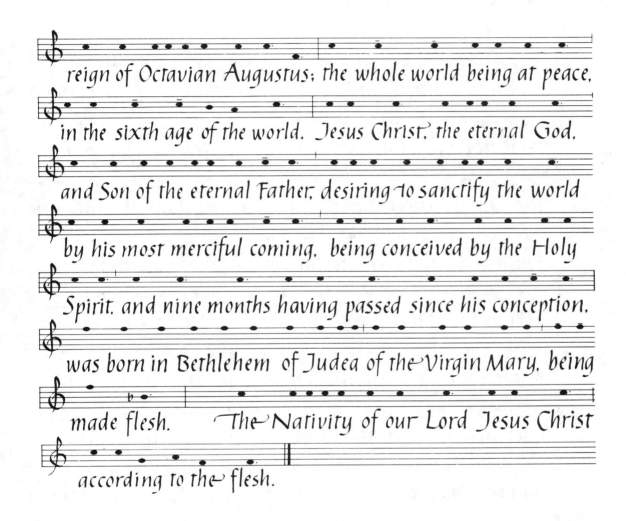

reign of Octavian Augustus; the whole world being at peace, in the sixth age of the world. Jesus Christ, the eternal God, and Son of the eternal Father, desiring to sanctify the world by his most merciful coming, being conceived by the Holy Spirit, and nine months having passed since his conception, was born in Bethlehem of Judea of the Virgin Mary, being made flesh. The Nativity of our Lord Jesus Christ according to the flesh.

Suggestions for using the Christmas proclamation:

This proclamation, taken from the ancient martyrology entry for December 25, could be sung at the beginning of the Midnight Mass. It should be done without explanation, with great simplicity and reverence in the silence and darkness as the assembly keeps vigil.

Acolytes with lighted candles might accompany the cantor to the ambo or another appropriate place before the assembly. The cantor may indicate with a gesture that the assembly is to stand; when all are standing the proclamation begins. The tradition calls for the assembly to kneel after the words "having passed since his conception . . ." and to rise before

"The Nativity of our Lord . . ." The cantor should stop at both times to allow this to take place. The acolytes should know beforehand so that they can model for the assembly the kneeling and the rising.

When the proclamation is concluded, the entrance rites of Midnight Mass—which have truly begun with this chant—can continue with song.

Text copyright © 1989, United States Catholic Conference (USCC), 3211 Fourth Street NE, Washington, D.C., 20017-1194. All rights reserved. Text was prepared by Fr. Richard Wojcik. Chant based on an adaptation of the original chant by Msgr. J. T. Kush. Calligraphy by Dolores Dehaan.

PROCLAMATION OF THE DATE OF EASTER

Dear brothers and sisters, the glory of the Lord has

shone upon us, and shall ever be manifest among us, until

the day of his return. Through the rhythms of times and

seasons let us celebrate the mysteries of salvation.

Let us recall the year's culmination, the Easter Triduum

of the Lord: his crucifixion, his burial and his rising

celebrated between the evening of the twelfth of April

and the dawn of the fifteenth of April. Each Easter, each

Sunday the holy Church makes present that great and

saving deed by which Christ has forever conquered sin

and death.

From Easter come forth and are reckoned all the days we

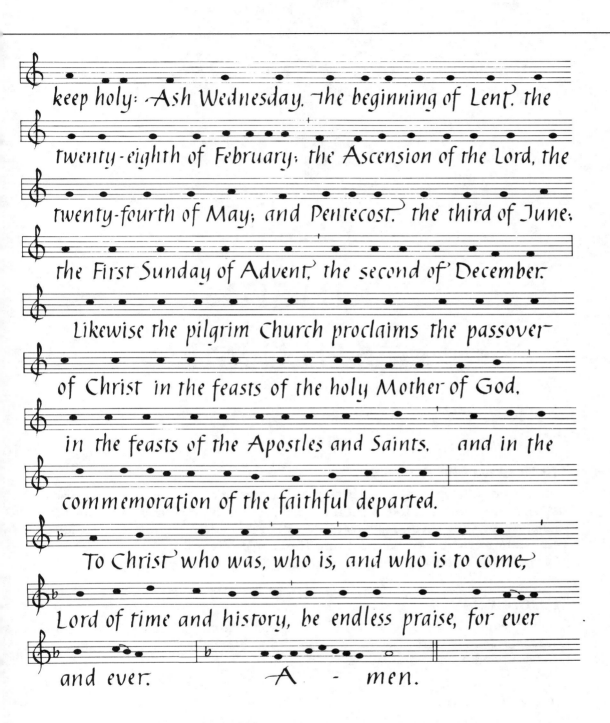

keep holy: Ash Wednesday, the beginning of Lent, the

twenty-eighth of February; the Ascension of the Lord, the

twenty-fourth of May; and Pentecost, the third of June;

the First Sunday of Advent, the second of December.

Likewise the pilgrim Church proclaims the passover

of Christ in the feasts of the holy Mother of God,

in the feasts of the Apostles and Saints, and in the

commemoration of the faithful departed.

To Christ who was, who is, and who is to come,

Lord of time and history, be endless praise, for ever

and ever. A - men.

Suggestions for using the Epiphany proclamation:

This proclamation, announcing the date of Easter and the various dates that depend on Easter, is chanted by a cantor following the gospel reading or homily on the solemnity of the Epiphany. The proclamation can be sung from the ambo with lights and incense as at the gospel. The line, "Each Easter, each Sunday, . . ." may sound like an error when chanted. The Italian sacramentary reads: "Every Sunday, as in a weekly Easter, . . ." Cantors: take note of the key change in the final lines. These lines require great solemnity and proper timing.

LENT
·◆·
TRIDUUM
·◆·
EASTERTIME

LENT

OFFICIAL DESCRIPTION

Lent is a preparation for the celebration of Easter. For the lenten liturgy disposes both catechumens and the faithful to celebrate the paschal mystery: catechumens through the several stages of Christian initiation; the faithful, through reminders of their own baptism and through penitential practices. (*General Norms for the Liturgical Year and Calendar*, 27)

RESOURCES

The following bibliography is useful for Lent, Triduum and Eastertime. These seasons are truly part of a single season—the paschal season—and must be discussed and prepared together.

Historical Background

Adam, Adolf. *The Liturgical Year* (New York: Pueblo Publishing Co., 1981).

Cobb, Peter G. "1. The History of the Christian Year," under "The Calendar" in *The Study of the Liturgy*, Cheslyn Jones, Geoffrey Wainwright, Edward Yarnold, eds. (New York: Oxford University Press, 1978).

Martimort, A. G., et al. *The Church at Prayer*, vol. 4: *The Liturgy and Time* (Collegeville: The Liturgical Press, 1986 edition).

Nocent, Adrian, OSB. *The Liturgical Year*, vols. 2 and 3 (Collegeville: The Liturgical Press, 1977).

Talley, Thomas J. *The Origins of the Liturgical Year* (New York: Pueblo Publishing Co., 1986), 163–230 (Lent), 1–54 (Triduum), 54–77 (Eastertime). This reading is indispensable for anyone who wants to understand what it is we are about in planning for Lent, Triduum and Eastertime. Here is a sense of the historical and spiritual *communio* in which we stand and of which we are a part.

Liturgical/Preaching Help

Hopko, Thomas. *The Lenten Spring* (Crestwood, New York: St. Vladimir's Seminary Press, 1983). Hopko offers a wealth of observations on the lenten themes and disciplines, written from the Orthodox tradition and oriented toward their liturgical observances, but providing much helpful material for any Christian observance of the season.

Huck, Gabe. *The Three Days: Parish Prayer in the Paschal Triduum* (Chicago: Liturgy Training Publications, 1981).

Huck, Gabe, and Simcoe, Mary Ann, eds. *A Triduum Sourcebook* (Chicago: Liturgy Training Publications, 1983).

Huck, Gabe; Ramshaw, Gail; Lathrop, Gordon, eds. *An Easter Sourcebook: The Fifty Days* (Chicago: Liturgy Training Publications, 1988).

Irwin, Kevin W. *Lent: A Guide to the Eucharist and Hours* (New York: Pueblo Publishing Co., 1986).

Lawrence, Emeric, OSB. *Believe the Good News* (Collegeville: The Liturgical Press, 1982). Continuing his homiletic reflections in the style of his Advent-Christmas book referred to previously.

Lawrence, Emeric, OSB. *Risen and Still with You* (Collegeville: The Liturgical Press, 1985).

Liturgy (Journal of the Liturgical Conference), vol. 3, no. 1. Entitled "Easter's Fifty Days," this issue is filled with historical information, model celebrations, Easter-in-the-home ideas, and much more. An issue that makes a wonderful introduction to this journal, if you're not already familiar with it.

Merton, Thomas. *Seasons of Celebration* (New York: Farrar, Straus and Giroux, reprinted 1983), 113–24 (Ash Wednesday), 125–43 (Christian self-denial), 144–57 (Eastertime).

Nocent, Adrian, OSB. *Liturgical Year,* vol. 2 (Collegeville: The Liturgical Press), 3–56 (biblical and liturgical reflections); 161–73 (structures and themes); 173–83 (lenten weekdays, including a chart that might be particularly helpful for those who participate in daily Mass and/or liturgy of the hours during Lent). Vol. 3, 146–258 (structure and themes of Eastertime).

Ratzinger, Joseph. *Journey to Easter* (New York: Crossroads Press, 1987). Especially 13–61 and reflections on the paschal mystery, 92–117.

Schmemann, Alexander. *Great Lent: Journey to Pascha* (Crestwood, New York: St. Vladimir's Seminary Press, 1974). A classic: Don't start Lent without it! Orthodox calendar and liturgy as reference points, but universally applicable meditations on fasting, discipline, celebration. Lent as pilgrimage.

Simcoe, Mary Ann, ed. *Parish Path through Lent and Eastertime,* second edition (Chicago: Liturgy Training Publications, 1985).

A SENSE OF THE SEASON

The word "Lent" means springtime. This word comes from the same root as "lengthen," since daytime lengthens during Lent. The northern hemisphere turns toward the sun, the source of life, and winter turns into spring. In Hebrew the word for repentance is *teshuvah,* rooted in *shuvah,* "to turn," like the turning of the earth to the sun, like the turning of soil before planting.

"Even now, says the Lord, turn to me." (Joel 2:12) The word "sin" means separation. We are called to turn from our separate selves, from our sin, to come together in community. Self-denial is the way we express our repentance. In the lengthening brightness from Ash Wednesday until Holy Thursday afternoon, our holy Lent, we turn away from sin and death. We turn to God as our source of life.

Self-denial is three-fold, advises chapter six of Matthew's Gospel. We *pray:* "Go to your room, close your door, and pray to your Father in private." We *fast:* "No one must see you are fasting but your Father." We give *alms:* "Keep your deeds of mercy secret, and your Father who sees in secret will repay you." Self-denial is an exercise, a workout, a getting into shape. Through the lenten exercise of prayer, fasting and almsgiving we spring-clean our lives, sharpen our senses, put tomorrow in its place and treasure the day at hand.

Why is Lent 40 days? It took 40 days for sinfulness to drown under the flood before a new creation could inherit the earth (Genesis 7:4). It took 40 years for the generation of slaves to die before the freeborn could enter the promised land (Numbers 14:33–35). For 40 days Moses and Elijah and Jesus fasted and prayed to prepare themselves for a life's work.

Forty is symbolic of a journey. It is the journey of the catechumens to baptism. They sail over the waters toward the rainbow, and march to the promised land of God's reign. Forty is symbolic of a lifetime, the lives of all the baptized. We pattern our lifelong work according to the gospel.

At the beginning of Lent the bishop calls out the names of the catechumens who seek to be baptized at Easter. He writes them in the book of the "elect," the "chosen." God has chosen them, and they have chosen to turn to God. Lent is the 40 days before the baptism of the elect. In more and more parishes, the already baptized are able to share the excitement and the struggles of the elect, and they come to rediscover the meaning of baptism in their own lives. During the 40 days, both catechumens and the already baptized journey together to the holy font.

We keep Lent *together.* We turn together, as a parish, as a church of so many colors, ages and ways of life. We put aside our business-as-usual to support each other in prayer, fasting and almsgiving. We turn to God to enlighten us and purify us throughout the lengthening brightness of our holy Lent.

"For now is the acceptable time! Now is the day of salvation!" (2 Corinthians 6:2)

PREPARING THE PARISH

A couple of generations ago, over a third of the days on the Catholic calendar were fast days: Fridays (and in some homes, Wednesdays as well), ember days, vigils, as well as the seasons of Advent and Lent. Nowadays, just mentioning the word "fasting" can bring on accusations of antiquarianism, or worse, of being holier-than-thou. Perhaps these reactions indicate that we've lost something more important than the traditions of fasting.

The liturgical year has precious few occasions for genuine lamentation, for expressions of brokenness and pain, for decrying injustice and pleading for assistance, for the trembling and tears that often accompany repentance, forgiveness and healing. Although no gathering of Christians is an occasion for despair or facile emotions, at the same time no assembly deserves to have its sorrows masked with a smile button.

And yet that is what so often happens to Lent and to Advent, to funerals and to services of reconciliation in parishes. As an example, even if we sing during worship the great psalms of Lent, such as Psalm 52 ("A clean heart create for me, O God"), Psalm 91 ("Be with me, Lord, when I am in trouble"), Psalm 130 ("Out of the depths") or Psalm 137 ("By the streams of Babylon"), the musical arrangements we employ can turn the words into marshmallow, with "friendly" musical styles that make them sound like a Broadway showtune or advertiser's jingle.

We are products of our culture. We are easily engulfed by its entertainment and escapism that can mask the depth of feelings within the parish, the brokenness of lives, the suffering and loneliness—and indeed life's joys and pleasures as well. When we prepare the liturgy, especially during Lent, we need to ask if we have been daring enough, bold enough to strip the sugar from our liturgical expressions, to encounter fully the power of its psalms and prayers, the often discomforting challenge of its scriptures, the discipline required of disciples.

If we take away the sugar coating, we will need to prepare an honest answer to the inevitable accusation that the lenten liturgy is not "upbeat," that it doesn't leave everyone with a smile, that it fails "to meet our needs" and offers little therapeutic escape from the realities of the world.

Lent cannot arise in a vaccuum: Preparing the parish for Lent involves year-round attention to the disciplines of fasting and prayer and almsgiving. How does the parish keep Fridays all year long? Are there ever communal rogation or ember days—days of supplication, days to call down God's blessings, days to remember great tragedies in our history? What preparation goes into the vigils of great feasts or the vigil of every Lord's Day?

How consistent is this coming Lent with the spirit of previous Lents? Is it being preempted by some artificial "theme"—an unfortunate gimmick popular in the '70s—for example, "This year, Lent in our parish is going to be about 'peace'"? (No matter how worthy the theme, the season of Lent cannot be boxed even for a year into a single approach.) What will be done to help the community make the

lenten psalms, hymns and prayers part of individuals' and the households' private prayer? Will the parish school and religious education be using the psalms and songs from Sunday worship as part of their own liturgical prayer?

The RCIA comments on the meaning of the season in this way: "In the liturgy and liturgical catechesis of Lent the reminder of baptism already received or the preparation for its reception, as well as the theme of repentance, renew the entire community along with those being prepared to celebrate the paschal mystery, in which each of the elect will share through the sacraments of initiation. For both the elect and the local community, therefore, the lenten season is a time for spiritual recollection in preparation for the celebration of the paschal mystery." (RCIA, 138)

Does Lent in our parishes fit the RCIA model of the season? Is Lent to be a focal point of every day in every way, in all parts of parish life including religious education programs and the parish school, or is Lent to be isolated moments that come around in the clockwork of Sunday Mass? Is it an appendage to our lives or the body of our existence? Such questions challenge a parish to be clear and consistent in how this season is embraced. By joyful invitation—to eucharist, to Morning and Evening Prayer, to weekly home meetings, to organized parish fasting and almsgiving, to recycling drives and cleanup projects, to stations of the cross and other devotions—and by consistent example—suspension of meetings, weddings, baptisms, fund-raisers, parties (and that includes St. Patrick's dances)—the parish lays the foundation for an ongoing, annually repeated tradition of initiation, repentance and renewal that is both life-giving and liberating.

It cannot be emphasized too strongly that such a Lent begins with the parish staff, with the parish council and others who do their ministry in a public manner. For them, and for all, these must become 40 very different days, days when there is the awareness of Lent permeating the waking hours and even the sleeping hours. Remember: Lent is serious, it is about struggle, it is about the nature and price of salvation. But it is not gloom. Alexander Schmemann speaks of the "bright sadness" that is Lent. How can we hold those two words together? Let the lenten liturgies teach us!

WORDS

Clay of the ground, serpent, we have sinned, be merciful, death began its reign, condemnation, acquittal, desert, 40 days, tempted by the devil, not on bread alone, go forth from the land of your kinsfolk, bear your hardship, robbed death, brought life, led up a high mountain, out of the cloud came a voice, thirst for water, strike the rock, tested the Lord, harden not your hearts, hope for the glory, Christ died for us, give me a drink, God's gift, an hour is coming, Spirit and truth, open your eyes, testimony, we have heard for ourselves, the Lord looks into the heart, the spirit of the Lord rushed upon David, live as children of light, awake, rise from the dead, I was blind, now I can see, to make the sightless see and the seeing blind, open your graves, out of the depths, the Spirit of God dwells in you, the dead man came out, branches from trees, blessed be he who comes, entered Jerusalem, set my face like flint, Jesus Christ is Lord, this was the Son of God.

VESTURE

Purple, but different from the colors of Advent. Some argue that a royal purple (a deep, bloody purple) is especially appropriate as the color of the *vexilla regis,* the banner of the king who "reigns from the tree." Others argue that traditional lenten vesture was an almost-black, somber blue-violet. (In practice, a region's particular shade of purple had more to do with the source of dyes than any secondary significance.) The common denominator in these traditions is avoiding a gaudy purple, as is often found in the polyester vestments of church supply stores. Also avoid appliqué symbols; Lent is not a six-week-long Passiontide. Colors as accents include grays, blacks, reds, browns. In Anglican usage unbleached linen is an option, and some Lutheran liturgical books suggest somber ash tones. Perhaps more important than color is plainness and simplicity.

THE MASS

Introductory rites: (See the suggestions noted under "Music.") This rite is particularly sober throughout Lent. The entrance could be silent throughout the season, or accompanied by appropriate instrumental music, such as the *Audi benigne conditor* or one of the other classic lenten chants, or a simple refrain. *Attende Domine* is still popular in several translations, for example, "Draw near, O Lord, our God." The penitential rite could be celebrated with the entire community kneeling as a sign of repentance. Everyone, presider included, should kneel (with the possible exception of the cantor who will sing the lines of the Kyrie). Such kneeling should not be rushed or brief. We need to become accustomed to the use of this posture, in church and at home, as one of penance. Even in churches that have no kneelers attached to the pews, people can still kneel— and with all the more sense for the meaning of this posture. Silence is in order here for pondering and praising God's mercy. Consider consistent use of the *Confiteor* or Form C, or a *Kyrie,* perhaps retaining the Greek, from the collection of beautiful chants found in our old (and new GIA edition) *Kyriale* or *Graduale Romanum.* (The sprinkling rite is entirely inappropriate during Lent.)

Planners with the best of intentions might employ a penitential rite that itemizes our faults: "For the times we have . . ." However, such itemization would likely get tedious every week and is best left to communal reconciliation.

Liturgy of the word: Each year of the three-year Sunday lectionary, the lenten readings are geared to a different group: the catechumens (Cycle A), the faithful (Cycle B) and the penitents (Cycle C). This year, Cycle A, notice how the readings especially of the third, fourth and fifth Sundays of Lent address rebirth, resurrection, death to self and new life in Christ. While this year may include the archetypal readings of initiation, every year, no matter which cycle, the readings speak on many levels to all three groups.

Those privileged to proclaim the word during Lent might be inspired and encouraged to meet for practice and prayer as part of their lenten observance and their gift to the community. Too much is at stake in the proclamation of the word to allow anything less than the best possible efforts.

Moments of silence are an integral part of every Mass, especially the silence that should follow each of the readings. During this season, however, those silences

could become a notch longer. Remember that the quiet is never there to make people restless or to distort the rhythm of the eucharist. Silence is a reasonable and regular pause that invites the assembly to reflect—together—while painstakingly chipping away at the myth that being quiet is wasting time. Try adding just enough silence for people to notice.

Let the one psalm that will be used *throughout* Lent establish itself as the assembly's common prayer and "sound of the season." Psalms 51, 91 and 130 are the common psalms of Lent.

Catechumenal rites: (Discussion of the rite of election, the presentations and the scrutinies are found on the proper lenten Sundays in "The Calendar.") "Gradually the catechumens should be admitted to the first part of the celebration of the Sunday Mass. After the liturgy of the word they should, if possible, be dismissed, but an intention for them is included in the general intercessions." (RCIA, 83) The dismissal of the catechumens and those who are candidates for full communion takes place before the liturgy of the eucharist (*during* the liturgy of the word, *before* the general intercessions). After the dismissal, they may gather elsewhere with catechists for continued discussion and prayer. The RCIA envisions that *this is not something unique to Lent* but is the parish practice throughout the year—whenever there is anyone in the community who has been admitted to the order of catechumens but not yet baptized.

The rite provides two texts for dismissing catechumens (67):

A. Catechumens, go in peace, and may the Lord remain with you always.

B. My dear friends, this community now sends you forth to reflect more deeply upon the word of God which you have shared with us today. Be assured of our loving support and prayers for you. We look forward to the day when you will share fully at the Lord's Table.

These texts make the spirit of the dismissal very clear. Other words may be used, but any dismissal should convey this concern and affection. Especially if the catechumens are being dismissed to continue reflection on the scriptures, the dismissal should commend them to their catechists.

A text is provided in the RCIA, 136, which is especially appropriate to the time between election and the first scrutiny:

My dear elect, you have set out with us on the road that leads to the glory of Easter. Christ will be your way, your truth, and your life. Until we meet again for the scrutinies, walk always in his peace.

Similar forms are provided for the scrutiny Sundays.

This ritual exclusion of the catechumens can be an incentive to personal conversion for the faithful: "Why can I stay when they can't? What's so special about being in this community?" This ritual exclusion can also have effects—positive and negative—on the elect who, like all of us, are challenged to grow but must be accepted and respected for who they are: "Why can't I stay and they can? What's so special about this community?" These concerns must be handled with prudence and vision.

Liturgy of the eucharist: The eucharistic acclamations should be consistent week after week, including Palm Sunday. A unique set of music can be chosen for

this one season or for the entire time from Ash Wednesday through Pentecost. Some communities link Lent and Eastertime by using the same memorial acclamation ("Dying, you destroyed our death . . ." or "Lord, by your cross and resurrection . . .") from Ash Wednesday to Pentecost.

Lenten Preface IV is prescribed for all fast days, presumably because of a Latin phrase that is not translated literally in the ICEL version. *Corporali ieiunio,* literally "bodily fasting," becomes "lenten observance" in the English version. While a literal description might be too narrow to describe all the lenten disciplines, "observance" is too general. Perhaps we might say:

> Through our lenten observance,
> *our prayer, fasting and almsgiving,*
> you correct our faults and raise our minds to you.

Read through the nine different prefaces in the sacramentary for use on weekdays and the first five Sundays of Lent (in Cycle A), plus the prefaces within the eucharistic prayers for reconciliation. Select one eucharistic prayer that will be used throughout Lent; many communities use one of the two eucharistic prayers for reconciliation. Both prayers contain beautiful words and images that nurture a sense of the season.

The communion rite begins with the Lord's Prayer. The sacramentary offers an introduction to the prayer in words appropriate for use throughout this season:

> Let us ask the Father to forgive our sins
> and bring us to forgive those who sin against us.

The Italian sacramentary suggests:

> Before sharing in the eucharistic banquet,
> that sign of reconciliation and bond of unity,
> let us pray together as the Lord has taught us.

Concluding rites: In the pre–Vatican II liturgy, this was the only season that featured the "bow your heads to the Lord" in the prayer over the people. The bowing of heads bespeaks submission of repentant hearts, and the blessing sends us forth with the assurance that God goes with us on our journey. Consider Prayer over the People #6 for use throughout the first part of Lent (first through fourth Sundays). Memorize the text chosen and repeat it weekly or daily. Then Prayer over the People #17 or the Solemn Blessing for the Passion of the Lord can be used for the conclusion of Lent (fifth Sunday and Palm Sunday).

If no bowing is to take place, then we obviously should omit the words "Bow your heads. . . ." If they are said, then let everyone, including the presider, bow for some moments of silence. An assembly will need some guided reflection to understand and perhaps to practice this gesture.

"Go in the peace of Christ," and a silent recessional would send everyone off in a reflective spirit throughout the season. But if the entrance was accompanied by silence, song at this point might be appropriate. The Congregation for the Sacraments and Divine Worship recently reminded us about the lenten discipline of instruments remaining silent unless they are accompanying voices; this would be a powerful silence throughout Lent, certainly a very old tradition worth respecting both in the spirit and letter of the law.

MUSIC

Gathering: The repeated use of the same gathering song coupled with the same "Lord, have mercy" or "Kyrie eleison" can develop a sense of the season as well as establish a ritual language for the parish. Sometimes one can find a combination that is tonally and thematically related, highly singable and easily remembered from Sunday to Sunday. Marty Haugen's "Tree of Life" (GIA, G-2944) works well with one of Richard Proulx's plainsong settings of the penitential rite (GIA). A through-composed Kyrie eleison such as David Hurd's (GIA, G-2258) makes a gentle gathering experience. All of these transfer easily into the reconciliation service(s) the parish undoubtedly schedules during Lent.

Psalmody: Other antiphon and verse settings of the psalms are Paul Inwood's "Remember, remember your mercy, Lord/Psalm 25" (OCP, #7101) and Christopher Walker's "Preserve me, God/Psalm 30" (OCP, #7144). *Psalms for the Church Year,* volumes 1 and 2, by Marty Haugen and David Haas, contain highly serviceable responsorial psalms.

The RCIA is linked inextricably to the lenten Sundays and provides some new areas to use music. Usually this calls for the assembly to sing (a litany of intercession, an acclamation); but there are times when, to enable the assembly to keep their eyes on certain of the rites, it would be desirable for the vocal ensemble or the cantor to sing an item alone. Texts that sing of the call or journey into the community serve well, for example, "I want to walk as a child of light" (GIA, G-2786) by Kathleen Thomerson, and "Lead me, guide me" (in *Lead Me, Guide Me,* GIA) by Doris Akers. From the black gospel tradition is Thomas Dorsey's "Precious Lord, take my hand" (*Songs of Zion,* Abingdon Press). Washington Gladden's unabashed romantic text, "O Master, let me walk with thee," is not known in most Catholic churches. It has two settings in *The Hymnal 1982.* One is by Calvin Hampton with his tune "de Tar" and the other is the more traditional tune of "Maryton."

Although most lenten hymnody is excessively literal, reminding us all too often that Lent is "these 40 days," there are several beautiful texts set to beautiful melodies. "Amazing grace" is fitting lenten fare. "I heard the voice of Jesus say" echoes the lenten scriptures and is set to many tunes, "Kingsfold" perhaps the most popular. The early American tune "Restoration" fits the text "Come, ye sinners poor and needy." The poetry has the delightfully antiquarian refrain, "I will arise and go to Jesus; he will embrace me with his arms. In the arms of my dear Savior, oh, there are ten-thousand charms." Susan Byler has done an SATB setting that is easy and satisfying and found in the collection "New Heaven, New Earth" (Word, Inc., purveyed by OCP).

The lenten acclamations for the eucharist need not be changed from the ones the assembly already knows. Or if there is a special "paschal set" of music for the eucharist—something that is developed over the years—there are different patterns possible: A special set can be used from Ash Wednesday through Pentecost, or one for Lent and another for Eastertime. Communion processionals take easily to the Taizé mantras: "Jesus, remember me" and "Adoramus te, Christe" are found in many sources. "Domine Deus, filius patris, miserere nobis" carries with it the psalm verses for "Out of the depths."

Recessional: Occasionally, singing the refrain that gathered the assembly as the recessional item lends a more flexible quality to the liturgy. Perhaps the use of a metrical hymn at the beginning and the closing of the lenten Sunday liturgies tends to speak too strongly of Ordinary Time—something extraordinary is needed between Ash Wednesday and Pentecost.

THE WORSHIP ENVIRONMENT

Simplification: Christian discipline requires a stripping away and emptying of our very selves. During Lent, as we celebrate and symbolize this discipline, that translates roughly into the austerity, simplification and stripping of the worship environment. A thorough cleaning, yes. A removal of anything extraneous, yes. But Lent requires even more. After all, our worship space should always be free of clutter, always clean. Perhaps most of the art and statuary can be removed or covered. Plain earthenware or wicker can be used instead of metal or glass vessels. Plants and flowers can be removed. Use unbleached beeswax candles and unbleached cloth. The stripped-down worship environment is so that we can focus on what is most important: the assembly, the penitents, the elect.

The lenten season has traditionally been a time for renewing the ancient forms of rite, for restoring a purer, simpler, more transparent style of worship—the genius that is the Roman rite. One such ancient expression is placing the cloth on the altar *only* from the preparation to communion. Another is gathering substantial gifts for the poor during the preparation. Another is lively attention to— and participation in—Sunday Evening Prayer.

Even after being stripped, the worship place during Lent can sustain a few uniquely lenten elements, both to keep it from merely looking gloomy and to express some of the distinctive characteristics of the season.

Lent is a journey through the desert. Some parishes dump sand somewhere in church and create an arrangement of cactuses and driftwood. This is a rather literal device that plays on a single word: desert. It can come off as a gimmick. However, it is in the nature of liturgy to keep many, many images juggled at once, and it's not easy putting cactuses somewhere without drawing too much attention to and then limiting this single image of "desert."

Perhaps it's all in the placement: There's a world of difference between placing sand and cactuses in front of the altar (where they *demand* attention) and placing them somewhere in the gathering area, perhaps near where folks can pick up lenten take-home materials (where they simply call attention to something else). When playing with this image of the desert, also keep in mind the related images of thirst, of wasteland and of journey in your own part of the world. There are few things more dry and lifeless than a March landscape north of the Mason-Dixon line. The "wasteland" we are concerned about is not really the desert with its cactus but the waste we are making of God's creation and even of one another. A generation ago the word "wasteland" was applied with great force to television programing. Perhaps, instead of a cactus . . .

Lent is an exile. Psalm 126, "By the rivers of Babylon," becomes our lenten song. We give up our Alleluias, our harps, "for how can we sing the Lord's song in a foreign land?" (The ceremony of bidding goodbye to the Alleluia is described on February 25 in "The Calendar.") Weeping willows and late winter seem to go

together; their golden color makes them one of the cheeriest plants, and yet they appear doleful, waiting patiently to turn green with the first warmth of the season. Like the catechumens, willows are thirsty for water. The lenten image of exile was the reason we used to cover statues with cloth. It was a sign that paradise was closed to us, that we have been cut off both from our past (the remembrance of our ancestors) and our future (the vision of heaven).

Many parishes place their Good Friday cross in the church throughout Lent. But why? Lent is not an extended meditation on the Passion. During Lent we are waiting for the Triduum, when our gracious Gardener will plant the cross in our midst as the tree of life. Just as we are waiting for the water and light of the Paschal Triduum, so too we await the cross. That is a reason why it has long been customary in Western tradition to veil or remove the cross throughout Lent.

Whatever your decisions about the worship environment, don't attempt to do something different every Lent. Keep it similar year to year.

A strong part of something that must be cared for every year is the appearance and quality of the parish library, bookracks and other places where educational materials are offered. These are good places to advertise how and why the parish is keeping Lent, including the worship schedules and the descriptions of whatever was agreed upon as the focus for parish-wide fasting or almsgiving. If the parish has pledged a particular charity as the recipient of its alms, a large vessel for collecting that money could be placed prominently in church—a giant mite box of sorts.

Many parishes seal the baptismal font, draining it (and all holy water stoops), covering it, making it unavailable (also emptying the ambry of chrism— the oil of gladness). The way you do this depends on the style of your font; sometimes simply leaving it dry makes it look like someone forgot to put water in it. If your font has a permanent lid, perhaps it can be bound in cords or veiled. Lent's ashes can be kept in a clay vessel nearby, a *memento mori,* a reminder of death.

As a final suggestion: Advertise the season to the neighborhood. An arrangement of strips of fabrics in, say, a monochromatic array of purples, hung outside the church building, would be a simple way to announce that this community is preparing the Passover.

OTHER RITUAL PRAYER

Evening Prayer: Lent provides a wonderful opportunity to introduce the community to Sunday Evening Prayer, and possibly to weekday Morning and Evening Prayer as well. During Lent, people are usually more inclined to make these liturgies part of the joyful discipline of each day.

Various settings of Psalm 141, the penitential psalm that accompanies the burning of incense, are available in *Praise God in Song* (GIA), the *Lutheran Book of Worship* and many other traditional and contemporary settings. The setting of Psalm 141 in *Evening Prayer: The Leader's Book* (LTP) uses the *tonus peregrinus* of the old Gregorian psalm tone system that is perfect for Lent. Choose a special tone that is used only during Lent. The old *Kyriale* provided different Mass melodies for different seasons and feasts. You could tell by the opening notes of the Kyrie where you were in the calendar. Strive for that same sort of year-after-year consistency.

Many parishes use a special scent of incense for each season. For example, "Gethsemani" for Lent and "Jasmine" for Eastertime are available from Holy Transfiguration Monastery, 278 Warren Street, Brookline MA 02146; 617/734-0608. A small point, but sounds and smells, as well as words—no, even *more* than words—are needed to root a community in tradition.

After the candle lighting, and before the incense psalm, a fine text for the thanksgiving for light appears in GIA's *Praise God in Song,* but another possibility would be this adaptation of the prayer "for the sanctification of the fast" from the Byzantine liturgy of the presanctified:

> It is truly right to offer you this evening sacrifice of praise
> for you are the Lord Most High, dwelling in light inaccessible,
> who created the whole universe in wisdom
> and who, with love beyond all telling, have brought us to the acceptable time,
> to these days of salvation:
> > for the purification of our souls and bodies,
> > for our growth in self-control and sacrificial love,
> > for renewing within us the hope of resurrection.
> As you led Moses to 40 days of prayer before receiving the Law
> and as you strengthened your own Son through 40 days of desert prayer,
> so enable us, O Good One, to fight the good fight:
> > to persevere through the course of this fast,
> > to keep the faith,
> > to crush underfoot the heads of invisible serpents,
> > to be victorious over sin,
> > and so, without reproach, to reach the solemnity
> > of his death, burial and resurrection,
> Jesus Christ, to whom with you and the Holy Spirit be all glory and honor,
> now and unto endless ages of ages. Amen.

Friday evening stations of the cross is a form of prayer hallowed by tradition in this country. Think about reviewing or revitalizing your community's experience of it. LTP publishes a scriptural form of this devotion that uses the Hebrew Bible well and avoids the verbosity of some updated forms of the stations. The nicely arranged version found in the Episcopal church's *Book of Occasional Services* has been published in booklet form (Church Hymnal Corporation, 800 Second Avenue, New York NY 10017). This publication includes a good translation of the *Stabat mater.* While venerable and fitting, this hymn is not mandatory at stations. LTP's booklet has a translation of the *Vexilla regis,* the hymn that celebrates the triumph of the cross. There is no reason why other hymns or psalms could not be used during this devotion.

Fasting suppers: A weekday Evening Prayer or stations might well be preceded by or concluded with a fasting meal and/or a *Paschal Mission* gathering. Fasting suppers need not always be held on Fridays; fasting is part of every lenten weekday. These suppers can take on some of the characteristics of a "St. Joseph's Table," featuring lenten song and psalms, meatless and dairyless shared dishes, a collection for the poor and an open door to those who cannot afford the meal—as well as the "eat and run" style that indicates that this is not a party or social event.

Sample Prayer Texts for Lent

Sample texts for Passion (Palm) Sunday may be found on April 8 in "The Calendar" section of this Sourcebook.

Introductory Rites

GREETING

Especially during weeks 1 through 4:
The grace and love of Jesus Christ, who calls us to repentance and conversion, be with you all.

Or:

The Lord, who guides our hearts in the love and patient endurance of Jesus Christ, be with you all.

Especially during weeks 5 and 6:
Brothers and sisters: chosen and destined by God our Father, and sanctified by the Spirit for obedience to Jesus Christ and to receive sprinkling with his holy blood: grace and peace in abundance be with you all.

INTRODUCTION

If an introduction seems superfluous, the introduction can be combined with the invitation.

First Sunday of Lent:
Lent is a mirror-image of life: an ongoing journey. For those catechumens who will be called this day to prepare for the Easter sacraments, Lent marks the final steps toward the waters of rebirth. For those of us already initiated, Lent is at once a journey back to our beginnings in Christ and forward to the future God has prepared for us.

Second Sunday of Lent:
On this Second Sunday of Lent, the Lord gathers as a people the faithful and the penitents, (the catechumens and the candidates). Here we are given a glimpse of the glory to come as we journey through the desert of these Forty Days toward the life-giving celebration of the Lord's Pasch.

Third Sunday of Lent:
We gather on this Third Sunday of Lent to prepare to draw water joyfully at the springs of salvation. Christ is the foundation from which we receive the life-giving word, and he is himself the living bread come down from heaven. (Today we celebrate with our elect the first scrutiny, praying that they may find in Christ the fountain they long for, the Messiah they seek.)

Fourth Sunday of Lent:
On this Fourth Sunday of Lent, the Lord assembles us as a people delivered from the darkness of sin. But we do not yet see all things in the light of faith, and so our lenten journey of purification and enlightenment continues. (For our elect today we celebrate the second scrutiny, praying that Christ will be for them deliverance from the dominion of darkness and the dawning of unfailing light.)

Fifth Sunday of Lent:
On this Fifth Sunday of Lent we are shown the Lord Jesus, drawing near to a sentence of death, yet summoning Lazarus forth from the tomb into life. (For our elect we celebrate today the third scrutiny, preparing them for their deliverance from the tyranny of death and preparing them for their birth to new life in baptism.)

INVITATION TO THE PENITENTIAL RITE

For the entire season:
At the beginning of this eucharistic celebration, let us answer the lenten call to conversion of heart, the fountain of reconciliation and communion with God and our neighbor.

Or:

The Lord has said: Let the one without sin cast the first stone. Acknowledging that we are all sinners, let us pardon one another from the depths of our

CONTINUED

hearts, and let us ask pardon from God, who is merciful and just.

PENITENTIAL RITE

For the entire season:

It would be appropriate throughout Lent to recite the Confiteor followed by the absolution and then the six-fold or even nine-fold Kyrie (sung, of course, in English or in Greek). If another penitential rite is desired, here are alternatives:

You raise the dead to life in the Spirit: Lord, have mercy. You bring pardon and peace to the sinner: Christ, have mercy. You bring light to those in darkness: Lord, have mercy.

Focuses especially on the sacraments of initiation:
Lord, by water and the Holy Spirit, you have given us a new birth in your image: Lord, have mercy. Christ, you have sent your Spirit to create a new heart within us: Christ, have mercy. Lord, you have made us partakers of your body and blood: Lord, have mercy.

Focuses especially on reconciliation:
Lord, you command us to forgive each other before we come to your altar: Lord, have mercy. Christ, on the cross you asked the Father to forgive sinners: Christ, have mercy. Lord, you have entrusted to your church the ministry of reconciliation: Lord, have mercy.

Focuses on the Lord's Passion:
You made the tree of the cross the tree of our salvation: Lord, have mercy. You suffered for us, leaving us an example that we might follow in your footsteps: Christ, have mercy. You mounted the wood of the cross burdened with our sins, that dead to sin we might live in your justice: Lord, have mercy.

Introduction to the Readings

First Sunday of Lent:
The Hebrew Scriptures chosen for the lenten Sundays present stages in the journey of God's people toward salvation. The story begins with God's creative act and humanity's rebellion. Paul sees Jesus as the new Adam reversing the sin of the first Adam. Matthew portrays Jesus as a new Moses, reliving Israel's 40-year testing in the desert and emerging victorious.

Second Sunday of Lent:
God invites Abraham, father of all believers, to go forth in faith to a land he does not know. Abraham's obedience in the face of mystery and hardship contrasts sharply with Adam's disobedience, and Abraham's journey prefigures the struggle of all believers and of Jesus himself. But as Paul and Matthew remind us, the destiny is immortal glory!

Third Sunday of Lent:
The third lenten Sunday presents Israel's testing in the desert. At God's command, water flows from the rock to quench the thirst of the parched pilgrims. For us on our pilgrimage the gift Jesus offers is the Holy Spirit, a spring of living and life-giving water welling up in the hearts of those born again in baptism.

Fourth Sunday of Lent:
On this fourth Sunday David is chosen and anointed as a king whose reign would be a radiant light in Israel's history and whose dynasty would not fail. Jesus, the Son of David, the Anointed One whose reign will not end, is the source of light for all who come to him in faith.

Fifth Sunday of Lent:
The prophets begin to speak of Israel's return from exile in terms of a future resurrection. When Jesus summons Lazarus from the tomb, the hour of victory is at hand. Paul sees the same power that raised Jesus from the dead already at work in those born again in the death, burial and resurrection of baptism.

CONTINUED

General Intercessions

INVITATION TO PRAYER

For the entire season:
Behold, this is the acceptable time: the lenten springtime of the Spirit, the church's school of discipline and faith. Let us ask the Lord to render us docile to the word that, purified and renewed, we may come to the celebration of the holy Pasch.

Or:

In this lenten season the Lord invites us to be renewed in thought and deed, to respond from the heart to the needs of others. Let us ask God to accompany us on our journey to conversion with the abundance of grace.

Or:

With a living faith let us present our prayers to the Lord, giving voice to that longing for justice and peace that rises up from the hearts of all people of good will.

Or:

Let us offer our Sunday prayers for a reconciled world.

INTERCESSION FOR THE CHURCH

For the holy church of God throughout the world: that it may proclaim by word and action the mystery of the cross, the power of sacrificial love, as the path to real liberation and true joy: let us pray to the Lord.

Or:

For the pilgrim church on earth: that by walking the path of prayer, penance, and charity it may become more visibly like Christ its Lord, and so follow him in the exodus that leads to true liberation and the paschal feast of the kingdom: let us pray to the Lord.

INTERCESSION FOR THE ELECT

For our elect, those to be baptized at the Easter Vigil: that they be seen by our community as the Father's great gift, meant to stir up within us a longing to live without compromise the vows of our own baptismal covenant: let us pray to the Lord.

Or:

For our elect, for their godparents and catechists: that, accompanied by our prayers and strengthened by our witness, they may reach the goal of their journey at the font of rebirth and renewal: let us pray to the Lord.

INTERCESSION FOR THE WORLD

For those who govern nations and guide human destinies: that, by their conversion to peace and justice, the immense resources of earth and of humanity may be utilized for the relief of the multitudes who suffer misery and hunger: let us pray to the Lord.

Or:

For the world in which we live: that the lives of believers may be a blessing for it, as the followers of Christ gladly join all people of good will to work for human rights, true justice and lasting peace: let us pray to the Lord.

INTERCESSION FOR VARIOUS NEEDS

For the sick, the suffering, the neglected and marginal: that they may see themselves to be a primary concern of this community, as we pray and struggle with them, love and serve them, journeying together toward Christ's paschal victory: let us pray to the Lord.

Or:

For those who because of injustice or the crosses they bear, come to despair of the future: that fellow Christians may help them rekindle hope by respecting their human dignity and sharing their burdens: let us pray to the Lord.

INTERCESSION FOR THE ASSEMBLY

For all of us assembled here: that our lenten journey may culminate in a

CONTINUED

heartfelt celebration of reconciliation and a joyous Easter communion, the sacramental signs of our conversion and renewal: let us pray to the Lord.

Or:

For all of us returning to the font of baptism: that the lenten discipline may render us more attentive to the liberating power of God's word and the needs of all our brothers and sisters: let us pray to the Lord.

Or the intercession for the assembly may be based on the scriptures of the day:

First Sunday of Lent:
For all of us here present: that victorious in Christ over the temptations of Satan, we may never bow before false idols of money, power or prestige, but place all our hope in the saving word of God: let us pray to the Lord.

Second Sunday of Lent:
For this eucharistic assembly: that with our hearts fixed on the hope of glory and our eyes fixed on Jesus, we may bear courageously the difficulties of life and selflessly bear the burdens of others: let us pray to the Lord.

Third Sunday of Lent:
For this community of faith: that we may come to a fuller understanding of the gift of God which we have received in our relationship with Christ, and so begin to see and live life in a new and deeper way: let us pray to the Lord.

Fourth Sunday of Lent:
For ourselves: that with unblinded eyes we may be granted insight into the person of Christ and a more committed response to the challenge of the gospel: let us pray to the Lord.

Fifth Sunday of Lent:
For this assembly, summoned to new life in the Spirit: that we may bear in our lives the harvest of good fruit borne by those who have died to sin and who have been reborn in baptism: let us pray to the Lord.

CONCLUDING PRAYER
These concluding prayers for the intercessions were selected from among opening prayers for Mass (based on the readings from Cycle A) of the Italian sacramentary, Messale Romano, © 1983 by the Libreria Editrice Vaticana (translated by Peter Scagnelli).

First Sunday of Lent:
O God, you know how fragile is our
    human nature,
wounded as it is by sin.

Help your people to enter upon the
    lenten journey strengthened by
        the power of your word,
so that we may be victorious over the
    seductions of the Evil One
and reach the paschal feast in the joy
    of the Holy Spirit.

We ask this through
    our Lord Jesus Christ, your Son,
who lives and reigns with you
    in the unity of the Holy Spirit,
one God, for ever and ever.
—From the Italian sacramentary

Second Sunday of Lent:
O God, you called our ancestors
    to faith
and have given us grace to journey
    toward the light of the gospel.

Open our ears to listen to your Son,
so that accepting in our own lives the
    mystery of the cross,
we may be able to enter into the glory
    of your kingdom.

We ask this through
    our Lord Jesus Christ, your Son,
who lives and reigns with you
    in the unity of the Holy Spirit,
one God, for ever and ever.
—From the Italian sacramentary

Third Sunday of Lent:
O God, the fountain of life,
to a humanity parched with thirst
    you offer the living water of grace
that springs up from the rock,
    our savior Jesus Christ.

Grant your people the gift
    of the Spirit,

CONTINUED

that we may learn to profess our
 faith with courage
and announce with joy the wonders
 of your love.

We ask this through
 our Lord Jesus Christ, your Son,
who lives and reigns with you
 in the unity of the Holy Spirit,
one God, for ever and ever.
—From the Italian sacramentary

Fourth Sunday of Lent:
O God, the Father of light,
you look into the depths of our hearts.

Never permit us to be dominated
 by the powers of darkness,
but open our eyes by the grace
 of your Spirit,
that we may see the one
 you have sent to illumine the world,
and may believe in him alone,
Jesus Christ, your Son and our Lord,
who lives and reigns with you
 in the unity of the Holy Spirit,
one God, for ever and ever.
—From the Italian sacramentary

Fifth Sunday of Lent:
Eternal Father, whose glory is the
 human person fully alive,
we see your compassion revealed
 in the tears of Jesus for Lazarus,
  his friend.

Look today upon the distress
 of your church,
mourning and praying for her
 children dead in their sins.
By the power of your Spirit
 call them back to life.

We ask this through
 Lord Jesus Christ, your Son,
who lives and reigns with you
 in the unity of the Holy Spirit,
one God, for ever and ever.
—From the Italian sacramentary

Passion (Palm) Sunday:
*A concluding prayer may be selected from
one of the opening prayers in the sacramentary for today or for the early part of this
week. (The opening prayer for Monday in
Holy Week is particularly fitting.)*

Communion Rite

INTRODUCTION TO THE LORD'S PRAYER

For the entire season:
Let us ask our Father to forgive our
sins and to bring us to forgive those
who sin against us.

Or:

Let us turn our hearts toward our
heavenly Father, that God might forgive our sins and preserve us from evil.

PRAYER FOR PEACE

For the entire season:
Lord Jesus Christ, through your death
on the cross, God our Father made
peace between heaven and earth: Look
not on our sins, but on the faith of your
church. . . .

INVITATION TO COMMUNION

During the first four weeks:
This is the Lamb of God, who takes
away the sins of the world: who for our
sake endured temptation and suffering. Happy are those who are called to
his supper.

During the fifth and sixth weeks:
This is the Lamb of God, who takes
away the sins of the world: who has
ransomed us for God by his blood shed
upon the cross. Happy are those who
are called to his supper.

Concluding Rite

BLESSING AND DISMISSAL

*The prayer over the people was a tradition
during the lenten season in the Tridentine
rite ("Humiliate capita vestra Deo"). Rather
than a constantly changing one, however, it
might be good to pick one for the first part of
Lent (Weeks 1–4), for instance, #6, which
speaks of a complete change of heart; and
another for the second part of Lent (Week 5–
6), for instance, #17, which speaks of the
Lord's Passion. These are found in the sacramentary after the Order of Mass and the
Solemn Blessings.*

Sample Bulletin Insert for before Lent

The following will need to be adapted to reflect your own diocesan and parish situations. Include in this insert reminders and explanations of the special ways in which your own parish will be keeping the lenten disciplines as a community.

The lenten regulations for this year are as follows:

1. *Abstinence* from meat is to be observed by all Catholics 14 years old and older on Ash Wednesday and on all the Fridays of Lent. Abstinence from all festive foods is encouraged on every day of Lent as part of the common discipline of this holy season.

2. *Fasting* is to be observed on Ash Wednesday by all Catholics who are 18 years of age but not yet 59. Those who are bound by this may take only one full meal. Two smaller meals are permitted only if necessary to maintain strength according to one's needs, but eating solid foods between meals is not permitted.

As St. John Chrysostom reminded us, "Fasting is a medicine, strengthening the weak and helping Christians grow healthy." Daily fasting—especially eating less at meals, skipping meals if possible and not eating between meals—is encouraged on all weekdays throughout Lent.

The lenten discipline of fasting and abstinence, according to the best of our tradition, is always to be accompanied by prayer and almsgiving (the giving of charity and works of mercy). In the words of St. Augustine, "Prayer needs two wings to fly to heaven: fasting and almsgiving."

"Lent is a preparation for the celebration of Easter. For the lenten liturgy disposes both the catechumens and the faithful to celebrate the paschal mystery: the catechumens, through the several stages of Christian initiation; the faithful, through reminders of their own baptism and through penitential practices." (*General Norms for the Liturgical Year,* #27)

"By the threefold discipline of fasting, almsgiving and prayer the church keeps Lent from Ash Wednesday until the evening of Holy Thursday. All of the faithful and the catechumens should undertake serious practice of these three traditions. Failure to observe individual days of penance is not considered serious, but failure to observe any penitential days at all or a substantial number of such days must be considered serious.

"[On] weekdays of Lent, we strongly recommend participation in daily Mass and a self-imposed observance of fasting. In the light of grave human needs which weigh on the Christian conscience in all seasons, we urge, particularly during Lent, generosity to local, national and world programs of sharing of all things needed to translate our duty to penance into a means of implementing the right of the poor to their part of our abundance." (U.S. bishops' statement on penitential observances, 1966)

A Penitential Procession for the First Sunday of Lent

The Circular Letter Concerning the Preparation and Celebration of the Easter Feasts *(January 1988) suggests that an appropriate way to mark the First Sunday of Lent with penitential solemnity would be to begin the liturgy with a procession during which the litany of the saints is chanted. Reference is made to the new* Ceremonial for Bishops *(not yet available in English translation), specifically to #261 in that document that describes how this procession is held. For those communities that might like to have such a procession before the principal Mass—and it would be a fine link to the processions of Palm Sunday and Easter Eve—here is the straightforward procedure:*

1. The community assembles in a place apart from the place where Mass will be celebrated while a gathering song is sung.

2. The presider (who may be vested in a cope) then greets the assembly, and (a deacon or other minister) offers a brief introduction, for example:

We have come to the beginning
    of our lenten spring,
the holy Passover that will bring our
    catechumens to the saving waters
    of rebirth,
the Passover that will be,
    for those of us already initiated,
    a pilgrimage of conversion.

Lent is a journey with the Lord who
    longs to draw us more closely
    to himself
that he might speak to our hearts.
Along the way we will be challenged
    to recognize Christ in the
    scriptures we read,
in those we love and serve,
and in those whom we so
    often neglect to love and serve
—for surely Christ is most specially
    present in them.

Therefore, let us begin the journey!
Our procession is in the spirit
    of the pilgrimage of the Israelites,
our forebears in faith.
We call upon the saints,
    our holy ancestors,
who remind us that we do not
    journey alone.
Let us move forward in faith,
keeping our eyes fixed on Jesus.

3. The presider offers a collect, either that of the Holy Cross, September 14, or "For Forgiveness of Sins" in the back of the sacramentary, #40, or from the prayers over the people in the sacramentary, or perhaps even this beautiful text from the *Book of Common Prayer:*

Almighty God,
whose most dear Son went not up to
    joy but first he suffered pain,
and entered not into glory before he
    was crucified:
Mercifully grant that we, walking in
    the way of the cross,
may find it none other than the way
    of life and peace;
through Jesus Christ your Son
    our Lord.

4. Incense is placed in the thurible and the deacon announces: "Let us go forth in peace."

5. The litany of the saints is sung as the procession moves to the church. When the ministers reach the altar, the presider reverences it, kisses it and may incense it. The presider goes to the chair (changing from cope to chasuble) and, when the litany ends, chants the opening prayer of the Mass, omitting the penitential rite.

TRIDUUM

This section of the *Sourcebook* includes an overview of this three-day "season" and then examines its principal liturgies. Turn to pages 178–81 in "The Calendar" for a discussion of other aspects of keeping the Triduum, such as gathering the parish for the continuous vigil, the liturgy of the hours, seder meals, fasting suppers and the Easter breakfast.

OFFICIAL DESCRIPTION

Christ redeemed us all and gave perfect glory to God principally through his paschal mystery: dying he destroyed our death and rising he restored our life. Therefore the Easter Triduum of the passion and resurrection of Christ is the culmination of the entire liturgical year. Thus the solemnity of Easter has the same kind of preeminence in the liturgical year that Sunday has in the week. The Easter Triduum begins with the evening Mass of the Lord's Supper, reaches its high point in the Easter Vigil, and closes with Evening Prayer on Easter Sunday.

On Good Friday and, if possible, also on Holy Saturday until the Easter Vigil, the Easter fast is observed everywhere.

The Easter Vigil, during the holy night when Christ rose from the dead, ranks as the "mother of all vigils." Keeping watch, the church awaits Christ's resurrection and celebrates it in sacraments. Accordingly, the entire celebration of this Vigil should take place at night; that is, it should either begin after nightfall or end before the dawn of Sunday. (*General Norms for the Liturgical Year and Calendar*, #18–21)

RESOURCES

Lent, Triduum and Eastertime must be discussed and prepared as a whole. For resource material on historical background and liturgical help, see the bibliography beginning on page 46.

A SENSE OF THE SEASON

Triduum means "three days." The Paschal Triduum is the three-day season, counted sunset to sunset, from Holy Thursday night to Easter Sunday evening. During these days we keep one festival—our Passover, our Easter. We join with all the people of our parish—and in spirit with all Christians in every time and place—to fast, pray and keep watch. It is the Passover of the Lord!

Why three days? For three days Esther fasted and Judith kept vigil, the exiles came home to Jerusalem and the Hebrews marched to the waters of Marah. For three days darkness afflicted the Egyptians, Hezekiah lay mortally ill, Jonah was entombed in the belly of a fish and Paul waited in blindness. On the third day Abraham offered his firstborn son, God came down in fire and wind upon Sinai, the boy Jesus was found in "his father's house," and the man Jesus "performed the first of his signs at Cana of Galilee." Echoing the words of Hosea, Jesus announced the three-day Passover of his death, rest and resurrection.

The Paschal Triduum, the "Three Days of Passover," are for us days of death, rest and resurrection. We march to the waters of baptism. We keep watch for light

and for liberation. For three days we climb Mount Moriah, Mount Sinai, Mount Golgotha. Those who were lost are found, and those who were exiled come home.

The first day of the Passover, from Holy Thursday sunset until Good Friday sunset, is the sixth day of creation, when God formed us from the clay of the earth and the breath of the Spirit. In dying on this day, the Lord Jesus fell asleep—like Adam—that we might be formed from his own open body—like Eve. In dying, Jesus breathed forth his Spirit to renew the face of the earth. On this first day of the Passover we wash each other's feet in tender humility. We begin the paschal fast, for who can even think of eating during these days? And we come to the holy cross as if it were Eden's tree of life.

The second day of the Passover, from Good Friday sunset until Holy Saturday sunset, is the paschal sabbath, the day of rest. In burial the Lord Jesus rested, and we rest in him. But this day is also a mysterious image of the timelessness before time began, of the chaos before creation. In burial, the Lord Jesus entered the "formless void." Jesus died the death we fear the most—utter lifelessness, utter nothingness. On this second day of the Passover we continue our fasting with the anxiety of separated lovers, with the grief of the newly widowed. We keep watch, learning the lessons of restfulness, silence and darkness. We reserve this day, unique in all the year, to do nothing at all.

The third day of the Passover, beginning Holy Saturday sunset, is the great surprise, the Easter surprise! This third day begins with the holiest night of the year, the vigil of Easter leading into the day of days, the "queen of seasons bright." On this glorious night, light is kindled in darkness. Order is born from chaos. Life tramples death by death. The rainbow appears and the Red Sea opens. The River Jordan skips and Jonah swims with the whale. Daniel curls up with lions and the three youths play with fire. And a slaughtered lamb rises to become our Good Shepherd.

That's why we make Easter Eve shine like day. That's why anyone and everyone in the parish must come together to keep the Easter Vigil. For on this night we witness resurrection in our very midst as the newborn children of God rise from the waters of baptism, are christened with the fragrant oil of confirmation, and are led to partake of eucharist. Why is this night different from all other nights? Tonight Christ is risen! And as the darkness of Saturday night passes over into Sunday dawn, our Passover is accomplished, and irresistible Easter overwhelms the world.

PREPARING THE PARISH

Attendance during the Triduum is poor in many parishes. But what should be considered *good* attendance? Our festival of Passover beckons every living thing into its house—that in its beginning it may shut the door against the angel of death, that in its ending it may open the door to the bridegroom. If we are convinced of the paramount importance of these days, if we believe the life of the parish is expressed in its liturgy, then it is our responsibility to ensure authentic and well-crafted liturgy *and* excellent attendance, not only for the principal liturgical moments of *Pascha* but throughout all its many hours.

How much of the lenten homilies have been directed at welcoming and encouraging folks to come to the Passover? Do we present these days as holier than any holy day of obligation, and that our obligation to attend the Triduum goes beyond legalities? We must be blunt and honest enough to explain that attendance at Easter Sunday Mass is important, but that it is secondary to attendance at the Easter Vigil, and that a large part of being a Catholic Christian means Sunday observance every week of the year *and* Triduum observance once a year. It's not that the Easter Triduum is more important than a Sunday; rather, the Triduum is a Sunday celebrated with all our might.

Do we speak openly to parish children, to the senior citizens, to teens, to all of the parish's organizations about their obligation to take part in the Triduum? Then do we put the effort into preparing these folks to sing its songs and hear its scriptures? The Passover is something kept not only around our parish table, but our home tables as well, in the paschal fast, in the paschal feast, in forgoing entertainment, work, anything that distracts us from the Passover of the Lord.

Yes, all this involves asking people to break household customs, to approach Easter with a new mind-set, to juggle schedules and to engage in the arguments and agreements involved in coming to church for so much time. This "new mind-set" is nothing less than the spirituality of baptism, confirmation and eucharist, our eagerness to descend into the waters of death and rebirth, to rise christened with the aroma of Christ, to take our seats at the supper of the Lamb. We must rehearse each other in the discipline of eternity, coming to the Triduum fully prepared to put aside our clocks and to experience something of the timelessness of heaven. Last Easter Vigil someone asked, "What time does this start?" The reply was tongue-in-cheek: "Well, it all began Thursday at sunset, and, God willing, it will end tomorrow at dawn."

An undercurrent in the discussion of the liturgy of *Pascha* is an intangible quality we must hold dear, something easily lost in all our preparations and hard work, something easily lost even in the midst of liturgy done well. *Pascha* is a mystery we enter, a cloud of God's presence that envelops us, a "three-day space," to use a term dear to the fathers and mothers of the church, that descends over us as we enter into the darkness of Holy Thursday night. This holy *Pascha* is Christ. And that is, at heart, why we must be there for all of the paschal liturgy. We must come to meet Christ, our beloved spouse. In the mystery of *Pascha,* we ourselves are lifted from the watery grave of baptism and escorted into a wedding feast that will have no end.

VESTURE

In former days, from Holy Thursday through Easter Sunday the vestments changed from violet to white, back to violet, then to black, back to violet, then from violet to white for the deacon alone, back to violet, then everyone finally in white. (Whew!) Things are simpler now—but that doesn't mean sloppier. There still are many decisions to be made about vesture, colors, appropriate fabrics and patterns—and all these decisions should be made when there's still time to do something about it.

Holy Thursday: Rubrically, the evening Mass on Thursday is in white, although that white should be as plain as possible, certainly not the Easter vestments that deserve to be seen for the first time at the Vigil. Some parishes use red accents on plain vesture, inasmuch as this night is Good Friday Eve. It is the first day of the Triduum and this day lasts from Thursday evening until Friday evening. The liturgy tonight is rich in references to blood, to the cross, to the paschal sacrifice begun with the meal we remember this night.

If the main cross (or other crosses anywhere else) cannot be removed, it is to be covered. A logical choice for this cover would be gray- or ecru-colored cloth, not flashy red or purple, but something that makes the cross fade away, not a wrapping at all but a flat curtain that hides the cross and not just the corpus. It makes sense to do this at the same time the church is cleaned earlier in the week.

Good Friday: Red is the color for the day, plain, without ornament (certainly without Pentecost symbols pasted on). The sacramentary calls for red Mass vestments—meaning chasuble for the presider, dalmatic for the deacon. Since there is no Mass, *there should be no concelebration*. Perhaps red copes could be worn by the lectors for the passion. Every parish will have to decide based on the best available vesture.

Holy Saturday morning and afternoon: The vesture for Morning Prayer or for the preparatory rites of the RCIA could stay red, or perhaps only a simple alb would be worn by the liturgical ministers—the white garment that is the property of all the baptized.

Easter Vigil and Sunday: Let the vesture to be worn throughout the Fifty Days of Easter be worn for the first time on Easter Eve. White is more than the rubrically correct color—it is the color of the bride and bridegroom, the color of robes worn by the baptized, the color of the Lamb. A way of adding solemnity is to vest cantors and lectors, especially the person who will sing the Exsultet, in albs. The book that contains the Exsultet should be especially beautiful, perhaps bound in the same fabric and trims of the Easter vesture.

THE WORSHIP ENVIRONMENT

The vigiling of the entire parish throughout the Triduum cannot be disturbed by last-minute preparations and fussing. That means that Holy Saturday is entirely too late to do the parish's Easter cleaning. In other words, when it comes to Easter, the "last minute" is sundown on Holy Thursday. After that, everything has to be in place.

The sacramentary is clear: "The tabernacle should be entirely empty." That implies the veil is removed, the vigil light is removed, the doors are left open. That implies that the entire church is stripped and cleaned—without candles or cloths or a single piece of unnecessary furniture from the choir area to the shrines to the vestibule. That further implies a certain startling bareness, an iconoclasm that in our broad tradition has included removing statues, veiling bright windows, covering art—so our attention can be given to the ritual actions and objects and people that are the ways we celebrate the Passover.

See the Eastertime section of "The Seasons" and the Triduum section of "The Calendar" for continued discussion of the worship environment for these days.

THE PASCHAL FAST

There is a fast called for on Good Friday through the Easter Vigil, a fast given repeated emphasis in nothing less than the *Constitution on the Sacred Liturgy,* the *Rite of Christian Initiation of Adults* and the *General Norms for the Liturgical Year and Calendar.* It is the Easter fast, the paschal fast. This fast is to be presented to the parish as unlike that of Lent (now over). It is a stricter fast. It is not the penitential fasting of Lent, but a fasting of anticipation, of anxiousness, of yearning. Nor is it bare-minimum observance of Good Friday alone. The paschal fast extends fully from Holy Thursday night through Good Friday and through Holy Saturday as well.

The paschal fast is also a fast from the sacraments. The parish has a great responsibility to instruct people in the significance of this interruption in the sacraments. It all comes down to a basic way of defining the Triduum: The Three Days are not a preparation for Easter. They *are* Easter.

The parish bulletin and certainly the lenten homilies have to invite everyone to keep the fast and make clear the distinction between the lenten fast and this paschal fast. Also, we should address the remembrances from over 30 years ago when the fast ended at noon on Holy Saturday. It may be 30 years since anyone heard anything about this fast except for the barest of legalities tucked once a year into the parish bulletin. Perhaps the best way to bring about a consciousness of the paschal fast is to provide parish-wide fasting meals both on Good Friday and Holy Saturday. One approach is to point out to people that this fast is like the fast before Sunday eucharist: a fast of preparation, of readiness, of being so wrapped up in what is to come that there is no thought to meals and such.

HOLY THURSDAY EVENING
The Mass of the Lord's Supper

What is the liturgical focus of this night? In the Last Supper the Lord Jesus was not recognized in the breaking of the bread. Instead, the disciples began an argument about who was best. The supper sank into betrayal, denial, total abandonment. Even our holy kiss of peace was turned inside out. When we prepare the liturgy of Holy Thursday, especially if we entertain romantic notions about the institution of the eucharist or of the priesthood, we should keep in mind just what the synoptics tell us of this night: It was the beginning of the passion of the Lord. For centuries the church did *not* celebrate eucharist tonight, so painful was the thought of how our worship can be twisted into a travesty of itself. (Also, it simply didn't make sense to have a eucharistic feast just as the paschal fast was beginning, or to hold a liturgy separated from the guests of honor—the elect.)

If we read the surrounding verses of the second reading from the liturgy, 1 Corinthians 6:23–26, we see it is set in the context of a warning: Our eucharist

can be a judgment against us. It is the judgment of the cross. The other two readings this night contain life and death ultimatums: The angel of death descends to execute judgment; a sacrifice is required to guarantee protection. If we are unprepared to be each other's slaves, then we can have no part with Jesus, the sacrificial lamb who offers freedom and life. The liturgy of Holy Thursday evening puts those warnings clearly before us as it sweeps us into the Passover. Any additions to this night, such as the renewal of priestly vows or the commissioning of ministers or even first communions, are dishonest to the liturgy and incompatible with its scriptures.

INTRODUCTORY RITES

Today these rites introduce the assembly not only to the Mass of the Lord's Supper, but to the entire Triduum. How can these rites most eloquently receive the assembly into the Triduum? The different ordering of the very first moments of the eucharist might be one way to suggest that somehow this night is different.

The gathering song, if the proper entrance antiphon in the sacramentary is not used, should keep with the imagery of that antiphon. Adapted from Galatians 6, it reads: "We should glory in the cross of our Lord Jesus Christ, for he is our salvation, our life and our resurrection; through him we are saved and made free." *Thursday's opening song should not be about the eucharist.* "Eucharist" is not Holy Thursday's "theme." Rather, we sing about the whole paschal mystery —Christ's passion, death, rest, resurrection, ascension and sending of the Spirit —that is our song especially as we enter into *Pascha.* An ancient text that echoes the entrance antiphon is "Sing, my tongue, the song of triumph," and it fits well to the tunes of "Picardy" and "Lauda Anima." (The text is found in *A Triduum Sourcebook,* LTP, and in *Worship, #437,* GIA.)

For simplicity's sake, consider omitting the penitential rite this evening. The opening prayer for Holy Thursday was poorly written, with little attention to the fullness of the paschal mystery. The simple opening prayer for the Tuesday of Holy Week is fitting, as is the beautiful opening prayer (A) for the Votive Mass of the Holy Eucharist.

The use of an elaborate Gloria at this time bears the same caveat as its use at any other time: There is a danger of overloading the gathering rite with such an item that diminishes the liturgy of the word. Especially at this time, "less is more." The custom of ringing bells can be adapted: One parish lets their tower bells peal from the time the sun sets to the time the people gather; then the bells are silenced. Parishes with automated bells should of course keep them silent from now until the Vigil.

The practice of singing the Gloria with bells as the gathering song underlines the completion of Lent and the beginning of the great Three Days. The mood created by such a festive beginning would contrast sharply with the mood created by the singing of a Taizé ostinato, such as "Ubi caritas," which lends a quiet and centering attitude. If also used during the mandatum or during the collection of alms or as the communion processional, a connectedness would be generated—a quality most desirable during these Three Days. The connecting power of a musical item should not be underestimated.

Receiving the oils. There is an Order for the Reception of the Holy Oils now approved for use on this day in the *Book of Blessings*. The oils blessed by the bishop at the Chrism Mass can be presented to and received by the parish community. This can be incorporated into the Mass of the Lord's Supper with the ministers carrying the vessels of blessed oil during the entrance procession. Coming to the altar, they place the vessels on it, and then incense the oils along with the altar. After the greeting the priest may say a few brief words about the oils and their significance in the life of the local faith community (although such words are unnecessary if the parish has learned during Lent the meaning of this ritual reception). The oils are then carried reverently to the place where they are reserved.

A suggestion: One parish begins the Triduum each year by bringing an enormous branch of flowering plum—a proclamation of spring—along with all the material things used during the Triduum into a completely stripped and cleaned church: the holy cross, the unlit paschal candle (held horizontally), the holy books, great vessels of water, the white robes, the oils and chrism, a bucket of kindling for the fire, even the towels to be used in tonight's washing of the feet. It takes over 20 ministers and a single rehearsal earlier in the week (to ensure that this procession takes place slowly and gracefully). Each item is placed near where it will eventually be used, either by the font or in the vestibule or some other place outside of the area around the altar, ambo and chair. After that, no one need spend time taking care of the environment. All is ready. (After the Vigil, attention goes to the Easter flowers and decorations that are really the environment of the Fifty Days.)

LITURGY OF THE WORD

Tonight's scriptures are clearly about entering into the Passover. Don't miss the keynote words of the first reading, that this month is to be our new year, that this festival is to be a perpetual institution, that the great mystery of the *Pascha* has now surrounded us. (These are words that would well be chanted.)

The psalm: Several of the paschal psalms are called the *Hallel*—so named because of their many shouts of Hallelujah. Psalms 114–118 (the Hallel) and Psalm 136 (the grand Hallel) receive in the sacramentary and psalter of the lectionary an important place within the liturgy of the Triduum. The setting of the psalm tonight should be chosen as much for its melody as its words.

THE WASHING OF FEET

The homily should lead naturally into the washing of feet. Don't add any other words of introduction. Throughout these days, no matter how unusual the rituals, "explanations" of any kind often become graceless and condescending; they frequently sound as if the assembly has no idea why they're there. If we have only a vague idea what is about to transpire the next three days, we need to go back and start Lent over.

Substituting the washing of hands or some other gesture for the washing of feet is dishonest. Sometimes one hears the argument that the foot-washing ritual is alien to our culture or that washing feet makes it inconvenient for

everyone to participate. Of course it is inconvenient. Peter obviously thought it was unseemly, disgusting and downright strange. And Jesus responded to Peter with what has to be the worst threat he ever uttered: "If I don't wash your feet, you will have no share in my heritage."

Certainly the washing of the feet will involve many parishioners washing each other's feet. Jesus' command is explicit: "As I have done, so you must do." This is not a tableau attempting to recreate a scene from the gospel but a sacramental rite that must engage the entire assembly, either directly and physically or indirectly by way of witness. Make sure all chairs are set up ahead of time. What could be uglier than rearranging furniture during the liturgy? Generous towels, sturdy washbasins, pitchers of warm, scented water—all these can be brought from the sacristy (or as part of the entrance rite as discussed previously) with a broad gesture as the singing begins and the participants move to their places.

The music of the mandatum has as many interpretations as there are parishes. Its length, its elaborateness, its style of execution dictates the type of music used. What is clear, though, is that the assembly's singing should not prohibit their watching and taking part in the action of the washing of the feet— that rather eliminates a hymn in its traditional construction. Also, this is a ritual (like the transfer of the eucharistic bread) that deserves a unique melody that returns every year. Antiphon and verse, ensemble piece, or reading with background music are a few solutions. Two comparatively new pieces are gaining popularity in American parish usage: Chrysogonus Waddell's "Jesus took a towel" and "Jesu, Jesu," a simple song from Ghana (both in *Worship,* GIA). Christopher Walker has designed a lush antiphon with a verse description of the scripture account of the washing. Its title is "Faith, hope and love" (OCP, #7149). M. D. Ridge uses 1 Corinthians for her "The greatest of these is love" (OCP, #8893) and sets it for a two-part choir and keyboard.

Wash everyone's feet? There are parishes that gracefully, beautifully, within a reasonable time conduct the washing of everyone's feet. Yes, it involves a Lent's worth of instruction and preparation (no stockings and especially no panty hose) and even a running joke about making sure that socks don't have holes. Earlier in the day, simple two-chair stations are set up throughout the body of the church (about 30 stations in a 1000-seat church). As the singing begins, people move to these stations as to a communion station, first washing the feet of a person already seated, then sitting down to have their own feet washed. Shoes can be removed either at the station or beforehand at seats. The deacon and presider act as water and towel bearers, and there are ushers to help also. No one is compelled—even as no one is compelled to go to communion.

The dismissal of the elect and the general intercessions follow the washing of feet. The length of this evening's liturgy is no excuse to skip the intercessions. The dismissal of the elect is one of those unsolvable quandaries in the liturgy of this night, and tomorrow as well. Surely they are not to take part in eucharist, especially if they were dismissed all through Lent. And surely there is no place to which we can send the elect; the entire parish has gathered in mystery and no one is to be dismissed. Their godparents, their catechists, the

parish RCIA coordinator—it can't be right to have these people absent from the paschal assembly! Until such time as the Triduum liturgies are reformed to acknowledge the presence of the elect, there are two courses of action, neither of which makes all that much sense liturgically: Either the elect are not dismissed and are asked merely to watch the eucharist without participating, or (a better choice) the elect move without a formal dismissal to a private place by themselves, somewhere close to the worship space, during the intercessions and eucharist today, and during the intercessions and the communion rite tomorrow, coming back to the assembly afterward. On Good Friday that involves rejoining the assembly after the intercessions for the veneration of the cross and then departing after they have each venerated the cross.

LITURGY OF THE EUCHARIST

This is the one celebration of the year when it is appropriate to bring forth something in addition to bread and wine during the preparation of the gifts: "gifts for the poor" says the sacramentary. Canned goods for a food bank or gifts for a parish's sister parish could be collected for this procession. Especially appropriate is the bringing forward of the parish lenten alms and the collection of parish mite boxes, such as the Operation Rice Bowl proceeds. This is made more visible if a big hamper was in place all Lent for collecting these alms.

The appointed song for the preparation is *Ubi caritas*. No other preparation rite has a song given it. Proulx's setting for unison choir/cantor and congregation, "God is love," is good (GIA, G-3010). So is Berthier's setting in music from Taizé (GIA, G-2433). It is difficult to imagine a more deservedly popular song from the '60s than Benoit's "Where charity and love prevail" ("Christian love"), which has recently received a bit of editing to change the exclusive language and can be found in the *People's Mass Book* (World Library Publications).

Eucharistic prayer: Preface of the Holy Eucharist I (P 17) is called for, but other texts are probably more appropriate to the Triduum (e.g., see the Preface of the Sacred Heart or of the Triumph of the Cross). Remember there are special inserts for Eucharistic Prayer I. Although Lent is over, it's perhaps best to retain the acclamations used throughout that season, especially if these were understated and simple. Save a new setting for the Vigil.

If there are concelebrants taking part, they need to know the text of the eucharistic prayer and who will be responsible for offering different parts of it: Some sections are reserved for the presider alone, but some parts can be read by a concelebrant. Also work out the details of where people stand. Remember that concelebration is not co-presiding. No one may usurp the position of the presider *or the deacon*. These details need to be settled well before Mass begins. The solemnity of the proclamation of the eucharistic prayer is satirized in the scene of concelebrants pointing their way through the sacramentary, or in their crowding around the altar, or even in their working out the details of who does what in the sacristy ten minutes before Mass begins—a poor witness to other liturgical ministers.

The communion rite: A strong custom this night was to forgo the sign of peace. It's absence was a reminder of many things, including the sense in which the

liturgy this night is meant to be incomplete, awaiting the Vigil. The sign of peace is never a facile handshake but a pledge of fidelity not to be made without consequences. Communion music can be chosen from versions of the *Ubi caritas*. Peloquin's "Faith, hope and love" (GIA, G-1893), using Psalm 136 as it verses, is a haunting piece uniting the paschal grand Hallel with Paul's words. What is used during communion as the processional could be repeated at the Good Friday liturgy in addition to its use at the Easter Vigil. Bob Hurd's "In the breaking of the bread" (OCP, #8776) sings almost by itself as does James Moore's "Taste and See" (GIA, G-2784).

After communion, the consecrated bread for tomorrow's liturgy is placed on the altar. After a goodly period of silence, the prayer after communion is said. There is no blessing, no dismissal, and there are no casual announcements. Remember, this is just the beginning of the Triduum—a single, three-day liturgy.

TRANSFER OF THE HOLY EUCHARIST

All the elements of this ceremony should be well known to the presider and assistants. We are doing something very simple here. We are putting the holy bread away for communion tomorrow. The rubrics in the sacramentary suggest little more than what we might do any Sunday in solemnly reserving the bread for the sick. This is not a Corpus Christi procession or benediction. The eucharist we have just celebrated was not deficient; it does not need a further show of affection for the presence of Christ in the eucharist. (The reason wine is not reserved is the same reason that wine is generally not reserved for the sick; it's simply not our tradition to reserve eucharistic wine—although this can be done for the sick when it is appropriate.)

Standing before the altar, the presider puts incense into the thurible, kneels and incenses the eucharist. The presider puts on the humeral veil, takes the vessel with the eucharist in it, and covers this with the ends of the veil—like the tabernacle veil with its image of the *shekinah,* the tent that God has pitched among us. The presider carries the holy bread to the place of reposition. Cross, candles and incense accompany the presider. (Although perhaps using the processional cross does not make much sense on this night.)

The hymn "Pange lingua/Sing, my tongue" should be sung as much for its melody as for its words. It is a touchstone in Catholic ritual music. One verse in Latin and one verse in English, with subsequent verses done in the same manner, assures its sustenance in the life of the parish. It is customary to sing the final two verses when the bread is placed in the repository. That is why it is important to have the repository somewhere other than in the main church space—so everyone can join the procession.

Arriving at the place, the presider sets the holy bread down and removes the humeral veil. The presider kneels and incenses the bread, and then places it in the repository and closes it. A period of silent adoration follows. A Taizé mantra introduced at this point would carry the assembly into the mood of quiet watchfulness, a mood that continues through the night and to the beginning of the Good Friday liturgy. Good choices are "Jesus, remember me," "Stay with me," and "Peace, I leave you." "De noche iremos" and "Dans nos obscurités" are

equally effective. At this point it makes most sense for the ministers to take their places with the people to begin the nightwatch.

The place of reposition is described in the rubrics as "a chapel suitably decorated." What is "suitably decorated"? Remember that it is Good Friday Eve. Save the lilies for Saturday night. The Italian ordo suggests that the decor be "in keeping with the sobriety and simplicity befitting the liturgy of these days." Still, it's only human nature to lavish energies on the beauty and drama of the Pasch—and a private chapel can definitely absorb more decoration (candles and flowers) than a space in the midst of the worship hall. Everyone can be invited to bring springtime garden flowers here to this chapel; these flowers in turn can be used as a bed on which to place the holy cross tomorrow.

The rubrics don't envision the assembly trying to jam into the chapel to keep watch. Since the eucharist is supposed to be reserved in a chapel of its own throughout the year, perhaps what is envisioned is the placement of the holy bread in that chapel in the regular tabernacle. It seems like the rubrics were written to suggest that if the regular tabernacle is located in an irregular location—such as in the main body of the church—this tabernacle is not to be used for reservation of the bread tonight.

When to close the church: The rubrics say "no solemn adoration after midnight." *This does not mean that the church itself be closed,* but that formal adoration stop within the eucharistic chapel. Night Prayer can close eucharistic adoration and begin the all-night vigiling, which should continue uninterrupted in the worship space of the church. If the repository is within the body of the church, then when the period of adoration ends, the eucharist is moved to another place, perhaps in the sacristy. (See the notes in the Triduum section of "The Calendar" in this *Sourcebook* for a discussion about a focus for keeping watch.) It should be clear why "a chapel" is preferred by the official rubrics: A place of repose in the main church distracts from the sobriety and intensity of Good Friday. Wherever the eucharist is kept, a lamp is kept lit nearby.

STRIPPING THE CHURCH

The altar is stripped without ceremony. Crosses are to be removed from the church or veiled. Holy water is to be removed from the stoops. However, the removal of water or crosses is a logical part of the church cleaning that precedes the Triduum. (Removing water is something many parishes do even before Lent begins.) There should be little to "strip" from the church tonight—which would only disturb the quiet vigiling that is beginning—except perhaps the altar cloth and the furniture used in the mandatum.

Although there is no ceremony for this removing of the altar cloth, it only makes sense to strip the altar with ritual reverence and dignity, realizing that this simple action was for years a strong sign of our entering into the paschal fast. This action took place while singing Psalm 22 in conjunction with Night Prayer.

KEEPING WATCH

See additional discussion on pages 178–79 of "The Calendar" in this *Sourcebook.* The vigiling and fasting begun tonight come as a direct command: "Stay awake

and pray" (Luke 22:46). The old liturgy's stripping of the altar during Compline, such ceremonies as tenebrae and "the three hours," the round-the-clock prayer kept by various church societies—all these can be sorely missed by people who take seriously the importance of the vigiling begun this evening. What is needed is not a restoration of these separate customs so much as a renewal of the entire Three Days as a period of constant prayer and fasting *in ecclesia,* as an assembly. And this renewal will happen most readily in parishes that are learning how to pray the liturgy of the hours.

Here is a suggested way to start the vigiling tonight, beginning right after the reposition of the eucharist: After the ministers have taken their seats among the assembly (everyone is kneeling at this point), darken the worship space somewhat and begin Berthier's continuous ostinato "Stay with me" (*Music from Taizé,* vol. 2, GIA, G-2778—see also the previously mentioned suggestions.) Let the ostinato continue, very hushed, while the deacon goes to the ambo and motions everyone to rise. Without the introductory dialogue, he reads Matthew's account of the agony in the garden (Matthew 26:36–45; or 26:36–56) from the gospel book (mark the verses in Palm Sunday's Passion reading); the deacon then returns to his place among the assembly. The church can be darkened further, and the choir can sing something such as the Early American round by Billings, "When Jesus wept," and then they can take their seats with the assembly. Finally, the deacon rises and says: "My friends, let us keep watch in peace," and all respond, "Thanks be to God."

The beginning of this vigiling will make a few people uneasy since there isn't any dismissal. The only way to make clear that the church will remain open and the vigil will continue is to spend some time during Lent preparing for this pattern, and perhaps a note can be put in the worship aid about keeping silent when leaving. The church doors should be kept well lit to invite coming and going throughout the night.

Tenebrae: Of course, Night Prayer, the Office of Readings and eventually Morning Prayer belong to this night, as to every night. "Tenebrae" was the paschal title for the Office of Readings ("Matins") combined with Morning Prayer ("Lauds") during which candles were extinguished as morning came. Traditional readings, psalms and responsories for prayer during this night, and through Friday and Saturday as well, can be adapted from "Tenebrae" in *The Book of Occasional Services* (The Church Hymnal Corporation). A beautiful tradition tonight is the reading of the Last Discourse (John, chapters 14–17). Avoid using the ambo-altar-chair area during any of this vigiling.

GOOD FRIDAY AFTERNOON
The Celebration of the Passion of the Lord

For additional notes on the keeping of Good Friday, including notes on the liturgy of the hours, keeping vigil throughout the day and parish fasting meals, see pages 178–81 in "The Calendar."

Silence prevails. There is no procession to speak of (no cross, candles, incense). The presider and deacon rise from where they have been sitting with the vigiling

assembly and then go before the altar and reverence it with a bow. This is a true and clear indication that the church keeps itself in prayer and vigil all through these days.

The sacramentary specifies that the liturgy begins in silence. Silence means absence of sound. The choir does not perform a motet or anthem as a prelude, tympani do not pulse out a sinister rhythm. This does not mean music cannot be used sometime before the hour of the liturgy. Musical meditations on the stations of the cross or the seven last words, however, should end well before the liturgy begins.

Falling prostrate: As the service begins, the presider and assistant ministers prostrate themselves full length. Everyone else kneels in silence. If the physical arrangement of the room allows, anyone in the assembly could join in the prostration. Kneeling is only a poor substitute for this profound gesture; ideally, kneeling would be done only if health or available space prevent this posture. Prostrate or kneeling, then, all pray silently as the sacramentary suggests "for a while," that is, long enough to let the banging of kneelers and the clearing of throats yield to an intense silence, then longer as this silence turns to true communion. The time for this silent posture to begin and end might be signaled by a sharp sound, such as a knocking on wood.

Opening prayer: Going to the chair, the presider neither greets the people—remember the Triduum greeting took place last night—nor invites them with the traditional "Let us pray." Instead, with hands joined, the presider simply offers the prayer and sits down for the liturgy of the word. (The second, longer alternative prayer is more traditional. "Adam" can be "Adam and Eve," and "manhood" can be "humanity.") Certainly, all the presidential prayers these days should be chanted.

LITURGY OF THE WORD

The word (in length and content) is a central part of today's celebration. The poetry of Isaiah, the confirming reassurance in Hebrews, and the lengthy Gospel of John unraveling the victorious passion of Christ—together these can draw the assembly more fully into the celebration or cut them off from the remainder of the liturgy. Everything depends on the manner of the proclamation.

The liturgy does not call for melodramatics or passion plays. It only assumes that the best lectors are invited to spend a great deal of time and prayer in preparing for this celebration. If that translates into having the readings memorized, fine. If that translates into having a choral reading of the gospel, fine. If that translates into an articulate, sincere and faith-filled reading from behind the pulpit and straight from the lectionary, fine. The primary concern should be to invite readers who are willing to make the prayer of their talents a service of love to the rest of the assembly.

The psalm: This is the first music of the liturgy. Keep in mind the tradition of not using musical instruments during much of the Triduum. It is a remarkably powerful absence. Whether or not parishes use instruments today, you may want to repeat the setting of Psalm 22 used on Passion Sunday. This psalm is the seasonal psalm for Holy Week, so it is suitable throughout this week. Hughes's

"God, my God, why have you abandoned me" (*Psalms for All Seasons*, NPM) has a very strong refrain coupled with a formula psalm tone that permits articulation of the text. Peloquin's "My God, my God, why have you abandoned me" (GIA, G-1658) is very dramatic—in the good sense—moving from despair to an intense cry of glory, requiring a cantor capable of full control of dynamics and voice coloration.

The Passion: The singing of the Passion by three strong singers should be given priority over any other means of proclamation. The rubrics in the sacramentary permit the nonordained to sing it. The assembly can interpolate the verses of a hymn during the Passion, but the song chosen must respect the unique character of the Johannine account. "Sing, my tongue, the song of triumph" (set to the haunting French carol "Picardy" in *Worship*, a melody that is familiar to many parishes) or "The royal banners forward go" are much more in keeping with John's passion than "O sacred head surrounded."

Several missalettes involve the congregation in the reading of the Passion with a "crowd" part. The proclamation of the scriptures is never to be a read-along. Communities that use such missalettes would do well to invite the congregation to relinquish the "crowd" lines, put down the missalettes, and listen to the word as proclaimed, not as read.

"A brief homily may be given." These sacramentary rubrics are strengthened in the recent letter from the Congregation for Divine Worship. The text there says, "A homily *should* be given, at the end of which the faithful may be invited to spend a short time in meditation." Remember that apathy in any form—by failing to prepare a homily, or even by skipping the homily as a "favor" to everyone—shows contempt or condescension to the people who have gathered for the Pasch.

The general intercessions follow. The *Saint Andrew Bible Missal* offers a brief note on the lengthy, stylized form these prayers take today: "On this day the form of these prayers goes back to the ancient usage of the Roman church. They are truly universal, for no one and no thing is exempt from the saving power of Christ's cross." The general intercessions are taken from the sacramentary texts within the Good Friday celebration. The most direct way of leading the assembly in these prayers would be for the deacon (or another minister) at the ambo to introduce each petition and then to invite everyone to kneel in silent prayer. When this is over, the presider (at the chair) stands, with everyone standing as well. Then the presider sings the prayer, and the assembly seals it with their sung Amen. Pacing is all-important since there is a tendency to rush.

VENERATION OF THE CROSS

There is a period of silence as the cross is prepared for veneration—not a busy time for a collection. Baskets inviting our aid for the upkeep of the holy places in Jerusalem can be placed in the vestibule so that the general intercessions lead directly to the veneration of the cross.

There are two formats possible for the showing of the cross: The "uncovering" and the "bringing-in." If the "uncovering" form is chosen, note carefully what the rubrics try to say: The veiled cross is not carried in and unveiled in stages along the way. Rather, the gradual unveiling takes place entirely in one place. This would seem to suggest that the cross being considered is the one referred to in the words of the Holy Thursday rubrics: "It is desirable to cover any crosses which remain in the church." If at all possible, the year-round stationary cross can be taken down for the unveiling and veneration.

The "bringing-in" is the preferred format (if the cross is other than the stationary cross) both because of its graceful simplicity and especially because of its ritual movement. The presider or deacon moves through the assembly with the cross, making three stops: at the entrance of the worship space, in the middle of the assembly, in front of the assembly. This movement is patterned after the bringing-in of the paschal candle, a nonverbal link between Good Friday and the Easter Vigil. Other ministers can surround the crossbearer with bowls of incense and candles, like a gospel procession. The cross is not held over the shoulder like a holy card picture of Jesus ascending Calvary, but in the way one holds a processional cross. At the three stations, the cross must be hoisted as high as possible and held steadily, a feat that is possible if rehearsed well a few days earlier. After the final station, assistants should come to help hold the cross, and the candles and incense can be placed nearby.

Some parishes make sure the cross is always held by people during the veneration, and some parishes simply lay it flat on a large carpet or on a bed of flowers. It should not be propped up lackadaisically on furniture or railings, much less on the altar. *Nor should the cross be plunked into a stand*—this makes it look more like a stage prop than a holy sign. For the veneration, the assembly comes forward to reverence the cross. There is a simple genuflection "or another sign of reverence, . . . for example, kissing the cross." Local custom in many places means both a genuflection (or total prostration) and a kiss. It's best not to explain to the assembly how to venerate the cross; that only reduces the intense mystery of the rite to a set of prosaic instructions. After all, we wouldn't think of informing loved ones how to embrace one another. Let the first people who come to venerate the cross do so with broad, authentic gestures, enabling those who come after to feel free to worship the holy wood with affection.

Going barefoot: A beautiful, powerful gesture on this day is for all ministers— indeed, all the people—to come to the cross barefoot or in stocking feet. This sort of tradition happens over years but begins with catechesis during Lent. This tradition, observed by many monastic orders and mentioned by ancient writers in the context of the veneration of the cross, calls to mind several images: Isn't the holy cross like the burning bush? Isn't this place holy ground? Read the powerful words of Song of Songs 5:2–8. We have removed our shoes and washed our feet, a preparation for entering the bath of baptism. Now we stand barefoot before the tree, eager to be restored to the innocence of Eden.

Cross or crucifix? What we honor today is what we proclaim: Behold the *wood* of the cross. We are declaring that this wood, be it oak, cedar, pine or any other

tree, is truly the wood of the holy cross. Wood is the sign. It is the material from which was built the great ship that preserved creation from the flood, the pyre prepared for the sacrifice of Isaac, Aaron's blossoming rod and Moses' mighty staff held over the Red Sea to open before us a highway to freedom. The wood of the cross is the tree of life and the ark of the covenant—this wood, here now, here among us.

One cross or several? To expedite the veneration, some parishes add two or three crosses. But what does that say about the significance of the grand procession of all the people, the chanting, the kneeling? And what does that say about the holy cross that was just brought in? Allow for the procession of the people to come forward and venerate the one cross. The alternative—and it's really a very poor alternative—is the presider inviting the people to venerate the one cross by holding it up for them to worship from their places in silence.

Music for the veneration: The ritual's spirit is that we present the cross as trophy, as triumphant symbol. The music can enhance that symbol immensely. The use of the "Agios, o Theos/Holy is God" composed by Howard Hughes (in *Praise God in Song,* GIA, G-2270) certainly creates the mood after the invitation to come and adore is sung by a cantor near the cross. The long procession to venerate the cross cannot be rushed. It is an opportunity to mix congregational singing with choir pieces, using several different styles. Begin with something that involves the assembly, choir and cantor, perhaps one of the Taizé ostinatos, such as "Adoramus te, Domine I" or "Jesus, remember me," then move to an American spiritual, such as "Calvary" sung by choir and soprano, then back to the assembly's singing, ending the veneration with a strong hymn, such as the haunting and lovely song "Alas, and did my Savior bleed" ("My Savior," *Worship II, #7,* GIA) or "What wondrous love is this." Many other musical solutions are possible during the veneration. Dan Schutte and Roc O'Connor's "Jesus the Lord" (NALR, SJ41-SLJ-SM), Stainer's "God so loved the world," and "No greater love" (GIA, G-3141) by Michael Joncas are but a few items that could intensify that liturgical action.

One caution: While Roman Catholic liturgy welcomes into its use the music of so many different traditions, the spirit of this ritual—and of all liturgy—does not have a place for facile sentiment. As an example, "The old rugged cross" may have served Tennessee Ernie Ford very well, but it's unsuited to the liturgy— particularly because it makes the saving death of Christ "long ago and far away."

HOLY COMMUNION

This is a very recent addition to Good Friday. When the liturgies of these days were taking shape, the church fasted from the eucharist throughout the Triduum until the Easter eucharist. Communion and the general intercessions today bring with them the question of the dismissal of the catechumens and the elect. Dismissing anyone from the Triduum liturgies is alien to the spirit of the Triduum. Last night's eucharist and this afternoon's communion service leave completely unresolved the role of the elect—demonstrating what a late addition these rites were to the liturgies of the Pasch. See the discussion beginning on page 72 about possible temporary solutions. The communion rite is clearly

intended to be carried out simply and with reverent dispatch, perhaps singing the same thing as was sung last night during communion. This is the only use of the altar in today's liturgy and it should be minimal.

CONCLUDING RITES

Without the traditional greeting—which says that we are still within the Triduum—the presider extends hands toward the assembly and offers the prayer over the people. There is no dismissal (that will come only after the Vigil), and there should be no recessional of ministers. The ministers—including the music ministers—should return to sit with the vigiling assembly.

Paschal silence: Immediately following any liturgy is a time recognized as an occasion for socializing. Today all are urged to keep silent for the benefit of those remaining in vigil, keeping the paschal fast in speech as well as food. Mention this in the bulletin and in the worship aid, but the best teacher is the example of the ministers themselves as they take their places in the assembly to continue vigiling. Perhaps such "silence" can be ensured by the soft singing of a Taizé ostinato, possibly the same one sung last evening, while those who must leave make their departure. Or try what they sometimes find necessary at the Taizé liturgies: You are greeted at the door with a smile and a large sign—"Silence!"

CONTINUING THE WATCH

(See the discussion of the liturgy of the hours, fasting meals and the continuous vigil on pages 178–81 in "The Calendar" of this *Sourcebook*.) The Celebration of the Passion is not to be repeated. It is supposed to take place in the afternoon, before sundown, so that it is celebrated on the first day of the Triduum. Sundown on Good Friday marks the beginning of the second day, the paschal sabbath. Many parishes offer a "lesser" service in the evening, often stations of the cross, presumably to accommodate people who could not attend afternoon worship.

But that's not exactly what a parish should be striving for. In the first place, lenten catechesis should have led the parish to understand that business-as-usual must be set aside for the Triduum. The only parishioners to be "accommodated" are those very few people working in jobs that cannot be set aside. And in the second place, what we're trying to make happen is not a Triduum made up of three distinct liturgies but a Triduum of ongoing liturgy—the principal services in tandem with the liturgy of the hours, with devotions such as stations of the cross and with continuous vigiling, so that the church is never empty.

Are the more important liturgical services of the Triduum—such as the liturgy of the hours—getting more attention and better attendance than the less important services—such as stations of the cross? Designing a schedule for the services means accommodating not those people who can attend only one service but those parishioners who choose to attend *all* the services. (See the Sample Triduum Schedule on page 93.) That is why the services cannot be redundant; as has been said before, the services within the Triduum have no greetings and no dismissals. We are called to remain together in holy conclave until the first light of Easter dawn.

HOLY SATURDAY
The Paschal Sabbath

(See pages 180–81 in "The Calendar" for additional notes on this day.) The rubrics for "Sabbatum Sanctum" in the sacramentary specify its character:

> On Holy Saturday the church waits at the Lord's tomb, meditating on his suffering and death. The altar is left bare, and the sacrifice of the Mass is not celebrated. Only after the solemn vigil during the night . . . does the Easter celebration begin, with a spirit of joy that overflows into the following period of 50 days. On this day holy communion may be given only as viaticum.

The paschal fast from food, work, shopping and entertainment continues until the Easter Vigil. The public celebration of the Office of Readings before Morning Prayer is strongly recommended. (What an incomparably beautiful patristic reading that office features!) Midday Prayer and Evening Prayer should also be celebrated. See the already-mentioned *Book of Occasional Services;* this has fitting material that can be adapted to this day in the section on "Tenebrae."

Today is not a day for blessing foods. Although many parishes have the custom of blessing Easter foods today, this is a throwback to the era when the Easter Vigil was held Saturday morning. Restore this beautiful custom to its proper liturgical place, and hold the blessing of foods after the prayer after communion during the Easter Masses, *especially* the Vigil.

The character of this day gets lost in most of the usual ways parishes observe Holy Saturday: as the day "in between," as the day for cleaning, decorating, filling fonts and rushed rehearsing. Certainly there will be preparations, but most of this activity is what Lent was for. Even something as seemingly necessary as Easter decorating cannot disturb the Triduum; it can, in fact, become an integral part of the parish's round-the-clock vigil, a way for all parishioners to remain together in fasting and watching. After all, what is more important, the Easter decorations or the Easter sabbath?

The RCIA outlines a service of "preparation rites" on Holy Saturday (which can be kept some other day): song and greeting; reading the word of God and homily; celebration of certain rites (e.g., "giving back" the creed, *ephphetha* rite, choosing a baptismal name, the anointing with the oil of catechumens). If these rites are kept today, they are part of the parish keeping of the Pasch and are not private affairs for the soon-to-be-initiated. Make sure they are part of the distributed Triduum schedule, and invite everyone to attend. See what was said earlier about rehearsals and the elect.

THE EASTER VIGIL
Nightwatch of the Resurrection

When do we begin? The sacramentary rubrics say of the Easter Vigil: "It should not begin before nightfall." That doesn't mean twilight; it means after dark. The sacramentary continues: ". . . it should end before daybreak." Since

nightfall on Easter Eve this year comes about 1½ hours later than in 1989 (thanks to Daylight Savings Time and a later Easter), schedules need to be adjusted. One Polish-American community keeps a *real* vigil: They kindle the new fire after dark, then keep the church open and an informal vigil going on all night. The formal Vigil begins around 3:00 AM so that when it is completed the community walks out of the church into the early dawn of Easter Sunday morning. Is any attention ever paid to choosing this morning end of the time spectrum for the Vigil, or to continuing all night?

The *Circular Letter Concerning the Preparation and Celebration of the Easter Feasts,* issued from the Congregation for Divine Worship in Rome, January 16, 1988, adamantly confirms these rubrics regarding the time of the Easter Vigil, speaking with particular harshness to those who begin the Vigil too early: "This rule is to be taken according to its strictest sense. Reprehensible are those abuses and practices that have crept into many places in violation of this ruling, whereby the Easter Vigil is celebrated at the time of day that it is customary to celebrate anticipated Sunday Masses" (#78).

Whatever time is chosen between nightfall and daybreak, remember that the Vigil can make sense only in the context of that darkness. That means lots of details like turning off and taping over the switches of all lighting in the church, outside the church, even in the parking lot. It means growing accustomed to the darkness and not running about with flashlights or flicking lighters. It means not staring at watches, and not worrying when the fire begins (and just plain *not worrying*), and allowing the assembly to sit and wait in darkness and silence for the holy things about to happen. It means letting this night be odd—different from all other nights—even if that requires a rally and rehearsal with the ushers earlier in the week, or asking teenagers to help escort people in the darkness, or asking all liturgical ministers, especially the choir, to set the example by being quiet and contemplative.

The results are in and are clear from those parishes that have prepared well every ministry, then let the Vigil run its course. It can be hours long and *no one complains!* People do not complain about beauty and mystery and the very heart of their existence being celebrated.

THE SERVICE OF LIGHT

The service of light is an integral part of this evening's celebration. Still, the lamp lighting, *lucernarium,* must be given only that time and solemnity that will keep it proportionate to the rest of the Vigil. The ideal structure of the rite is straightforward:

A fire is kindled. The Latin word for this fire is *rogus,* "bonfire." That means a real fire, outdoors, a bonfire that gives off heat and brilliant flame. Even if the assembly stays inside, the fire stays out. Setting a fire indoors of any size is ridiculous, necessitating the snuffing out of the fire to prevent smoke. A bonfire set within 20 feet of the main doors will cast cheery light throughout the inside of church. Some parishes save their Christmas greens to burn. A bonfire can be built right on a lawn with no harm if a thick tarp is put down, then about ten inches of sand laid over it—a good job for the scouts! A large trough made for

watering livestock can also be used to contain the wood, providing that sand is placed underneath as insulation.

If you plan to gather everyone outside around the fire, consider having everyone meet first in a place that has chairs, other than the worship hall. Don't fret the inconvenience of being outdoors. The worse the weather, short of a downpour, the more the assembly will welcome cheerful fire. So often we try to protect people from their own best interests. It's ironic that in churches with a tradition of outdoor ceremonies it is often the oldest and feeblest who are most eager to take part. Put out 20 or so chairs with signs "For the infirm" if you want. The words of blessing over the fire should be spoken from memory. (The ordinary greeting and blessing of the fire, moving into the "Light of Christ," are all the words that are needed; the presider's "instruction" in the sacramentary has little purpose.) Careful rehearsal can settle ways for this rite to be done well, with broad gestures, few words and no fumbling for pages in books. If the presider or deacon is weak-voiced, perhaps a strong cantor can substitute. A lovely gesture at this point is to cast a handful of incense into the flames.

The paschal candle is prepared and lit. It's a shame that so many parishes do not perform the symbolic decoration of the paschal candle, although it can be a wordy intrusion in the liturgy at this point. (One parish does this preparation as part of Good Friday Night Prayer, inserting the incense grains and anointing the cross, the numerals of the year and the alpha and omega with myrrh while the traditional words are chanted solemnly.) A tight bundle of thin wooden sticks can be used to carry the fire to the candle (wax tapers melt down near a bonfire instead of lighting).

The deacon carries the candle (held high, the sacramentary says) and leads the procession into church. Accompanying the candle is an incense bearer, other ministers, and the one who will chant the Exsultet—at least wearing an alb, but why not wearing a cope?—holding a fine book or scroll with the Exsultet. The people of God marching together while the pillar of fire guides them home—here is one of the most powerful images of Easter! Sure, it is much more convenient to forgo the procession of the people from the fire into the church and simply bring the paschal candle into a darkened church already filled with the assembly, but realize what gets lost. If this procession is kept, the "Light of Christ/Thanks be to God" becomes the processional song of sorts.

The candle is incensed when it is placed in its stand; a bowl of incense put beneath the candle during the Exsultet is wonderful, allowing a cloud of smoke to curl around the candle.

When do the people's candles get lit? There are several patterns possible: If there is a procession of everyone walking from the place around the outdoor fire to the church, the sacramentary suggests that everyone's candles (and not the ministers' first and then the people's) are lit at the doors when the second "Light of Christ" is sung. (What the sacramentary seems to imply is that the people light their candles directly from the paschal candle as they enter the church.) If there is no procession of the assembly, the people's candles can be lit when the paschal candle is lowered at each of the three stations. (It's graceless to have acolytes transfer the holy flame from the candle to the people. Allow the members of the assembly who are closest to the candle to reach out for the light.)

If the fire is built some distance from the church, and the procession therefore is to be of a good length, you might consider having a beautiful glass windguard built for the candle. The people's candles can be lit before the procession if you also have windguards for these. Paper cones are available; some Orthodox church goods stores have pretty red plastic windguards designed to be placed on the substantial candles they use in their Easter processions.

Or here's a pattern for the lighting of candles that you may not have considered: The people are not given candles at the beginning of the service (it seems odd to blow them out and then relight them for the baptisms). The Exsultet can be chanted to the light of just the paschal candle, or perhaps a smattering of tapers around the candle (placed near the ambo). This single area of light surrounded by darkness is dramatic, and it functions well throughout the entire liturgy of the word. In this way the assembly keeps watch in relative darkness. Responsorial psalmody and the gospel acclamation would then be chosen to make reading from a worship aid unnecessary. After the homily (and imagine what sort of preaching would be evoked by such an atmosphere), candles are distributed and then lit during the litany of the saints as the elect are brought to the font. The rites of initiation thus take place with everyone holding candles. When the newly baptized are handed their lighted candles, then the circle of light is complete.

The Exsultet begins after the assembly and ministers have taken their places. The Exsultet is a blessing and thanksgiving for the paschal light. The cantor's diction needs to be good. Electric lights should be off; there really isn't any need for them.

The Exsultet is one of the most beautiful vestiges of solo repertory that has survived the nearly 2000-year history of Christian music. Like the presidential prayers, it is solo music, sung by deacon, cantor or presider, but solo music nonetheless that comes from the tradition of the cantor/deacon office of hundreds of years ago. For a single cantor, the edition by Batastini (GIA, G-2351) is a smooth working of the text to the traditional melodies. The setting by Walker (St. Thomas More/OCP, #7151) is for cantor and SATB choir. The assembly enters only for the concluding Amens. (Although this should go without saying, if you don't have a cantor able to sing the Exsultet, you won't have an Exsultet. A trained singer, well rehearsed, is essential.)

A caveat: Music publishers are coming out with settings that masquerade as Exsultets. For example, "The Easter Proclamation" by Conry substitutes marshmallow for the actual text of the Exsultet—an unfortunate thing to put an assembly through. A much finer piece of music is Haugen's "The Light of Christ," which is so lovely that it's tempting to ignore the lightweight words that truncate the actual words of the Exsultet and that fail to perform the anamnetic function of this chant in recounting the wonders of this night. "The Light of Christ" makes a good song at Evening Prayer or even a good communion song for Eastertime, but it is *not* an Exsultet.

When the structure of this *lucernarium* is understood, one will treat it in the way it is meant to be: "the lighting of the lamps that will fill the night with light for us" (Rupert Berger in *Celebrating the Easter Vigil,* Pueblo, 42).

LITURGY OF THE WORD

The proclamation of the word in a prolonged fashion is the foundation of any vigil service. On this "mother of vigils," the church meditates on all the wonderful things God has done from the beginning. In truth, this is the night the *mirabilia* happen in our midst. This is the night of creation, of liberation, of resurrection. Solid catechesis and liturgical practice can help prepare the community for the lengthy proclamation of the scriptures.

We take time to rehearse ourselves in timelessness. Just as important as catechesis, however, is the need to consider how that understanding is ritualized in the Vigil. The layouts of most of our churches are such that people would almost never consider standing up to stretch, walking to the back of the church for a while, stepping outside of the building for a few moments (or even going home for a time?), only to come back again to the Vigil celebration. This is a healthy style of worship sometimes found among Orthodox Christians. While considering the need for listening to *all* the readings offered for this great night—which is really a consideration of just how long we expect people to stay together *in ecclesia* during the Pasch—concerns such as these need to be addressed.

How many readings to read? See LTP's *A Triduum Sourcebook* for tables of all the traditional readings for the Vigil if you choose to add to the nine readings in the lectionary. Yes, *add*. Certainly there is a place this night alongside the stories of creation, of Abraham and Isaac, of Moses and Miriam, for the stories of the great flood, of Daniel in the lions' den, of Esther and Mordechai, of Jonah and the whale, of the three youths in the fiery furnace, of passages from the Song of Songs. What it really comes down to is that we all approach this night *demanding* to hear these stories—because we know that this is the night they happen in front of our eyes. Standing with us this night are all the people of these stories, our ancestors. After hearing how God delivered Daniel, how God freed the Hebrews, how God set the spangled stars in the sky, we come to hear the gospel of resurrection not with confusion or even surprise but rather with a confident "of course!"

The readings could be done by candlelight, following this structure: reading, silence, sung psalm, presider's collect. When all is said and done, the lectors' and cantors' abilities within this part of the night's liturgy make or break the Vigil. One cannot compensate for their abilities by embellishing the readings with gimmickry. Is there anything more splendid than a single reader reading well? Practice, practice, practice. Lectors will be some of the most excited members of the assembly as they sweat away at their preparation for this night.

Psalmody this night has infinite possibilities. While it seems reasonable to draw from the psalms that are sung throughout the year, you certainly want a few that are unique to this night. Here's one suggestion: the Gelineau setting of the grand Hallel, the glorious paschal Psalm 136, is a classic. Verses 1–3 can be used after the creation reading and then the remaining verses can be sung— adding tambourines—after the reading from Exodus. Every song-leading group in the parish needs to be involved with the music of the Vigil. Rehearsals in the

dark are necessary so that the minimum of lights can be used, and then only for those who need it and only during the psalm that group is leading.

The gospel acclamation: Berger suggests that the odd division of readings between Hebrew Scriptures and Christian Scriptures by the Gloria and the opening prayer does not serve well. He suggests that we omit both Gloria and prayer, and let the solemn, festive intonation and repetition of the Alleluia, accompanied by bells, lead naturally into the proclamation of the gospel. No matter what the yearlong parish practice for the gospel procession, tonight's gospel demands a long-as-possible procession, an Alleluia that enables us to sing our praise for all the scriptures we have heard this night and for the good news of resurrection we are about to hear.

Whichever way this is decided, note that the Alleluia is prolonged on this night: There are verses from Psalm 118, with the Alleluia refrain echoing again and again. Surely this could be a liturgy at which to chant the gospel (GIA publishes a challenging adaptation of the old Gregorian solemn melody). The chant triple Alleluia pushes the assembly to their vocal limits. One solution to its preservation and performance would have a cantor (or deacon, if he is up to it) sing the Alleluia with the choir repeating it in its three-fold pattern. During that singing, the gospel book is carried in procession and held aloft each time the Alleluia is sung by the solo singer. After the completion of this unit, the organ and instruments introduce the Alleluia of the assembly. A cymbal crash would announce the singing of the acclamation in no uncertain terms!

The choice of the acclamation is directed by the elaborateness of the procession. The assembly should view all the stuff that is going on—incensations, bells swinging, banners waving, all the movement. A printed page bearing a complicated text gets in the way—so a many-time repeated Alleluia is what's needed. Alleluia X from Taizé fits the need. Hutmacher's "Gospel processional" (GIA, G-2450) is a hypnotic melody that should begin quietly and be allowed to build with each repetition. There are options for chorus, organ and brass. Hughes's "Gospel processional" (GIA, G-2505) can be done in a similar manner. This can be the Alleluia that will be heard throughout the Fifty Days—and at no other time during the year. After the gospel it is important to break into either a vigorous setting of the Gloria or an Easter carol—something very familiar like "The strife is o'er." The gospel reading this night just about demands a merry hymn afterward—with plenty of Alleluias.

For an example of what the homily should do this holy night, read John Chrysostom's paschal sermon, reprinted in LTP's *A Triduum Sourcebook*. The homily this night, like the scriptures themselves, should leave us babbling our Alleluias as we invite all creation to celebrate our festival.

LITURGY OF INITIATION

The absence of anyone to be baptized at the Vigil is a great loss for the entire community. Indeed, this absence is reason for the parish to examine how it has been witnessing to the life and love of God: Why doesn't anyone want to join our number? (Of course, this can never mean that hopefuls are rushed through a crash course on religion and processed through the Vigil in the hope that faith

will someday catch up. The many rites of the RCIA, which are meant to unfold over a period of several years, are also meant to ensure that those to be baptized this night are long familiar to the parish and much of its liturgical life.)

First things first: These lengthy initiation rituals *can* be done in a manner that is graceful, beautiful, prayerful. You will need to believe that tedium sets in not necessarily when ritual takes a long time, but when it is done poorly. To insure this gracefulness, imagine, prepare and rehearse the ritual first *without any words.* Concentrate on the people involved, their comfortableness, their postures, their clothing, the life and death solemnity yet gentle playfulness of their part in the ritual, even the expressions on their faces. Tonight we are conducting something far more mysterious than the word "initiation" implies. We are observing the funeral and the birth, the royal anointing and the coronation, the nuptials of the body of Christ.

How will they come slowly forward to the font? Where will everyone stand? How can gestures be as visible as possible? Then concentrate on the physical things to be used. For example: How are the white robes put on? How will the baptismal candles be kept burning brightly throughout the eucharist? How will candidates for reception into the church be treated distinctly from the elect? Only after everything can be done in mime should song be woven through the rituals. And then only after that should words—as sparingly as possible—be added.

The presentation of the candidates, invitation to prayer and litany of the saints: The presentation is given several possible formats in the RCIA, 219. Almost every parish can make fine use of Form B, regardless of the placement of the font. The summoning of the elect to the font should be done solemnly and slowly, calling their names loudly and adding no additional words. The litany of the saints is the "processional song" as the elect and godparents come forward, perhaps following the deacon who carries the paschal candle at the head of the procession. This not only signifies the slaves being led by the pillar of fire through the water to the promised land, it gets the candle from the ambo to the font in a gracious manner. This procession should take as long a route as possible through the church to the font.

The litany of the saints has been treated in many ways by many composers. What has endured is the chant setting. It must move as a litany, that is to say, a rapid movement from invocation into intercession. It cannot drag. (The litany goes quickly, with as many names as possible, but the procession moves at a snail's pace.) If we are true to the meaning of its text, the invitation to prayer should precede the blessing of the water instead of preceding the litany.

Welcoming water: Something happens tonight that sometimes gets lost within the initiation rites. Just as we greet and bless the return of light, so we greet and bless the return of water. Here's one parish's welcome to water: Immediately after the litany of the saints, with the assembly seated, the Canticle of Isaiah (Isaiah 12) is begun (for example, "You will draw water joyfully," Batastini, GIA, G-2443). During the singing, porters carry great jugs of water through the assembly and pour the water into the font. (Beautiful, serviceable containers can often be found in restaurant supply stores.)

The blessing of water: After the elect and their party have assembled around the font, the water is blessed. (So that sight lines are maintained between the assembly and the font, make sure that everyone won't huddle together tonight too close to the font.) This prayer of blessing can include repeated sung acclamations, even Alleluias; it is, after all, a eucharistic prayer over the water—although it seems odd that the blessing of the water does not begin with the ordinary prefatory dialogue: "The Lord be with you. . . . Lift up your hearts. . . . Let us give thanks. . . ."

Renunciation of sin and profession of faith: Liturgical scholars remind us that the profession of faith is the heart of baptism, the immediate prelude to the water bath. Notice what the rite suggests (RCIA, 224–225)—and please ignore the options given "if there are a great many to be baptized": The presider "questions all the elect together" for the renunciation of sin. In contrast, the presider "questions the candidates individually" in their profession of faith. The individual is then baptized immediately. So profound is this connection between the profession of faith and the water bath that in some traditions, past and present, the baptismal vows are spoken while the individual stands in the water so that they can be plunged under the water immediately afterward. In ancient tradition, the elect faced west to renounce evil (and sometimes spit in that direction!) and then faced east to profess their faith.

Baptism: If your parish baptizes by immersion, the only advice we can offer is to keep up the good work. If you *want* to baptize by immersion, you will need to use your imagination to construct a pool (preferably in relationship to the parish's font), perhaps from a large-as-possible shallow planter, perhaps from an inexpensive pool liner and bricks, perhaps from a great horse-watering trough. Test it outside first for leakage—and sturdiness—and the ability of the people to step in and out of it. Immersion baptism is being done by an ever-increasing number of parishes—who are now unable to imagine doing baptism any other way.

The assembly's sung acclamation is needed as each person rises from the water. The form of call and response—the cantor singing the line, the assembly repeating—can help free up the assembly to watch the ritual. Most acclamations need to be sung at least twice to work well. Some parishes set their tower bells pealing during the baptisms. Suggestions for acclamations are: "You have put on Christ," Hughes (GIA, G-2283), and "Blessed be God who chose you in Christ," Chepponis (GIA, G-2442), or any rousing Alleluia.

The clothing with a baptismal garment and presentation of a lighted candle: These are not major rites in themselves, but simple necessities following upon the water bath. The explanatory words in the rite are really not necessary. Godparents should know what to do for the newly baptized at this point, assisting them in drying off and robing, handing them their candle. All of this might take place somewhere privately, and then the newly baptized and their sponsors can be ritually led into the assembly transfigured by their robes and lights. (Full albs are fine baptismal robes, and the plain, smallest-size paschal candles—with followers—available from church supply stores make good baptismal candles.)

Celebration of confirmation: The RCIA, 231, says that a song may be sung between baptism and confirmation. Consider a piece of music here only if there is ritual movement from the font to the sanctuary. (The Taizé ostinato "Beati in domo domini" is perfect for this entrance.) One of the most dramatic aspects of certain ancient baptismal liturgies was this movement of the newly baptized, wet and oily, who came by torchlight into the assembly (baptism took place in private because of the required nakedness).

Confirmation itself has three parts: invitation, laying on of hands, anointing with chrism. The suggested words of the invitation (RCIA, 233) are not very clear; at this point in the ritual, what does it mean to be made "more like Christ"? The invitation in the "anointing after baptism" (RCIA, 228) is simple and beautiful, and includes the words, ". . . Priest, Prophet and a King"—images curiously lacking in the celebration of confirmation. It's an ancient custom to crown the confirmed with a wreath of flowers after the fragrant chrism is poured over their heads. Why not pour from a pitcher to anoint them generously rather than anointing with a mere thumbprint of chrism? Surely the container for the chrism must also be a sign of the lavishness of the outpouring of the Spirit. If it is not fragrant enough, add flower oils or essences (which can also be used to daub the church building itself). During the entire rite of confirmation, one of the Taizé ostinatos such as "Veni, Sancte Spiritus" or "Confitemini Domino" can be sung throughout, becoming much quieter during the prayer.

The renewal of baptismal promises. Because the assembly has just heard the promises asked of the elect, the renewal of promises cannot help but appear an unnecessary duplication. It is true that before the baptisms the questions were asked of the elect and of no one else, and that's how it should be. Each person deserves that moment when they individually profess their faith. But should we ask all of those questions all over again? Isn't our very *witness* of baptism the way we renew our own promises? The Italian sacramentary suggests this solution:

> 1. While the elect are making their renunciation of sin and profession of faith and during the baptisms and confirmations, the faithful hold lighted candles. (These are our baptismal candles, which, as was suggested earlier, might be lit for the first time during the litany of the saints and burn throughout the rites of initiation.) Our very witnessing of the vows and initiation of the elect in our midst is our nonverbal reaffirmation of our own baptismal covenant.

> 2. The verbal renewal of baptismal vows by the assembly is omitted.

> 3. The presider, after a brief word of exhortation, offers the prayer: "God, the all-powerful Father of our Lord Jesus Christ . . ." (RCIA, 240).

> 4. Then the faithful are sprinkled with baptismal water, and the neophytes are led to "their place among the faithful."

The music of the sprinkling should connect with the following Sundays. Whatever is used at the Vigil should be used during the great Fifty Days. Music does make connections. Marty Haugen's "Song over the waters" (GIA, G-3096) is a masterpiece of ritual music that can be tailored for the length of the ritual. David Haas's "Water of life" (in *As Water to the Thirsty,* GIA, G-3062) is a playful round that children would enjoy as well as their parents.

Combining rites: When there are also candidates to be received into full communion in the Catholic church, this takes place following the baptisms (and

following the assembly's renewal of baptismal promises, if that takes place). Only then are these candidates called forward by name and asked to make their profession of faith. Then those who have been received join the newly baptized in being confirmed. (Because of this order, they may also join in the procession of the newly baptized from the font to the place of confirmation.)

The order followed is from Appendix I of the RCIA:

> Celebration of Baptism (same as above)
>
> Renewal of Baptismal Promises (see the suggestions on the previous page)
>
> Celebration of Reception
> Invitation
> Profession by the Candidates
> Act of Reception
>
> Celebration of Confirmation (same as above)
>
> Liturgy of the Eucharist

Perhaps the sprinkling of the assembly can be kept *after* confirmation—since it is such a beautiful finale to these rites of initiation.

In this matter of celebrating the baptism of the elect along with reception of the candidates into the church—especially in the early stages of planning the parish's use of the RCIA and its Triduum liturgies—the pastor and others involved should study the relevant sections of the RCIA, such as 206–217, 473–486 and 562–565.

Intercessions: Tonight the Creed is not recited since its function has been fulfilled in the baptismal promises. The general intercessions bring the newly baptized for the first time into one of the central tasks of the church: to constantly lift up the needs of the world and church to God. Surely these intercessions will neither be omitted nor simply spoken. Turn to the many Taizé Kyries, and execute them in proper, rapid Byzantine style.

LITURGY OF THE EUCHARIST

The preparation of the gifts is the perfect time for the choir to show its artistry. Preparing the altar deserves special attention: Up until now, the altar should be completely stripped, left bare since Holy Thursday. The placing of the cloths, with candles and flowers set nearby perhaps, will require some choreography, but it is a wonderfully gracious action that speaks of our moving now from fasting into feasting. The neophytes bring up the bread and wine for the eucharistic banquet in which they will share for the first time. The processional cross can be used to escort them back and forth.

The eucharistic prayer: Preface of Easter I is used with the words, "on this Easter night." In Eucharistic Prayer I there are special inserts. Intercessory inserts for the newly baptized are to be used in Eucharistic Prayers II and III. These inserts will be found in the back of the sacramentary under "Ritual Masses, Christian Initiation, Baptism." Eucharistic Prayer IV would not be used at the Vigil since it has a fixed preface. The many acclamations of the Eucharistic Prayer for Masses with Children II seem a fitting musical style to celebrate the paschal eucharist. Many settings of this prayer make it the musical high point of the liturgy (such as the truly splendid eucharistic prayer *Unless*

You Become of Alexander Peloquin, GIA, G-2311), a very real concern and need during a night as liturgically rich as this one.

The communion rite: During the communion rite the new ritual notes that: "Before saying 'This is the Lamb of God,' the presider may briefly remind the neophytes of the preeminence of the eucharist, which is the climax of their initiation and the center of the whole Christian life." One might wonder what more could, should and needs to be said to the neophytes after their journey to and participation in this night. If any comment is necessary, remember that it is to be brief.

Concluding rites: The dismissal of the Vigil, with its double Alleluia, could be sung to the old Gregorian melody. In the Episcopal church's revised books this dismissal is sung throughout the Fifty Days. Be sure to have Easter water—and even the holy fire—available for people to take home tonight and tomorrow. Pint-sized deli containers make fine water vessels. A cathedral parish purchased fairly large, plastic-enclosed vigil lights for the people to use as their individual candles (costing about twice what ordinary small tapers cost), with the added bonus that the assembly could easily take home the holy fire.

THE BLESSING OF FOOD

(See the discussion of the parish Easter breakfast on page 181 in "The Calendar" of this *Sourcebook*.) Right after the prayer after communion—or at the beginning of the parish Easter breakfast—is a good time to bless the foods in baskets that have been brought to the Vigil. This can take place at tables set up near the entrance: Remember, it was dark when people first entered. If you also distribute Easter eggs and have a parish Easter breakfast this night, include these foods in the blessing.

Easter eggs: A venerable custom this night is the egg-crack game. It costs about $50 to purchase enough eggs for 1000 people. These are hard-boiled, dyed (red is the traditional color) and refrigerated earlier in the week, and then distributed (by the communion ministers?) before the blessing of foods. A grocery store in a Greek neighborhood will stock red food dye. Cake dye or even Rit works well. The choir can sing something during the distribution (see the Russian carol "Easter eggs" in the *Oxford Book of Carols*). The presider and the deacon then lead the way in introducing egg-cracking: One person says "Christ is risen!" to which the other person responds "Christ is truly risen!"—and then they try to break each other's egg with their own. Christ has shattered the tomb like an eggshell!

EASTER SUNDAY

For purposes of preparing the liturgy, the Masses of Easter Sunday morning are the first Masses of the great Fifty Days. (The Triduum and the Fifty Days of Eastertime overlap.) See the notes on this day beginning on page 182 in "The Calendar" of this *Sourcebook*. The concluding liturgy of the Triduum is Easter Sunday Evening Prayer—an important liturgy that deserves our attention. See a complete order of service in *A Triduum Sourcebook* (LTP), as well as a brief discussion of this service in "The Calendar."

A Sample Triduum Schedule

Holy Thursday, April 12

6:00 PM PARISH MEAL
We conclude Lent by coming together in the cafeteria to share a final meal before entering into the paschal fast.

8:00 PM MASS OF THE LORD'S SUPPER
We welcome the Passover
The liturgy of the word
The washing of feet
The collection for the poor

Please bring your household's lenten almsbox tonight.

The liturgy of the eucharist
The watch begins

The church will remain open throughout the night as we begin to keep watch in prayer and fasting in the spirit of Gethsemane. Adoration of the eucharist ends at 11:00 PM.

11:00 PM NIGHT PRAYER

Good Friday, April 13

The church will remain open throughout the day as we continue to keep watch in prayer and fasting.

9:00 AM MORNING PRAYER

12:00 NN MIDDAY PRAYER

3:00 PM THE CELEBRATION OF THE PASSION OF THE LORD
We prostrate ourselves in silence
The liturgy of the word
We make intercession for the world
The veneration of the cross
Communion

5:00 PM PARISH MEAL
All are invited to join together in the school cafeteria to share a simple meal in the spirit of the paschal fast.

8:00 PM NIGHT PRAYER OF THE BURIAL OF THE LORD

The church will remain open throughout the night as we continue to keep watch in fasting and prayer.

Holy Saturday, April 14

The church will remain open throughout the day as we continue to keep watch in fasting and prayer.

9:00 AM MORNING PRAYER

12:00 NN MIDDAY PRAYER

3:00 PM THE RITES OF PREPARATION OF THE ELECT
We gather as a parish with the elect for a final time before their baptism, confirmation and eucharist tonight.

5:00 PM PARISH MEAL
All are invited to gather in the school cafeteria to share a simple meal in the spirit of the paschal fast.

6:00 PM EVENING PRAYER

Nightwatch of the Resurrection, April 14–15

10:00 PM THE EASTER VIGIL
We keep watch in darkness
The Easter bonfire
We give thanks for light
The liturgy of the word
We give thanks for water
The liturgy of baptism and confirmation
The liturgy of the eucharist
The Easter blessing of food

Please bring a glass vigil light or other container to bring home the holy fire. Easter water in containers will be provided. Also please remember to bring your Easter foods for the blessing tonight.

12:00 MM PARISH MEAL
The Easter Vigil eucharist breaks our fast. The feast begins. All are invited to come together in the

school cafeteria to share in the Easter breakfast. Bring treats! Our guests of honor this night are the newly baptized.

Easter Sunday, April 15

6:00 AM MORNING PRAYER

8:00 AM EASTER MASS

10:00 AM EASTER MASS

12:00 NN EASTER MASS

A reminder: The blessing of Easter foods and baskets will take place after every Mass. The church will remain open throughout the day. You are invited to visit with family and guests.

6:00 PM EASTER EVENING PRAYER AND CAROLING

Sample Bulletin Insert for before the Triduum

You might adapt this insert regarding the paschal fast along with the parish worship schedule for the Triduum as well as any special reminders (for example, to bring lenten alms to Mass Holy Thursday evening and Easter foods for the blessing after the Vigil). Of course, a bulletin insert is only meant to bolster other, more personal forms of catechesis that encourage the parish to a full, rich celebration of the Paschal Triduum.

Regulations for the Paschal Fast of Good Friday and Holy Saturday

"The Easter fast is sacred on the first two days of the Triduum [Good Friday and Holy Saturday], in which according to ancient tradition the church fasts 'because her Spouse has been taken away.' Good Friday is a day of fasting and abstinence. It is also recommended that Holy Saturday be observed with fasting so that the church with a welcoming heart is ready to celebrate the joys of the Sunday of Resurrection." (From the Vatican Letter *Concerning the Preparation and Celebration of the Easter Feasts,* 1988)

On Good Friday all Catholics age 14 and older are to abstain from meat, and those who are age 18 but not yet 59 are to fast (taking no more than one full meal; two smaller meals are permitted to maintain strength but no solid foods between meals). The church strongly encourages that this fast and abstinence *be kept also on Holy Saturday* until the Easter Vigil. Catechumens are likewise urged to fast in preparation for their baptism.

This is not the penitential fast of Lent that we keep on Good Friday and Holy Saturday. (Lent ends on Holy Thursday afternoon.) This fast is called the "Easter fast" or "Paschal fast." It is to be a fast of anticipation as we look forward to the Easter feast and most especially to the baptisms at the Easter Vigil. The fasting of Friday and Saturday, by strong and ancient tradition, includes also a "fasting" from normal work and from entertainment. Catholic Christians must be a witness to the world in this. We must put aside our business-as-usual for these holiest of all our holy days—and that means not shopping, not opening our places of work, keeping the television and other electronic entertainment turned off.

These most unusual of days call for a most unusual way of life. Prayer and fasting, the reading of scripture, attention to the needs of others, and especially attendance at *all* the services in church: These should fill our lives and prepare us for the great Vigil of Easter, the most holy, most splendid, most astonishing night of the year.

EASTERTIME

OFFICIAL DESCRIPTION

The 50 days from Easter Sunday to Pentecost are celebrated in joyful exultation as one feast day, or better as one "Great Sunday" (Athanasius). These above all others are the days for the singing of the Alleluia. The Sundays of this season rank as the paschal Sundays, and after Easter Sunday itself, are called the Second, Third, Fourth, Fifth, Sixth and Seventh Sundays of Easter. The period of 50 sacred days ends on Pentecost. The first eight days of the Easter season make up the octave of Easter and are celebrated as solemnities of the Lord. On the fortieth day after Easter the Ascension is celebrated. . . . The weekdays after the Ascension until the Saturday before Pentecost are a preparation for the coming of the Holy Spirit. (*General Norms for the Liturgical Year and Calendar*, 22–26).

RESOURCES

Lent, Triduum and Eastertime must be discussed and prepared as a whole. For resource material on historical background and liturgical help, see the bibliography beginning on page 46.

A SENSE OF THE SEASON

Fifty days are a seventh of the year, and so we keep our 50-day Eastertime as a long Lord's Day, the "Great Sunday." Fifty days are a week of weeks plus a day, a symbol of eternity. And so we keep Eastertime "playing heaven," living as if God's reign had already come. Christians—both the newly baptized and the long baptized—are to live in the wedding feast of heaven and earth, like a honeymoon, no fasting, no mourning, endlessly singing our Alleluias.

In more and more parishes Eastertime is not just remembering something that happened long ago. It is Christ dead, buried and risen in our midst. It is the Spirit breathing in us today. For Easter is made present in the neophytes, the newly baptized among us. Easter is made present in the newly confirmed and those who are brought to the table to make their first eucharist. And it is baptism and anointing and eucharist that tell us what to do with these Fifty Days. Initiation has its consequences. There is a great mystery to learn and a great mission to begin. Eastertime is a season for learning the language of the Spirit, for climbing Mount Sinai that the Law might be etched in our hearts, for accepting anew the challenging apostolic commission of the Risen Lord to "go, therefore, and make disciples of all nations. . . ."

We celebrate Eastertime with all the signs of the Risen One. We open our doors in springtime hospitality and bring healing peace to all whose hearts are wintry. We renew our efforts to restore this good earth to the freshness of creation. The risen Spirit of Jesus bids us to spill out into the streets, like the apostles on Pentecost. The good shepherd calls us into verdant pasture. The wonderful gardener brings us home to paradise.

PREPARING THE PARISH

Even if many Christians are unaware of these Fifty Days, no season gets more liturgical preparation than Eastertime. Isn't that a function of Lent? And the Triduum is Eastertime's pep rally: A parish that has kept the Triduum well is going to be filled with parishioners unable to constrain the possibilities opened up by *Pascha*. If you've experienced a good Triduum, you know this enthusiasm. For many it feels something like, "Why can't we be like this all year round?"

In a real sense, the mystagogy, the learning of mystery that must now be the endeavor of the neophytes, is a channeling of the energies unleashed by baptism. Many experienced RCIA ministers can tell horror stories about what happens when the newly baptized are not cared for, what happens when Eastertime is disorganized. In contrast, those parishes that treat initiation as a lifelong liturgy, renewed each time we gather around the holy table, will understand what Eastertime is. As Sunday is to the week, so these Fifty Days are to the year.

Eastertime is the season to channel energy and learn mystery. And the process is deceptively simple, beginning perhaps with questions prompted by the paschal liturgy itself. After all, doesn't the great babble of Easter Eve release a great flood of whys and hows? Such questioning may be groundwork for the paschal seasons in years to come, groundwork for the catechumenal adventure of others who are now but inquirers in the faith.

This time of year comes with its own problems. Parishes begin to scatter; it's harder and harder as the season progresses to locate ministers. The liturgical ministers can wind up beating their heads against the wall, preparing Eastertime liturgical celebrations in parishes that put the festival away on Easter Monday. Pentecost is invariably a source of great stress for the liturgically minded. The day is not kept in homes, and so often its observance gets eclipsed by something else, like Memorial Day weekend, weddings, graduations or—like last year—Mothers Day. Perhaps the popular observance of Pentecost (at home and not just in church) is a litmus test in a parish's liturgical life, because it comes about only after that remarkable combination of enthusiastic catechesis and year-by-year consistency. The same can be said for all of Eastertime.

Eastertime is springtime. Year by year, the households of the parish should find a one-day-only Easter to be insufficient. We should gently lead people into recognizing that keeping Eastertime is something we have been doing every spring: Washing windows, breathing in the fragrance of newly mown grass, standing under the shower of petals from an apple tree, preparing confirmations and first communions, visiting our mothers on the second Sunday in May, weaving a crown of daisies for mother Mary, planting window boxes with geraniums, waiting for newly planted crops to emerge, checking the horizon for rain, organizing neighborhood cleanups, planting a tree on Arbor Day, mourning the victims of war, mourning the victims of genocide, attending graduations and spring weddings and even family barbecues and baseball games.

All these are signs of the season, and those who have been initiated into the language of the Spirit will surely recognize, year by year, the voice of the turtledove, the voice of the beloved calling "arise."

WORDS

Alleluia, Christ is truly risen, witnesses, things above, the day the Lord has made, I shall not die, early in the morning, communal life, new birth, rejoice with inexpressible joy, like newborn children thirst for milk, peace be with you, we have seen the Lord, your sojourn in a strange land, stay with us, the breaking of bread, the Lord is my shepherd, by his wounds you were healed, I am the sheepgate, imposed hands on them, a living stone, an edifice of spirit, I am the way, life in the realm of the spirit, another Paraclete, a cloud, clap your hands, a blare of trumpets, the fullness of him who fills the universe, I am with you always, I will not leave you orphans, confused the speech of all the world, came down upon Mount Sinai in fire, bone joining bone, from the four winds come, all creation groans, a strong driving wind, tongues as of fire, renew the face of the earth, baptized into one body, coolness in the heat, as the Father has sent me so I send you, alleluia.

VESTURE

White, silver and gold, springtime pastels, tapestry prints: Use the finest the parish has to offer! Remember, "on more solemn occasions more precious vestments may be used, even if not the color of the day" (*General Instruction*, 309). Eastertime is springtime: Many parishes commission glorious white Eastertime vesture with springtime colors as accents. This is a bit unorthodox, isn't it? We usually think of vesture trimmed with rich, deep colors and patterns; but why shouldn't vesture worn in April and May reflect the colors of the season?

Eastertime is Fifty Days: There should not be one set of vesture for Easter Sunday and then other white fare for the rest of the season. This is nonverbal teaching: Let the clothing itself say that these days are one unit of time and celebration. Of course, Pentecost is the exception. Our white is transformed into fiery, bloody, summer-hot red. This red vesture might be unique to the day, not like the more somber vesture of the Passion. Ideally, whatever fabrics and trims were chosen for vesture, altar cloths, book covers, etc., for the previous Sundays of Eastertime can be reflected in the Pentecost vesture. Only the colors would change, thereby establishing a strong connection.

The paschal white vesture might also be the parish's funeral set, worn also on Assumption, All Saints, and most rites of initiation outside Lent.

THE MASS

Introductory rites: Eastertime needs a festive entrance procession with antiphons or hymns with lots of Alleluias. During this, clouds of Easter-smelling incense—such as the many flower fragrances available from certain Orthodox monasteries—can honor the altar, candle, font, cross and assembly. This says without words what we are focusing on during these days. Then the long form of the greeting, as a contrast to Lent's simplicity, perhaps a sung Kyrie with paschal invocations (Form C5 in the sacramentary is appropriate), then Easter's Gloria and the collect.

A better variation on this would be the sign of the cross and greeting, then a thanksgiving over the Easter water and a resumption of the opening song or the

Gloria while the presider (and assistants, if necessary) noisily fill the buckets and take branches to sprinkle everyone generously with water. The entrance then concludes with the collect.

Whatever decisions are made, make sure the entrance rite is planned as a whole. It needs to be understood by the presiders, deacons, musicians and other ministers long before the opening moments of the Mass. A meeting, or a letter sent to all ministers beforehand, will guard against the introductory rites becoming a casualty of last-minute details—but an actual rehearsal is best. The order of the rite should be kept through Pentecost. After several years of using a strong entrance rite that is only for Eastertime, it will belong to everyone.

Liturgy of the word: This season calls once again for readers who will proclaim the word articulately and with faith. Take time now also to consider what the gospel procession looks like. Some parishes use the old Sanctus bells to call the assembly to stand, and during Eastertime these are rung through much of the acclamation. The Eastertime gospels just about demand a reprise of the Alleluia afterward. (Let the reader conclude as usual, "This is the gospel of the Lord," with the assembly's response; then the organ or other instruments return the Alleluia.) Do not deprive your community of the Easter and Pentecost sequences—marvelous melodies that have several incarnations as chant or as metrical carols. (For example, the Easter sequence *Victimae paschalis* is the progenitor of the carol melody "Christ ist erstanden" and the chorale "Christ Jesus lay in death's strong bonds.") There are many other songs that can be sung in celebration of the words of the scriptures. In fact, many popular hymns and carols have their origin as sequence hymns. Some parishes sing a "hymn for the day"—sort of a sermon in song—after the gospel.

The seasonal psalms for Eastertime are Psalm 118, "This is the day the Lord has made," and Psalm 66, "Let all the earth cry out." Psalm 47, "God mounts his throne," and Psalm 104, "Lord, send out your Spirit," are the seasonal psalms from Ascension to Pentecost. The choices in excellent psalm settings are enormous—that's why it's so important to choose a few and stick with them year after year instead of experimenting with different settings, lovely as they all might be.

In this *Sourcebook* we harp on this principle of year-after-year consistency. Musicians sometimes forget how long it takes some people to get a song into their psyches, to make it their prayer, to come to a point where they remember with delight a particular melody as part of a season or feast. (The not-very-well-known season of Eastertime especially needs its characteristic sounds.) In contrast, so often in the exhilaration that follows a workshop or music reading session, music ministers come home and unnecessarily revamp the parish repertory. There's got to be a balance between new and old, but the key word is "repertory." Something sung once or just a few times never has a chance to become part of the parish repertory.

Liturgy of the eucharist: Along with the unity of the season achieved by vesture, ritual patterns and music, the choice of texts is crucial as well. The Easter prefaces are a rich treasury of scriptural reflection and provide a solid "paschal orientation." Look over the titles and texts. Choose one or two to use until Ascension Day. A good text will continue—or just begin—to reach us with

this repetition. It is important to establish a regular annual pattern of using the various choices of eucharistic prayers. Perhaps Eucharistic Prayer III could be used, even on weekdays, throughout Eastertime. This would be especially appropriate if one of the reconciliation prayers was heard throughout Lent.

Concluding rite: The sacramentary's "Solemn Blessings" section has a text (#6) for the Vigil and Easter Sunday, and another (#7) to use throughout the Sundays of Eastertime. For Pentecost, the Holy Spirit text (#9) should begin "This day . . ."

MUSIC

No day in the time of the great Fifty Days of the paschal feast should be without a profusion of Alleluias—in the hymns, in the acclamations, in the choral pieces, in the church bulletin, everywhere. Everything should resound with the explosion of praise that the Triduum ignited. One good way to excite that experience is to start off the Sunday liturgy with Fintan O'Caroll's and Christopher Walker's "Celtic Alleluia" (St. Thomas More Centre/OCP). With such a contagious melody and such powerful paraphrases of the Exsultet text, an assembly would have to be cast in stone not to respond. The use of such an acclamation as the processional piece creates a much more flexible experience of the gathering rite that would flow easily into the sprinkling with blessed water.

Mary Francis Reza and Frank Brownstead have produced an exciting setting of Kiko Arguello's "Resucito" (OCP, #8879) with trumpet parts that add to the fiesta. Marty Haugen's "Easter Alleluia" (in *Gather*, GIA) is set in a 6/8 rhythm that comes probably as close to the original intent of the ancient poet and musician whose rhythmical modes enlivened medieval music. "Song of the Risen One" (in *Gather*, GIA) by David Haas captures the same excitement. "Easter Vigil" (World Library Publications, #8505) with typically great words by Omer Westendorf and music by Eugene Englert provides another refrain and verse processional.

Hymnody: That is not to say there is no value in the metrical hymn serving as the processional song. "Jesus Christ is risen today" with the tune "Lyra Davidica" connotes Easter celebrations in the hearts of Christians of all faiths. "The strife is o'er" with the tune "Victory" wields similar power. There are many more hymns for the Easter celebration available today than the church has seen in one time. We need only compare the five English hymns and three in Latin in the 1920 *St. Gregory Hymnal* with the 27 entries in the Easter section of GIA's *Worship* to see a massive shift in the awareness of the importance of Eastertime.

As well as the traditional and contemporary storehouse of music, there is a nearly untapped source in African-American spiritual hymns. A relatively new item is James Moore's "I will be with you" (GIA, G-2803). It speaks strongly of the Ascension and could be used with the mystagogical gatherings of the neophytes. Music can exert a welcoming experience on the neophytes. Used also during Lent, "Precious Lord, take my hand," and "I want to walk as a child of the light" can quickly become their favorites. Familiar items such as Marty Haugen's "Canticle of the sun" (GIA, G-2788), Michael Joncas's "On eagle's wings" and Paul Inwood's "Center of my life" (OCP, #7136) are representative of a body of music that the parish might already know and could pass on to the new members.

The embracing power of shared song crystallizes hospitality—an important value within this time of mystagogy. The welcoming that familiar music affords can last longer than a name tag and an occasional cup of coffee.

Choirs, vocal ensembles and instrumental groups should capitalize on these days to pull out their best pieces to celebrate the season of new life. From gospel music to Handel's "Hallelujah chorus," the parish musicians should nourish their assembly with the richest and finest fare. Musical icons from the parish treasury enrich the assembly. Renaissance choral pieces expertly edited by Eugene Lindusky make up volume 4 of the *Classical Choral Series* (OCP, #8618) and provide a fulfilling collection for the SATB choir whose abilities are modest. Marty Haugen's *Shepherd Me, O God* collection (GIA, G-3107) is geared more to the "contemporary group"—not that an SATB choir that sings Renaissance music is not contemporary. James Marchionda's "Mass of the Children of God" (World Library Publications, #7663) contains two attractive gospel acclamations that should not be restricted to children's celebrations.

Pentecost boasts the chant sequence, *Veni, sancte Spiritus,* whose strong meter adapts well to the rhythmical mode of long, short; long, short, etc. Richard Proulx's relatively new setting of the Pentecost psalm, "Lord, send out your spirit" (GIA, G-3064), requires a French horn and cello in addition to the keyboard and voices. The cantor needs to be aggressive to make the verses work in this very elegant responsorial-style psalm. (Other musical suggestions for this longest liturgical season are located in "The Calendar" of this *Sourcebook*.)

THE WORSHIP ENVIRONMENT

First off, when do you decorate for Easter? Possibly this could be a parish event immediately after the Easter Vigil, after the paschal sabbath. Why not? Staying up all night is the thing to do on Easter Eve. Whether before or after the Easter Vigil liturgy, make the decorating a part of the way the parish keeps watch, with an invitation for everyone to turn out to help. (Cleaning and as much preparation as possible should be done well before the Triduum begins on Holy Thursday evening.)

The baptismal font: Parishes with handsome fonts will keep them overflowing, surrounded by flowers and lights, perhaps a ribboned maypole set nearby or a flower-studded victory wreath hung overhead. Parishes that have fonts that are hidden away sometimes display a large bowl of water somewhere up front. That may seem like a reasonable thing to do, but it would be far more sensible to keep attention fixed on the font no matter where it is located, rather than mess up the altar-ambo-chair area with what often looks like a punch bowl on a table. During the sprinkling rite maintain some association with the font, even if that means drawing a bucketful of Easter water from it and then carrying this water into the assembly for the prayer of thanksgiving.

The Easter candle should be purchased before Christmas. Have you ever had your candle arrive broken? If you've had success in making your own candle, more power to you. Thanks to demand, commercial candlemakers are creating suitably enormous candles. While there is something grand about a huge, undecorated paschal candle, the traditional symbols are important. They can be fashioned from leaf-thin sheets of wax (available from Hearthsong: A Catalog for Families, PO Box B, Sebastopol CA 95473; 800/325-2502). The wax nails included with most store-bought paschal candles are just a colorful way to attach the grains of incense—which are the real symbol. Chunks of frankincense can be melted a bit and stuck in place; they look like jewels.

Throughout Eastertime keep the candle surrounded with spring flowers, something made easier by this trick: Find an angel food cake pan with a center hole wide enough to accommodate the candle. Fill the pan with cut blocks of "oasis" (the green, styrofoam-like substance that absorbs water) and add blossoms and foliage that will bend over the edges of the pan, such as asparagus fern.

Where to put the candle? When baptistries were in separate rooms, the candle got taken out of the baptistry and put where everyone could see it during Eastertime; specifically, it was placed so that the gospel could be read by its light. If the font is in plain view, however, it makes sense to keep the candle near it. Another idea is to place the candle smack dab in the center of the assembly—the Risen One in our midst. Wherever it is put, it should be kept lit for every possible gathering. Also, it should be shining brightly even before people gather: The idea is that once it is lit on Easter Eve, it is never extinguished, at least publicly. That is why we need a large candle. Other candles are always lit from it, a gracious gesture at the beginning of any liturgy during this season.

The Easter cross: Good Friday is the day we plant the holy cross in our midst. That day is within the Triduum, our Passover. Isn't the Passover our invitation to come into the presence of the burning bush, the tree of life, the vine that gives its life to the branches? The scripture readings of Lent prepare us to recognize the bare wood of the cross as a living tree, and Good Friday is the moment we welcome this tree, now kept alive in our midst throughout Eastertime, surrounded by flowers and lights. (That's why it does not seem appropriate to use the Good Friday cross as a sanctuary decoration during Lent—the cross is much more than decoration.) If you have the Good Friday cross in a place of honor during Eastertime, make sure it isn't redundant to a processional cross or to some other fixed crucifix. Why can't the Good Friday cross *be* the processional cross in Eastertime?

Fabric arts: Great swaths of color, like a shroud, like a rainbow, like the wind, can draw the eye upward. This year we read extensively from the First Letter of Peter, rich with baptismal imagery such as "new birth," "unblemished lamb," "returning sheep to the shepherd," "living stones," "life in the spirit." However, no matter how lovely a phrase is, it is cheapened to be used billboard-style on a banner. If you decorate the worship space with banners that employ Eastertime images, do not duplicate the imagery already present in the worship environment, such as water, candle, font, cup, book. Eastertime suggests lightweight fabrics, movement, transparency, things that look well in sunlight. Any of this large-scale decoration should direct attention to—and not draw attention from—the altar, ambo, chair, font, paschal candle and cross. Keep most of it out of the vicinity of the altar; use decoration to grace the assembly's space.

Nor should decoration be limited to the indoors. The whole world should know of our joy with springtime wreaths on the church doors, banners and

bunting merrily waving in the breezes, continual effort to keep Eastertime in the spirit of Arbor Day, with renewed attention to the church's landscaping and the neighborhood's cleanliness. A versatile decoration for outside are as-big-as-possible nylon windsocks, set to swivel freely on poles. The poles can be put up on parish property, placed in wide-enough steel piping pounded into the earth. Perhaps someone can fashion these maypole-like windsocks out of sail or parachute fabrics in a rainbow of colors: That way they can be used for various feasts and seasons, for example, spring colors for now, summer colors for the great June and August feasts, autumn colors for November.

Mary's shrine: A lovely way to decorate the Marian shrine during Eastertime is with a calligraphied parchment of the chant *Regina caeli* (most parishes have members who are gifted with this craft). One parish commissioned an icon of the resurrection painted on an ostrich egg, which was then suspended within the shrine. This is also a good place for any Eastertime icon, such as the harrowing of hell or Jesus' appearance to the disciples. Several old customs associate Holy Mary with Easter eggs: Legend has it that she brought red-dyed eggs to the disciples to spread the good news of resurrection. The bloody red shell, a symbol of mortal life, breaks open into the white and gold of immortality.

Other beautiful Easter symbols that seem suited to placement within a shrine, or at least somewhere they can be touched, smelled or otherwise enjoyed (remember this when placing flowers in the church), are honeycomb, sprouting grain, pussywillows and peacock feathers. Some parishes construct an Easter shrine akin to the Christmas crèche, with symbols of the passion such as dice, lance and vinegar, as well as the shroud and a crock of myrrh. This shrine can become a beloved tradition, especially since these items just about beg to be explained to children. Icons of the resurrection, ascension and descent of the Holy Spirit can be included. However, just like a Christmas crèche, any of these things are unsuited to placement within the line of sight of the altar, ambo and chair—placement in a shrine, the vestibule or the gathering area is better.

OTHER RITUAL PRAYER

Marian devotions: May brings Eastertime and devotion to Mary together, images wondrously woven in the poem by Gerard Manley Hopkins, "May is Mary's month." See Ann Johnson's beautiful prayer texts of the Magnificat in her book, *Miriam of Nazareth*. Some of her poems could be used as part of May devotions. Several texts published by the U.S. Catholic Conference for the 1988 Marian Year remain available; they contain many excellent texts from the tradition. A weekday evening May crowning might be made the conclusion of Night Prayer, complete with the song "Regina caeli/Be joyful, Mary."

This year, the feast of the Visitation (May 31) falls within Eastertime and also within the novena of watchfulness for the coming of the Spirit, a perfect occasion to gather in honor of Mary, mother of the church (see the prayer texts in the sacramentary in the Appendix, "Additional Presidential Prayers"). Include the reading of Acts 1:12–14, about Mary and the other disciples' nine-day vigil in the upper room, the first reading on the Seventh Sunday of Easter this year.

The liturgy of the hours: Eastertime is a season to invigorate Morning and Evening Prayer. Does Morning Prayer include a baptismal memorial, with a thanksgiving over Easter water and a signing with this water? Does Evening Prayer include a *lucernarium,* the lighting of candles from the already—and seemingly continuously—burning paschal candle, perhaps repeating the Vigil's "Light of Christ/Thanks be to God"?

What about a Saturday night resurrection vigil? This should be part of the parish's liturgical life. If we look back at the Easter Vigil and ask ourselves why we weren't bursting at the seams with attendance, perhaps one answer lies in the year-long practice of the parish regarding vigils, especially the vigil of the resurrection that should be part of our keeping of every Lord's Day. In other words, the "Great Sunday" of the year can be even greater if all the Sundays of the year are kept well.

Rogation Days customarily fall during Eastertime, both on St. Mark's Day (April 25) and on the three days that precede Ascension Day (see April 25 and May 15 in "The Calendar" of this *Sourcebook*). Spring's seedtime and birthing time are pretty frightening. It's a season of hail, vicious storms and tornados. And especially before the trees leaf out, it's a season of frequent fires and duststorms—all threats to the newborn herds and newly planted crops, to pollinating orchards and even to human life and limb. Why not keep an Eastertime Rogation Day in solidarity with both the threat and the promise of this season of the year? For beautiful Mass formularies for a Rogation Day, look up in the lectionary the Masses for Various Occasions: For Various Public Needs, #846–850, "Blessing of Human Labor" (#25 in the sacramentary), or #851–855, "For Productive Land" (#26 in the sacramentary). The *Book of Blessings* contains orders of blessings for fields and flocks, and also for the seedtime.

Sample Prayer Texts for Eastertime

Introductory Rites

GREETING

For the entire season:
The God of life, who broke the bonds of death and raised Jesus from the tomb, be with you all.

Throughout Eastertime you may want to add to the greeting, with appropriate catechesis, the greeting and response:

Christ is risen, alleluia!
Christ is truly risen, alleluia!

INTRODUCTION

If an introduction seems superfluous, the introduction can be combined with the invitation.

Easter Sunday:
In the holy night just passed, the Christian community has celebrated its passover in Christ from death to risen life. From the font, from the womb of Mother Church, children have been born again of water and the Spirit. Now we gather in the light of Easter morning: a new creation in the Risen Christ.

Second Sunday of Easter:
On this eighth day of the Easter feast, the "octave" day, we continue the celebration of the "today" of Christ's resurrection. For the newly baptized and for all those who have renewed their baptismal promises, the presence of the Risen Christ in our midst must be a powerful—and daily—reality.

Third, Fourth and Fifth Sundays of Easter:
This is the day the Lord has made! Throughout the Great Fifty Days of Easter, the Good Shepherd gathers his flock together, opens our minds to understand the scriptures, and reveals himself in the breaking of the bread.

Sixth Sunday of Easter:
On this Sixth Sunday of Easter, the Risen Christ begins to instruct the disciples about the Paraclete Spirit whom he will pour forth, in every generation, upon those who show their love by keeping the commandments.

Ascension:
The Solemnity of the Lord's Ascension is a celebration of Christ's glorious return to the Father. The Lord has not abandoned us but, rather, goes before us to prepare a place for us and to intercede for us at the Father's right hand.

Seventh Sunday of Easter:
On this Sunday between the Ascension and Pentecost, in the midst of the novena—the nine days—of prayer, the Christian community assembles in anticipation of a new outpouring of the Holy Spirit, who forever breathes in our midst and forever renews the face of the earth.

Pentecost:
The great Fifty Days of Easter culminate in this Solemnity (Vigil) of Pentecost. This harvest festival becomes a proclamation of God's superabundant generosity, a vindication of Lord Jesus' sacrificial suffering, a celebration of the community's faith made fruitful by the gift of the Holy Spirit.

RITE OF SPRINKLING

Dear brothers and sisters: Let us implore the blessing of God that this rite of sprinkling may revive in us the grace of baptism through which we have been immersed in the redeeming death of the Lord, that we might rise with Christ to new life.

O God Most High, from the Lamb sacrificed for us upon the cross you have made spring up for us fountains of living water:

CONTINUED

R. Cleanse and bless your people.

Or:

R. Glory to you, O Lord.

O Christ, you have renewed the youthfulness of the church with the cleansing water and with the word of life: *(R.)*

O Spirit, you have brought us up from the waters of baptism as the firstfruits of a new humanity: *(R.)*

Almighty God, who in the sacred signs of our faith renews the wonders of creation and redemption, bless + this water and grant that all who have been born again in baptism may be heralds and witnesses of the paschal mystery, which is forever renewed in your church. We ask this through Christ our Lord. Amen.

Introduction to the Readings

Easter Sunday:
On this Sunday of Sundays, the day which the Lord has made, the church sets before us the witness of Peter and the challenge of Paul. Accepting their testimony and building on their faith, we too eat and drink with the Risen Lord, but this requires us to become a new creation and to refocus our sight upon the dominion of God.

Second Sunday of Easter:
Throughout Easter's Fifty Days we trace in the Acts of the Apostles the history of the infant Christian community. This year we also read from the First Letter of Peter, which challenges those born again in baptism to persevere in faith and bear witness with courage. With Thomas we proclaim: My Lord and my God!

Third Sunday of Easter:
As for the disciples at Emmaus, so also for us: Jesus explains the scriptures and reveals himself in the breaking of bread. In the Acts of the Apostles we hear Peter's proclamation of Jesus as Messiah. Then from the First Letter of Peter the reminder that we, the baptized, are of inestimable worth, for we have been ransomed by the precious blood of Christ, the Lamb of God.

Fourth Sunday of Easter:
In the Acts of the Apostles we see the pattern of discipleship: witness, conversion, baptism, the Spirit's gift and life in community. Peter's First Letter sets Christ before us as our model, a model of the suffering that holiness brings, a model of pain borne fearlessly under the watchful eye of our Good Shepherd.

Fifth Sunday of Easter:
The influx of gentile converts brings unforeseen problems, but the Spirit present in the guidance of the Twelve finds an unforeseen solution in the new ministry of deacon. Peter reminds us that we are all living stones being built into a temple established on Christ, our way, our truth, our life.

Sixth Sunday of Easter:
As we approach the day of the Ascension, the reading from Acts emphasizes the gift of the Spirit by which the Lord confirms his abiding presence. It is in the power of the Spirit, says Peter, that we must bear respectful but committed witness to Christ.

Ascension:
In the first lines of the Acts of the Apostles, the ascension of the Lord is described as a moment of gifts: a blessing, a promise, a challenge. Under his domain and adorned with the Spirit's power, we are to baptize all nations into the new life of discipleship.

Seventh Sunday of Easter:
The Acts of the Apostles tells of the first novena of prayer. Led by Peter and gathered around Mary, the infant church awaits the Spirit. A share in Christ's sufferings is inevitable, the First Letter of Peter reminds us, but Christ prays for us at the Father's right hand and promises us glory.

Pentecost:
The ancient feast of Pentecost—the 50th day—is a celebration of the gift of

CONTINUED

the Law and the bounty of the grain harvest. According to the Acts of the Apostles, the infant church receives the gift of the Spirit on the 50th day with a mission to reap the harvest of the nations. One body with many gifts, says Paul, the community of the baptized in every generation continues to proclaim Jesus as Lord.

General Intercessions

INVITATION TO PRAYER

On Easter Sunday and the octave:
On this most holy day in which the power of the Spirit makes us a new creation in the image of the Risen Lord, let us pray with one mind and heart that the joy of Easter may be shared by all the world.

During Eastertime:
By the resurrection of the Son, God has given us a new birth unto a living hope. Even those who do not know God depend upon God's mercy and loving kindness. Let the longing of the whole world find voice now in the prayers we offer together.

Or:
In Christ Jesus, crucified, buried and risen, we recognize the saving will of God and come to believe in God's overwhelming love. In this paschal faith, together let us pray.

On Ascension:
The Lord Jesus, conqueror of death, sits at God's right hand and intercedes for all as our advocate and mediator. With this confidence, we implore God's mercy.

After Ascension:
Imitating that first community of the apostles, gathered together with Mary in the cenacle, let us live in expectation of the full fruit of Easter: the gift of the Holy Spirit to the church and to the world. With one mind and heart, let us offer our prayers to God.

Pentecost:
The Spirit of the Lord, long awaited and prayed for, descends today upon the church to bring to completion, even in our own time, the great wonders of Pentecost. Let us open ourselves to the working of that Spirit, announcing and witnessing to all the liberating power of Easter's resurrection.

INTERCESSION FOR THE CHURCH

During Eastertime:
For the church of God: that it may grow in awareness of its identity as a paschal community, born of Christ's humiliation on the cross and Christ's glorification in resurrection: let us pray to the Lord.

Or:
That the Christian community may preserve the paschal faith of our forebears and bear witness to the transforming power of the Spirit, especially in works of justice and peace: let us pray to the Lord.

Or:
That the church of Christ may enjoy stability and true peace throughout the world, growing in love and reverence for God the Father, filled with the consolation of the Holy Spirit: let us pray to the Lord.

Ascension and Seventh Week:
For the holy church of God, on pilgrimage through time: that it may experience that missionary impulse that inspired the first Christians to carry the gospel even to the ends of the earth: let us pray to the Lord.

Pentecost:
For the church, dispersed throughout the world, that it may have a living awareness of its call to be the holy people of God, whose law is love, whose spirit is the freedom of God's children, let us pray to the Lord.

CONTINUED

INTERCESSION FOR THE NEOPHYTES

For all the newly baptized: that washed in the blood and water springing forth from the side of Christ, they may persevere in their new birth and the Spirit's gift: let us pray to the Lord.

Or:

For those who have been born again in baptism: that they may recognize God's gift and their responsibility to carry the light of faith to the non-believers of our own time: let us pray to the Lord.

INTERCESSION FOR THE WORLD

For all the human family: that the whole world may hear the good news that, in Christ, true peace has been established between God and humanity, within the human heart and among all who live upon this good earth: let us pray to the Lord.

From Ascension to Pentecost:
For every person on earth who loves truth, who suffers for justice or who seeks for liberation and peace: that the Holy Spirit may renew the wonders of Pentecost and rekindle hope in every heart: let us pray to the Lord.

INTERCESSION FOR THOSE IN NEED

For all who are afflicted with any kind of suffering: that they may not let themselves be conquered by their burdens, but through the power of faith and the experience of solidarity with their brothers and sisters, know that the Lord is near to them and concerned for them: let us pray to the Lord.

Or:

For those who are persecuted for whatever reason: that the Risen Lord will strengthen them through their trials and let them reap the harvest that will blossom from what they have endured: let us pray to the Lord.

INTERCESSION FOR THE ASSEMBLY

For all our parish family: that every household may celebrate the true meaning of Easter, sharing with others the Lord's many gifts and offering Christian hospitality to the little and the lowly, the poor and the suffering: let us pray to the Lord.

Or:

For our community: that, growing together with the newly baptized as a family united in the Lord, we may listen attentively to the word of God, persevere in prayer, and bear witness to the gospel through loving service: let us pray to the Lord.

Or:

For this holy assembly: that the Spirit of the Risen Christ may help us to understand the prophetic signs of our times and work to make the gospel present to the world in which we live: let us pray to the Lord.

Ascension to Pentecost:
For all of us here present: that the Holy Spirit, sent for the forgiveness of sin, may help us to understand that we are always in need of pardon and conversion, and so to help us in turn to forgive our brothers and sisters: let us pray to the Lord.

Or:

For all of us who work daily in the many and varied dimensions of human activity: that we may have a living awareness of having been sealed with the gift and message of the Spirit for the building up of a new world: let us pray to the Lord.

CONCLUDING PRAYER

These concluding prayers for the intercessions were selected from among opening prayers for Mass (based on the readings from Cycle A) of the Italian sacramentary, Messale Romano, © 1983 by the Libreria Editrice Vaticana (translated by Peter

CONTINUED

Scagnelli), as well as from ICEL *original opening prayers based on the scripture readings of the day,* © *1983, 1986, 1987, 1988, International Committee on English in the Liturgy, Inc. (ICEL). All rights reserved.*

Easter Sunday:

You may want to use one of the sacramentary's opening prayers for today that wasn't used for the opening prayer, or an opening prayer from one of the days of the octave. Easter Tuesday's prayer is appropriate ("sons" can be "children").

Second Sunday of Easter:
Lord our God,
in your great mercy
you have given us a new birth
    unto a living hope
through the resurrection of your Son.

Increase within us that paschal faith
founded upon the witness
    of the apostles:
believing in Christ and clinging
    to him.
Although we have not seen him,
may we receive the fruit of new life.

We ask this through
    our Lord Jesus Christ, your Son,
who lives and reigns with you
    in the unity of the Holy Spirit,
one God, for ever and ever.
—From the Italian sacramentary

Third Sunday of Easter:
O God of mystery,
out of death you delivered Jesus
and he walked in hidden glory
    among his disciples.

Stir up our faith,
that our hearts may burn within us
at the sound of his word,
and our eyes be opened
    to recognize him
in the breaking of the bread.

We make this prayer through Jesus,
    the risen Lord,
who is with you and the Holy Spirit,
one God, living and reigning
in the world without end.
—Coypright © ICEL

Fourth Sunday of Easter:
O God our Father,
in your Son you have reopened for us
    the gate of salvation.

Pour forth into our hearts the
    wisdom of the Spirit,
that in the midst of this world's lies
    and empty promises
we may learn to recognize the voice of
    Christ, the Good Shepherd,
who offers us life,
    life in all its fullness:
Christ who lives and reigns with you
    and the Holy Spirit,
one God, for ever and ever.
—From the Italian sacramentary

Fifth Sunday of Easter:
Father, you have revealed yourself
    to us in Christ,
our teacher and our redeemer.

Grant that, drawing near to Christ,
    the living stone,
rejected by humankind but chosen
    and precious in your sight,
we too may be built up in him
into a nation of priests, a holy people,
a temple of your glory.

We ask this through
    our Lord Jesus Christ, your Son,
who lives and reigns with you
    in the unity of the Holy Spirit,
one God, for ever and ever.
—From the Italian sacramentary

Sixth Sunday of Easter:
Faithful God,
who love us in Christ Jesus,
send your Spirit of Truth
    to dwell with us
that we may always recognize
    what is godly,
live by the commands of Christ,
and be true to the love entrusted
    to us.

We make this prayer through Jesus,
    the risen Lord,
who is with you and the Holy Spirit,
one God, living and reigning
in the world without end.
—Copyright © ICEL

CONTINUED

Seventh Sunday of Easter:
Merciful Father,
in the power of your Spirit
you have glorified your Son,
handed over to death for our sake.

Look upon your church,
gathered together as were
    the disciples
with Mary in the Upper Room:
Grant that in the joy
    of that same Spirit,
we too may taste the blessedness
    of those
who have shared in the sufferings
    of Christ:
who lives and reigns with you
    and the Holy Spirit
one God, for ever and ever.
—*From the Italian sacramentary*

Pentecost:

One of the several opening prayers from the sacramentary for Pentecost Vigil or Day may be used as a concluding prayer to the intercessions.

Communion Rite

INTRODUCTION TO
THE LORD'S PRAYER

For the entire season:
We are a chosen race, a royal priest-hood, a people God claims as God's own; and so we have the courage to say:

PRAYER FOR PEACE

For the entire season:
Lord Jesus Christ, on the day of your resurrection you greeted your disciples saying: "Peace be unto you." Look not on our sins, but on the faith of your church. . . .

From Ascension to Pentecost:
Lord Jesus Christ, you sent the Holy Spirit to endow the infant church with the gifts of unity and peace: Look not on our sins, but on the faith of your church. . . .

INVITATION TO COMMUNION

For the entire season:
This is the Lamb of God, who takes away the sins of the world, (*from Easter Sunday until Ascension:* Christ our Passover who was sacrificed for us:) (*from Ascension to Pentecost:* who has poured into our hearts the gift of his Spirit:) Happy are those who are called to his supper (*or, as in the Latin:* Blessed are those who have been called to the wedding feast of the Lamb).

Concluding Rite

BLESSING

For the entire season:

The Episcopal Church's Book of Occasional Services *has a one-paragraph blessing, long but not as long as the solemn blessing, which might be good if one desires to add solemnity to the dismissal throughout the full Fifty Days:*

The God of peace, who brought again from the dead our Lord Jesus Christ, the great Shepherd of the sheep, through the blood of the everlasting covenant make you perfect in every good work to do God's will, working in you that which is well-pleasing in the Lord's sight; and the blessing of almighty God. . . .

A Vigil Service for Pentecost Eve

In the Circular Letter Concerning the Preparation and Celebration of the Easter Feasts *(January 1988), the Congregation for Divine Worship encouraged a "prolonged celebration of the Mass in the form of a vigil, whose character is one of urgent prayer after the example of the apostles and disciples who persevered together in prayer with Mary, the Mother of Jesus, as they awaited the Holy Spirit" (107). In the February 1988 issue of its publication* Notitiae *the Congregation offered these texts and rubrics for the Pentecost Vigil. A translation of the Latin follows, with adaptations.*

In churches where the Vigil Mass is celebrated in an expanded form, the Vigil may be celebrated in the following way:

IN THE CONTEXT OF EVENING PRAYER

If Evening Prayer I immediately precedes the Mass, the celebration begins either with the introductory verse ("O God, come to my assistance") and the hymn "Veni, Creator Spiritus" or the entrance antiphon from the Pentecost Vigil Mass while the procession enters. The priest greets the people, omitting the penitential rite (cf. General Instruction on the Liturgy of the Hours, *94 and 96).*

Evening Prayer may begin with a lucernarium, the thanksgiving for light, except that the paschal candle would already be lit privately before everyone gathers.

The psalmody of Evening Prayer then follows up to, but not including the short reading. After the psalmody, the priest offers the prayer "God our Father . . ." (Pentecost Vigil Mass, second text).

IN THE CONTEXT OF AN EXTENDED LITURGY OF THE WORD

If Mass begins in the usual way, after the Kyrie the priest offers the prayer "God our Father . . ." Then the priest addresses an introduction to the people in these or similar words:

Dear brothers and sisters: we have begun this Pentecost Vigil after the example of the apostles and disciples who, with Mary, the Mother of Jesus, persevered in prayer, awaiting the Spirit promised by the Lord. Let us listen now with quiet hearts to the word of God. Let us contemplate how much God has done for us, and let us pray that the Holy Spirit, whom the Father sent upon those first believers, will bring God's work to perfection throughout the world.

The readings follow as given in the lectionary in the following order (which means that all the "first readings" from the Vigil Mass in the lectionary are proclaimed):

READING I

Introduction: The building of the Tower of Babel represents the human folly of rebellion against God. The result is always division and confusion. But this is reversed at Pentecost as the Spirit builds a community drawn together in love from all nations and languages.

Reading: Genesis 11:1–9

"It was called Babel for there the speech of the whole world was put to confusion."

Psalm 33:10–11, 12–13, 14–15

Prayer: Grant, we pray you, almighty God, that your church may always be that holy people gathered together by the unity of the Father and of the Son and of the Holy Spirit, so that it may manifest to all the world the mystery of your unity and holiness and itself come to the perfection of your love. We ask this through Christ our Lord.

READING II

Introduction: In the fire on Mount Sinai God sealed a covenant with the people of Israel. In parted tongues of fire, the God who raised Jesus from the dead seals a new covenant with the people of the church.

Reading: Exodus 19:3–8, 16–20

"The Lord descended on Mount Sinai in the sight of all the people."

CONTINUED

Canticle of Daniel 3:52, 53, 54, 55, 56
Or:
Psalm 19:8, 9, 10, 11

Prayer: O God, who in smoke and fire upon Mount Sinai gave the old law to Moses, and who this day revealed the new covenant in the fire of the Spirit: grant, we pray, that kindled by that same Spirit which you wondrously poured forth upon your apostles, and gathered from among all peoples to be the new Israel, we may receive with joy the eternal commandment of your love. We ask this through Christ our Lord.

READING III

Introduction: As in the beginning, so in Ezekiel's vision, the Spirit breathes and creation comes to life. Pentecost marks a new breathing of the Spirit and a new creation, the birth of the church.

Reading: Ezekiel 37:1–14

"Dry bones, I will send spirit into you and you will see."

Psalm 107:2–3, 4–5, 6–7, 8–9

Prayer: Let your people ever exult, O God, renewed in youthfulness of soul by your Holy Spirit: that we, who have been restored to the glory that is ours as your adopted children, may look forward in sure and certain hope to that great day of resurrection and reward. We ask this through Christ our Lord.

READING IV

Introduction: Joel's vision of the end of time included an abundant outpouring of the Spirit and a call to judgment. Pentecost signals the dawning of the last days, as the Spirit descends and the church goes forth to gather the harvest of the nations.

Reading: Joel 3:1–5

"I will pour my Spirit upon my servants and handmaids."

Psalm 104:1–2a, 24 and 35c, 27–28, 29bc–30.

Prayer: Graciously fulfill, O Lord, the promise you have made in our regard: that your Holy Spirit, when the Spirit comes to us, may make us witnesses before all the world to the gospel of our Lord Jesus Christ, who lives and reigns with you forever and ever.

GLORIA

OPENING PRAYER

Taken from either the first or alternative opening prayers in the sacramentary. After the opening prayer, the liturgy of the word continues with the reading from Romans and the gospel, and Mass continues in the usual way.

———

If Evening Prayer is combined with Mass, after communion the Magnificat is sung with its antiphon from Evening Prayer ("Come, Holy Spirit"); then the prayer after communion is offered and the concluding rite takes place as usual.

In dismissing the people, the deacon or the priest adds a double Alleluia to the invitation, as do the people to their response.

ORDINARY TIME

OFFICIAL DESCRIPTION

Apart from those seasons having their own distinctive character, 33 or 34 weeks remain in the yearly cycle that do not celebrate a specific aspect of the mystery of Christ. Rather, especially, on the Sundays, they are devoted to the mystery of Christ in all its aspects. (*General Norms for the Liturgical Year and Calendar*, 43)

RESOURCES
On Ordinary Time

Adam, Adolf. *The Liturgical Year* (New York: Pueblo Publishing Co., 1981).

Cobb, Peter G. "1. The History of the Christian Year," under "The Calendar," *The Study of the Liturgy,* Cheslyn Jones, Geoffrey Wainwright, Edward Yarnold, eds. (New York: Oxford University Press, 1978).

Martimort, A. G., et al. *The Church at Prayer,* vol. 4: *The Liturgy and Time* (Collegeville: The Liturgical Press, 1986, new edition).

Nocent, Adrian, OSB. *The Liturgical Year,* vol. 4 (Collegeville: The Liturgical Press, 1977).

Talley, Thomas J. *The Origins of the Liturgical Year* (New York: Pueblo Publishing Co., 1986).

On the Lord's Day

Adam, Adolf. "Sunday as the Original Celebration of the Paschal Mystery," *The Liturgical Year* (New York: Pueblo Publishing Co., 1981), 35–51.

Huck, Gabe. "Eucharist on Sunday," *Liturgy with Style and Grace* (Chicago: Liturgy Training Publications, 1984), 72–73.

Jounel, P. "Sunday and the Week," *The Church at Prayer,* vol 4: *The Liturgy and Time* (Collegeville: The Liturgical Press, 1986), 11–25.

Kavanagh, Aidan. *On Liturgical Theology* (New York: Pueblo Publishing Co., 1984), 55–69.

Kollar, Nathan R. "Worshiping on the Lord's Day," *Liturgy* (Journal of the Liturgical Conference), vol. 6, no. 2, 15–21.

Marshall, Paul. "The Little Easter and the Great Sunday," *Liturgy,* vol. 1, no. 2, 27–31.

Nocent, Adrian. "The Lord's Day: A Theology of Sunday," *The Liturgical Year,* vol. 4: *Ordinary Time* (Collegeville: The Liturgical Press, 1977), 9–19. This essay is followed by commentary on the collects and prefaces of Ordinary Time.

Rahner, Karl. "The Sunday Precept," *The Practice of the Faith* (New York: Crossroads Press, 1983), 179–85.

A SENSE OF ORDINARY TIME

> Ordinary Time is not very ordinary at all. Ordinary Time, the celebration of Sunday, is the identifying mark of the Christian community which comes together remembering that on this first day of the week the Lord of life was raised up and creation came at last to completion. Sunday as a day of play and worship is a sacrament of redeemed time. How we live Sunday proclaims to the world what we believe about redeemed time now and forever.
>
> What happens in our churches every Sunday is the fruit of our week. What happens as the fruit of the week past is the beginning of the week to come. Sunday, like all sacraments, is simultaneously a point of arrival and departure for Christians on their way to the fullness of the kingdom. This is not ordinary at all. This is the fabric of Christian living. *(Saint Andrew Bible Missal)*

Dorothy Day observed: "The words 'Ordinary Time' in our own prayer books put me in a state of confusion and irritation. To me, no time is ordinary." The term "Ordinary Time" really means not ordinary but ordinal—counted—time. It's simply the way the church organizes liturgical books, assigning each Sunday a number, counting each week one after the other. The term "Ordinary Time" is not meant to have significance in itself; *it is not a season,* nor should it be turned into a living part of liturgical spirituality—the way Lent-Triduum-Eastertime and Advent-Christmastime are. In other words, the only reason for knowing that it is the "Seventeenth Sunday in Ordinary Time" is so that a person knows where to turn in the lectionary, the sacramentary or perhaps at home in a missal to prepare for Sunday Mass.

Dorothy Day is right. No time is ordinary. The church has a tradition of calling the least of its days *feriae,* feasts. All Christian time within the liturgy is an entrance into the endless feast of God's reign.

PREPARING THE PARISH

Preparing for what? We just finished saying that Ordinary Time is not a church season but merely a term useful for organizing our liturgical books. Even still, this "counted time" that comprises over half of the year is when we must be laying the groundwork for the parish's yearlong liturgical life: the discipline of keeping the day (with Morning, Evening and Night Prayer at home or in church); the discipline of keeping the week (especially in the rhythms of Fridays and

Sundays); the discipline of keeping feast days (learning what it means to take time off to "play heaven"); the discipline of keeping a lifetime (turning to our ritual tradition at times of births and deaths, weddings and anniversaries, and all the many other occasions of joy and sorrow that mark our lives).

Ordinary Time also provides a breather in the round of the year when we perhaps can better find the time to attend to building up the liturgical ministries, to get the ball rolling for parish renovation and parish stewardship, to review and make adaptations in our worship, especially Sunday Mass. And it isn't only liturgical personnel who should respect the calendar and make good use of Ordinary Time for their business. All parish leaders should have the sense to schedule ongoing programs or special events *outside* of the liturgical seasons.

VESTURE

> Variety in the color of the vestments is meant to give effective, outward expression to the specific character of the mysteries of the faith being celebrated and, in the course of the year, to a sense of progress in the Christian life. . . . Green is used in the Offices and Masses of Ordinary Time. (*General Instruction of the Roman Missal*, 307, 308)

Of course, there are many shades of green and many effective combinations of green with other colors. Forest green with stark white, silver and brown fit winter; bright greens and turquoise with yellow, orange or even pastels fit summer. (Fabrics should change as well; the summer vesture should accommodate the heat and humidity.)

Whatever is chosen, be consistent from year to year so that the assembly can begin to associate certain vesture with certain times of year. In autumn, the month of November in particular, deeper and richer earth tone shades would echo the change of seasons in nature as well as hint at the imminence of Advent. (And, as a caveat, the "off the rack" green vestments in the mostly polyester materials available from some church supply stores are generally awful—both in colors and in fabrics unsuited to comfort or beauty.)

THE MASS

The character of Ordinary Time encourages a review of fundamental questions and concerns of liturgical celebration—an opportunity to get back to basics. Consequently, much of what follows pertains to year-round liturgy. These comments appear now to take advantage of a period in our calendar that gives the space to merge time and inclination into parish evaluation and reform.

Hospitality: The gathering of the community does not begin at the introductory rites. It climaxes there. Well before the entrance song, the people are already gathering and being gathered into a community at prayer. Before considering the introductory rites, first consider how the vestibule and bulletin boards, the ushers who welcome, and the general environment of everything from the sanctuary to the parking lot bespeak hospitality. Hospitality, after all, is a concern of all the faithful. For example, could involving *all* the liturgical ministers at any given Mass in greeting people at the doors discourage those ministers from huffing into the church 30 seconds before the entrance procession

begins? Have your ushers received training and encouragement in their ministry? Consider the inside and outside of the church building, parking spaces, traffic patterns, snow removal, provisions for the handicapped, chairs/pews, decorations. All help "the faithful come together to take on the form of a community and prepare themselves to listen to God's word and celebrate the eucharist properly." (*General Instruction,* 24)

If the "four hymn syndrome" still holds sway in your community, now is the time to break with it. An easily memorized entrance antiphon could provide an alternative to a hymn or other song. A chanted litany—Taizé-style—might also be appropriate. Is the opening song at least in the same spirit as the entrance antiphons of the sacramentary? To those who expend energy belaboring a "theme" for a Mass by trying to match song lyrics to the readings, just take a good look at these entrance antiphons: There is no attempt to match them with the readings for the day.

Entrance song: The entrance procession begins *after* the first verse or refrain of the entrance song/antiphon. This avoids the impression that the congregation is standing and singing to greet the ministers in the procession. Thought must be given to the pace, posture and positioning of those entering in procession, the objects they carry (cross, candles, lectionary, thurible), and the path they take (from the back of the church, the side, the front?), and how all these variables can be best adapted to the simplicity of Ordinary Time.

After the ministers have reverenced the altar, they go to their assigned positions. At this point the presider greets the assembly with the sign of the cross. The presider initiates the gesture not with trite informality nor starched piety but slowly, prayerfully and with reverence. The presider then offers a scripturally based greeting. Through this greeting the presider declares to the assembled community that the Lord is present. (In a fashion, this says the same thing as the use of the processional cross as the only cross in the worship place. It is plunked down in our midst to declare that Christ is with us.)

The greeting and the assembly's response express the mystery of the gathered church (*General Instruction,* 28). Casual words and personal thoughts are better saved for one-to-one greetings before and after the liturgy. Let's face it: If a presider feels it necessary to add folksy bits of commentary during the liturgy, turning the liturgy into a private conversation, that same freedom should be given the assembly in its responses.

The penitential rite during Ordinary Time is brief and concise, with a simple introduction and clear invocations. The well-known sacramentary texts can convey a sense of Ordinary Time and contrast nicely with composed or unearthed texts for seasonal use. Keep in mind that a lot of wordiness here will make it very difficult for the assembly to give themselves over to the exultant praise of the Gloria—or to wholehearted attention to the liturgy of the word.

The singing of the Gloria is often reserved for high holy days and other special occasions. At first, it might seem reasonable to recite the Gloria during Ordinary Time—but the Gloria is an ancient *hymn* in which the church, assembled in the Holy Spirit, praises and entreats the Father and the Lamb. (*General Instruction,*

31) Is it better left unsaid if it isn't sung? Remember the form and style of the processional song and the penitential rite, and then consider the various ways in which the Gloria might be sung: Every parish should be comfortable with just a few of the excellent musical settings available.

Ordinary Time is never an occasion to get a Mass done as quickly as possible. Some silence is necessary after the invitation to the opening prayer.

Liturgy of the word: Feel the rhythm of this liturgy—sitting down and settling in, scripture, silence, psalm, scripture, silence, standing up, acclamation, scripture, again sitting down, homily, silence, standing up, (profession of faith,) intercessions. Have we let the assembly learn this rhythm through purposeful silence after the readings? Do we always sing the responsorial psalm—and *always* a psalm—perhaps by choosing and repeating one psalm throughout a season or a block of Ordinary Time. (See the "Common Texts for Sung Responsorial Psalms" [seasonal psalms] in the lectionary, #175, especially the several psalms given for use in Ordinary Time.) Do we sing the Alleluia not as a separate part of the liturgy but as a welcome to the gospel, so that when it begins *all* stand—without any minister standing beforehand—and by the time it ends the deacon or presider is at the ambo with the gospel book or lectionary open, and immediately says, "The Lord be with you"?

General intercessions can be composed for use throughout blocks of Ordinary Time, individual petitions being changed as necessary, with a new set of petitions being reworked every four to six weeks. Review the outline of the divisions within the Gospel According to Matthew on page 135 to help decide logical Sundays to change intercessions. (See samples on page 128.)

The liturgy of the word and the catechumens: The Rite of Christian Initiation of Adults speaks of the challenges this liturgy of the word presents to catechumens. Within that text can readily be seen the invitation for all the faithful to reflect on the meaning and potential of the word and to question what kinds of challenges this liturgy continues to present in their lives:

> Celebrations of the word of God [for the catechumens] have as their main purpose: 1. to implant in their hearts the teachings they are receiving: for example, the morality characteristic of the New Testament, the forgiving of injuries and insults, a sense of sin and repentance, the duties Christians must carry out in the world; 2. to give them instruction and experience in the different aspects and ways of prayer; 3. to explain to them the signs, celebrations and seasons of the liturgy; 4. to prepare them gradually to enter the worship assembly of the entire community. (RCIA, 82)

The preparation of the altar and gifts: The altar has been bare up until now, as the *General Instruction* says (no "permanent" corporals, laminated cue cards, missal stands, Mass-intention sheets, etc.). At the beginning of the liturgy of the eucharist the bread and wine are brought to the altar by the people. This part of Mass is called the "preparation of the altar and gifts," *not* the offertory. (The Roman rite has not had anything called an "offertory" for 20 years!) Give some thought to the procedure for selecting people for this preparation: Who selects them? When are they asked?

The preparation of the altar and gifts is, indeed, a simple and functional rite. But its function is as essential to a beautiful celebration of the eucharist as the careful setting of an attractive table is to the hosting of a meal. There is beauty in its very simplicity. Still, something that becomes second nature by its simplicity cannot be carried out without a second thought. The simplicity of the rite emerges out of careful attention to details. The preparation is a bridge between word and eucharist. Both a sense of rhythm and a sense of transition can be maintained here as the words over the bread and wine are done *silently* while the congregation sings or is silent. Instrumental music is certainly appropriate as the deacon or presider quietly and with reverence prepares the altar table. When all movement (including the collection) has ceased, then comes the invitation: "Pray, brothers and sisters. . . ."

The eucharistic prayer: We have eight prefaces for Sundays in Ordinary Time and nine approved eucharistic prayers. Determine a schedule for the use of the various prefaces and prayers throughout the year. The prayer should not be changed every week. Rather, a particular eucharistic prayer might be selected for use throughout a season or during a series of weeks within Ordinary Time (see "The Calendar" in this *Sourcebook* for suggestions). Occasionally there are bits of noninclusive language in the prefaces. These will disappear in the revision of the sacramentary being prepared for the early to mid-1990s. Of course, the presider has a responsibility to read over carefully all the texts of a particular celebration well beforehand—and not ten minutes before Mass begins.

When a parish has more than one presider (resident or regular visitor), there can be no question but that they see decisions about the eucharistic prayer and other facets of the liturgy as belonging to all who prepare the liturgy. In this way, the decision to use during September, for example, the second of the two eucharistic prayers for reconciliation, will be honored by all who preside.

The communion rite begins with the Lord's Prayer and embolism/acclamation. It continues with the sign of peace and the Lamb of God litany while the bread of Christ's body is broken and the cup of Christ's blood is poured into various cups (*just now* brought to the altar). *Pastoral Care of the Sick* offers examples of the "moderate amplification" that may take place in the invitation to holy communion:

> This is the bread of life.
> Taste and see that the Lord is good.
>
> Jesus Christ is the food for our journey;
> he calls us to the heavenly table.
> Happy are those . . .
>
> This is the Lamb of God
> who takes away the sins of the world.
> Come to me, all you that labor and are burdened,
> and I will refresh you.

As with any words of address or invitation where a response is expected, both the words themselves and the tone must invite that response ("Lord, I am not worthy . . ." in this case). Thus the final line to which the assembly is accustomed, "Happy are those who are called to his supper," should normally conclude the invitation.

The communion rite continues through the communion procession and song, then a silent time and the prayer after communion. Communion from the cup is to be and is becoming the norm at parish Sunday Masses. This demands care in design and habitual reverence. Occasionally evaluate the communion procession, considering ways in which it might flow with the least congestion and backups. Don't be shy about altering the patterns if they don't seem to be smooth; in many parishes they couldn't get any worse. If you are someone who does not experience the assembly's pattern of going to communion—if you are a presider or a musician—the only way to understand the pattern is to be part of it.

After communion, the assembly (that means everyone present) needs sacred silence. The quiet can occasionally be filled with a sung meditation. This time is followed by the prayer after communion. Announcements are not part of the communion rite, and so they come, if at all, only after the Amen concludes the prayer after communion. (See the introduction to the lectionary, 27.)

Concluding rite: Try banning announcements for a while and then evaluate the effects it has on parish life. (Why, after all, do we go to the trouble of printing those bulletins?) This rite should evoke a sense of being sent out. The RCIA (75.3) refers to a sense of being empowered before even being able to participate in worship. Together, being empowered and sent out can converge into a keen and profound sense of mission. This is handled within the rite with the prayer over the people, the blessing, the dismissal and the recessional (if any—a recessional song is *not* an official part of the Roman rite). One of the prayers over the people or one of the solemn blessings for Ordinary Time can also be chosen to repeat throughout a block of weeks.

MUSIC

The promulgation of the *Constitution on the Sacred Liturgy* spawned some of the most important writing and directives on the use of music—quite a contrast to an Austrian emperor's restrictive decree in the eighteenth century that no Mass was to last longer than 45 minutes! What today's musicians have is immense freedom in the choice of music and ultra-clear directions on how and where that music is to be used. For some musicians this enormous repertory becomes much more inhibiting than the 45-minute liturgy Haydn or Mozart faced; there are many choices that have to be made many times. Of course, choices are dictated by taste, and taste is something that should be shaped by an understanding of how music is used in the liturgy. Important sources for gaining an understanding of this "how" are the directives given in the *General Instruction of the Roman Missal* (an entire issue of *Pastoral Music* was devoted to the subject, Volume 13:4), *Music in Catholic Worship* and *Liturgical Music Today* (the latter two documents issued by the American bishops and found in LTP's *The Liturgy Documents*). What follows is a breakdown of the Mass in the spirit of these directives.

A fundamental concept links all the parts of Mass: The normative liturgy of the Roman rite is a sung liturgy. Why? Liturgy is the voice of Christ singing to the Father. Christ sings because Christ is the Song. For the Word of God, *Logos* in Greek, *Dabar* in Hebrew, is a sung word, a chanted word. And the liturgy of heaven, in which all the holy ones join in praise of God and the Lamb, is a sung

liturgy. The rubrics in the lectionary for the singing of the gospel acclamation come close to expressing a principle of all of liturgy: It is omitted if it is not sung.

What all this means is that any spoken parts of the Mass are to be regarded as unusual, abnormal. Chanting is the normal way the presiders and deacons and lectors—and the assembly—should communicate in the liturgy. That may not be the way we do things in most North American parishes, but the chanting of our communal worship is a common heritage that links the Roman rite to most of its sister Western rites, to the many Eastern rites, even to the synagogue and to the mosque. Until we begin to feel the abnormality of spoken liturgy, somewhere deep down, it's not likely that we'll ever really appreciate what singing is within the liturgy.

However, parish liturgy does fall short of being "normative" since we regularly speak the prayers and the readings. Certainly on important occasions these should be chanted. Maybe it's better to make liturgy more festive (more normative) by concentrating on including these chants, instead of adding hymns and other music to the liturgy. For example, on a festive occasion or during the seasons (even before adding a song to the preparation of the gifts or another anthem to the choir's repertory), think about ensuring that the eucharistic prayer is sung.

The gathering song: The use of metrical hymns, songs and carols has been restricted in the Roman liturgy of Mass. While they became a standard part of Morning and Evening Prayer, in Mass their use was restricted to the occasional hymn before the gospel: the sequence. In general the musical form in use was the "responsorial" form with the assembly singing an easily memorized refrain and the cantor interpolating selected verses of a psalm. (The 1985 sacramentary keeps the refrains of these musical forms for the entrance, preparation and communion. Is there a parish that makes use of them?)

This should give us some pause in our use of hymnody at Mass. The "four hymn syndrome"—a stopgap measure in our first attempts at vernacular liturgy—is embedded in much of our thinking. For most parishes, a gathering song will be the most common use of the hymn form. The choice should be seasonal during the major seasons of the year, and on the other Sundays of the year probably should reflect the larger outlines of the gospel—and might also reflect the spirit of the entrance antiphons of the sacramentary. For instance, in 1990 from August 5 to September 16—the Eighteenth Sunday through the Twenty-fourth Sunday in Ordinary Time—the thrust of the readings deal with the marvelous deeds of Jesus that resound in the kingdom of heaven and in its image here on earth—the church. The thrust of the entrance antiphons throughout the late summer and fall is an earnest plea for salvation and safety, for a speedy arrival of the reign of God to right all wrongs. Rather than trying musically to portray on each separate Sunday those marvelous gospel deeds of feeding the 5,000 or walking on water, a better approach would be to select texts and music that embrace all of those things. There is no heresy in repeating an item such as a hymn in the course of these seven weeks. (In "Suggested Parish Repertory," beginning in a few pages, specific items are suggested for the course of Ordinary Time.)

Ritual dialogue includes the greeting, the penitential rite, the dialogue before and after the readings, the preparation rite, the preface dialogue, the concluding

rite. Ritual words deserve ritual music—chant that stays basically the same all year through even if some of the texts shift a bit. Ritual dialogue always requires "cue words" (like ". . . for ever and ever" or "This is the word of the Lord") that lead directly to the assembly's response. Since the assembly does not have the prerogative to alter its responses, the presider, deacon or readers should not ad lib their words either.

The way a parish handles such ritual dialogue is something of a diagnostic test of its liturgical health. Murmured recitation of ritual dialogue is one of the saddest aspects of worship in many parishes. An assembly should be able to respond vigorously, eventually *in parts,* to the full-throated chanting of its ministers.

The Gloria: This is our Sunday song of praise. Originally composed for Easter—a song begun by the angels, taken up by the crowds as Jesus entered Jerusalem, now sung by all the redeemed around the throne of the Lamb—the Gloria became part of every morning office in much of the East and the Sunday eucharist in much of the West.

But the Gloria is problematic. It follows too closely to the gathering hymn. In its placement in the middle of the entrance rites, it is difficult to think of it ever being sung by the choir while the rest of the assembly sits. Its length makes one approach with caution the learning of a through-composed setting. A simple chant usually works better, such as the one by John Lee. Settings that use a refrain for the assembly—of which there are many—are useful, but when does such a device become monotonous?

We have all participated in Masses that begin with a vigorous hymn followed three minutes later with the lackluster reciting of a second hymn—the Gloria. Some parishes employ the Gloria as their gathering song. Some parishes confine the singing of the Gloria to Easterime, Christmastime and on feast days. This would be in line with the concept of "progressive solemnity" (hymns or other songs sung when appropriate in addition to the irreducible minimum of sung psalm, gospel acclamation, intercessions, eucharistic acclamations, litany at the breaking of the bread and communion song).

The psalm: The psalm is sung scripture, the domain not of the lector but of the cantor leading the assembly. Singing something besides a psalm at this point in the liturgy of the word is the same thing as reading Gibran's *The Prophet* instead of the scriptures. Despite what is written to the contrary, the psalm is not a "response" to the first reading.

The word "responsorial" refers to the style of singing, like the words "metrical" or "antiphonal." True, many—not all—of the psalms within the lectionary for Mass were chosen to reflect the first readings, but the first readings were chosen to reflect the gospels, and one wouldn't call the first reading a "response" to the gospel. (Also, why then wouldn't the second reading and the gospel merit a similar "response"?) Our true response to the scriptures is none other than the praise and thanksgiving of the eucharist. Nevertheless, the psalm *does* function as a "response" in this restricted sense: The beauty and power of the psalms can enable a gathered people to sing before God the songs of Israel. This comes about when the psalms are allowed to arise from the silence after the first reading and are allowed to happen without rush. It happens if psalms are done with whatever craft the musical style demands. It happens if the musical arrange-

ments of the psalms are true to their texts (just scan the great sweep of emotions found in the familiar Psalms 22, 23 and 24).

The lectionary also proposes a series of "common psalms" for the seasons and for Ordinary Time. The same arrangement of a particular psalm sung over a period of several weeks, returning each year at a given season, enables a parish to make a number of psalms its own. (The latest setting of a particular psalm sung at the latest workshop should be "forbidden fruit" to music ministers who want to serve the prayer of their parishes. One of the few good reasons to make a change is because one has made a mistake in the first place.) Further, such a "common psalm" becomes a season's theme song (a season of the liturgy or a season of the earth). For example, phrases like "Be with me, Lord, when I am in trouble" or "Out of the depths I cry to you, O Lord" will begin to sound like Lent to the parish and will more readily come to people's lips in private prayer both during Lent and throughout the year.

In choosing settings of the psalms, consider arrangements that are compatible with the various musical leaders the parish regularly uses at the Sunday Masses. Can a guitarist lead this setting or is it only suitable for keyboard? Is there room for the choir either to sing some of the verses or embellish the refrain once the congregation has it firmly in mind? Will a cantor be able to handle it alone? If the verses are through-composed, can a less-experienced cantor sing the verses to a simpler formula?

There are many collections of the common psalms that fulfill these requirements. However, most collections are uneven. You'll need to pick and choose from several. For settings that are sensitive to inclusive language, take a look at the collection *Psalms for All Seasons: From the ICEL Liturgical Psalter Project* (NPM, 1987). For a look at metrical, rather than responsorial-style psalmody (especially useful at Morning or Evening Prayer when many psalms are used in succession, and you might want to vary the style), see *A New Metrical Psalter,* edited by Christopher L. Webber (The Church Hymnal Corporation, 1986).

The gospel acclamation: If this acclamation is not sung, it is to be dropped entirely. Many parishes "surround" the reading of the gospel with this acclamation, reprising the refrain (but no verses) after the gospel. Most parishes can sustain a wide repertory of Alleluias. Because they are acclamations, they should be fairly short. Expand it with additional verses to accommodate the gospel procession. Stick to the discipline of using a particular arrangement for a particular season, then choose a few that are used only during Ordinary Time.

On great feasts some parishes sing a hymn either after the gospel or after the homily—akin to the tradition of the sequence, maybe actually singing the sequence for the day as a hymn. Some parishes may even sing such a hymn every Sunday, dubbing it "the hymn for the day." Many of our more didactic or poetic hymns seem to fit this part of the liturgy, like homilies in song. Who wouldn't appreciate a good song as part of the homily?

The general intercessions: The intercessions are a litany and litanies should be sung. After the reading of the gospel, the homily, and the recitation of the Creed, what the assembly does not need is more verbiage. Music ministers owe the assembly the ability to make litanic prayer their own. And it is by singing that the assembly joins its one voice to Christ who is our intercessor. That is why

the refrain "Lord, have mercy" is traditional for the intercessions and should have its place today along with the now more familiar "Lord, hear our prayer." Aside from these, however, the number of responses used should be few and should never be given to the assembly just at that moment, as in "Our response today will be. . . ."

The cantor should first sing the refrain and then have everyone repeat it. Then a series of short petitions using only the formula "For . . ." or "That . . ." is begun. It is better to have many short petitions than only a few long ones. Only in parishes with a strong tradition of singing the intercessions should you consider changing the refrain from season to season.

The eucharistic acclamations: Three or four well-chosen settings of these acclamations would serve any parish well for at least ten years. They should become so well known that they can be sung by the assembly with the leadership of the accompaniment or a voice alone. Changing these acclamations wisely over the course of the year will give the needed variety to the various seasons. A well-developed program might use a unique set of acclamations for Advent/Christmastime (simple during Advent, embellished during Christmastime), a set for Lent, a set for Eastertime, and *two other settings for the Sundays of Ordinary Time.* More than that will probably result in less for the assembly.

In the manner of the interpolated Hosannas of the second eucharistic prayer for children, perhaps a part of the preface acclamation can be repeated as additional acclamations during the eucharistic prayer. There's an art involved here, insuring that the acclamation is neither too short nor too long and that there's enough of a warning when to come in. Sometimes singing a short acclamation twice through works better than singing it only once.

The litany at the breaking of the bread: Like the eucharistic acclamations, three or four settings should be all a parish needs. All settings should be flexible enough to contain the entire rite of breaking and pouring.

Look for settings where the assembly sings "You take away the sins of the world: have mercy on us/grant us peace." Many settings that have the assembly singing only the final words do not work as well. There are a few lovely settings where the assembly sings an ostinato refrain while the cantor or choir sings the acclamations over them. If the assembly is capable of holding its own voice, this works well. If the people can be taught to sing in parts, this works great.

The communion processional: Here again, a repertory of seven or eight songs will be more than adequate for the entire year. Because the assembly will be moving in procession and sharing the bread and cup, the responsorial form—where the assembly sings a memorized refrain—is what is needed. Finding good music for the communion procession takes digging and imagination and maybe even some editing of music and texts. For instance, one could use the refrain from a responsorial psalm and couple it with verses from that or other psalms. Verses from Psalms 23, 34 and 104 are appropriate year-round. Especially in parishes where singing the psalm in the liturgy of the word or singing during the communion procession is not yet all that successful, try using the same refrain from the psalm that was sung after the first reading.

It's possible to adapt a hymn to the responsorial style: The assembly sings the first two lines of the first verse of a hymn as a refrain, with the cantor singing the actual hymn. Some parishes sing a hymn immediately after communion. This works if there is no recessional song. The Roman rite does not include a recessional song, although many parishes do. Perhaps when we are told to "go in peace" we are expected to do just that.

SUGGESTED PARISH REPERTORY FOR ORDINARY TIME

These suggestions are meant first to illustrate liturgical principles, and then second to recommend certain pieces of music. This section of the *Sourcebook* is an exercise in thinking through annual parish repertory, showing how certain pieces fit into the overall picture. Building repertory is a tremendous responsibility for the parish music ministers, made much more difficult if your parish has not emerged from that frightening wall that was erected when church music began to be regarded as either "traditional" or "folk" (as if the categories were exclusive of each other). A hallmark of church music in the '80s was certainly the slow erosion of that wall as musicians recognized that style is not as important as quality and appropriateness to the demands of public worship.

Perhaps the next stage in the progress of church music will be a renewed appreciation of what parish repertory is: why it is better to aim for fewer pieces of music done splendidly than more and more pieces of music done in a mediocre way; why year-to-year consistency is better than endless novelty; why building repertory means teaching the parish only the best—of whatever style—rather than settling for music that may be immediately gratifying but that does not abide. An excellent, brief discussion of this enormous topic is LTP's new book *How Can We Keep from Singing?* The book was written by the "certified non-musician" Gabe Huck.

In "The Calendar" section of this *Sourcebook,* the Sundays of Ordinary Time are broken down into "blocks" of several weeks each; on the first Sunday of each block (and throughout the Sundays as well) we recommend how to handle certain same-every-Sunday elements for each of these blocks. Here we deal with the musical elements:

The Sundays between Christmastime and Lent

January 14–February 25, 1990

Ordinary Time needs three, possibly four psalms whose settings have a high lyricism that are a delight to sing over and over again. Marty Haugen's "The Lord is kind and merciful" (Psalm 103) and David Haas's "The Lord is my light and my salvation" (Psalm 27) wear very well. Both are in GIA's *Psalms for the Church Year* (G-2664). Ed Walker's "Bless the Lord, O my soul" (Psalm 103 in the OCP *Music Issue*) asks for a cantor who is able to sing with some expression to insure the success of the verses and the beautifully balanced antiphon. Taizé repertory can be introduced and used later in the seasons of Lent and Triduum.

Choral items that are different settings of the same psalm provide a consistency for two or three Sundays. The text of Psalm 34, "Taste and see," has been set by many composers in the past few hundred years. A newer one that is most attractive is by Stephen Dean (OCP, #7114). It could be used later as a communion procession with the congregation singing the antiphon.

The communion procession takes on a new message if the text reflects the gospel story in some way. For example, the Beatitudes are taught by Jesus in the gospel assigned to the Fourth Sunday. There are numerous musical expressions of the Beatitudes—although, as in certain settings of Psalm 23, the music sometimes turns our most profound words into saccharin. Two fine processional pieces relevant to this time sequence are "Trust God" by James Chepponis (World Library Publications, #8512) and "I will sing to the Lord" by Noel Goemanne (World Library Publications, #8510).

Hymns should be chosen to expand the parish's collection of "kingdom" hymns—a genus that is most useful. These Sundays provide an opportunity to learn a hymn tune to which the assembly has yet to be exposed. Some favorite common meter (8686) tunes are "Azmon" ("O for a thousand tongues to sing") or "Land of Rest" or "St. Agnes." The inspection of any tune index can reveal much untilled musical soil.

The Thirteenth Sunday through the Seventeenth Sunday

July 1–July 29

Psalmody that can be used in other celebrations throughout the year with a particular kinship to these Sundays should be selected from the musician's "wish list"—plotting out on paper just what comprises parish repertory and just what *should* comprise such repertory. With July's overriding sense of praise in the mystery of God's kingdom in the gospels, the choice of Psalm 88 and/or 145 would be good. David Haas's Psalm 145, "I will praise your name," always works well. Roc O'Connor and Elizabeth Staehler have set Psalm 138 ("Rise up in splendor," NALR) in a rather contagious 3/4 setting that children would have a great time singing. Chris Walker's "Preserve me, God," Psalm 30 (OCP, #7144), is haunting and can be used at either reconciliation or anointing services. Always consider using the responsorial psalm of one Sunday as the communion processional for another Sunday.

Red, white and blue music: Even though the Fourth of July falls within this time period, please resist the urge to use only patriotic texts with patriotic tunes. Although "America the beautiful" (Materna) would be a good choice for the day, instead of using patriotic songs, use early American songs—useful also during November (which is American Music Month). "Inculturation" of liturgy means more than bowing to the worldwide commercial culture in which we find ourselves. It means, in part, gaining a respect and delight in Quaker tunes, spirituals, Shaker hymns, Appalachian folk carols, New England shape-note psalms—and in the Old World roots of so much of these traditions. There are many fine early nineteenth-century American tunes that are begging for use. Tunes such as "Land of Rest," "Holy Manna," "Dunlap's Creek" and "Resignation" with their useful metrical schemes serve the musician well as new tune possibilities for the common poetic meters in which many hymn texts are set.

The Eighteenth Sunday through the Twenty-fourth Sunday

August 5–September 16

There seems to be a revival in the use of Gelineau's psalmody, the psalmody that served in the first years of liturgical reform. The introspective quality and small musical demands placed on the cantor are two important elements to consider during these late-summer Sundays. Psalm 8 with its antiphon, "How great is your name," and Psalm 94 with its antiphon, "Come ring out our joy," are good possibilities that reflect the mood of this time period. *Psalms for the Cantor* by World Library Publications in two volumes—WLP 2510 and WLP 2512—is a new possible source. Robert Kreutz's Psalm 65, "The seed falls on good ground," is assigned to the Fifteenth Sunday, but it can be easily used during this entire time as either responsorial or processional music.

The Bryan Rees text, "The Kingdom of God," provides an exuberant inclusion of all the things that make up this dominion: "justice and joy," "mercy and grace," "challenge and choice." Wedded to the tune "Laudate Dominum" by Charles H. H. Parry, both text and tune would be welcome additions to the parish's hymnody. It is found in GIA's *Worship,* third edition. "Pan de Vida" by Bob Hurd (OCP, #9110) provides a bilingual communion processional with a refrain that is unencumbered and instantly learned.

The Twenty-fifth Sunday through the Thirtieth Sunday

September 23–October 28

For many folks the "real" liturgical year begins during this period. This is the time when school, family and the new TV scheduling get solidified. It's also the time when the parish musician begins in earnest the preparation of the ensembles for the seasonal liturgies. It's the best time to start the assembly in its preparation for those seasons.

The scriptures of early autumn anticipate the advental scriptures of late autumn; one could almost say that in Cycle A, Advent begins in September. Psalms 98 and 72 are appropriate year-round psalms for gathering or responsorial pieces (the common psalms for Christmastime). Many churches already know David Haas's and Marty Haugen's "All the ends of the earth" (in *Psalms for the Church Year,* GIA, G-2664). An energetic treatment of Psalm 134, "Come and Praise the Lord," is by Randy DeBruyn (OCP, #8137). He has structured a vibrant antiphon that demands energy and commitment from the assembly. The choral parts are easy and approachable by any choir. One could easily utilize Bernard Huijber's "Hold me in life" (in *Vigil: Christmas,* OCP, #8535) as processional music, and it fits into many slots during these Sundays with their many kingdom parables. "In the Lord" by Jacques Berthier from the Taizé community is most useful as a hymn-like mantra.

The Thirty-first Sunday through Christ the King

November 4–November 25

All Saints and All Souls, then Christ the King and Thanksgiving frame the month of November and along with the Sundays give this month its character. "Rejoice and be glad" by David Haas and Richard Proulx's setting of the Beatitudes in GIA's *Worship* contrast in style, but the effect is rather similar. If the choir is up for it, there are many versions of "requiem" texts. One of the most recent, of course, is Webber's *Pie Jesu* (Hal Leonard Publishing Company) for two soprano soloists.

The ingathering of the harvest—so richly reflected in the liturgies of this time of year—calls to mind the final day, the ingathering of all people in God's holy city. The chestnut, "How lovely is your dwelling place," from Brahms's *German*

Requiem is a beautiful choice, but its length almost precludes its use during a eucharistic celebration, unless as a prelude. Evening Prayer or a memorial service would be more likely places.

It's about this time the musician is at wit's end for choosing the responsorial psalm: Psalm 122, "I rejoiced when I heard them say: let us go up to the house of the Lord," is the common psalm for the "last weeks of the year," and it is a gem. Again the observation needs to be made: Use something that is singable and repeatable. Most psalm collections, such as the ones already cited, have an arrangement of Psalm 122.

Ralph Verdi's Psalm 138, "I will give thanks to your name," in *Psalms for the Cantor,* Volume IV (World Library Publications, #2506), is the assigned psalm for Thanksgiving Day, the day that appears to be a new "holy day of obligation" for the American church. The musician is cautioned to take the metronome marking 72–88 seriously. Otherwise the antiphon becomes lethally dull.

"Thanksgiving" music fits all of this month. (All Saints is the harvest homecoming of the church.) Good alternatives (or companions) to "We gather together" are "Sing of the Lord's goodness" by Ernest Sands (OCP, #7100), "Confitemini Domino" by Jacques Berthier from the Taizé community, and "Father, we thank thee who hast planted" with the tune "Rendez a Dieu." One needs only to look in the topical indexes in most hymnals under "harvest" or "thanksgiving" and one finds just that.

THE WORSHIP ENVIRONMENT

This year Ordinary Time comprises three seasons of the earth: winter (January 8 to February 27), summer (June 4 to September 22), autumn (September 23 to December 1). How will the natural seasons be reflected in the worship place—birch trees in February, cattails in July, sunflowers in August, asters in September, cornstalks in November—or whatever is native to your neck of the woods? (Remember, anything like this always looks better in a single huge clump instead of being scattered around, and it serves the liturgy better if it graces the assembly's space rather than complicating the immediate vicinity of the altar, ambo and chair.) And how will the environment echo the season just past and prepare for the season to come? As with music, ritual and texts, so too with decoration: If you stay consistent from year to year, the community can come to remember and feel at home with its worship.

See the many suggestions for the worship environment for these weeks in "The Calendar" of this *Sourcebook.* Note in particular Matthew's abundant use of field and vineyard images, especially during summer and autumn this year.

OTHER RITUAL PRAYER

Liturgy of the hours: Ordinary Time is the time of year when parish patterns for Morning and Evening Prayer need to be established. Although we tend to think of the public celebration of the liturgy of the hours as something special to do during the seasons, we cannot expect either parish consciousness about this form of prayer or attendance at this prayer to increase unless the liturgy of the hours becomes part of the ordinary fabric of parish liturgy.

Ordinary Time presents a series of feasts, many with blessings associated with them. Become familiar with the incredible variety of texts in the *Book of Blessings* and in *Catholic Household Blessings and Prayers*. Call the parish's attention to the blessings in the latter book via the parish bulletin so this book can better become part of home prayer. The feasts during Ordinary Time should grow in popular observance and become one of the ways we are Catholic Christians, one of the ways we live our lives. And perhaps it all starts by the way the parish keeps these days, not as obligations but as joyful expressions of the mystery of Christ. Here's a list of important and ancient festival days that fall during Ordinary Time this year:

> Presentation of the Lord (2/2/90)
>
> Birth of John the Baptist (6/24/90—a Sunday this year)
>
> Saints Peter and Paul (6/29/90)
>
> Transfiguration of the Lord (8/6/90)
>
> Assumption of Mary (8/15/90)
>
> Triumph of the Cross (9/14/90)
>
> Michael, Gabriel and Raphael (9/29/90)
>
> All Saints Day (11/1/90)
>
> All Souls Day (11/2/90)
>
> Dedication of St. John Lateran (11/9/90)

The parish's patronal day should be kept with vigor. A patronal day is always ranked as a solemnity for the parish itself. (So is the anniversary of the dedication of a church.) These celebrations involve a sense of rededication of the people and the properties of a community. Flowers and lights can be placed at the four corners of the church and perhaps also at the incised crosses of the altar. A great wreath of fresh seasonal flowers makes a splendid decoration for the statue or image of the parish's patron saint. One or more texts might be borrowed from the many formularies available for the dedication of churches and altars, in addition, of course, to any proper texts for the parish's patronal feast.

A fine piece of music for such an occasion is Margaret Daly's "Church of God, chosen people" based on images from the First Letter of Peter. The piece is found in the *ICEL Resource Collection* (GIA). An SATB arrangement of the same piece is available in *Choral Praise,* vol. 1 (OCP, #8723). A patronal festival or anniversary of the dedication might be an occasion for which the parish commissions a piece of liturgical music. A "parish song" might evolve over the years, brought back again and again for such a festival day.

If your parish's feast falls at a poor time for celebrating it, such as during Advent or Lent or close to major feast, do what communities have always done: Transfer your feast to Ordinary Time, especially anytime in high summer, so the day can be kept with a parish picnic or potluck as well as worship—only keep the day consistent from year to year. A patronal day should always include outreach to marginal parishioners and to the civic community as well, enabling others to join in the celebrations. Greetings and flowers (and intercessory prayer) are gracious gifts to neighboring parishes on their patronal feasts.

Sample Prayer Texts for Ordinary Time

General Intercessions

The following are taken from the Italian sacramentary, Messale Romano, *copyright 1983 by the Libreria Editrice Vaticana. Translation by Peter Scagnelli.*

INVITATION TO PRAYER

Called to become one body and one spirit, let us turn to God who is in all and works through all.

Or:

With that childlike confidence that the Spirit of Christ raises up within us, let us offer our common prayer to God our merciful Father.

Or:

Our faith tells us that, for those who love God, all things work together unto good. Let this certainty of ours be evident now in the spirit with which we present our needs before God.

Or:

God's bountiful goodness, shared with us in baptism, has made us part of the great plan of salvation. As we pray, may the Lord open our eyes to see the events of every day in the light of loving providence.

INTERCESSION FOR THE CHURCH

For the church: that in its every word and deed there may shine forth more clearly the Christ in whom we hope and believe: let us pray to the Lord.

Or:

For holy church: that, guided by the Lord's Spirit, believers may learn to recognize in everyday life the challenging signs of God's presence: let us pray to the Lord.

Or:

For the holy people of God: that the church may manifest fidelity to the gospel message of love toward our enemies and solidarity with all: let us pray to the Lord.

Or:

For God's holy people: that for all the human family the church may be the beginning of redemption and a fertile seed yielding a harvest of unity and hope: let us pray to the Lord.

INTERCESSION FOR THE WORLD

For the world in which we live: that it may become a place of peace, mutual respect, and concern for the rights of all: let us pray to the Lord.

Or:

For the health of our planet: that the peoples of the world cooperate with wisdom to safeguard the environment and to restore our earth to the freshness of paradise: let us pray to the Lord.

Or:

For those responsible for nations and international relations: that their consciences may be stirred to seek authentic human progress, and not corrupted by the seductions of money and power: let us pray to the Lord.

Or:

For the needs of all who live on this good earth: that the Lord may give us the imagination to create an atmosphere of respect for one another in a world so distraught by anxiety and fear: let us pray to the Lord.

INTERCESSION FOR THOSE IN NEED

For families torn by discord and dissension: that loving hearts and helping hands may touch their lives with healing and their homes with new hope: let us pray to the Lord.

Or:

CONTINUED

That those who labor may receive a just wage for satisfying work that ennobles their human dignity and helps them to provide for the needs of their households: let us pray to the Lord.

Or:

For those dedicated to the service of the marginal or excluded: that the Lord may grant them the spirit of the good Samaritan to persevere as true servants of God: let us pray to the Lord.

Or:

That the Lord may give modern society eyes to see and hearts to help the new poor in our midst: the disabled, the mentally ill, the elderly and the displaced: let us pray to the Lord.

INTERCESSION FOR THE ASSEMBLY

For all of us who celebrate this eucharist: that we may learn to forgive as we have been forgiven and so become instruments of reconciliation and peace: let us pray to the Lord.

Or:

For all of us in this holy assembly: that the call of God may resound in the depths of our spirits and guide us to true conversion of heart: let us pray to the Lord.

Or:

For all of us here present: that the word of God may challenge us to face our limitations and acknowledge the contradictions in our lives, that we may grow together as one family through our sharing in the eucharist: let us pray to the Lord.

Or:

For all of us gathered here before the Lord: that a daily familiarity with God's word may bring us to a mature discernment of God's will in the concrete circumstances of our daily lives: let us pray to the Lord.

CONCLUDING PRAYER

These concluding prayers for the intercessions were selected from among opening prayers for Mass (based on the readings from Cycle A) of the Italian sacramentary, Messale Romano, © 1983 by the Libreria Editrice Vaticana (translated by Peter Scagnelli), as well as from ICEL original opening prayers based on the scripture readings of the day, © 1983, 1986, 1987, 1988, International Committee on English in the Liturgy, Inc. (ICEL). All rights reserved.

*Second Sunday
in Ordinary Time (1/14/90):*
Merciful Father,
you sent your Son, the Lamb of God,
to bear the sins of the world.

Make our lives holy,
and unite us with all who invoke the
    saving name of Jesus the Christ,
for he is the Lord,
who lives and reigns with you
    and the Holy Spirit,
one God, for ever and ever.
—Copyright © ICEL

*Third Sunday
in Ordinary Time (1/21/90):*
O God, you have founded your church
upon the faith of the apostles:

Grant that this community of ours,
enlightened by your word
and united by the bond of your love,
may become a sign of salvation
    and hope
for all those who,
    dwelling in darkness,
long for the radiance of your light.

We ask this through
    our Lord Jesus Christ, your Son,
who lives and reigns with you
    in the unity of the Holy Spirit
one God for ever and ever.
—From the Italian sacramentary

*Fourth Sunday
in Ordinary Time (1/28/90):*
O God,
teach us the hidden wisdom
    of the Gospel,
so that we may hunger and thirst
    for holiness,
work tirelessly for peace,
and be counted among those

CONTINUED

who seek first the blessedness
    of your kingdom.

We ask this through
    our Lord Jesus Christ, your Son,
who lives and reigns with you
    and the Holy Spirit,
one God, for ever and ever.
—*Copyright* © ICEL

*Fifth Sunday
in Ordinary Time (2/4/90):*
O God, who in the folly of the cross
reveal how great is the distance
between your wisdom and the logic
    of this world:

Grant us the true spirit
    of the gospel,
so that fervent in faith and tireless
    in love,
we may become light and salt
    for the world.

We ask this through
    our Lord Jesus Christ, your Son,
who lives and reigns with you
    in the unity of the Holy Spirit,
one God, for ever and ever.
—*From the Italian sacramentary*

*Sixth Sunday
in Ordinary Time (2/11/90):*
O God, you have revealed that law is
    brought to fulfillment
in that new justice which is based
    upon love:

Grant that the Christian people,
gathered to offer you the
    perfect sacrifice,
may live according to the demands
    of the gospel,
and become for everyone a sign
    of reconciliation and peace.

We ask this through
    our Lord Jesus Christ, your Son,
who lives and reigns with you
    in the unity of the Holy Spirit,
one God, for ever and ever.
—*From the Italian sacramentary*

*Seventh Sunday
in Ordinary Time (2/18/90):*
God of peace,
the Gospel of Jesus

challenges us to renounce violence
and to forsake revenge.

Teach us to recognize as one with us
even our enemies and persecutors
and to love without measure
    or discrimination.

We ask this through
    our Lord Jesus Christ, your Son,
who lives and reigns with you
    and the Holy Spirit,
one God, for ever and ever.
—*Copyright* © ICEL

*Eighth Sunday
in Ordinary Time (2/25/90):*
Eternal God,
your care for us surpasses
even a mother's tender love.

Renew our confidence
    in your provident care,
that we may abandon our
    self-protective ways
and seek first your kingdom.

We ask this through
    our Lord Jesus Christ, your Son,
who lives and reigns with you
    and the Holy Spirit,
one God, for ever and ever.
—*Copyright* © ICEL

*Thirteenth Sunday
in Ordinary Time (7/1/90):*
All-powerful God,
your word commands our loyalty
and offers us true life.

Give us ears attentive to the voice
    of your Son
and hearts generous in answering
    his call.
May we take up our cross with trust
    in his promises.

We ask this through
    our Lord Jesus Christ, your Son,
who lives and reigns with you
    and the Holy Spirit,
one God, for ever and ever.
—*Copyright* © ICEL

*Fourteenth Sunday
in Ordinary Time (7/8/90):*
O God, you reveal yourself
    to the little ones

CONTINUED

and give to the gentle the inheritance
    of your kingdom.

Make us poor in spirit,
    free and filled with joy
that we might imitate Christ
    your Son,
carry with him the sweet yoke
    of the cross,
and proclaim to all the joy
    that comes from you.

We ask this through
    our Lord Jesus Christ, your Son,
who lives and reigns with you
    in the unity of the Holy Spirit,
one God, for ever and ever.
—*From the Italian sacramentary*

Fifteenth Sunday
in Ordinary Time (7/15/90):
Increase within us, O God,
    by the power of your Spirit,
an openness to receive the seed
    of your word,
which you continue to sow in the field
    of humanity,
that it may bear fruit in works
    of justice and peace
and reveal to the world the blessed
    hope of your kingdom.

We ask this through
    our Lord Jesus Christ, your Son,
who lives and reigns with you
    in the unity of the Holy Spirit,
one God, for ever and ever.
—*From the Italian sacramentary*

Sixteenth Sunday
in Ordinary Time (7/22/90):
Almighty God,
may the power and patience
    of your love ever sustain us.
Let your word, the church's mustard
    seed and the church's yeast,
      bear fruit within us.

May this revive the hope of seeing
    grow that new humanity,
which the Lord, upon his return,
will cause to shine like the sun
    in his kingdom.

We ask this through
    our Lord Jesus Christ, your Son,

who lives and reigns with you
    in the unity of the Holy Spirit,
one God, for ever and ever.
—*From the Italian sacramentary*

Seventeenth Sunday
in Ordinary Time (7/29/90):
O God, font of wisdom,
you have revealed to us in Christ
the hidden treasure and the pearl
    of great price.

Grant us the Spirit's gift
    of discernment,
that, in the midst of the things
    of this world,
we may learn to appreciate the
    inestimable value
    of your kingdom,
and be ready and willing
    to renounce everything
for the sake of gaining the gift
    you offer.

We ask this through
    our Lord Jesus Christ, your Son,
who lives and reigns with you
    in the unity of the Holy Spirit,
one God, for ever and ever.
—*From the Italian sacramentary*

Eighteenth Sunday
in Ordinary Time (8/5/90):
O God, in the compassion of your Son
toward the poor and the suffering
you have manifested your
    parental goodness.

Grant that the bread multiplied
    by your providence
may be broken and shared in charity,
and that our communion
    in your sacred mysteries
may open us to enter into genuine
    dialogue with all people.

We ask this through
    our Lord Jesus Christ, your Son,
who lives and reigns with you
    in the unity of the Holy Spirit,
one God, for ever and ever.
—*From the Italian sacramentary*

Nineteenth Sunday
in Ordinary Time (8/12/90):
God of all power,

CONTINUED

your sovereign word comes to us
in Christ.

When your Church is in danger,
make firm its trust;
when your people falter,
steady their faith.

Show us in Jesus your power to save,
that we may acclaim him as
your Son,
who lives and reigns with you
and the Holy Spirit,
one God, for ever and ever.
—*Copyright © ICEL*

*Twentieth Sunday
in Ordinary Time (8/19/90):*
Father, in the self-emptying
of your Son,
gentle and humble of heart,
you have accomplished your
universal plan of salvation.

Clothe us in his gentleness
and humility,
so that by word and deed we too
may bear constant witness
to your eternal and steadfast love.

We ask this through
our Lord Jesus Christ, your Son,
who lives and reigns with you
in the unity of the Holy Spirit,
one God, for ever and ever.
—*From the Italian sacramentary*

*Twenty-first Sunday
in Ordinary Time (8/26/90):*
Living God,
you sent your Son among us
to reveal your wisdom
and make known your ways.

Increase our faith,
that we may confess Jesus
as your Son,
take up his work upon earth,
and trust in his promise to uphold
the Church.

We ask this through Jesus the Christ
who is one with you
and the Holy Spirit,
true God, for ever and ever.
—*Copyright © ICEL*

*Twenty-second Sunday
in Ordinary Time (9/2/90):*
Renew us with your Spirit of truth,
God most high,
so that we may not allow ourselves
to be deceived
by the seductions of the world.

As true disciples,
gathered together by your word,
may we discern all that is good
and pleasing to you,
and so carry our cross every day
in the footsteps of Christ, our hope,
who is God, living and reigning
with you and the Holy Spirit,
for ever and ever.
—*From the Italian sacramentary*

*Twenty-third Sunday
in Ordinary Time (9/9/90):*
O Father, you hear all those who ask
you for anything in the name
of your Son:
Give us a new heart and a new spirit,
that we may become sensitive
to the needs of every brother
and sister
according to that commandment
of love
which is the fulfillment of the law.

We ask this through
our Lord Jesus Christ, your Son,
who lives and reigns with you
in the unity of the Holy Spirit,
one God, for ever and ever.
—*From the Italian sacramentary*

*Twenty-fourth Sunday
in Ordinary Time (9/16/90):*
O God, most high,
you are slow to anger and rich
in compassion.

Keep alive in us the memory
of your mercy,
that our angers may be soothed
and our resentments dispelled.
May we discover the forgiveness
promised to those who forgive
and become a people rich in mercy.

We ask this in the name of Jesus,
the Lord,

CONTINUED

who is one with you
and the Holy Spirit,
true God, for ever and ever.
—*Copyright © ICEL*

*Twenty-fifth Sunday
in Ordinary Time (9/23/90):*
O great and just God,
you give equally to the last worker
as to the first,
for your ways are as far above
our ways
as the heavens are above the earth.

Open our hearts
to understand the words of your Son,
that we may comprehend the
inestimable privilege
of working in your vineyard
from daybreak until evening.

We ask this through
our Lord Jesus Christ, your Son,
who lives and reigns with you
in the unity of the Holy Spirit,
one God, for ever and ever.
—*From the Italian sacramentary*

*Twenty-sixth Sunday
in Ordinary Time (9/30/90):*
O God, ever quick to welcome sinners
as soon as they open themselves
to repentance of heart:
you promise life and salvation
to everyone who turns from injustice.

May your Spirit render our hearts
docile to your word
and give us the same mind
that is in Christ Jesus,
who is God, living and reigning
with you and the Holy Spirit,
for ever and ever.
—*From the Italian sacramentary*

*Twenty-seventh Sunday
in Ordinary Time (10/7/90):*
Yours, O God, is the vineyard,
yours the harvest,
yours the kingdom of justice
and peace.
You have called your people
to tend its growth.

Make us worthy of your trust.
Guide our efforts

and bless the work of our hands,
that we may offer to you
an abundance of just works,
a rich harvest of peace.

We ask this in the name of Jesus,
the Lord,
who is one with you
and the Holy Spirit,
true God, for ever and ever.
—*Copyright © ICEL*

*Twenty-eighth Sunday
in Ordinary Time (10/14/90):*
Father, you have invited
the whole world
to the wedding feast of your Son.

Give us the wisdom of your Spirit,
that we may be able to bear witness
to how great is the hope to which we
have been called,
and that no one may ever have to be
refused entrance
to the banquet of eternal life.

We ask this through
our Lord Jesus Christ, your Son,
who lives and reigns with you
in the unity of the Holy Spirit,
one God, for ever and ever.
—*From the Italian sacramentary*

*Twenty-ninth Sunday
in Ordinary Time (10/21/90):*
O God, through the mysterious and
free interacting of human wills,
every creature obediently serves
your providential purpose.

Grant that none of us may ever abuse
the power you have given us,
but may every authority serve the
good of all
according to the Spirit and word
of your Son.

We ask this through
our Lord Jesus Christ, your Son,
who lives and reigns with you
in the unity of the Holy Spirit,
one God, for ever and ever.
—*From the Italian sacramentary*

*Thirtieth Sunday
in Ordinary Time (10/28/90):*

CONTINUED

Your love, O God, is boundless.
We who once were strangers
have been brought
    into your household.
We who once were nameless
have been called your children.

Remind us of your deeds of mercy,
that we may love you
    with our whole heart,
and love our neighbor
    as our very self.

We ask this in the name of Jesus,
    the Christ,
who is with you and the Holy Spirit,
one God, for ever and ever.
—*Copyright* © ICEL

Thirty-first Sunday
in Ordinary Time (11/4/90):
Sovereign God,
we have no father but you,
no teacher but Christ.

Conform our lives to the faith
    we profess;
preserve us from ambition
    and pretence,
and teach us the greatness
    of humility and service.

We ask this through
    our Lord Jesus Christ, your Son,
who lives and reigns with you
    and the Holy Spirit,
one God, for ever and ever.
—*Copyright* © ICEL

Thirty-second Sunday
in Ordinary Time (11/11/90):
O God, whose wisdom goes
    in search of all those
who will listen to your voice,
make us worthy to share
    in your banquet
and make the oil in our lamps
    increase,
that they may not be extinguished
    as we wait.

When you come, may we be prompted
    to run and welcome you,
and enter with you into the
    wedding feast.
We ask this through
    our Lord Jesus Christ, your Son,
who lives and reigns with you
    in the unity of the Holy Spirit,
one God, for ever and ever.
—*From the Italian sacramentary*

Thirty-third Sunday
in Ordinary Time (11/18/90):
Rouse us from our complacency,
    O God,
that we may heed your word
and become your watchful servants,
your tireless workers.

Free us from our narrow caution,
that we may venture beyond security
and serve your kingdom well.

We ask this in the name of Jesus,
    the Lord,
the judge of our lives,
who is one with you
    and the Holy Spirit,
true God, for ever and ever.
—*Copyright* © ICEL

Christ the King (11/25/90):
God most high, you have established
    Lord Jesus Christ
as king and shepherd of all people
to build from all the painful events
    of history
your kingdom of love.
Increase within us the certainty
    of faith:
so that we may look forward
    to that day,
when, having destroyed even our
    final enemy, death,
Christ will hand over to you the work
    of redemption,
that you may be all in all:
Christ, who lives and reigns
    with you and the Holy Spirit:
one God, for ever and ever.
—*From the Italian sacramentary*

An Introduction and Outline of the Gospel of Matthew in Ordinary Time

The following has been drawn from the Pope John Sunday Missal, *copyright © 1978 by Kevin Mayhew, Ltd., England. This missal includes fine notes about the lectionary cycles, as well as brief introductions to the Sundays, the sacraments and the symbols of our tradition.*

The new series of readings from scripture that we hear every Sunday at Mass has rightly been called the catechism of the church. The Second Vatican Council stressed the centrality of scripture as the perpetual source of our spiritual life. St. Jerome reminds us that "ignorance of the scriptures is ignorance of Christ."

What distinguishes Matthew's account of the gospel story from the others is his concentration on the *words* of Jesus. His portrait of Christ is basically that of the master, the teacher of the new law. His technique is simple. He gathers the sayings of Jesus into five major discourses or "sermons" and uses them as the skeleton around which he builds his gospel. The five sermons are:

The sermon on the mount, Chapters 5–7

The mission sermon, Chapter 10

The parable sermon, Chapter 10

The community sermon, Chapter 18

The final sermon, Chapters 23–25

These "sermons" represent the core of the catechetical instruction of the liturgy this year. Matthew's Gospel underlines his conviction that the Lord is with the church, "always to the end of time." This is the theology that Matthew offers us. The abiding presence of the Lord has guided the evangelist in his choice of themes. Each theme gives us an insight into the nature of the church and Christ's activity through it. The mystery of the church is the center of Matthew's theology, and this leads us to the theology of the church and the theology of the sacraments.

The narrative parts of the gospel are intertwined with the five discourses to give us a carefully worked out catechetical construction of the whole gospel. From a very early stage Matthew's Gospel was recognized as "the ecclesiastical gospel." He starts with a principle in theology, "Christ the sacrament of the encounter with God," and develops it in line with the present experience of the Lord's abiding presence and activity in the church, namely, through the sacraments. The Gospel of Matthew, therefore, essentially deals with the mystery of the church and the sacramental life.

With these principles before us we can begin to appreciate the riches of the gospel that the church puts before us. Our lives are intimately linked with the church, and we share the life of our Lord through the life-giving power of the sacraments.

Stage One: *Sundays 1–2*

THE FIGURE OF JESUS THE MESSIAH

1. (a Monday in 1990, 1/8/90) The baptism of Jesus (Matthew 3:13–17)

2. (1/14/90) The witness of John the Baptist (John 1:29–34)

Stage Two: *Sundays 3–9*

CHRIST'S DESIGN FOR LIFE IN GOD'S KINGDOM

3. (1/21/90) The call of the disciples (Matthew 4:12–23)

4. (1/28/90) The sermon on the mount (Matthew 5:1–12)

CONTINUED

6. (2/11/90) The sermon on the mount (Matthew 5:17–37)

7. (2/18/90) The sermon on the mount (Matthew 5:38–48)

8. (2/25/90) The sermon on the mount (Matthew 6:24–34)

9. (not in '90) The sermon on the mount (Matthew 7:21–27)

Stage Three: *Sundays 10–13*

THE SPREAD OF GOD'S KINGDOM

10. (not in '90) The call of Levi (Matthew 9:9–13)

11. (not in '90) The mission sermon (Matthew 9:36—10:8)

12. (not in '90) The mission sermon (Matthew 10:26–33)

13. (7/1/90) The mission sermon (Matthew 10:37–42)

Stage Four: *Sundays 14–17*

THE MYSTERY OF GOD'S KINGDOM

14. (7/8/90) The revelation of the simple (Matthew 11:25–30)

15. (7/15/90) The parable sermon (Matthew 13:1–23)

16. (7/22/90) The parable sermon (Matthew 13:24–43)

17. (7/29/90) The parable sermon (Matthew 13:44–52)

Stage Five: *Sundays 18–24*

GOD'S KINGDOM ON EARTH— CHRIST'S CHURCH

18. (8/5/90) The feeding of five thousand (Matthew 14:13–21)

19. (8/12/90) Jesus walks on the waters (Matthew 14:22–23)

20. (8/19/90) The Canaanite woman (Matthew 15:21–28)

21. (8/26/90) Peter's confession (Matthew 16:13–20)

22. (9/2/90) The passion prophesied (Matthew 16:21–27)

23. (9/9/90) The community sermon (Matthew 18:15–20)

24. (9/16/90) The community sermon (Matthew 18:21–35)

Stage Six: *Sundays 25–33*

AUTHORITY AND INVITATION— THE MINISTRY ENDS

25. (9/23/90) Parable of the laborers (Matthew 20:1–16)

26. (9/30/90) Parable of the two sons (Matthew 21:28–32)

27. (10/7/90) Parable of the wicked vinedressers (Matthew 21:33–43)

28. (10/14/90) Parable of the marriage feast (Matthew 22:1–14)

29. (10/21/90) Paying tribute to Caesar (Matthew 22:15–21)

30. (10/28/90) The greatest commandment (Matthew 22:34–40)

31. (11/4/90) Hypocrisy and ambition (Matthew 23:1–12)

32. (11/11/90) The final sermon (Matthew 25:1–13)

33. (11/18/90) The final sermon (Matthew 25:14–30)

Stage Seven: *Sunday 34*

GOD'S KINGDOM FULFILLED

34. (11/25/90) Christ the King (Matthew 25:31–46)

THE CALENDAR

ADVENT

DECEMBER 1989

3 First Sunday of Advent. "Advent begins with the proclamation of its perennial promise: The Lord will come. We enter into a season of paradox, when we celebrate the long vigil we keep in preparation for the one who has already come." (*St. Andrew Bible Missal,* Brooklyn: William J. Hirten Co., Inc., 1982) See more on Advent in "The Seasons," beginning on page 11.

◆ A MYSTICAL VIGIL: The Advent season begins at sundown on December 2— and an early sundown it is, just about the time many parishes have their Saturday evening Mass. The beginning of the season deserves attention, and evening seems the finest time of day to celebrate. Some parishes announce well in advance that the Saturday evening liturgy before the First Sunday of Advent is their principal Mass that weekend, and then give this Mass extra attention. Or they reschedule the Saturday Mass so sundown can be marked by Evening Prayer, or a vigil of Advent readings, psalms and hymns. In any case, "Advent Eve" is one of the mystical moments of the year, and the resurrection vigil that should mark every Saturday night takes on special significance as we begin this season of expectancy.

◆ USING THE SACRAMENTARY: Either opening prayer is fitting this day, but the first prayer is less wordy. Advent Preface I is used until December 16 ("As a man" can be rephrased "as our brother" or "in our flesh"). Advent Preface II is used from December 17 to 24. So this year Preface I is used the first two Sundays of Advent, and Preface II the last two.

The solemn blessings and prayers over the people—which can be used as a conclusion to any liturgy, including Mass—are located together in the sacramentary after the order of Mass. For some reason, they are duplicated scattershot in the sacramentary in the proper of the seasons, making it appear as if they were suggested concluding rites for particular Sundays. It's probably best to keep a single format for the concluding rite throughout a season. Select one text from among the many options, make several copies, and then place a copy in the sacramentary on every Sunday of a season rather than relying on flipping pages to find the text. In the solemn blessing for Advent, "live with us as man," might be rephrased, "live as one with us."

◆ BLESSING THE ADVENT WREATH: See the advice about Advent wreaths on page 19. The church's *Book of Blessings,* which is scheduled to be published in English and in use by this Advent (check with a bookstore or with The Liturgical Press), contains an order for the blessing of the wreath on the First Sunday of Advent. Interestingly, if it takes place during Mass, the blessing of the wreath and the lighting of the first candle come as the conclusion to the general intercessions. The rubrics specify that no additional rites or prayers about the wreath are used at Mass after the First Sunday.

The blessing of the wreath most appropriately takes place as part of the thanksgiving for light, the *lucernarium,* during Evening Prayer. Kindling

According to their importance, celebrations are distinguished from each other and named as follows: solemnities, feasts, memorials.

Solemnities are counted as the principal days in the calendar and their observance begins with Evening Prayer I of the preceding day. Some also have their own vigil Mass for use when Mass is celebrated in the evening of the preceding day. The celebration of Easter and Christmas continues for eight days, with each octave governed by its own rules.

Feasts are celebrated within the limits of the natural day and accordingly do not have Evening Prayer I. Exceptions are feasts of the Lord that fall on a Sunday in Ordinary Time and in the Christmas season and that replace the Sunday office.

Memorials are either obligatory or optional. Their observance is integrated into the celebration of the occurring weekday in accord with the norms set forth in the General Instruction of the Roman Missal and the Liturgy of the Hours. Obligatory memorials occurring on lenten weekdays may only be celebrated as optional memorials. Should more than one optional memorial fall on the same day, only one may be celebrated; the others are omitted.

On Saturdays in Ordinary Time when there is no obligatory memorial, an optional memorial of the Blessed Virgin Mary is allowed. (*General Norms for the Liturgical Year and Calendar,* #10–15)

December 1989

3 SUNDAY
First Sunday of Advent (#1)

Isaiah 2:1–5
Romans 13:11–14
Matthew 24:37–44

4 MONDAY
Advent Weekday (#176)
John Damascene,
  priest and doctor
OPTIONAL MEMORIAL
Isaiah 4:2–6
Matthew 8:5–11
St. Barbara's Day

5 TUESDAY
Advent Weekday (#177)
Isaiah 11:1–10
Luke 10:21–24

6 WEDNESDAY
Advent Weekday (#178)
Nicholas, bishop
OPTIONAL MEMORIAL
Isaiah 25:6–10
Matthew 15:29–37

7 THURSDAY
Ambrose, bishop and doctor
MEMORIAL (#179)
Isaiah 26:1–6
Matthew 7:21, 24–27

8 FRIDAY
Immaculate Conception
SOLEMNITY (#689)
Genesis 3:9–15, 20
Ephesians 1:3–6, 11–12
Luke 1:26–38

lights—Advent candles included—is something ordinarily done in the evening. That's why Advent candles are lit in the home for the evening meal, and each new Advent candle is lit on a Saturday evening, which is also the most appropriate time to light and bless the first candle. Advent and Christmastime evenings cry out for the celebration of Evening Prayer, if only to bless God for the light shining in the darkness.

◆ DO WE NEED AN ADVENT WREATH LIGHTING CEREMONY AT MASS? On Sunday mornings, Advent candle(s) should already be glowing as people gather for worship. (It's not any different than what is fitting for the paschal candle during Eastertime: Because the candle is lit and blessed as part of the Vigil on Easter Eve, on Eastertime mornings it should be merrily shining and not publicly lit or extinguished before, during or after worship.) Perhaps a wordless incensation of the altar and wreath during the entrance rites of Mass, rather than the lighting of the candles, can best focus attention on the growing light of the wreath.

◆ THE CATECHUMENATE: In some parishes inquirers are admitted to the catechumenate today, although the RCIA does not suggest a date for this rite. In fact, many authorities suggest that the rite of acceptance not be given a fixed date but occur whenever the parish determines the readiness of an inquirer.

◆ IMMACULATE CONCEPTION: Announce Friday's holy day. Are there plans to make the day itself special beyond an hour of worship? Perhaps Friday evening lends itself to a parish potluck, or at least some sort of hospitality after Mass.

6 **Nicholas, bishop of Myra (Turkey), fourth century.** Tradition has immortalized Nicholas and catapulted him to popularity for his generosity. He's the patron of children, brides, sailors and pawnbrokers, as well as Greece, Sicily and Russia.

A visit from Nicholas is not supposed to be a pleasant occasion. In fact, the festivity begins only after the gruff old man leaves. He's very judgmental and is quick to point out anything he regards as unjust. If you stage a visit from Saint Nick, leave out the "ho, ho, hos" and allow him to be who he truly is: a no-nonsense pastor and teacher who turned the diocese upside down in his attempt to end unscrupulous business practices. At least that's what many legends attest.

8 **Immaculate Conception.** In this celebration we affirm that the Blessed Virgin Mary was filled with God's grace at the moment of her conception. This dogma was proclaimed by Pope Pius IX in 1854, although the feast of the conception of Mary in her mother's womb is very ancient. Under this title, Mary is patroness of the United States.

◆ MAINTAIN THE ADVENT SPIRIT. It would be difficult to imagine a more advental liturgy than today's. Since the angel's message and Mary's response perfectly match the expectancy of the season, let almost everything stay the same as worship on Sunday. A few possible changes include: a simple Gloria; a petition for the rights and dignity of all the people of the United States; some Marian music that fits the mood of Advent, such as "O Sanctissima"; floral and candle arrangements near the image of Mary—although attention to this image is fitting throughout the season.

◆ IMMACULATE CONCEPTION OR VIRGIN BIRTH? A special greeting and introduction would be helpful today, if only to clarify the confusion that still exists in most people's minds—complicated by today's gospel reading—between the "immaculate conception" of Mary and the "virgin birth" of Jesus. One possibility:

> Grace, light and peace from God our Father,
> and the Lord Jesus, be with you all.
>
> Today we honor holy Mary,
> who on this day was conceived in the womb of her mother.
> (Mary is called the Immaculate Conception,
> and by this title we honor her as patroness of our nation.)
>
> Praising God,
> who kept her sinless from the first moment of her life,
> and who is gracious and quick to forgive,
> let us humbly acknowledge our sins.

◆ USING THE SACRAMENTARY: The alternative opening prayer is beautiful. Use the proper preface for today. In the proper solemn blessing "mankind" can be "humanity" (but the concluding rite used on all the Advent Sundays would be appropriate today as well).

◆ MOST PEOPLE WILL LIKELY GATHER FOR AN EVENING MASS, so make the most of the season's darkness: Let the gathering be done by candlelight, and allow people to remain in prayer afterward in a dimly lit church. A morning liturgy in parishes with schools will likely involve the students. Such holy day liturgies can be gifts the school offers the parish at large, especially if prepared responsibly and well. For a complete discussion of school liturgies and of the liturgy for December 8, see *Hymnal for Catholic Students* and its *Leader's Manual* (both published by LTP and GIA).

10 **Second Sunday of Advent.** USING THE SACRAMENTARY: The alternative opening prayer is difficult to comprehend, especially when spoken aloud—which is a shame because several of its images are lovely. The prayer after communion is a beautiful proverb. Although John the Baptist steps forward this weekend to begin his yearly challenge to our complacency, remember *not* to use Advent Preface II which mentions him. That preface waits until December 17 (next Sunday).

◆ COMMUNAL PENANCE: There are but two weeks left until Christmas Day. Let the words of John the Baptist invite the parish to join in communal penance and the sacrament of reconciliation sometime soon. Appendix II of the *Rite of Penance* offers a complete service for the Advent season. Sample copies of the examination of conscience from the *Rite* would be a helpful handout for this weekend, in leaflet form from Pueblo Publishing Company.

◆ ORDERING CHRISTMAS FLOWERS: With the image of Christmas as a foretaste of eternal spring (notice the first reading at Mass for December 21, the winter solstice: Song of Songs 2:8–14) there has always been a great delight in getting flowers to bloom at midwinter. Poinsettias may seem obligatory, but why not add equally long-lasting cyclamens, azaleas, rieger begonias, tulips or primulas in compatible colors? A display of any of these plants looks better if you cluster several together—knocked out of their pots—in giant containers, with perlite as a base. Kalanchoes and potted spring bulbs such as crocuses or daffodils look great tucked into the straw around the manger, as if the straw itself was coming to life. Branches of forsythia and flowering cherry culled from backyards can be forced into bloom and would certainly be a cheerful sight.

9 SATURDAY
Advent Weekday (#181)
Isaiah 30:19–21, 23–26
Matthew 9:35—10:1, 6–8

10 SUNDAY
Second Sunday of Advent (#4)
Isaiah 11:1–10
Romans 15:4–9
Matthew 3:1–12

Thomas Merton died this day in 1968.

12 **Our Lady of Guadalupe.** This Advent feast recalls the events in 1531 when Mary appeared to the Mexican Indian Juan Diego and left with him a picture of herself on his cloak—pregnant, as an Indian herself, shining like the sun and moon together. Under this title Mary is patroness of the Americas. New texts for the liturgy of the hours on this day have been published by the Bishops' Committee on the Liturgy. Check with your diocesan worship office.

13 **Lucy, martyr, died 304.** Most of the saints on whom we focus in "The Calendar" of this *Sourcebook* are those holy women and men who seem to capture—in their lives and in the lore that surrounds their honor—the spirit of a season, and St. Lucy is a fine example. She was martyred in Sicily and her name means "light." Yet she is often associated with Sweden, mainly because a Stockholm department store, capitalizing on a rural folk custom, began promoting a December "Lucy Queen," not unlike American department stores hiring Santas to sell their wares. (Nicholas's association with Holland is because of the worldwide publicity he gets from an Amsterdam department store.) What sometimes gets lost in the attention to Nicholas and Lucy is perspective—they aren't any more important than many other saints on our calendar who also have marvelous legends, folk customs, and glorious, inspiring life stories to tell in celebration of their memorial days.

Despite the commercialism, Christians everywhere have found reason to honor Nicholas and Lucy as their Advent guides. And all the rich traditions that surround St. Lucy's Day take as their jumping off point the beautiful advental gospel of the wise and foolish bridesmaids, Matthew 25:1–13.

16 **Las Posadas.** Tonight the Advent novena begins (called in Mexico *Las Posadas,* "lodgings"). This novena is popular in much of Latin America and the Philippines. It is patterned on the nine days before Pentecost of waiting for the coming of the Spirit, and commemorates the journey of Mary and Joseph from Nazareth to Bethlehem. The customs of this novena, especially the nighttime or early dawn processions, if observed according to their original significance, mystically weave together Advent vigilance, hospitality and social justice.

17 **Third Sunday of Advent.** It is Gaudete Sunday, the day traditionally called "rejoice." This title comes from the first word of the Latin entrance antiphon. (Every Sunday had such a Latin title.) In most places, the rose-colored vestments for this day have quietly passed from the scene, so unless your community has worthy rose vestments that it uses on this Sunday and on the Fourth Sunday in Lent, it doesn't make sense to single out this week with a pink candle in the wreath.

◆ LITURGICAL TRIVIA: Some people mourn the loss and some people rejoice in the loss of such once-or-twice-a-year things as rose vestments, processional canopies, the lenten veiling of statues, clappers replacing bells during the Triduum, the "breathing" upon the baptismal waters in the shape of a Greek letter, the sequence hymns sung before the gospel on great feast days—even all the pomp that went into the annual pastoral visit of the bishop. In perspective, the loss of any one these things, when considered separately, is not very important. And in perspective, the loss of nearly all the "once-a-year" things, when considered together, has left our worship poorer in several ways.

That's the key word to consider: *perspective.* When the important aspects of a parish's worship and communal life are healthy, then some fine once-a-year traditions have their place. They are small treasures that need to be polished up occasionally and reformed just as all worship needs reform. But if the important aspects of parish liturgy are not well cared for, then these treasures are out of place, even comical, something akin to sticking jewelry on rags.

◆ USING THE SACRAMENTARY: Remember to use Advent Preface II from now until December 24. The alternative opening prayer contains a rare reminder, "the earth rejoices," that Christ comes to set all creation free. The first opening prayer and the prayer after communion offer the imprecise word "birthday" as a translation for the Latin "day of birth." That's an enormous difference! In both prayers, "birthday" should read "birth." What's at stake here is an understanding of a Christian festival as something far more than a historical commemoration. In our holy Christmas—as in all our festivals—we enter the mystery of God's own timelessness where we can declare in truth: Today is born our Savior, Christ the Lord. To quote St. Leo, "Although all the children of the church are separated from each other by intervals of time, yet as the entire body of the faithful—being born in the font of baptism—is crucified with Christ in his passion, is buried in his burial, is raised in his resurrection and placed at the Father's right hand at his ascension, so with Christ are they born in his nativity." (Sermon 26, "On the Feast of the Nativity")

◆ A SEASON OF JUSTICE: Is our sober joy during Advent visible in a commitment to justice? Is there a food bank and a soup kitchen for the hungry; a collection of winter clothing for the poor; a letter-writing campaign for those far away from home, perhaps to college students, perhaps to those in branches of the armed services; home visiting to reach out to the elderly, the infirm, the alone? Have you made available the phone numbers of hotlines or other services that can help people deal with the great stress that this month can impose?

◆ CHRISTMAS STRAW: From December 17 to 24, the empty crèche, without flowers or ornament, with only the cow and manger perhaps, can be set up with several bales of straw for people to bring home handfuls. Yes, it's messy, but it's the sort of custom that weds the home and the church. Getting the crèche in place for this weekend will ease the rush of next weekend.

18–23 Late Advent weekdays.

The liturgist Pius Parsch spoke eloquently about this final week of Advent, comparing it to the longing of a soon-to-be bride and bridegroom; or to the utter stillness and expectancy during the final moments of the night, just as dawn is about to break; or to the end of pregnancy when the child kicks in the womb, as if eager for birth.

◆ RELIGIOUS EDUCATION PROGRAMS AND PARISH BUSINESS SHOULD BE SUSPENDED from now until after Christmastime, which ends this year on January 8. In keeping with the tone of the week's liturgies, the general intercessions or Evening Prayer might be concluded with one of the "lost collects," those prayers buried in the back of the sacramentary under headings rarely averted to, in the Common of the Blessed Virgin Mary, #4 (Advent), #5 (Christmastime). The word "man" can be "flesh" in the Advent prayers.

◆ O-ANTIPHONS: Yesterday began the week of the O-Antiphons, customarily the antiphon of the Magnificat during Evening Prayer, and now also prayed

18 MONDAY
Late Advent Weekday (#195)
Jeremiah 23:5–8
Matthew 1:18–24
O Adonai!

19 TUESDAY
Late Advent Weekday (#196)
Judges 13:2–7, 24–25
Luke 1:5–25
O Flower of Jesse's Stem!

20 WEDNESDAY
Late Advent Weekday (#197)
Isaiah 7:10–14
Luke 1:26–38
O Key of David!

21 THURSDAY
Late Advent Weekday (#198)

Peter Canisius, priest and doctor
OPTIONAL MEMORIAL

Song of Songs 2:8–14
 or Zephaniah 3:14–18
Luke 1:39–45

O Daystar!

Winter Solstice

22 FRIDAY
Late Advent Weekday (#199)

1 Samuel 1:24–28
Luke 1:46–56

O King and Lawgiver!

Hanukkah begins at sundown.

23 SATURDAY
Late Advent Weekday (#200)

John of Kanty, priest
OPTIONAL MEMORIAL

Malachi 3:1–4, 23–24
Luke 1:57–66

O Emmanuel!

24 SUNDAY

Morning:
Fourth Sunday of Advent (#10)

Isaiah 7:10–14
Romans 1:1–7
Matthew 1:18–24

Adam and Eve's Day

---

during Mass as the gospel acclamation. The O-Antiphons are set metrically in the hymn "O come, O come, Emmanuel." Why not sing the appropriate verse during the gospel acclamation or at any gathering this week?

◆ REHEARSALS AND DECORATING: Will there be a special practice this week for the lectors, servers, musicians and presiders? Is everyone in the parish invited to participate in the cleaning and decorating of the worship space, guided by the environment ministers, making this an "all hands on deck" parish effort? Unless you are explicit, most folks assume that only a small coterie is really invited to help. Since the evening of the Fourth Sunday of Advent is Christmas Eve, it's especially important this year to line up the key people who help in decorating for Christmas. You will need some sort of game plan as to which of the Christmas decorations can be put up for the Fourth Sunday and which must wait to be put up on Sunday afternoon. For suggestions, see notes on the Christmastime worship environment on pages 31 and 32.

22 Hanukkah begins tonight, the Jewish, eight-day feast of lights. Tradition has it that at the rededication of the Temple, after the tyrant Antiochus left the Holy City in ruins, the Jews found only a small portion of oil for the sacred lamp. It miraculously burned for eight days until new oil was prepared. There are remarkable lessons in this festival against the dangers of cultural assimilation and the abandonment of religious tradition—good lessons for all people during this month.

24 Fourth Sunday of Advent. Most everyone in the assembly will be filled with expectancy. Don't undo this mood by jumping the gun on Christmas. Keep the liturgy like the previous three Sundays.

◆ USING THE SACRAMENTARY: The first opening prayer is a rewrite of the old Angelus collect, although it's hard to recognize in this draft. "Man" can be "flesh." Use Advent Preface II.

◆ A HECTIC WEEKEND: Although it may not seem all that dreadful as you're reading this, no doubt on December 24 you'll be thinking that there ought to be a liturgical law against back-to-back celebrations. Christmas on a Monday *does* create problems, and as a liturgical minister, you will need to prepare this long weekend carefully to avoid mayhem.

Consider the parish Mass schedule. Both last Sunday and this Sunday, publish this weekend's schedule for the Saturday night Masses through all Christmas Masses (and perhaps add in next weekend while you have people's attention). It seems logical to avoid inviting people to two Masses on one day, Sunday. It also seems proper to do all that can be done to help people gather for the eucharist of the last Sunday of Advent and then gather again for Christmas. Perhaps, then, there should be special emphasis on Saturday evening liturgy and a reduction in the number of Sunday morning Masses. As for Sunday afternoon/evening, is it even reasonable—especially this year—to have more than one parish liturgy on Christmas Eve? Emphasis would then go to the Midnight Mass and to the Masses on Christmas Day. (Notice that Sunday's gospel is the same as the short form of the Christmas Vigil gospel—underscoring a redundancy that crops up in several places in the liturgy of this Fourth Sunday and in the liturgy of the Christmas Vigil.)

Work something out with janitors to have a person on duty all weekend. A common frustration during a hectic period is trying to find and then put away ladders, tools and cleaning supplies—and the keys to the places in which these are stored. Don't attempt to do too much yourself; ask for help and secure that help weeks, maybe months in advance. Scheduling is especially critical for musicians. Consider hiring extra people along with the regulars, rather than overburdening any individual.

 **CHRISTMASTIME**

24 **Christmas Vigil.** See pages 26–45 in "The Seasons" for more on Christmastime.

◆ THE CHRISTMAS MASS SCHEDULE: The Roman rite on Christmas follows the sun—at its setting, at its lowest point at midnight, at its dawning and at its highest point at noon. So there are four Mass formularies: Vigil, Night, Dawn, Day. The time matters a great deal. In its own way, the turning of a day is an encounter with Christ, a sacrament of the mystery of God. That's why it's not in the spirit of the liturgy to use the Midnight readings at the Vigil or during the Day, as is sometimes done.

The framers of our liturgy presumed that Christians would be so enthusiastic about the birth of Christ that they would want several celebrations on this day and throughout the season. When we plan Christmas Day, do we share this enthusiasm and think in terms of a day-long liturgy? At the very least, will we encourage people to attend—and put our best energies toward—both the Mass at Midnight and the Mass during the Day, the most ancient and most important of the Christmas eucharists? How will each Mass be different—even in the way we illuminate the worship space to reflect the time of day?

◆ CHRISTMAS EVE OR CHRISTMAS DAY? The past ten years in many parishes there has been an upswing in attendance early on Christmas Eve—and a downswing on Christmas Midnight and Day. The main reason given for this shift is "convenience." A secondary reason—as disturbing a reason as "convenience"—is that late afternoon on December 24 has become a popular time for the school or religious education program to sponsor a "family Mass." These liturgies are sometimes transformed into children's pageants.

Are people truly observing the festival of Christmas if they regard worship on Christmas Day to be inconvenient? And how is the liturgy of the church supposed to function as a school of Christian formation if it can be molded into any shape we wish? What's at stake here?

The people who come to an early evening Mass on Christmas Eve often are disappointed to hear the Vigil readings—and so these are substituted with the Midnight readings, all with the assurance that such substitution is "legal." (It is legal, but as explained above, it is hardly in the spirit of the liturgy.) What may draw us to use the same readings at most of these liturgies is their beauty and familiarity. What we neglect is the beauty and appropriateness of the assigned readings—and the zeal we should have that they become *more* familiar. The genealogy of the gospel at the Vigil Mass, for example, is a strong text, one of

24 SUNDAY

Evening:
Christmas Vigil (#13)
Isaiah 62:1–5
Acts 13:16–17, 22–25
Matthew 1:1–25 *or* 1:18–25

Christmas Eve

those that is exactly right to the moment of its reading. It leaves us where we should be: hungry to hear more! That hunger is what may draw us back to hear other rare words ("In the beginning was the Word . . .") on Christmas Day.

◆ IF THE COMMUNITY CELEBRATES A VIGIL MASS, make it truly a vigil, scheduled later than a Saturday evening Mass and preceded by a well-developed liturgy of the word (see page 39). Or direct parish energies toward a single vigil and eucharist on this night, the holy night when the bridegroom comes, the master returns. (The alternative opening prayer for Midnight reminds us that the Midnight Mass is also in the spirit of this vigiling.)

25 **Christmas: Mass during the Night.** See page 39 for a pre-Mass vigil, and see page 42 for the Proclamation of the Birth of Christ.

◆ NIGHTTIME HOSPITALITY: Especially if you're planning a vigil or choir concert, why not greet folks who've come early to keep watch—and to get a good seat— with a cup of hot cider? A parish in Oregon greets everyone with a branch of holly—green branches to welcome the Messiah! A parish in New Jersey begins the vigiling by lighting real candles on a fresh, apple-hung fir tree—for the coming of Christ opens the gates of paradise. ("Fresh" is the key word here.) A parish in Texas festoons the worship place with softly illuminated papier-maché stars. The parking lot and doorways are made cheery with a hundred paper-bag *luminaria*. Allow folks the luxury of vigiling by candlelight. Yes, all this is hard work; it's the work of hospitality.

◆ SILENT NIGHT: Is the assembly given the respect of a worship space free from last-minute preparations? Is the darkness being used to full advantage? Is it possible to keep vigil by candlelight alone, at least for some period of time? Is the beginning of liturgy bright and boisterous or awe-filled and gentle? Is "O come, all ye faithful" the best choice for this night, or is it better to turn to lullaby carols, such as "Lo, how a rose," "Away in a manger," "I wonder as I wander," or any of the hundred ethnic and Appalachian carols that convey great tenderness and peace?

◆ INTRODUCTORY RITES: If the assembly has been keeping watch through a simple order of scripture readings, psalms, carols, choir pieces and instrumental music, the ministers should take their places before or during this vigiling, rather than entering in procession afterward. If you have a choir concert or a developed vigil, you can end it with the Proclamation of the Birth of Christ, the placing of the figure of Christ in the manger, an incensation of altar, crèche and congregation, then the greeting and Gloria leading into the opening prayer (the first option is ancient and succinct). Whatever custom suggests, much thought needs to go into this richer-than-usual introductory rite.

In all the preparations for the Christmas liturgies, keep in mind that these are not entertainment, nor is it simply one group (the choir, the readers, etc.) providing some uplifting moments for another group (the assembly). The liturgy can never appear to be just another Christmas special. Effort, graciously done, needs to be made to encourage participation rather than spectating.

◆ ETHNIC CUSTOMS: Don't be afraid to adapt and improve upon any ethnic traditions of this night. Recognize that many of these traditions crossed the Atlantic in bastardized form. Search out the ancient form of a custom—often a mystical reinterpretation of common liturgical practices, much as the lighting of the Christmas tree is really a *lucernarium* at heart—and reincarnate the ethnic

25 MONDAY
Christmas Day
SOLEMNITY

Mass at Midnight (#14)

Isaiah 9:1–6
Titus 2:11–14
Luke 2:1–14

Christmas roses

tradition into a form that makes sense in our reformed liturgy. Sometimes this takes a bit of genius, and certainly it takes a sense of wonder. However, customs should never be overloaded into the liturgy—and that includes newfangled ideas like gathering baby toys for the poor or having children dress up like angels. Perhaps customs can be expressed during a party after liturgy or on a later day in Christmastime. Even Christmas is not enough of an excuse to ignore liturgical good sense and norms just because "we've always done it that way."

◆ LITURGY OF THE WORD: Remember that, as long as it can be done well and with great clarity, the gospel can be chanted. The Episcopal altar missal outlines the two traditional Roman tones (found also in the old *Liber usualis*), and GIA offers a beautiful but challenging adaptation of more elaborate chants for a number of festal readings. A genuflection is to be made during the profession of faith at the words "by the power of the Holy Spirit . . ." Introduce the Creed in a way that cues the community to this change, then slow the recitation of the text and execute the genuflection in a way that clearly manifests reverence.

Scolding innuendo (mock or serious) and good-natured ribbing directed at twice-a-year worshipers not only reduces them to outsiders but is also an effective guard against their becoming anything more than twice-a-year worshipers. Our best welcoming efforts are a must—without any tone of condescension.

◆ LITURGY OF THE EUCHARIST: Of the three, Christmas Preface I or II fits this liturgy well. Also note the special Christmas inserts that are part of Eucharistic Prayer I this day.

Christmas greetings can be expressed briefly just before the final greeting, blessing and dismissal. Indeed, such holiday wishes might well lead into the blessing spoken by the presider over the assembly. Avoid a tone that says that the staff or clergy somehow own the parish. Perhaps the finest way to permit parishioners to extend wishes to one another is to offer refreshments after Mass.

Christmas: Mass at Dawn. What has been hidden from the learned and the clever is revealed to the marginal poor, the shepherds, who hasten from the Judean hillside to see God, who has become a child in their midst. And in most parishes, a few humble souls will gather for the early Mass on Christmas morning. Many times the elderly are here, or those whose children are grown and gone and whose grandchildren are miles away. The spirit of this Mass seems always to have been rather quiet and contemplative, as the church, like Mary, ponders the mystery in the silence of its heart. But quiet need not be translated as dull. Music at all the usual times certainly needs to be present here.

◆ USING THE SACRAMENTARY: The alternative opening prayer is clear and beautiful. See the note above about genuflecting during the Creed. Again we have the word "birthday" (discussed in the Third Sunday of Advent) in the prayer after communion; let it read "birth." Use the same concluding rite for all the liturgies of the Christmas season. It can be the solemn blessing for Christmas; copy, cut and paste it into the sacramentary for all Christmastime liturgies rather than relying on whatever option is duplicated in the sacramentary.

◆ MORNING HOSPITALITY: If a number of folks who live alone participate in this early morning Mass, perhaps some kind of breakfast gathering immediately after Mass is fitting. Such a gathering could be hosted by others who are alone on

25 MONDAY
Christmas Day
SOLEMNITY
Mass at Dawn (#15)
Isaiah 62:11–12
Titus 3:4–7
Luke 2:15–20

this morning: clergy and religious staff persons or the widowed who minister in the community.

25 MONDAY
Christmas Day
SOLEMNITY

Mass during the Day (#16)

Isaiah 52:7–10
Hebrews 1:1–6
John 1:1–18 *or* 1:1–5, 9–14

26 TUESDAY
Stephen, first martyr
FEAST (#696)

Acts 6:8–10; 7:54–59
Matthew 10:17–22

First Day of Christmas

27 WEDNESDAY
John, apostle and evangelist
FEAST (#697)

1 John 1:1–4
John 20:2–8

Second Day of Christmas

Christmas: Mass during the Day. Everything about walking into church this day should proclaim what the entrance antiphon puts into words: "A child is born for us, a son given to us; dominion is laid on his shoulder, and he shall be called Wonderful-Counselor!"

◆ USING THE LECTIONARY AND SACRAMENTARY: "Man" and "him" in the first opening prayer can be "humankind" and "us." The readings just about ask to be chanted. Although rubrics permit the interchangeable use of the four sets of Christmas readings, the prologue to John's gospel is a venerable tradition at this Mass. It speaks of light, the brightness of the noonday sun now streaming in the windows. See the note above about the genuflection during the Creed.

◆ A "FAMILY MASS": Is it ever appropriate to designate a eucharist as a "family Mass"? It's only fair to ask when is the single folks' Mass, the seniors' Mass, the unwed mothers' Mass and the married couples without children's Mass. Especially at the principal parish Mass, go to great pains to include all ages and ways of life. There might even be a piñata party afterwards in the gathering area or a larger vestibule of the church. If a children's pageant at Mass is a much-loved tradition in the parish, does it have to be on Christmas Day? Why not make merry on one of the Twelve Days of Christmas?

◆ CHRISTMAS DAY AFTERNOON: If your church decorations are splendid, consider leaving the church open throughout the day. Announce it as an invitation at all Masses. You'd be surprised how many households would enjoy stopping in with their guests to show off their parish home. No doubt all worship personnel are exhausted, but Christmas Day afternoon or early evening is just the time many folks are looking for something Christmasy to do—like a carol-sing or Evening Prayer.

◆ WE THREE KINGS (AND QUEENS, TOO!): Be sure to place the statues of the magi somewhere in church heading toward the crèche. Keep a few vigil lights burning around them just to catch the eye. Then move them closer to the crèche day by day throughout Christmastime until they arrive at Epiphany. This simple custom is guaranteed to be much appreciated.

26 **Stephen, first martyr.** Throughout these feasts of Christmastime, remember that, first and foremost, these are the days of Christmas, a season of carols, extra hospitality, extra solemnity even for the daily Mass—and good reason for keeping Evening Prayer with carols each evening of Christmastime. Today is the "First Day of Christmas"—the Feast of Stephen when "Good King Wenceslaus looked out." It's a day for charity to the poor, since Stephen was a deacon who distributed the wealth of the church.

27 **John, apostle and evangelist.** Because legend has it that John drank poisoned wine without harm, and because wine can be a drink of joy and conviviality as well as suffering and destruction, it's customary to bless and drink wine today, toasting each other with the words, "I drink to you the love of Saint John." The First Letter of John is traditional reading both during Christmastime and Eastertime. The resurrection gospel for the day—as well as so many of the Christmastime prayers and readings—are glorious reminders that Christmas is a paschal celebration.

28 **Holy Innocents, martyrs.** Ember days: If there is a developing tradition in the parish of keeping ember days, the following may be used without permission in the bulletin:

> Christmastime never hesitates to tell the whole story. That is why it would not be out of place to propose an ember day—a day of prayer, fasting and works of charity—on Thursday, December 28, the Feast of the Holy Innocents. In the midst of the joyous feasting of Christmastime—all the days from December 25 to January 8—we can keep a single day of fasting. When we observe Christmastime according to what is best in our tradition, we know that the great mystery of the season is not grasped apart from the killing we call the Holy Innocents. The Christmas red of poinsettias and holly berries is also the red of today's vestments, the red of blood and martyrdom and slaughter. We know how Rachel is weeping for her children as much as we know how the angels are singing their Glorias. We know all this in a way that is at the same time terribly sad and yet transcendent.
>
> This day of fasting could be kept by us who bitterly mourn the way we kill the unborn and let the world's children die. Read Matthew's story of the children of Bethlehem (Matthew 2:13–18) as the cornerstone of such an observance. Let our common memory and our conviction enter the life of our households: in prayer and fasting, in turning off entertainment and in dimming for this one night our festive lights, in actions that allow us to make our voices heard. This would not at all depart from the spirit of Christmastime, but it would probably bring to that spirit something it often lacks. For example: Write a Christmas card to your senator or representative or other official about one or more of the issues relating to our respect for life.

29 **Today is the anniversary of the massacre of native Americans at Wounded Knee, South Dakota, in 1890.** Every age and every generation has its holy innocents, for Rachel has not ceased her weeping.

31 **Feast of the Holy Family.** Today, on the "Sixth Day of Christmas" —which is also the seventh day in the Octave of Christmas, which is also the first Sunday of Christmastime, which is also New Year's Eve—Roman Catholics keep a feast in honor of the Holy Family. We marvel at the ordinariness of it all. Imagine: God takes up residence in a human family! At the same time, we are reminded that there is holiness in the ordinary.

◆ DO NOT MAKE UNNECESSARY WORK FOR YOURSELF. The liturgy for this Sunday does not fixate on the word "family"—and neither should you. Rather, both today and tomorrow are *Christmas* liturgies, with Christmas readings, prayer texts, melodies and environment—and extra after-worship hospitality. For parishes that have a Sunday evening Mass, are there diocesan guidelines whether this Mass must be the Sunday (Holy Family) or Monday (Mary, Mother of God) liturgy? Make this confusing point clear earlier in December.

◆ REMIND PEOPLE OF THE BLESSING FOR FAMILIES IN *CATHOLIC HOUSEHOLD BLESSINGS AND PRAYERS*. This is a good time of year to make this book available to all parishioners. Parishes may wish to order the book in quantity (at discount prices) and make it available on the Sundays before Christmas as a gift for

---

28 THURSDAY
Holy Innocents, martyrs
FEAST (#698)

1 John 1:5—2:2
Matthew 2:13–18
Third Day of Christmas

29 FRIDAY
Fifth Day in the Octave
of Christmas (#203)

Thomas Becket,
bishop and martyr
OPTIONAL MEMORIAL
1 John 2:3–11
Luke 2:22–35
Fourth Day of Christmas

30 SATURDAY
Sixth Day in the Octave
of Christmas (#204)

1 John 2:12–17
Luke 2:36–40
Fifth Day of Christmas

31 SUNDAY
Holy Family
FEAST (#17)

Sirach 3:2–6, 12–14
Colossians 3:12–21
Matthew 2:13–15, 19–23

St. Sylvester's Day
Sixth Day of Christmas
New Year's Eve

parishioners to buy for their own families and for friends and relations. The bishops of the United States have offered this book as something to be kept and used in every household, along with the family Bible, as a source for forming us— all through life—in the faith we entered at baptism. *Catholic Household Blessings and Prayers* should be as familiar and as much used in the rectory and the parish center as it is in the homes. It is truly a way for the spirit of the liturgy to become the spirit of our lives. If the parish missed the opportunity to make this book available this year, now is the time to schedule a consignment purchase for next year. The book is published by the United States Catholic Conference (and is available from LTP). This book is not to be confused with the *Book of Blessings* (mentioned above in connection with the blessing of the Advent wreath). The *Book of Blessings* is a book for large and small assemblies, often with an ordained minister presiding. *Catholic Household Blessings and Prayers* is exactly that: for the household.

◆ USING THE SACRAMENTARY: The first opening prayer is succinct. The alternative prayer can be made inclusive by changing "man" and "men" to "humanity" and "people." There is no proper preface for the day; Christmas Preface II is beautiful ("mankind" can be "humankind") and deserves to be used often. It is perhaps superior to the English of Christmas Prefaces I and III which in proclamation can be difficult to comprehend.

◆ WHAT DOES THE WORD "FAMILY" MEAN? Whole families or broken families? Single-parent families, the retired, the childless, single people, those who live in institutions—these are probably the majority of parishioners! All people need to expand their notions of the word "family." Choosing nuclear families (father, mother, children) today to act as liturgical ministers (preparing the gifts, offering hospitality), as is done in some parishes, runs the risk of excluding in an insensitive manner most of the households in the parish. The feast of the Holy Family is not a celebration of the nuclear family or of "family" values or of "family" life. True, the institution of marriage is in trouble, and parishes must address this trouble head on. But liturgy is not therapy; nor is it education; nor is it a soapbox to expound on an issue, worthy or not. Liturgy is an ascent into mystery. Happily, this encounter with mystery often has, as some of its fruits (not its goals), education, moral development and mental health.

◆ KEEP UP THE SPIRIT: Advertisers preach in their own way that the Christmas season ends on December 26—just take a look at all the "after-Christmas sale" ads in the paper this past week. Many of us were raised to believe that the "holiday season" ends on January 1, losing sight of Epiphany and Candlemas, much less the carnival season that leads to Lent. Considering the tremendous cultural pressure to abandon the celebration on December 25, we need to be blunt in reminding everyone that Christmas continues for many more days, and that it is antagonistic to our Christian way of life to take our trees down and turn off our festival lights before Christmastime is past. And parishes need to do more than give this problem lip service—they have an obligation to offer communal celebrations during Christmastime so that the season can be expressed beyond an hour or so of Sunday or holy day worship.

◆ NEW YEAR'S EVE: Providing a chance for folks to dance and sing on parish property tonight is a favor to the entire parish. Even something less ambitious, such as a great burst of church bells, a bonfire or some other hoopla at midnight would be a marvelous gathering, especially if it is well advertised. What's in the works? See page 33 about the appropriateness of a watchnight service this evening.

JANUARY 1990

1 **Mary, Mother of God.** A parish has good reason to weigh its usual approach to this day. Is it just "Happy New Year"? Is it kept as one of the great days of the Christmas season? This feast has had many names over the years, but it always has been called the "Octave of Christmas." Other titles for the day focus on the naming and circumcision of the Lord eight days after his birth (Luke 2:21). The title "World Day of Peace" reflects the angel's message in Luke 2:14. In 1969 the Roman Catholic church restored an ancient feast of the motherhood of Mary—also focusing on a passage in chapter 2 of Luke's Gospel, "Mary treasured all these things. . . ." The title, *Theotokos*, "Bearer of God," dates from the Council of Ephesus (431). It says so much about Mary and it says so much about her Son. See LTP's *A Christmas Sourcebook* for reflections on this day.

◆ USING THE SACRAMENTARY: Everything about today's liturgy should continue the Christmas tidings, including the penitential rite and the concluding rite. The alternative opening prayer successfully weaves together several of the titles for this day mentioned above. Notice how the communion antiphon is a beautiful New Year song. Perhaps the collect prayer of the intercessions can be the opening prayer from the Masses and Prayers for Various Needs and Occasions; "For Various Public Needs," #24 "Beginning of the Civil Year."

◆ HANDING OUT PARISH CALENDARS yesterday or today can be done with style. Think ahead and have folks (perhaps the religious education program students or the senior citizens) wrap calendars in festive ribbons; the blessing of the New Year from LTP's *Welcome, Yule!* can be prayed over the calendars—which have been stuffed into a wicker basket and carried into the midst of the assembly after communion. Then the calendars are distributed to each household. (See also the appendix to LTP's *Parish Path through Advent and Christmastime*.)

2—5 **Christmastime weekdays.** Remember: Christmas continues all week. Keep the statues of the magi marching through church to Bethlehem. If the parish has a back-to-school liturgy, keep it Christmasy. This is an ideal week for the parish, including the school, to host parties, pageants and programs. The memorials this week, important as they are to the church in the United States and Canada, should be kept as Christmastime days, with the memorial reflected perhaps in the opening prayer, an intercession or the homily.

6 **Today is the Twelfth Day of Christmas** (it is Epiphany on the calendar of the universal church, although not on the calendar of the United States and of Canada). Remember to move the statues of the magi into the manger scene. Some parishes remove the shepherds, although if you want to be literal, the magi didn't visit Christ in a stall. They visited a house (Matthew 2:11). Of course, a Bethlehem scene is not a literal device. Perhaps it is more in the spirit of Epiphany to allow the scene to be cumulative, subtracting nothing. Many old-fashioned scenes depict ordinary townsfolk, Adam and Eve (and sometimes the

January 1990

1 MONDAY
Octave of Christmas

Mary, Mother of God
SOLEMNITY (#18)

Numbers 6:22–27
Galatians 4:4–7
Luke 2:16–21

Seventh Day of Christmas

New Year's Day

2 TUESDAY
Basil the Great and Gregory
  Nazianzen, bishops and doctors
MEMORIAL (#206)

1 John 2:22–28
John 1:19–28

Eighth Day of Christmas

3 WEDNESDAY
Christmas Weekday (#207)

1 John 2:29—3:6
John 1:29–34

Ninth Day of Christmas

4 THURSDAY
Elizabeth Ann Seton, religious
MEMORIAL (U.S.A.) (#208)

1 John 3:7–10
John 1:35–42

Tenth Day of Christmas

5 FRIDAY
John Neumann, bishop
MEMORIAL (U.S.A.) (#209)

1 John 3:11–21
John 1:43–51

Eleventh Day of Christmas

6 SATURDAY
Christmas Weekday (#210)

Blessed Andre Bessette, religious
OPTIONAL MEMORIAL (U.S.A.)

1 John 5:5–13
Mark 1:7–11

Theophany

Twelfth Day of Christmas

7 SUNDAY
Epiphany of the Lord
SOLEMNITY (#20)

Isaiah 60:1–6
Ephesians 3:2–3, 5–6
Matthew 2:1–12

Julian Calendar Christmas Day

Heath

snake, too!), John the Baptist and his parents, and even the animals that were aboard Noah's ark, all worshiping Christ.

Parishes with a large community of people who reverence the sixth of January may want to observe Epiphany today *and* tomorrow. That surely harmonizes with the spirit of the readings and prayer texts this weekend. A visit from the magi and the Epiphany blessing of the home—or any building—can be part of religious education and parish school functions earlier this week. See the blessing in the Epiphany handout of LTP's *Welcome, Yule!*

7 The Epiphany of the Lord. Three mysteries have been a part of this holy day over the centuries: Today the star leads the magi to the infant Christ, today water is changed into wine for the wedding feast, today Christ wills to be baptized by John in the River Jordan to bring us salvation.

◆ BRIGHTEST AND BEST OF THE STARS OF THE MORNING: Be especially conscious of the richness of this day and do not try to scale down or contain the celebration by focusing exclusively on a particular aspect. Today is the climax of Christmas. The day is also called "Theophany," "the appearance of God." Today's celebration should summon forth the brightest and best of the parish's vessels and vesture, music and merriment. In fact, as so many liturgical writers have reminded us— people such as Adolf Adam, Pius Parsch and Jean Danielou—Epiphany is the climax of the year of grace, an anticipation of the parousia, a foretaste of the fulfillment of the promise of Easter. All of Christmas, all of Advent, and even all of the time since Pentecost have led to this feast. And before you fret over the parish liturgy of the day, be concerned whether people are keeping Epiphany at home. Make your enthusiasm for the day infectious.

◆ USING THE SACRAMENTARY: Notice the entrance antiphon. It points up the redundancy in the calendar of the Solemnity of Christ the King. Today is the most ancient Christian feast of God's reign. The alternative opening prayer contains the important word "today" ("men" can be "people"), but it also has the ugly phrase "resplendent fact." The first prayer is ancient and direct. The proper preface is a gem. There are proper inserts to the Roman Canon. Be sure to use the Solemn Blessing for Epiphany.

◆ EPIPHANY IS AN OCCASION, MUCH LIKE PENTECOST, WHEN THE PARISH MASS SCHEDULE MIGHT BE CHANGED to allow the principal Mass to be celebrated without any rush, as exuberantly as possible. The various musical groups of the parish may join forces this day—something that requires ample rehearsal and forethought. A lovely tradition worth repeating year after year at this principal Mass is to proclaim not one but all three Epiphany gospels: Matthew 2: 1–2, Matthew 3:13–17, John 2:1–12, perhaps employing three readers, perhaps concluding the proclamation with a hymn in celebration of the "three wonders" of this day, such as "Songs of Thankfulness and Praise" or "Hail to the Lord's Anointed."

◆ ONE REGULAR CUSTOM FOR EPIPHANY is the ancient proclamation of the year's dates for Easter and the days that depend on Easter (see page 44). Even as this day completes the promise of Easter, so it looks forward in time to the next and perhaps the final Easter. Let today's celebration be bright with all the splendor the community can summon. Everything should proclaim the revelation of the Prince of Peace, our sovereign and Lord. Include preschoolers in the entrance procession, perhaps carrying silver stars on sticks and halos of garland in their hair; or they can escort the magi who come in search of Christ, entering after the prayer after communion. The magi can then offer the blessings over chalk, Jordan water and incense (see page 41); or these blessings can be offered by the deacon or presider, with everyone helping in the distribution.

◆ EPIPHANY CELEBRATIONS: Epiphany evening is a grand night for the parish Christmas choir concert. Precede it with Evening Prayer, and add lots of carols for everyone to sing—maybe with a visit from the magi themselves! Take note of the wonderful Epiphany verse to "O come, all ye faithful": "Lo, star-led chieftains . . ." in *Carols for Choirs* (Oxford University Press, 1961). Epiphany is a fine day for one of several annual parish potluck suppers.

8 The Baptism of the Lord. This final day of Christmastime is a continuation of Epiphany, with the Father's voice revealing Jesus as the "beloved." Jesus will "baptize . . . in the Holy Spirit," and this denotes urgency of mission. Note how these images are incorporated into the preface for this day.

Most years Christmastime concludes with the feast of the Baptism of the Lord a week after Epiphany. Not in 1990. In the United States and Canada, we transfer Epiphany from where it is on the Roman Calendar (January 6) to the first Sunday after January 1. That means it can fall anytime from January 2 to 8. Yet on the Roman Calendar, the Sunday after January 6 is the Baptism of the Lord. So when we transfer Epiphany to Sunday, January 7 (like this year), or Sunday, January 8 (like last year), we're moving Epiphany to the day kept as the Baptism on the Roman Calendar. And so in the United States and Canada we move the Baptism to the next day, a Monday.

The baptismal font can replace the nativity scene as the place to be honored today. The rite of sprinkling could be used at Mass today, using evergreen branches as an aspergillum. Surely the carol "Joy to the World" has a place in today's celebration. Evening Prayer can bring to a close our Christmastime.

ORDINARY TIME

9 Ordinary Time resumes today. Remember that the weekday readings are taken from Cycle II. On weekdays at Mass from now until Lent the church will be reading Mark's Gospel, the Books of 1 and 2 Samuel, 1 Kings and the Letter of James.

◆ LOOKING BACK AND LOOKING FORWARD: Were Advent and Christmastime clearly more than business-as-usual for the parish? Already those responsible for preparing Lent, Triduum and Eastertime should be organizing all that must be done not only for the liturgy and its music but for the adequate preparation of the people. What was the response to any home prayer materials made available for Advent and Christmastime? What is being purchased for Lent, Triduum and Eastertime? How did Advent and Christmastime touch every aspect of parish life: the parish council and its committees, religious education, the parish school, various parish organizations? How did our worship bear fruit in works of justice? Is the coming paschal season fully reflected in the parish calendar, or are parish events, fundraisers and meetings scheduled with little or no regard for Lent, Triduum and Eastertime?

8 MONDAY
Baptism of the Lord
FEAST (#21)
Isaiah 42:1–4, 6–7
Acts 10:34–38
Matthew 3:13–17

9 TUESDAY
Weekday (#306)
1 Samuel 1:9–20
Mark 1:21–28
First week in Ordinary Time
Carnival begins.

10 WEDNESDAY
Weekday (#307)

1 Samuel 3:1–10, 19–20
Mark 1:29–39

11 THURSDAY
Weekday (#308)

1 Samuel 4:1–11
Mark 1:40–45

12 FRIDAY
Weekday (#309)

1 Samuel 8:4–7, 10–22
Mark 2:1–12

Marguerite Bourgeoys, virgin
MEMORIAL (Canada)

13 SATURDAY
Weekday (#310)

Hilary, bishop and doctor
OPTIONAL MEMORIAL

BVM
OPTIONAL MEMORIAL

1 Samuel 9:1–4, 17–19; 10:1
Mark 2:13–17

14 SUNDAY
**Second Sunday in
Ordinary Time** (#65)

Isaiah 49:3, 5–6
1 Corinthians 1:1–3
John 1:29–34

14 Second Sunday in Ordinary Time. After the intense liturgies of Advent and the festive celebrations of Christmastime, these next seven Sundays should be marked by that "noble simplicity" for which the Roman rite is noted and for which the assembly will be grateful. However, the spirit of the liturgy during winter continues the comfort and joy—and the challenge—of Epiphany. Lutheran and Episcopal tradition calls the days between Epiphany and Lent "the Epiphany season." While the Roman calendar does not do this, notice how often the scriptures and psalms speak of such Epiphany images as the gathering of all nations, the reign of God's anointed one, the calling of disciples, the light shining in the darkness. Like the month of November, this winter part of Ordinary Time needs to be prepared as a unit with much thought to what it follows and what follows it.

◆ THE WORSHIP ENVIRONMENT DURING THE WINTER might not involve a total dismantling of the Christmas decorations. Because the next few Sunday's liturgies resonate strongly with Epiphany, surely there is a place during these weeks for simple, unadorned evergreens, birch branches, grasses and a foretaste of spring flowers. Winter's worship environment should not shock people with drabness, especially when contrasted to Christmas. In the South a progression of seasonal flowers can grace parish worship. One Christmas holdover that seems out of place is the red poinsettia. (White varieties do not appear so incongruous once Christmas is past.) Newer varieties refuse to die, although they can get mighty shabby, and it seems wasteful to chuck them; perhaps they can find a home somewhere besides the worship space.

◆ USING THE SACRAMENTARY: Entrances and exits should be neither as festive as the solemnities just past nor as reflective as the lenten ones to come. Choose a straightforward greeting, penitential rite invocations, eucharistic prayer, introduction to the Lord's Prayer and communion, blessing and dismissal. Homilies could be rather brief, with references to the coming demands of Lent. Eucharistic Prayer II with its own preface, spoken or sung from memory, can be used throughout winter. If another eucharistic prayer is used, the Preface for Sundays in Ordinary Time I recalls images from the Sermon on the Mount in Matthew's gospel, which is read from next Sunday until Lent.

◆ THIS WEEKEND THE UNITED STATES OBSERVES THE BIRTHDAY OF DR. MARTIN LUTHER KING, JR. Prepare ahead of time by ordering the packet of materials for bulletin inserts and ecumenical prayer services, prepared each year by the National Catholic Conference for Interracial Justice (NCCIJ), 1200 Varnum Street NE, Washington DC 20017; 202/529-6480. Some of the materials are given in Spanish also. Today's homilists will find help in these materials for preaching from this Sunday's scriptures about the vision shared with us in the work and words of Martin Luther King. This Sunday, too, is an occasion for the parish to make a contribution to the traditions that should come to mark this weekend. It is not a run-of-the-mill national holiday but a summons to celebrate by actions that carry on Dr. King's work for racial justice and world peace. The bulletin might carry a list of issues and the names and addresses of elected officals to whom letters could be written. There might be a list of products being boycotted for reasons of justice (at this writing such a list would include Shell Oil Company for their dealings in South Africa, all Nestle products because of that company's continued exploitation of mothers and infants in the Third World, California grapes because of the growers' continued use of pesticides that are dangerous to farm workers). Perhaps, as in many communities, the summons should be to examine individually and as a village or town or city our progress against racism.

◆ COMMISSIONING PARISH MINISTERS: Today's selection from John is the Baptist's announcement of Jesus as the chosen servant of God. This might be a good Sunday—not only because of the scriptures but also in terms of avoiding doing this kind of thing during the major seasons—for commissioning people who have been prepared to serve in the various ministries of the parish. If so, this would be the culmination of a period of preparation that began last fall. Beware of rites with verbal excess. For a model, look instead to the outline of the commissioning rites for lectors and acolytes in *Rites I* (Pueblo Publishing Company) or to the Episcopal *Book of Occasional Services*. The Episcopal book contains excellent texts for a wide variety of ministries: wardens and members of the vestry (parish council members), servers at the altar, catechists, evangelists, singers, musicians, lectors, eucharistic ministers, even parish visitors and members of prayer groups, and a general form for other ministries. Look also at the rites for commissioning in the new *Book of Blessings*. The rite takes place following the homily and replaces the profession of faith. If the parish is devoting attention today—as is appropriate—to the birthday of Martin Luther King, it may be too much to add these commissioning rites. There are other Sundays when they will be equally fitting.

◆ GREEN VESTURE: Many parishes have a wintertime-only set of green vesture. In most parts of the country, a deep evergreen color would be fitting, perhaps accented with white, or even the customary carnival colors of gold, green and purple. These colors look back to Epiphany's gold, frankincense and myrrh, and look forward to Lent's purple, springtime's green and Easter's gold.

◆ ABOUT THE CATECHUMENATE: These "ordinary" weeks are time to make final plans for the celebration of the rite of election (if this is to take place locally and not at the cathedral), for the scrutinies and for the presentations that will be celebrated during Lent. Remember to observe the careful distinction that the RCIA establishes between catechumens (unbaptized persons coming to Christian faith) and baptized Christians seeking reception into the full communion of the Catholic church (no longer to be called "converts").

15 Today is the birthday of slain civil rights leader Dr. Martin Luther King, Jr. The U.S. Catholic Conference in *Catholic Household Blessings and Prayers* offers a beautiful prayer in memory of Dr. King that would make a fitting conclusion to the intercessions today.

17 St. Anthony, abbot, 251–356. One of the first "desert fathers," Anthony lived in the wilderness after giving everything he owned to the poor. He is the founder of Western monasticism. Although the weather rarely cooperates, today is a customary day for blessing household pets, since Anthony kept company with several critters, including—legend has it—with fleas! Anthony wrote: "The prayer of the mind is not perfect until you no longer realize yourself or the fact that you are praying."

18—25 Week of Prayer for Christian Unity. Keep the Lord's desire "that all may be one" before the eyes of the parish through intelligent use of the texts provided in the sacramentary, especially the Mass

---

15 MONDAY
Weekday (#311)
I Samuel 15:16–23
Mark 2:18–22
Martin Luther King, Jr., Day (U.S.A.)

16 TUESDAY
Weekday (#312)
I Samuel 16:1–13
Mark 2:23–28

17 WEDNESDAY
Anthony, abbot
MEMORIAL (#313)
I Samuel 17:32–33, 37, 40–51
Mark 3:1–6

18 THURSDAY
Weekday (#314)

1 Samuel 18:6–9; 19:1–7
Mark 3:7–12

Octave of Christian Unity begins.

19 FRIDAY
Weekday (#315)

1 Samuel 24:3–21
Mark 3:13–19

20 SATURDAY
Weekday (#316)

Fabian, pope and martyr
OPTIONAL MEMORIAL

Sebastian, martyr
OPTIONAL MEMORIAL

BVM
OPTIONAL MEMORIAL

2 Samuel 1:1–4, 11–12, 19,
23–27
Mark 3:20–21

21 SUNDAY
**Third Sunday in
Ordinary Time** (#68)

Isaiah 8, 23—9:3
1 Corinthians 1:10–13, 17
Matthew 4:12–23 or 4:12–17

St. Agnes's Day

"For Unity of Christians" and the beautiful preface for Christian unity (P76). This intention should figure prominently in the general intercessions. The Benedictine liturgist Godfrey Diekmann once said that *no* Sunday liturgy should pass without prayer for the unity of all the churches of Christ.

The liturgy committee could take the initiative in organizing and inviting participation in ecumenical services during this week. The most appropriate form is Morning or Evening Prayer, liturgies in which all Christians can share and in which Christians of many liturgical traditions are comfortable. Besides the tremendous number of Roman and Byzantine resources, certainly the Episcopal *Book of Common Prayer* and the *Lutheran Book of Worship* offer excellent forms of Evening Prayer. Another resource is *Ecumenical Services of Prayer* (Paulist Press). Pueblo Publishing Company offers the *Lectionary for the Christian People,* an inclusive language emendation of the Revised Standard Version Bible, the translation used by most Christian churches. New this past year from Pueblo are *Intercessions for the Christian People* and *Homilies for the Christian People.*

21 **Third Sunday in Ordinary Time.** USING THE SACRAMENTARY: Continue the same greeting, penitential rite, eucharistic prayer, invitation to communion and Lord's Prayer, and concluding rite from the Second through Fifth Sundays in Ordinary Time, weeks that are imbued with an Epiphany tone. We are within the octave of Christian Unity; the Preface for Christian Unity (P76) fits well today.

♦ THE YEAR OF MATTHEW: Readings from Matthew begin this week, and a schedule of selections from now until Lent lines up like this:

January 21:	Matthew 4:12–23
	He came to Capernaum.
January 28:	Matthew 5:1–12
	Blest are the poor in spirit.
February 4:	Matthew 5:13–16
	You are the light of the world.
February 11:	Matthew 5:17–37
	You have heard it said . . . but I say to you.
February 18:	Matthew 5:38–48
	Love your enemies.
February 25:	Matthew 6:24–34
	Be not anxious about tomorrow.

We will be proclaiming the Sermon on the Mount, the great charter of the reign of God, throughout this winter Ordinary Time. See the Introduction and Outline of the Gospel of Matthew in Ordinary Time, page 135.

♦ SUNDAYS DON'T HAVE "THEMES"! Cycle A today begins a semicontinuous reading from 1 Corinthians and from Matthew's Gospel. So in general, the second readings and the gospels have no relationship to each other. The introduction to the lectionary offers an often-overlooked liturgical principle in a discussion about why the framers of the lectionary did not give each Sunday a "theme":

An organic harmony of themes designed to aid homiletic instruction . . . would be in conflict with the genuine concern of liturgical celebration. The liturgy is always the celebration of the mystery of Christ and makes use of the word of God on the basis of its own tradition, guided not by merely logical or extrinsic concerns but by the desire to proclaim the gospel and to lead those who believe to the fullness of the truth. (#68)

The scriptures are not to be manipulated into tidy thematics or messages. However, because the gospel—in common with most literature—employs certain organizing images that ebb and flow throughout its pages, a week-by-week reading of a particular gospel gives to certain stretches of weeks a cohesiveness of imagery. The month of January when we read of the call and commissioning of disciples, or the month of November when we read the warnings of the end time are two examples of stretches of weeks with overarching imagery. That is why this *Sourcebook* repeatedly suggests that Sundays be prepared not individually but in blocks, taking advantage of the naturally occuring ebb and flow of scriptural imagery.

Adrian Nocent (*The Liturgical Year,* The Liturgical Press, 1977) presents an outline of such images and even points out where the second reading does or does not fit in. Remember, the first reading has been chosen (many regret this) to shed light on one or several aspects of the gospel. It would be a service to the community to provide at the beginning of winter and summer Ordinary Time a handy "home guide" to the scriptures of the coming Sundays.

◆ VOLUNTEER SUNDAY: The call of the first disciples provides an opportunity to call forth the talents and gifts of the community. If your parish wants to have an annual "Volunteer Sunday" when folks are encouraged to list their names and talents for future reference and calls to service, this Third Sunday in Ordinary Time is a good choice every year. Invite new volunteers to begin interviews/training for the various ministries. If last week saw a well-celebrated commissioning rite, this might be the opportune time to nudge others toward thoughts of community service.

25 Conversion of Paul. This feast concludes the octave of prayer for Christian unity.

28 Fourth Sunday in Ordinary Time. These next few Sundays present homilists with an opportunity to offer the community a period of reflection on some of the issues that the church has been facing with new intensity in recent years. The Beatitudes, of course, turn the world's conventional wisdom upside down. Next week's challenge is to be salt and light, which Isaiah defines as sheltering the homeless, clothing the naked, dealing with the oppression hidden from our sight only because it is right before our eyes. This is a fitting time to provide the community with a refresher (by way of homilies and handouts) concerning the universal or national or local church's teachings on the issues raised so powerfully in the Sermon on the Mount. LTP offers its annual publication *The Pastorals on Sundays,* each edition beginning on the First Sunday of Lent, with weekly excerpts from conciliar documents, papal encyclicals and the U.S. bishops' pastoral letters concerning the church's social teachings—what many ecumenical commentators have called the church's "best kept secret."

◆ USING THE SACRAMENTARY: The general intercessions should include intentions related to these social concerns, and their concluding prayer might be taken from the section in the back of the sacramentary entitled "Masses and Prayers for Various Needs and Occasions," such as #21, "For the Progress of Peoples," and

---

22 MONDAY
Weekday (#317)

Vincent, deacon and martyr
OPTIONAL MEMORIAL

2 Samuel 5:1–7, 10
Mark 3:22–30

17th anniversary of the U.S. Supreme Court's decision "Roe vs. Wade."

23 TUESDAY
Weekday (#318)

2 Samuel 6:12–15, 17–19
Mark 3:31–35

24 WEDNESDAY
Francis de Sales,
 bishop and doctor
MEMORIAL (#319)

2 Samuel 7:4–17
Mark 4:1–20

25 THURSDAY
Conversion of Paul, apostle
FEAST (#519)

Acts 22:3–16 or 9:1–22
Mark 16:15–18

Octave of Christian Unity ends.

26 FRIDAY
Timothy and Titus, bishops
MEMORIAL

2 Timothy 1:1–8
 or Titus 1:1–5 (#520)
Mark 4:26–34 (#321)

27 SATURDAY
Weekday (#322)

Angela Merici, Virgin
OPTIONAL MEMORIAL

BVM
OPTIONAL MEMORIAL

2 Samuel 12:1–7, 10–17
Mark 4:35–41

Lunar (Oriental) New Year begins.

28 SUNDAY
**Fourth Sunday in
 Ordinary Time** (#71)

Zephaniah 2:3; 3:12–13
1 Corinthians 1:26–31
Matthew 5:1–12

29 MONDAY

Weekday (#323)

2 Samuel 15:13–14, 30; 16:5–13

Mark 5:1–20

30 TUESDAY

Weekday (#324)

2 Samuel 18:9–10, 14, 24–25,
30—19:3

Mark 5:21–43

*Anniversary of the assassination
in 1948 of Mohandas Gandhi*

31 WEDNESDAY

John Bosco, priest

MEMORIAL (#325)

2 Samuel 24:2, 9–17

Mark 6:1–6

#22, "For Peace and Justice." Notice how the entrance antiphon continues to echo Epiphany in the image of the gathering of peoples. In today's first opening prayer, "men" can be "people." The alternative prayer is remarkably beautiful.

◆ TIMELY ATTENTION TO THE WORD: The introduction to the lectionary is poetic as it describes what the word in the assembly is supposed to be:

> In the hearing of God's word the church is built up and grows, and in the signs of the liturgical celebration God's many wonderful, past works in the history of salvation are symbolically presented anew. God in turn makes use of the assembly of the faithful who celebrate the liturgy in order that God's word may speed on in triumph and God's name be exalted among all peoples.

> Whenever, therefore, the church, gathered by the Holy Spirit for liturgical celebration, announces and proclaims the word of God, it has the experience of being a new people in whom the covenant made in the past is fulfilled. (#7)

How can we help this happen? The introduction gives the answer: "in the hearing" of the word, and "in the signs" of the celebration. During this relatively long winter Ordinary Time, planners might reflect on this "hearing" and these "signs." Where and with what is the word proclaimed? The document says:

> There must be a place in the church that is somewhat elevated, fixed, and of a suitable design and nobility. It should reflect the dignity of God's word and be a clear reminder to the people that in the Mass the table of God's word and of Christ's body is placed before them. The place for the readings must also truly help the people's listening and attention during the liturgy of the word. (#32)

> Either permanently or at least on occasions of greater solemnity, the lectern should be decorated simply and in keeping with its design.

> Since the lectern is the place from which the ministers proclaim the word of God, it must of its nature be reserved for the readings, responsorial psalm and the Easter proclamation (Exsultet). The lectern may rightly be used for the homily and the general intercessions, however, because of their close connection with the entire liturgy of the word. It is better for the commentator, cantor or director of singing, for example, not to use the lectern. (#33)

What does our lectern look like? Who uses it and for what purpose? Does the sound system work well? Is there only one lectern used to proclaim the scriptures, and is it clearly more important than the cantor's music stand? How is the lectern decorated?

> Since, in liturgical celebrations the books too serve as signs and symbols of the sacred, care must be taken to ensure that they are worthy and beautiful. (#35)

> Because of the dignity of the word of God, the books of readings used in the celebration are not to be replaced by other pastoral aids, for example, by leaflets printed for the faithful's preparation of the readings or for their personal meditation. (#37)

These are blunt words that forbid missalettes from being used at the lectern. Notice that the document does not leave room for these "leaflets" being used during worship. Reading along with the lector is alien to the spirit of liturgical proclamation in our tradition.

FEBRUARY

2 Feast of the Presentation of the Lord. This is a very important feast, worth any effort to celebrate well—perhaps with a "pep talk" on the previous Sunday, encouraging people to observe the day and assemble for an evening Mass or Evening Prayer scheduled today. It's a day for carols such as "Hark, the herald angels sing," with its reference to the "sun of righteousness," and "Joy to the world." In many countries today the créche is surrounded with potted spring flowers—before being dismantled. The day has its own preface. In the opening prayer, "man" can be "human." The collection "Music from Taizé, vol. 1" has a gorgeous *Nunc dimittis* that works well during today's blessing of candles and procession and can be used again as a recessional.

The feast is called Candlemas because the church's candles are blessed on this day; the spirit of the blessing calls for something larger than the typical Easter Vigil candles. The boxed "Candlemas candle" sets are often overpriced—who needs the box anyway? Check an Orthodox church supply store—they should have simple, sizable beeswax candles at reasonable prices. They also should have unbleached beeswax candles—the orange, natural-colored candles that many will remember were used around the coffin during funerals.

Perhaps people can bring more substantial candles from home, including the candle that will become the home Easter candle this year, blessed but not lit today. There are parishes that also pronounce a blessing over the parish's new paschal candle—something curiously excised from the *Exsultet* of the Easter Vigil—and over all the other candles the church will use during the year ahead. With its embrace of the Christmas season and its looking forward to Easter, this feast is a sort of keystone in the year.

The Italian sacramentary offers this introductory note:

> This feast of lights (cf. Luke 2:30–32) has its origins in the East where it is called "The Encounter" (Jesus with Simeon and Anna; the Lord with the Lord's people in their temple). This feast of the Lord's presentation, with the image of Simeon uttering his prophecy to Mary (Luke 2:33–35), both closes the Christmas season and sets us on the road that will lead to the paschal mystery.

◆ SINCE THIS DAY FALLS IN CATHOLIC SCHOOLS WEEK, it's the perfect day for the special parochial school liturgy—although the primary focus of the day must be the feast. See the many fine suggestions for this feast in the *Leader's Manual* for the *Hymnal for Catholic Students* (LTP/GIA, 1989). For several years now Andrew Ciferni, OPRAEM, has put together excellent guidelines for celebrating the Presentation and the January 31 memorial of John Bosco during Catholic Schools Week. This "Liturgy Guide" should be available through your diocesan education office from the National Catholic Education Association, or write the NCEA, Suite 100, 1077 30th Street NW, Washington, DC 20007-3852. The Guide is $1.25, prepaid.

3 Blase, bishop of Sebaste, martyr, fourth century. For the celebration of St. Blase and the blessing of throats, the United States Bishops' Committee on the Liturgy has provided a fine updating with forms for use during Mass and apart from Mass (as a liturgy of the word). This booklet should be available from

February 1990

1 THURSDAY
Weekday (#326)

1 Kings 2:1–4, 10–12
Mark 6:7–13

2 FRIDAY
Presentation of the Lord
FEAST (#524)

Malachi 3:1–4
Hebrew 2:14–18
Luke 2:22–40 or 2:22–32

Candlemas

Snowdrops

3 SATURDAY
Weekday (#328)

Blase, bishop and martyr
OPTIONAL MEMORIAL

Ansgar, bishop
OPTIONAL MEMORIAL

BVM
OPTIONAL MEMORIAL

1 Kings 3:4–13
Mark 6:30–34

4 SUNDAY
**Fifth Sunday in
  Ordinary Time** (#74)

Isaiah 58:7–10
I Corinthians 2:1–5
Matthew 5:13–16

5 MONDAY
Agatha, virgin and martyr
MEMORIAL (#329)

I Kings 8:1–7, 9–13
Mark 6:53–56

6 TUESDAY
Paul Miki and companions,
  martyrs
MEMORIAL (#330)

I Kings 8:22–23, 27–30
Mark 7:1–13

7 WEDNESDAY
Weekday (#331)

I Kings 10:1–10
Mark 7:14–23

8 THURSDAY
Weekday (#332)

Jerome Emiliani
OPTIONAL MEMORIAL

I Kings 11:4–13
Mark 7:24–30

9 FRIDAY
Weekday (#333)

I Kings 11:29–32; 12:19
Mark 7:31–37

your diocesan worship office, or write: Publications Service, United States Catholic Conference, 3211 Fourth Street NE, Washington DC 20017-1194; Ask for publication #993. Beginning this year, this rite is also available in the *Book of Blessings* (available from several publishers).

The Rite of Blessing of Throats offers this historical perspective:

> According to various accounts, Blase was a physician before becoming a bishop. His cult spread throughout the entire church in the Middle Ages because he was reputed to have miraculously cured a little boy who nearly died because of a fishbone in his throat. From the eighth century he has been invoked on behalf of the sick, especially those afflicted with illnesses of the throat.

Although blessing throats is a fitting custom in the middle of the flu season, what is given more attention in your parish's liturgical life—yesterday's feast or today's memorial?

4 Fifth Sunday in Ordinary Time. WORKING TOWARD LENT TOGETHER: Jesus speaks bluntly about prayer, fasting and almsgiving in the Sermon on the Mount that we are reading over these weeks, and these three lenten disciplines must be the heart of any "lenten program" the parish undertakes.

What resources have been prepared for all the households in the parish to enter into Lent and beyond? Three specific items for distribution to individuals and families are available from Liturgy Training Publications. 1. *An Introduction to Lent and Eastertime* is a 16-page booklet that describes what it means to keep Lent and Eastertime with the church with attention to prayer and fasting and almsgiving. 2. *Keeping Lent, Triduum and Eastertime* is a pocket-sized prayer book for all the days of these seasons. 3. *Paschal Mission* is an every-Sunday handout that has lively reflections on the scriptures and a day-by-day calendar for Ash Wednesday through Pentecost activity.

Perhaps the liturgy team could invite other groups of parish leaders to a presentation and discussion on how Lent (and the Triduum and the great Fifty Days that follow it) can be *the* priority from February through June. It's important to muster all forces so that everyone is proceeding in the same direction; such coordination is an important pastoral role. And it's important to include those who may not at first see how the paschal season can imbue all of parish life, affecting the nonliturgical aspects of parish life such as social clubs, charity and justice ministries, youth and senior groups, the school and religious education, and even the janitorial staff.

Initial discussion should center on freeing up time: What can be put on the back burner—and what *must* be let go—during March and April? We can expect the world around us to make it difficult to keep Lent, Triduum and Eastertime, but it's ridiculous when our own parish's business-as-usual schedule makes it difficult. Once folks are on the same wavelength, we can begin to look at prayer, fasting and almsgiving from both a communal and individual perspective.

◆ A LENTEN COVENANT: Some parishes put together an attractively printed brochure, calling it their *Parish Lenten Covenant*. This brochure can be handed out or mailed as early as this Sunday so that individuals can ponder and prepare the coming season. The Covenant can offer suggestions for communal and household prayer, fasting and almsgiving, with an eye toward ways in which these disciplines can be embraced by individuals for the spiritual welfare of the whole parish. The Covenant can also include complete schedules of parish liturgies and devotions, brief explanations of some of the less familiar rites (such as communal penance or the catechumenal rites), an overview of the often surprising canons regarding the lenten disciplines (introducing people to the spirit of these laws rather than the bare-minimum regulations that most dioceses publish), and concrete ideas (with names and addresses) for almsgiving to local and global concerns.

Many parishes ask all members to pledge toward common lenten disciplines, such as a mealtime grace, fasting from eggs or salt, turning the TV off on the Wednesdays of the season, contributing to one or two specific charities. Any such common observances need to be chosen with care and presented with enthusiasm and sensitivity, avoiding anything that would make them appear to be "this year's gimmick." Individual written pledges toward communal disciplines could be gathered on Ash Wednesday or the First Sunday of Lent. Perhaps these pledges could be a form that must be filled out and returned to church—part of the Lenten Covenant.

◆ JANUARY AND FEBRUARY ARE THE BEST TIME OF YEAR to schedule parish social events. Carnival time, this year spanning most of winter, is a great way to build enthusiasm for the approaching paschal season. That means that the annual parish play, luau, fashion show, salad luncheon, auction, Las Vegas night or what-have-you belongs to this time of year and can be made an annual part of the carnival merriment. It takes some education and encouragement to help people think of these social events as part of not just the secular calendar but a fitting part of the liturgical calendar as well.

11 Sixth Sunday in Ordinary Time. USING THE SACRAMENTARY: Notice how the entrance antiphons for the next three Sundays take on a lenten cast. If your parish follows the principle encouraged so often in this *Sourcebook* of preparing the liturgy—choosing the same songs, psalm, entrance rites, eucharistic prayer, concluding rite, etc.—for several Sundays within a block of weeks rather than for each individual Sunday, the next three Sundays are one of these blocks.

"Mankind" can be "humankind" in the alternative opening prayer today. From now until Lent, the general intercessions could include a petition for the parish's growth in grace during the Forty Days ahead, as well as a petition for catechumens and candidates, although such a petition should be a regular part of the intercessions. The first eucharistic prayer for reconciliation would be a fine choice the next three weeks. Its preface is perfect:

> Now is the time for your people to turn back to you
> and to be renewed in Christ your Son,
> a time of grace and reconciliation.
> You invite us to serve the human family
> by opening our hearts to the fullness of your
>   Holy Spirit.

◆ A LENTEN COUNTDOWN: Today and the next two Sundays were in former times designated Septuagesima, Sexagesima and Quinquagesima—roughly 70, 60 and 50 days from Easter. (In Latin, "Lent" is Quadragesima, meaning "40-day span"—the root of our word "quarantine," which suggests that Lent is a time set

---

10 SATURDAY
Scholastica, virgin
MEMORIAL (#334)
1 Kings 12:26–32; 13:33–34
Mark 8:1–10

Tu b'Sh'vat, the Jewish New Year of Trees

11 SUNDAY
Sixth Sunday in Ordinary Time (#77)
Sirach 15:15–20
1 Corinthians 2:6–10
Matthew 5:17–37 or 5:20–22, 27–28, 33–34, 37

12 MONDAY
Weekday (#335)
James 1:1–11
Mark 8:11–13

Lincoln's Birthday

13 TUESDAY
Weekday (#336)
James 1:12–18
Mark 8:14–21

14 WEDNESDAY
Cyril, monk, and
  Methodius, bishop
MEMORIAL (#337)
James 1:19–27
Mark 8:22–26

St. Valentine's Day

15 THURSDAY
Weekday (#338)
James 2:1–9
Mark 8:27–33

16 FRIDAY
Weekday (#339)
James 2:14–24, 26
Mark 8:34—9:1

17 SATURDAY
Weekday (#340)

Seven Founders of the Order
  of Servites
OPTIONAL MEMORIAL

BVM
OPTIONAL MEMORIAL

James 3:1–10
Mark 9:2–13

18 SUNDAY
Seventh Sunday in Ordinary Time (#80)

Leviticus 19:1–2, 17–18
1 Corinthians 3:16–23
Matthew 5:38–48

19 MONDAY
Weekday (#341)

James 3:13–18
Mark 9:14–29

Presidents Day (U.S.A.)

20 TUESDAY
Weekday (#342)

James 4:1–10
Mark 9:30–37

21 WEDNESDAY
Weekday (#343)

Peter Damian, bishop and doctor
OPTIONAL MEMORIAL

James 4:13–17
Mark 9:38–40

22 THURSDAY
Chair of Peter, apostle
FEAST (#535)

1 Peter 5:1–4
Matthew 16:13–19

Washington's Birthday

23 FRIDAY
Polycarp, bishop and martyr
MEMORIAL (#345)

James 5:9–12
Mark 10:1–12

24 SATURDAY
Weekday (#346)

BVM
OPTIONAL MEMORIAL

James 5:13–20
Mark 10:13–16

25 SUNDAY
Eighth Sunday in Ordinary Time (#83)

Isaiah 49:14–15
1 Corinthians 4:1–5
Matthew 6:24–34

apart for introspection and healing.) The number 70 signified the 70 years of the Babylonian exile (Jeremiah 25:11; 29:10; Daniel 9:2), one of the strongest of lenten images. Perhaps it was wise that the liturgical reformers did away with these many-syllable Sunday titles, but this countdown warned a parish that Lent was upon us—a necessary warning.

◆ WARNINGS TAKE MANY FORMS: Remove clutter from vestibules, gathering places, parish halls and bulletin boards. Let colorful posters proclaim the approaching season and invite participation at every level. It's none too soon to dry-clean the lenten vesture—and to repair and clean the vesture used on Palm Sunday and during the Triduum. It's time for candle and palm orders, and for tracking down suppliers of anything out of the ordinary that can enhance paschal worship, such as unbleached candles, date palm fronds, windguard followers for processional candles, or attractive baptismal candles and robes. Make sure that the liturgical books to be used in the weeks ahead are in good shape, with the latest editions on hand. Any parish-wide mailings can be announced today and mailed out tomorrow. Reintroduce the catechumens and candidates publicly, and share the hopes and joys and fears of their journey to the Easter sacraments.

18 **Seventh Sunday in Ordinary Time.** See last week's notes on using the sacramentary and other suggestions for worship and for preparing the assembly for Lent. Church housecleaning should extend to the sacristy and worship hall. It's impossible to embrace Lent in its sober simplicity and seriousness of purpose while climbing over accumulated junk. This is the week for all such spring cleaning.

◆ MUSIC REHEARSAL: Provide an opportunity for the assembly to practice the music of the coming seasons. If held before Mass, any such rehearsal needs to be somewhat low-key and brief. One parish holds an annual prelenten evening of song during which the assembly receives spirited instructions about the history and lore surrounding much of the music to be sung during the Triduum. Attendance is fine—primarily because the evening is grand fun for all involved. The attendees become leaven in the assembly, encouraging everyone to sing.

22 **Chair of Peter.** Celebrated since the fourth century, the feast is a sign of the unity of the church—a Christian expression of an old Roman feast of the *Paternalia,* an ancestors' festival. An interesting coincidence places it on George Washington's birthday, the "father" of the United States.

23 **Polycarp, bishop of Smyrna, martyr, 69–158.** A disciple of John the apostle, Polycarp was known as one of the apostolic fathers because he was an immediate disciple of the apostles. Polycarp means "many fruits," and marks the traditional day the sap begins to rise in trees: Maple syrup making is a wonderful sign of the approaching spring throughout the north. Polycarp wrote: "United in truth, show the Lord's own gentleness in your dealings with one another, and look down on no one. If you can do good, do not put it off, because almsgiving frees one from death."

25 **Eighth Sunday in Ordinary Time.** USING THE SACRAMENTARY: See the notes on February 11 for suggestions and for ways to prepare the assembly for Lent. "Men" can be "people" in the alternative opening prayer. Solemn Blessing 12 or 14 is appropriate today, and the dismissal can include Easter's double Alleluia.

◆ CHOOSING BETWEEN THE OPENING PRAYERS always requires a careful reading. Do this out loud, and listen to yourself. In general the alternative prayers are longer than the first prayers. Sometimes the first prayers are too terse, with little to capture the imagination. And sometimes the alternative prayers are too convoluted, difficult to grasp.

◆ IT'S CARNIVAL SUNDAY! Today is the last Sunday for the Alleluia until Easter. Some communities (children and adults) have great fun saying goodbye to it with due pomp and fanfare. When it rings out again at the Easter Vigil it will truly be the victory shout of a people born again of water and the Spirit. Some parishes usher out a great banner with the word "Alleluia" on it (one of the few times words belong on a banner), or they "bury" the Alleluia—a medieval custom—by locking up the word in some sort of tomb or actually burying it in the ground. This ceremony has its own song: See the hymn "Alleluia, song of gladness," #413 in *Worship,* third edition. If you don't want to teach this melody to your parish, the words fit the song "Praise, my soul, the king of heaven."

The annual prelenten carnival isn't just an excuse for a good time—although we need all the help we can get to drive the cold winter away. A Mardi Gras potluck supper on Shrove Tuesday or this weekend, with a crowning of the carnival queen and king, a parish play, dance, bonfire, pantomime, magic show—anything—helps the parish come together to begin Lent.

27 Today is Mardi Gras, "Greasy Tuesday," a day needed by all those who will take lenten fasting seriously. Every culture adds its own gifts to the fun. At the very least, today's liturgy deserves some of the ceremony added to liturgies last weekend, especially the many Alleluias. Today is also called "pancake day," because the animal-product ingredients of pancakes were forbidden fruit throughout Lent. They had to be eaten up in the form of pancakes, crepes, doughnuts and crullers. To anyone responsible for parish fund-raisers: A pancake supper or doughnut fry today or this past weekend is a traditional part of carnival.

LENT

28 Ash Wednesday. For more information on Lent, see pages 46–64 in "The Seasons."

"The key word for this day is 'turn.' 'Turn to God,' Joel says, 'and perhaps God will turn to you and leave behind a blessing.' Human turning in selflessness hopes to meet God's free turning in blessing. In Christ God has turned to us that we might turn to each other and all together return to God." *(Saint Andrew Bible Missal)*

◆ THE ASHES USED TODAY come from the palm branches blessed the preceding year for Palm Sunday. The old gives way to the new. Some parishes make a ritual out of this palm burning; that can be done during a carnival bonfire yesterday or last weekend. The odor of burning palms has a unique, acrid quality that deserves to be part of the preparation for Lent. However, including the burning of palms as a part of the day's liturgy is not traditional. Lively fire today is not a

26 MONDAY
Weekday (#347)

I Peter 1:3–9
Mark 10:17–27
Orthodox Lent begins.

27 TUESDAY
Weekday (#348)

I Peter 1:10–16
Mark 10:28–31
Mardi Gras–Shrove Tuesday
Carnival ends.

28 WEDNESDAY
Ash Wednesday (#220)

Joel 2:12–18
2 Corinthians 5:20—6:2
Matthew 6:1–6, 16–18

Pussywillows

symbol; dead ashes are—ashes that wait for the fire of Easter. Note that Ash Wednesday services need not be eucharists, but even when the eucharist is not celebrated, the full liturgy of the word takes place whenever ashes are distributed. One parish places the six old funeral candles around a table on which is placed a large earthen bowl with the ashes. This is set up in the main aisle, not near the altar or ambo, and that is where the blessing is proclaimed—incensing the ashes rather than sprinkling them with water.

◆ PEOPLE SHOULD FEEL THE LENTEN SPIRIT TODAY BEFORE A WORD IS UTTERED OR A NOTE SUNG. Silence and song, movement and melodies, vesture and visuals must all be woven into the tapestry which, *over many years,* the community will come to call "Lent." Most parishes will want to ensure that from this very first day the worship environment is in its lenten array. Some parishes may find it better simply to strip the church for this day, adding any lenten array sometime before Sunday. Ash Wednesday is unique within Lent in the way a beginning of a journey is different from the journey itself.

◆ THE ASH WEDNESDAY LITURGY: The gathering rite is sober and simple—no penitential rite today, no Gloria throughout Lent—austerely announcing that we are about serious business. After the liturgy of the word (even when there is no eucharist to follow), ashes are blessed and imposed. No formal instruction is provided in the sacramentary to introduce this rite, which is surprising considering that well-written instructions are offered on Passion/Palm Sunday and even on the Presentation. The following Ash Wednesday instruction is adapted from a model provided by the Episcopal church:

> Dear People of God: We are approaching the days of our Lord's death, burial and resurrection, and so it is the custom of the church to make ready for these holiest of holy days by a season of penitence and fasting. This season of Lent is a time in which catechumens are prepared for holy baptism. It was also a time when those who have been separated from the body of the faithful were reconciled by penitence and forgiveness, and restored to the fellowship of the church. The coming Easter sacraments of initiation and reconciliation bring a message of pardon and absolution set forth in the gospel of our Savior, and of the need that all Christians continually have to renew their repentance and the promises of their baptism.
>
> I invite you, therefore, in the name of the church, to the observance of a holy Lent, by self-examination and self-denial; by prayer, fasting and the giving of charity; and by reading and meditating on God's holy word.

The music for the distribution of ashes should not be metrical hymns about Lent, such as "These forty days"; rather, the music should be processional in character, such as the penitential psalms, perhaps a Taizé ostinato with interpolated psalm verses. The words "Remember, [hu]man, that you are dust . . ." are powerful; it's difficult to understand why the sacramentary offers an alternative. Society tends to deny death or garland it with flowers. Ash Wednesday is a stark *memento mori,* a reminder of death. The day should slap us in the face with this threat: You are human, and you are going to die. Get your priorities straight and run, don't walk, in your journey to Easter.

Lenten Preface IV is prescribed for this day, although Preface III also speaks of self-denial as a form of expressing thanks, and it brings in the social dimension of fasting. (See the note about the language of Preface IV on page 53, as well as other discussion of the lenten Mass and Evening Prayer.)

MARCH

4 **First Sunday of Lent.** For more information on Lent, see pages 46–64 in "The Seasons," especially the penitential procession for this day described on page 64.

The Declaration of Intent within the Rite of Welcoming the Candidates (RCIA, 419) is a challenge to the entire community to enter into this season:

> Blessed be the God and Father of our Lord Jesus Christ, who in his great mercy has given us a new birth unto a living hope, a hope which draws its life from Christ's resurrection from the dead. By baptism into Christ Jesus, this hope of glory became your own. Christ opened for you the way of the gospel that leads to eternal life. Now, under the guidance of the Holy Spirit, you desire to continue that journey of faith.

The text then includes a sober invitation for all the faithful to commit themselves to this "journey of faith" during Lent: "Are you prepared to reflect more deeply on the mystery of your baptism, to listen with us to the apostles' instruction, and to join with us in a life of prayer and service?"

◆ USING THE SACRAMENTARY: The alternative opening prayer suits this Sunday's scriptures. The prayer would be more inclusive if "man" were "human beings," and "him" and "he" were "them" and "they." The Prayer over the People #6 can be used throughout the next four weeks.

Choosing a preface during this season can be confusing. The sacramentary first has four prefaces useful any lenten day from now until the fifth Sunday. After these four come prefaces composed for specific Sundays. However, for the third, fourth and fifth Sundays these prefaces are useful only in Year A—this year. In addition, the Preface of the Passion of the Lord I is used on weekdays during the fifth week of Lent, and the Preface of the Passion of the Lord II is used on Monday, Tuesday and Wednesday of the sixth week of Lent. Passion (Palm) Sunday has its own preface. Today's choice is easy: the Preface of the First Sunday of Lent, useful in years A, B or C.

◆ THE CATECHUMENS/ELECT: Their journey toward new birth invites those of us who are already baptized to travel again along a road most of us were too young to remember, to a font in which we experienced a dying and rising that the world seems bent on erasing from our memories. The presence of the catechumens challenges us to go back to the brink of the place where once we took the baptismal plunge—this Easter and every Easter.

The elect are—for communities blest by their presence—living symbols during these weeks. What if you have no catechumens? Certainly, with or without, this is the season to look at the community's internal life and its outreach in evangelization and witness. Or what if you have catechumens but no coordinated way of bringing them into the community? Then see Karen Hinman Powell's *How to Form a Catechumenate Team* (LTP); it will help you recruit, form and maintain the teamwork that supports those seeking membership in the church.

March 1990

1 THURSDAY
Thursday after Ash Wednesday
(#221)
Deuteronomy 30:15–20
Luke 9:22–25
St. David's Day

2 FRIDAY
Friday after Ash Wednesday (#222)
Isaiah 58:1–9
Matthew 9:14–15
World Day of Prayer

3 SATURDAY
Saturday after Ash Wednesday
(#223)
Katharine Drexel, virgin
OPTIONAL MEMORIAL (U.S.A.)
Isaiah 58:9–14
Luke 5:27–32

4 SUNDAY
First Sunday of Lent (#22)
Genesis 2:7–9; 3:1–7
Romans 5:12–19 or 5:12, 17–19
Matthew 4:1–11
Rite of Election
St. Casimir's Day

5 MONDAY

Lenten Weekday (#225)

Leviticus 19:1–2, 11–18
Matthew 25:31–46

6 TUESDAY

Lenten Weekday (#226)

Isaiah 55:10–11
Matthew 6:7–15

7 WEDNESDAY

Lenten Weekday (#227)

Perpetua and Felicity, martyrs
OPTIONAL MEMORIAL

Jonah 3:1–10
Luke 11:29–32

8 THURSDAY

Lenten Weekday (#228)

John of God, religious
OPTIONAL MEMORIAL

Esther C:12, 14–16, 23–25
Matthew 7:7–12

9 FRIDAY

Lenten Weekday (#229)

Francis of Rome, religious
OPTIONAL MEMORIAL

Ezekiel 18:21–28
Matthew 5:20–26

*Purim (meaning "lots") begins
at sundown, the Jewish feast
of Esther and Mordechai.*

10 SATURDAY

Lenten Weekday (#230)

Deuteronomy 26:16–19
Matthew 5:43–48

11 SUNDAY

Second Sunday of Lent (#25)

Genesis 12:1–4
2 Timothy 1:8–10
Matthew 17:1–9

◆ THE RITE OF "ELECTION" OR "ENROLLMENT OF NAMES" takes place today (or sometime this week). The questions posed to the sponsors during the rite of election provide an examination of conscience for the whole community: Have these candidates listened to the word? Have they translated it into action? Have they been part of the community's life of prayer and service? This rite ordinarily takes place on a diocesan level at the cathedral, and if that's the case, a preparatory rite in the parish is suggested. See the RCIA, "Sending of the Catechumens for Election," 106. Parishes that are preparing baptized but uncatechized adults for penance, confirmation and eucharist should study the RCIA, 446ff. This is the "Rite of Calling the Candidates to Continuing Conversion." Although combining rites for catechumens and candidates runs the risk of overburdening the liturgy and confusing the ritual, parishes that are preparing both catechumens and candidates, and that do not hold separate rites at separate times for these two groups, can make use of the "Parish Celebration for Sending Catechumens for Election and Candidates for Recognition by the Bishop," found in Appendix I of the RCIA.

Make sure the parish owns the beautiful *Book of the Elect* (Collegeville: Liturgical Press) or has created something equally worthy that is used for the enrollment of names and sometimes taken to the cathedral celebration by the parish catechumenate director.

10 **Purim, the festival of lots, begins at sundown.** This is a Jewish holiday that falls a month before Passover. It too is a festival of liberation, albeit a bit more raucous, a rejoicing in the events detailed in the Book of Esther. Queen Esther and her uncle Mordechai awaited the destruction of their people, but the destroyer was himself destroyed! They mortified themselves in ashes, but their fast became a feast! Interestingly, one of the few times the church reads publicly from Esther comes each year on the Thursday of the first week of Lent.

11 **Second Sunday of Lent.** The transfiguration of the Lord is celebrated on August 6 in both Roman and Orthodox traditions. The Lutherans have placed this feast on the Sunday preceding Lent, recognizing that this gospel event is an epiphany (thus closing an "Epiphany Season") that turns our eyes toward Jerusalem, to the cross and resurrection. That is the function of our hearing the transfiguration story today: It turns our gaze toward the mountain of Calvary. The story calls to mind the shining robes and candles of baptism. Is someone in the parish sewing ample baptismal garments? What will the elect wear before and during their baptism? Be sure that fat candles—nothing other than beeswax—have been ordered for those to be baptized at the Vigil. (The smallest size, plain paschal candles are good.) You might also order candle followers (beeswax drips miserably without one) and perhaps even holders to fit these candles as a parish gift to the newly baptized.

◆ USING THE SACRAMENTARY: The alternative opening prayer presents the imagery of this Sunday most sharply: "Restore our sight that we might look upon your Son who calls us to repentance and a change of heart." The Preface for the Second Sunday of Lent (not to be confused with the lenten Preface II) echoes today's gospel.

◆ PENITENTIAL RITE FOR THE CANDIDATES: Those parishes accustomed to celebrating the scrutiny rites for the elect on the next three Sundays should consider the use this Sunday of one of the rites that are part of the "Penitential Rite (Scrutiny)," RCIA, 459ff., for those who are baptized but uncatechized. Paragraph 463 of the RCIA reads:

> This penitential rite is intended solely for celebrations with baptized adults preparing for confirmation and eucharist or reception into the full communion of the Catholic church. Because the prayer of exorcism in the three scrutinies for catechumens who have received the church's election properly belongs to the elect and uses numerous images referring to their approaching baptism, those scrutinies of the elect and this penitential rite for those preparing for confirmation and eucharist have been kept separate and distinct.

In the rite of election the RCIA provides a "combined" rite, with catechumens and those already baptized at one service but always treated as separate groups; however, no combined rites are provided for the scrutinies. The scrutinies are only for those to be baptized. This is one reason that the parish staff and the catechumenate team must study the RCIA carefully as a whole.

17 **Patrick, bishop (385–461).** Patrick was born in Britain, but was kidnapped and sold into slavery in pagan Ireland. Six years after his abduction he escaped and returned to his homeland. After studying for the priesthood, he felt compelled to return to Ireland, bringing with him Christianity.

Patrick's feast day has strong lenten connections. The famous shamrock was a teaching device for the catechumens preparing to be baptized at Easter in the name of the Trinity. The legend of Patrick's chasing the snakes out of Ireland is but an image of Christ, who in his death, burial and resurrection routed the powers of hell. Green became the ritual color associated with penitents returning to the church at Easter, much as white is associated with the newly baptized. Patrick kindled the Celtic May Day bonfire as part of the *lucernarium* ritual of the Easter Vigil. Any parish observance of this day should have, as in Ireland, a strong lenten character. In most of Ireland, fish, not corned beef, is customary today as a symbol for Christ; it is served with a great bannock bread marked with the sign of the cross.

18 **Third Sunday of Lent.** USING THE SACRAMENTARY: The alternative opening prayer is a bit wordy; "brothers" should be "brothers and sisters." Use the Preface of the Third Sunday of Lent. Notice within the sacramentary how often prayer, fasting and almsgiving are echoed in the lenten texts. Obviously, something more intense is being referred to than once-a-week Friday abstinence. It's as if our prayer texts are a continual pep talk for the three lenten disciplines, asking God for and reminding all of us about the strength and inner conviction required for real fasting, almsgiving till it hurts and ceaseless prayer. What is the parish doing to teach about and encourage people in the discipline of genuine fasting and in the almsgiving and prayer that must accompany the fast?

◆ THE LITURGY DURING WHICH THE FIRST SCRUTINY IS CELEBRATED uses proper sacramentary texts found under "Ritual Masses. The Scrutinies." The names of the godparents of the elect must be mentioned in the special insert for Eucharistic Prayer I. The scrutinies are explained in the RCIA in this way:

> The scrutinies . . . are rites for self-searching and repentance and have above all a spiritual purpose. The scrutinies are meant to uncover, then heal all that is

12 MONDAY
Lenten Weekday (#231)
Daniel 9:4–10
Luke 6:36–38

13 TUESDAY
Lenten Weekday (#232)
Isaiah 1:10, 16–20
Matthew 23:1–12

14 WEDNESDAY
Lenten Weekday (#233)
Jeremiah 18:18–20
Matthew 20:17–28

15 THURSDAY
Lenten Weekday (#234)
Jeremiah 17:5–10
Luke 16:19–31

16 FRIDAY
Lenten Weekday (#235)
Genesis 37:3–4, 12–13, 17–28
Matthew 21:33–43, 45–46

17 SATURDAY
Lenten Weekday (#236)
Patrick, bishop
OPTIONAL MEMORIAL
Micah 7:14–15, 18–20
Luke 15:1–3, 11–32

18 SUNDAY
Third Sunday of Lent (#28)
Exodus 17:3–7
Romans 5:1–2, 5–8
John 4:4–42 or 4–15, 19–26, 39, 40–42

First Scrutiny

weak, defective, or sinful in the hearts of the elect; to bring out, then strengthen all that is upright, strong, and good. (141)

Presiders and all who prepare the liturgy should note carefully the order of the scrutiny rite. See 141ff. in the RCIA, and also 291ff. for special notes on the scrutiny rites when children are being initiated. The following is an outline of the scrutiny rite, beginning at the conclusion of the homily:

Invitation to Prayer. The elect and their godparents gather before the presider and the assembly. The presider invites the assembly to pray for the elect (very specifically that they be given a spirit of repentance, a sense of sin, the true freedom of God's children); he invites the elect to bow or kneel and pray. Silent prayer is to continue "for some time." Clearly, this is important and needs careful preparation. The presider, too, needs to enter into the silence and the prayer. As these scrutiny rites become annual expectations on the middle three Sundays of Lent, they should bring the expectation (much like the principal Mass on Palm Sunday or the Easter Vigil) that nearly everyone in the parish tries to be there. After all, this is our doing. This is the season of intense work together. These are our elect, and the business of this parish right now is to be here around them. Is the liturgy longer than usual? You bet it is! Will anyone notice? Not if we immerse ourselves in the proper celebration of word, scrutiny and eucharist.

Intercession for the Elect. Godparents place their hands on the shoulders of the elect, and the intercessions begin. Note that these are prayers *for* the elect and not the usual general intercessions. Separate prayers, based on the gospels, are provided for each Sunday the scrutinies are celebrated. The elect themselves are not to pray these prayers; rather, they themselves are being prayed for.

Exorcism. A strong and important part of the rite, this consists of two prayers (different options are provided for each Sunday). Between the prayers, the presider places his hands on each of the elect in unhurried silence. The rite suggests that the exorcism be concluded with an appopriate psalm or song. The community might select one of the suggested psalms, find a setting, and use it at each of the scrutinies (and at other gatherings of the elect during Lent, and perhaps once again within the Easter Vigil).

Dismissal. A peculiarly worded optional text is provided if the elect are not dismissed—an unfortunate option that goes against the intention of the other scrutiny texts, indeed, the spirit of the entire RCIA: Participation at eucharist, and not just reception of communion, is the sealing of initiation. Christian tradition insists that participation in eucharist is something baptized people can do and the unbaptized can't.

The faithful then continue the liturgy with the general intercessions. The RCIA, 156, allows that "for pastoral reasons these general intercessions and the profession of faith may be omitted." Perhaps the length of the scrutiny rite (which has included a form of intercessory prayer) is what the rite has in mind as a "pastoral reason." Still, something is broken, incomplete, if the baptized do not offer their Sunday intercessions for the church and for the world. If "Mass gets too long" (the people who complain about the length of liturgy are going to have a miserable time in heaven), consider forgoing the recessional song or the entrance song, or shortening the homily before forgoing the intercessions.

◆ IF THE PRESENTATION OF THE CREED IS TO TAKE PLACE THIS WEEK, and that of the Lord's Prayer during the fifth week, announce this and invite the community's participation. Time, day and place should be known to all: These rites lose much of their power when the community into which the elect are being baptized is not there. These rites will be found at 157 and 178 in the RCIA, but also 104 and 105 concerning the times of the presentations. Consult Nocent's *The Liturgical Year* for commentaries with rich references to these celebrations from ages past. The RCIA has notes on the presentations at 147–149.

◆ A CAUTION FOR THOSE WHO PLAN THE WORSHIP ENVIRONMENT: The next three Sundays we hear about the woman at the well, the man born blind and the raising of Lazarus. The great Johannine words "water," "light" and "life" recur throughout these gospels—and please notice that no particular word is unique to any one Sunday. Sometimes one can find in a few popular liturgical resources the suggestion that we incorporate symbols of water, light and life in the worship environment during the next three weeks. That's the same mistake as thinking that liturgy needs a "theme" and that such themes can be captured in a word. It's wrong to misuse imagery like this. For example, it would be wrong to add a sprinkling rite to a lenten Sunday just to capitalize on the word "water," or to fill the church with candles just because the gospel mentions "light," or to hang butterflies all over the place to drive home the word "life."

Lent is a season of darkness, of drought, of reminders of death, a season of yearning for purification and illumination for the elect and for all the baptized. Such lenten thirst is not slaked by tap water put into pretty bowls and scattered around the church, and its darkness is not enlightened by a bunch of candles used as decoration. During *Pascha,* the holy night of initiation, we will kindle a great fire and follow behind a great candle. We will witness the elect pass over the water into the land of the living—and this is the water and light that will shine from our candles and be poured over our bodies throughout Easter's Fifty Days.

◆ IT'S HIGH TIME TO POST SCHEDULES! By now the entire parish should have received a schedule of the Triduum liturgies and other activities—with a plea to mark all calendars. Also by now the various liturgical ministers and other folks helping in all the many ways needed should know who they are and have received a schedule of rehearsals. Is the parish hosting fasting meals during the Triduum and an Easter breakfast after the Vigil? Are there plans to accommodate special transportation needs for some parishioners? How are the various groups of the parish being united through the coming holy days—including seniors, youth, and students and teachers in parish school and religious education—and is their attendance encouraged? Especially, how can youth and children be integrated into the preparations and be enabled to share their unique gifts?

19 **Joseph, Husband of Mary.** He is the patron of the universal church, of fathers and of a happy death. The preface for the day sensitively ponders the life of St. Joseph: "He is that just man, that wise and loyal servant, whom you placed at the head of your family. With a husband's love he cherished Mary, the virgin Mother of God. With fatherly care he watched over Jesus Christ your Son, conceived by the power of the Holy Spirit." Notice how this first week of spring is made rich with the gospel stories of annunciation. This past Sunday, be sure to announce these two solemnities of Joseph and of Annunciation.

◆ JOSEPH TABLES: This splendid custom is meant to combine the three lenten disciplines in a single event: prayer, fasting and almsgiving. Prayers and songs—both for Joseph and for Lent—are customary. The Table features lenten meatless—and some would insist completely vegetarian—meals. A collection is made for the poor, not to pay for the food.

19 MONDAY
Joseph, Husband of Mary
SOLEMNITY (#543)

2 Samuel 7:4–5, 12–14, 16
Romans 4:13, 16–18, 22
Matthew 1:16, 18–21, 24
 or Luke 2:41–51

20 TUESDAY
Lenten Weekday (#239)

Daniel 3:25, 34–43
Matthew 18:21–35

Spring Equinox

21 WEDNESDAY
Lenten Weekday (#240)

Deuteronomy 4:1, 5–9
Matthew 5:17–19

22 THURSDAY
Lenten Weekday (#241)

Jeremiah 7:23–28
Luke 11:14–23

23 FRIDAY
Lenten Weekday (#242)

Turibius de Mogrovejo, bishop
OPTIONAL MEMORIAL

Hosea 14:2–10
Mark 12:28–34

24 SATURDAY
Annunciation of the Lord
SOLEMNITY (#545)

Isaiah 7:10–14
Hebrews 10:4–10
Luke 1:26–38

*Tenth anniversary of the
assassination of Oscar Romero
of El Salvador.*

Glory of the snow

25 SUNDAY
Fourth Sunday of Lent (#31)

1 Samuel 16:1, 6–7, 10–13
Ephesians 5:8–14
John 9:1–41 or 9:1, 6–9, 13–17,
34–38

Second Scrutiny

Laetare Sunday

24 Annunciation of the Lord. This solemnity, with which the church binds together the paschal and Christmas seasons, is transferred from March 25. Remember the custom, as on Christmas Day, of a solemn genuflection during the Creed. Evening Prayer would be an opportunity to sing many wonderful Annunciation carols such as the medieval "Angelus ad virginem," the Basque "The angel Gabriel from heaven came," or the Dutch "Linden tree carol."

Why do we celebrate a "Christmas" feast here in the midst of Lent? Thomas Talley offers an intriguing understanding of the connection between Annunciation and Easter—which is, at heart, the inseparable relationship of incarnation and redemption—set out in detail in his book *The Origins of the Liturgical Year* (Pueblo, 1986). Such an understanding (at the risk of oversimplifying)—that Christmas is a celebration of the completion of Easter and that Easter is the source of all other festivals—can revolutionize our understanding of Christian time and make much of our tradition come alive.

A small sketch in Pius Parsch's *The Church's Year of Grace* for Annunciation Day shows a diptych: On one side Mary in her garden is telling Gabriel, "Behold the handmaid of the Lord," and on the other side Lord Jesus in Gethsemane is telling the Father, "Thy will be done." This simple sketch expresses some of the profound paschal theology of March 25. It is, after all, the day on which the equinox is over; day is now longer than night, and light has conquered the darkness. It is no wonder that March 25 was once understood—in contrast with the movable lunar calendar date—as the fixed solar calendar date for Easter.

Unfortunately, neither of the opening prayers in the sacramentary expresses the paschal nature of this feast as clearly as does the *Angelus* collect:

> Lord,
> fill our hearts with your grace:
> once, through the message of an angel
> you revealed to us the incarnation of your Son;
> now, through his suffering and death
> lead us to the glory of his resurrection.
> We ask this through Christ our Lord. Amen.

25 Fourth Sunday of Lent. USING THE SACRAMENTARY: The first of the opening prayers is lovely, befitting this mid-Lent Sunday with its powerful image: "Let us hasten toward Easter." In other texts, "mankind" can be "humankind" and "men" can be "people." Use the Preface of the Fourth Sunday of Lent; "man" and "mankind" can be "human" and "humanity," and "Adam" can be "Adam and Eve." (Coincidentally, this preface fits the solemnities observed this past week.) When the second scrutiny is celebrated, be sure to use the proper texts found in "Ritual Masses. The Scrutinies."

◆ HOMEGROWN PALMS AND EASTER GRASS: Laetare Sunday is like a crest in a hill along our lenten journey; spread out before us the goal of our travels—Jerusalem, God's holy city! If you live in the north, ask everyone to cut backyard branches to sprout in water for Palm Sunday. No matter where you live, bringing homegrown branches to mix with the tropical palms makes a beautiful connection between home and parish, and during the next two weeks budding branches act as a reminder of the nearness of Easter.

Another ancient custom is the lenten blessing of grain for people to take home and sprout to make "resurrection gardens." All you need are small bags, a few pounds of rye or wheat seed and a few cubic feet of perlite or vermiculite. Add a cup of perlite to each bag and a tablespoonful of grain. Tie the bags with something colorful like pink, green and purple yarns. Toss them into a large wicker basket and bring it forward after the prayer after communion at Mass. Bless the grain and distribute it with an insert for the parish bulletin or a flyer to describe the custom:

Bulletin Insert

Christians have long kept the paschal custom of nestling red-dyed eggs into sprouting seedlings, called "resurrection gardens." The seed reminds us of Lord Jesus' own words: "Unless a grain of wheat falls in the earth to die, it remains but a single grain. But if it dies, it rises to produce abundantly." (John 12:14) The red eggs remind us of the newly baptized, "who have washed their robes white in the blood of the Lamb" (Revelation 7:14).

Start some "Easter grass" today. Place the blessed grain together with its growing medium in a festive bowl. Keep it moist but not waterlogged. When Easter arrives tuck in a few red-dyed eggs. Or you can sprout the seedlings in dyed eggshell cups.

Red eggs can be dyed *au naturel* with as many yellow onion skins as can be stuffed into a cooking pot. A 40-minute boil yields gorgeous, bloody, mahogany-colored eggs. A tracery effect can be produced by tying ferns and flowers to the eggs with thread before hard-boiling in the dye. Shine eggs with a buttery rubdown.

We who are baptized must become as buried grain, rising to a fruitful harvest. We must become as blood-washed eggs, opening into the white and gold of risen life. We ourselves must become the burial garden in which our wonderful gardener lives.

Blessing of Grain

My friends,
The Passover of the Lord comes in three weeks.
The earth itself prepares for our feast:
The world grows green; the birds return.
The moon waxes brighter each day
until at last it will be full and our feast will come.

Our eyes turn toward Jerusalem
and we run with joy to the holy city to keep the Passover.
It is time to plant our Easter grain.

We remember the words of the Lord Jesus:
"Unless the grain is buried in the earth, it cannot grow.
But if it is buried, it rises to bear fruit a hundredfold."

When we sprout this grain, we foretell the day of resurrection
when we will rise from our graves in the harvest of God's reign.

My sisters and brothers, let us bless the Lord:

Raise arms over the grain:

+ Blessed are you, Lord, God of all creation,
for you create the seeds of the earth,
and you raise the world to life.
All glory to you, almighty God,

26 MONDAY
Lenten Weekday (#245)
Isaiah 65:17–21
John 4:43–54

27 TUESDAY
Lenten Weekday (#246)
Ezekiel 47:1–9, 12
John 5:1–3, 5–16

28 WEDNESDAY
Lenten Weekday (#247)
Isaiah 49:8–15
John 5:17–30
*Ramadan, the Muslim month
of fasting, begins.*

29 THURSDAY
Lenten Weekday (#248)
Exodus 32:7–14
John 5:31–47

30 FRIDAY
Lenten Weekday (#249)
Wisdom 2:1, 12–22
John 7:1–2, 10, 25–30

31 SATURDAY
Lenten Weekday (#250)
Jeremiah 11:18–20
John 7:40–53

in the death, rest and resurrection of your Son,
our Lord Jesus Christ,
now and unto endless ages, and for ever. Amen.

◆ COMMUNAL PENANCE: This week or the next is appropriate for the parish communal reconciliation. The direction in which Lent moves—and any communal penance leads—is to the profound reconciliation and healing celebrated in Holy Thursday's foot washing, Good Friday's veneration of the cross and Easter's baptism, chrismation and eucharist. The Triduum is the seal on any rites of reconciliation during Lent. The Easter Triduum is how we make merry and slaughter the fatted calf when prodigals like ourselves come home. For consideration on general absolution, see the chapter on this subject in John Huel's *Disputed Questions in the Liturgy Today* (LTP).

APRIL

1 **Fifth Sunday of Lent.** "Lazarus, come out!" This Sunday we proclaim the gospel of the raising of Lazarus. Eastern rite churches celebrate this event as a major feast day the Saturday before Palm Sunday. In the East, Lazarus Saturday and Palm Sunday form a unit that functions as a ritual conclusion to Lent. This festival weekend is founded on the narrative of chapters 11 and 12 of John's Gospel; John is the only evangelist who tells us of the raising of Lazarus, who mentions palms and who gives us a precise day for the triumphal entry of Jesus into Jerusalem. Rome "borrowed" the palm procession from the East, appending it to the Roman liturgy of the Passion on the Sunday before Easter. This hybridization is a marriage between Eastern and Western liturgical spiritualities—and is the reason why "Passion (Palm) Sunday" may seem schizophrenic. Look up the many references to Lazarus Saturday in Thomas Talley's *The Origins of the Liturgical Year* (Pueblo, 1986) for a glimpse into a feast day—and a unique way of approaching Easter's baptismal theology.

◆ USING THE SACRAMENTARY: Notice that the entrance antiphon and both opening prayers are oriented to the Passion—a definite movement within Lent. Although the entire "lenten music set" of gathering song, greeting, penitential rite, responsorial psalm, etc., might remain the same from the First through Fifth Sundays of Lent, consider including a Passion-oriented hymn, such as "What wondrous love," "O sacred head" or "My song is love unknown," for the next two Sundays, perhaps replacing the gathering song or perhaps replacing the after-communion hymn, followed by a silent recessional. In the alternative prayer, "brothers" should be "brothers and sisters." Use the proper Preface of the Fifth Sunday of Lent; "man" can be "human being." Solemn Blessing 5, "Passion of the Lord," might be used from now until the Triduum. When the third, final scrutiny is celebrated, be sure to use the proper prayers found under "Ritual Masses. The Scrutinies." Alert the community to the presentation of the Lord's Prayer if this rite for the elect is to take place this week.

◆ PASSIONTIDE: Those familiar with the calendar in use prior to the reform of 1969 will remember that these last two weeks of Lent were designated "Passiontide." This period was a recognition that the center of the liturgical year was drawing near and that all the discipline of the season was leading us to the Lord's

Pasch. At one time Passiontide marked the full length of the pre-Easter fast. Why two weeks? The explanation is marvelous: In the earliest centuries of Christianity many churches kept the Jewish Passover as their own Passover. The 14 days between the new moon and Passover's full moon was a natural time of preparation. As noted above, the current liturgy *maintains* Passiontide's spirit although the term is no longer used. The old custom of veiling statues and images was a sign of exile. Our sinfulness got us tossed out of paradise, cutting us off from our rootedness in the goodness of creation. We are prevented from enjoying the company of our ancestors and the vision of heavenly glory, symbolized by the statues and images in our worship spaces. Veiling these images has much to recommend it either during these final two weeks or during the entire period of Lent, the season of exile.

◆ PREPARING THE PASSOVER: It's a busy weekend for last-minute reminders of rehearsals and preparations for Palm Sunday and for the Triduum. On top of all this is the need—all too often forgotten—of rehearsing the pattern of the Eastertime Sunday liturgies. Hour-by-hour vigiling during the Triduum (the origin of the custom of "Forty Hours") is an excellent way to observe the Christian Passover. See the explanation of this custom on page 178. This week is the latest the sign-up board for this vigiling should be put in the vestibule and the custom explained thoroughly to the parish. This is also a good weekend to remind everyone, both in the bulletin and face-to-face, of the responsibility for all parishioners, young and old, to participate fully in the liturgy of the Triduum.

☀ **8 Passion Sunday (Palm Sunday).** The title given in English liturgical books, "Passion (Palm) Sunday," is confusing. Those parentheses are a prosaic way of titling a day that has a rich history and significance. The Latin title, *Dominica in palmis de Passione Domini,* "the Lord's Day in palms of the Passion of the Lord," is certainly more poetic and more precise.

◆ THE PROCESSION WITH PALMS: "If we were to see in the procession only a crowd waving palms and singing joyous songs, we would miss its real significance in the Roman liturgy. That liturgy looks upon the procession not simply as a commemoration of Christ's entry into Jerusalem nor simply as a triumphal march, but as Christ's journey, together with his people, to Calvary and the great act of redemption." (Adrian Nocent, *The Liturgical Year,* vol. 2 [Collegeville: The Liturgical Press, 1977], 195)

The procession for Passion Sunday includes lots of people actually moving from the place where the palms were blessed to where the eucharist will be celebrated, bells ringing, trumpets blaring, everyone singing, palms waving—everyone not incapacitated by age or illness participating. People who feel that a real procession is likely to stir up trouble because of its difficulty should attend Orthodox Christian worship at Easter. Everyone joins in several processions; no one complains. You get the feeling that they would be ashamed if the processions were curtailed since that would only reflect poorly on the parish's spirit.

Note that rubrics restrict the procession to the principal Mass. Why? A single, unified parish liturgy is called for—just as during the Triduum. That tells us that musical forces need to be unified as well, a great gathering of the entire parish that may require unique Mass scheduling this day. The ordering of rites is straightforward:

4 WEDNESDAY
Lenten Weekday (#254)
Isidore, bishop and doctor
OPTIONAL MEMORIAL
Daniel 3:14–20, 91–92, 95
John 8:31–42

5 THURSDAY
Lenten Weekday (#255)
Vincent Ferrer, priest
OPTIONAL MEMORIAL
Genesis 17:3–9
John 8:51–59

6 FRIDAY
Lenten Weekday (#256)
Jeremiah 20:10–13
John 10:31–42

7 SATURDAY
Lenten Weekday (#257)
John Baptist de la Salle, priest
OPTIONAL MEMORIAL
Ezekiel 37:21–28
John 11:45–57

8 SUNDAY
Palm Sunday of the Passion of the Lord
Matthew 21:1–11 (#37A)
Isaiah 50:4–7 (#38A)
Philippians 2:6–11
Matthew 26:14—27:66
  or 27:11–54

Forsythia

Gathering: All assemble in a place "distinct from the church to which the procession will move." (Quotes are from the rubrical directions in the sacramentary).

Branches are distributed: Branches are already in the hands of the assembly *before* the presider and other ministers arrive (also holding branches). Red Mass vestments are worn. The person who reads the gospel may wear a cope.

Although plenty of tropical palms should be available, it's only right to ask people the past few weeks to bring backyard branches this morning to welcome the Messiah. Note the significance of budding branches in Matthew 24:32—words of Jesus spoken after his entry into Jerusalem. Springtime is a sign of warning for the coming of Christ!

Song: All sing the antiphon (Matthew 21:9) "or any other appropriate song."

Greeting: The presider gives the greeting and a *brief* introduction, if not the one in the book, at least one that good.

Blessing: The presider prays the blessing with hands joined, followed by silently sprinkling the branches with water—which means everyone gets wet since the branches are being held by people at this point. Especially if your parish has kept holy water fonts dry, consider incensing the branches rather than sprinkling them, which is also a good way to add honor to the reading (chanting?) of the procession gospel.

Gospel: The deacon or presider proclaims the gospel of the entry into Jerusalem.

Homily: "A *brief* homily *may* be given."

Procession: The deacon or presider invites the assembly to join in the procession, which takes this order:

> —thurifer
> —crossbearer, "with the cross suitably decorated" in celebration of Christ's triumph, flanked by candle-bearers
> —presider and assistants, presumably with the deacon bearing the lectionary or gospel book
> —assembly, perhaps with several members of the assembly interspersed throughout the procession carrying festive banners and flags, and even greenery and ribbons tacked to wooden poles

Entering the church: Although not suggested by the current sacramentary, it is traditional to make much of the entry into the church. A responsorial-style arrangement of Psalm 24 can be sung at the church doors. After each verse, the presider uses the butt end of the processional cross to knock loudly several times on the closed doors. Then they are opened by ushers or servers during the final verse. The customary "All glory, laud and honor" (St. Theodulph) can be sung with plenty of brass and bells as people enter, a sign that the victory of the cross has opened the gates of paradise.

Conclusion of procession: The presider venerates the altar with a kiss and with incense, if it was used in the procession, then changes from cope to chasuble and from the chair "begins immediately the opening prayer of the Mass which concludes the procession."

The procession can go in a straight line toward the church, and upon arrival it can circumambulate the church building, a powerful image of yearning to enter into Jerusalem. (Of course, a procession should never get unduly long.) Walk through the route beforehand, looking for trouble as you go. Will banners and cross fit through any tight places? Is the head of the procession visible, ideally because the cross and its decoration are colorfully prominent? Are there spots where part of the procession can bog down, where people can trip easily or get confused and take shortcuts?

◆ MUSIC IS A GREAT UNIFIER IN A PROCESSION and is best provided by instruments that can function well outdoors, like handbells and some brass. A repeated Taizé ostinato works well—even a round, one in which the front of the procession can sing out of sync with the back. Give this ostinato a strong beginning in the place where everyone has first gathered. Scatter choir members and song leaders throughout the assembly. This procession is time for pilgrimage music. The "Hosanna" refrain from Howard Hughes's Mass of the Divine Word (GIA, G-2415) provides a kicky 6/8 melody that expands well with tambourines, trumpet, finger cymbals and anything that is musical and portable. Christopher Walker's five-part round, "Paschal/Palm Procession" (OCP, #7128), is well worth the need for rehearsal and preparation. The sacramentary suggests Psalms 24, "Open wide the doors," and 47, "All you peoples, clap your hands," and any hymn in honor of Christ the King, although it's difficult to imagine how a cantor or even a schola can be heard in a procession using responsorial-style singing, or how a metrical hymn can be sung with vigor while walking.

◆ AT THE OTHER LITURGIES: Focusing the community's attention and the planners' energies on the principal celebration will mean, almost inevitably, a scaling down of the Commemoration of the Lord's Entrance into Jerusalem at the other liturgies. But again, this is in keeping with the sound approach to these holy days adopted by the rubrics: *one* Mass of the Lord's Supper, *one* solemn liturgy on Good Friday, *one* Easter Vigil. The only reason for duplicating a particular service is a church so crowded that safety is at stake—something that *does* happen on Palm Sunday. And it is a judgment against us that it rarely happens during the Triduum!

The "Solemn Entrance"—with the following adaptations—is a practical alternative for other Masses on Passion Sunday: Members of the assembly are handed palms as they enter church, perhaps with the singing of one of the Taizé ostinatos beginning a good ten minutes before Mass is scheduled to start. At that time, the presider and other ministers "go to a suitable place in the church outside the sanctuary so that most of the people will be able to see the rite." The choir loft or a raised dais near the doors is a fine place. In the same manner as in the principal Mass with the procession, the branches are blessed, the gospel of the triumphal entry is proclaimed, and then the ministers pass through the assembly toward the altar while everyone sings a hymn.

◆ USING THE LECTIONARY: There can't be a good reason short of calamity for taking advantage of the "pastoral reasons" clause about omitting the first two readings. No one who comes to the principal liturgy with its procession is going to be playing "beat the clock." Two powerful versions of Psalm 22 are by Howard Hughes, SM (*Psalms for All Seasons,* NPM) and by Alexander Peloquin (GIA, G-1658). This psalm is the seasonal psalm for Holy Week, and so can be used on Good Friday rather than Psalm 31. As always, the liturgy of the word will seem long only if it is poorly done. The lectors for the first two readings (and there should be two, not one) should get all the help they need in rehearsals.

Especially if your parish omits the gospel acclamation during Lent, consider the rubrics for today's reading of the Passion: no candles, no incense, no greeting, no signs of the cross, no kissing of the book afterward. This completely bare gospel procession may best be done in silence. A beautiful gesture throughout the Passion is for the assembly to hold fast to the holy branches, for they are our pledge of resurrection. The ministers, including the readers, can take up their branches to remind the assembly to do so, and some instruction for doing this can be included in the worship aid.

◆ THE PASSION is "read by the deacon or, if there is no deacon, by the priest." Note that reading in parts *may* but need not be done. Please do not have the assembly read "crowd" parts. A liturgical principle is at stake: The scriptures are to be listened to, never read along with the lector. A fine way to proclaim the Passion is to interpolate the verses of a hymn sung by everyone; mark the reading where these verses will be sung. "O sacred head surrounded" fits the synoptics' accounts. (Interestingly, interpolated congregational hymns are part of the power of the Bach Passions.) Or the singing of a Taizé mantra, such as "Jesus, remember me" or "O Christe domine Jesu," three or four times in the course of the reading can enhance the attentive attitude of the assembly. This practice is effective only if these mantras are already part of the parish's worship life and are not sprung on them at the time of the reading. The use of the same mantra at the recessional will bring the parish to the threshold of the Triduum.

◆ "A *BRIEF* HOMILY *MAY* BE GIVEN." (Is the sacramentary trying to tell us something?) However, it is condescending to the assembly to forgo a homily just because today's liturgy is long. Being left speechless by the proclamation of St. Matthew's account of the Passion is one thing, but offering the parish nothing by way of guidance only five days before the holiest days of the year is another thing entirely. The sabbath before the Jewish Passover is called the "Great Sabbath," called "great" because the rabbi is required by tradition to preach on the hows and whys of the observance of the coming festival, and then to ensure that no one is left uninvited. Surely that is a worthy tradition to embrace as we approach the Christian Passover. Make the homily a strong bridge, just several minutes long, between the procession and the scriptures and the work of these next days: an invitation to keep Lent up to its last minutes on Thursday, then to enter wholeheartedly into the parish's observance of the Triduum. This is an authoritative summons to give over the time from Thursday night until Sunday to the paschal fasting and vigiling and prayer—three days like no other in the year.

◆ USING THE SACRAMENTARY: In the first opening prayer, "man" can be "a human being." The alternative opening prayer is shorter than the first but difficult to comprehend. What does "estrangement might be dissolved" mean? The Preface of Passion Sunday is appointed for this day although the Preface for the Passion of the Lord II seems better suited, with its anticipation of the Triduum. Continue with whatever eucharistic prayer was used throughout Lent. The communion rite can keep the same music as during the rest of Lent. Use Solemn Blessing 5, "Passion of the Lord." A clear, attractively printed schedule for the Triduum should be distributed as people leave (see the sample schedule on page 93).

◆ DON'T STINT ON YOUR PALM ORDER. Try to acquire palms that are not stripped into smithereens, and decorate with fully open palm fronds so people can make some connection between the torn leaf in their hand and the actual plant. Keep in mind it's the date palm frond, native to the Mideast, that has such intense religious significance for many Muslims, Christians and Jews, not the palmetto frond, native to the American Southeast. Many palm retailers have date palm fronds available that can be purchased to honor the processional cross.

◆ A TRIUMPHAL ARCH, constructed with lumber and decorated with bundled pussywillows, ribbons, flowers and greenery, and then placed outside over the main doors of the church, makes a splendid announcement to the neighborhood of the coming of the high holy days of our year. The inside of the church deserves great austerity throughout the Triduum until the Easter Vigil, but the outside of the church deserves bright red banners, bunting, victory wreaths and other signs of our celebration as an invitation to all the world to enter into the Passover.

◆ CLEANING AND REHEARSALS: Monday, Tuesday, Wednesday and Thursday of this week are "preparation days" for the Triduum, which begins at sundown on Thursday. These are the days for any last-minute details, parish cleaning inside and out, and rehearsals. Even the liturgies of the Triduum are secondary to the continuous prayer vigil and fasting of the Three Days, to which all parishioners should be invited—and not prevented from keeping because of the distraction of rehearsals or preparations. When darkness falls on Holy Thursday, will the parish be ready to enter into *Pascha*? The ministers for the liturgies of the Triduum will have been selected early in Lent and may already have had one rehearsal. The lectors will need their own time to rehearse but should also be present for the general rehearsal so that the details of coordination can be worked out. The rehearsals must include presiders and key musicians.

Such rehearsals are not only about the general order of things (which the principal ministers should know by heart) but about the pace and the timing involved. Careful planning of the rehearsal will help prevent wasting anyone's time. Rehearsals are far more effective when people are unhurried: Don't schedule several rehearsals on the same evening, but plan to do the Holy Thursday liturgy on one night, Good Friday the next, and the Vigil the next.

There may be one great exception to the rule about getting everyone to the rehearsal. Should the elect attend a rehearsal for the Vigil? Probably not. There is great wisdom in the practice of the third and fourth centuries. The elect can know something of what to prepare for, but initiation isn't really something you can rehearse. The presider and all others (especially the godparents) who are key to the baptismal liturgy should know their parts very well—including the deacons and other assistants whose help will be needed with water and towels and oil. But the elect themselves can come free of concern and full of trust. The elect (and the candidates) should not be troubled with trying to remember what comes next; they should be graciously directed by their godparents to enter into a ritual and a mystery known to all those who have been christened. They will then have all of Eastertime to reflect on what happened.

◆ AT HOME: The new prayer book for use at home within the church in the United States, *Catholic Household Blessings and Prayers,* has a short rite for "Placing of Branches in the Home." Introduce the parish to the many other blessings and services of prayer for the coming festival and make this important book readily available to purchase.

10 First Day of Passover. Greetings are in order from the parish to the local Jewish community. Parishes that enjoy seder suppers might make a seder part of their annual keeping of Eastertime rather than Lent or the Triduum: Keep in mind that one of the great songs of the seder is "Hallelujah!" Or Christians might join together with Jews in a communal seder perhaps last night or tonight, perhaps sometime early next week. Whatever is done, the

9 MONDAY
Monday of Holy Week (#258)

Isaiah 42:1–7
John 12:1–11

On this day Dietrich Bonhoeffer died in 1945.

Passover begins at sundown.

10 TUESDAY
Tuesday of Holy Week (#259)

Isaiah 49:1–6
John 13:21–33, 36–38

11 WEDNESDAY
Wednesday of Holy Week (#260)

Isaiah 50:4–9
Matthew 26:14–25

12 HOLY THURSDAY
Morning:
Chrism Mass (#39)

Isaiah 61:1–3, 6, 8–9
Revelation 1:5–8
Luke 4:16–21

12 HOLY THURSDAY

Evening:

**Mass of the Supper
of the Lord**

(#40)

Exodus 12:1–8, 11–14
I Corinthians 11:23–26
John 13:1–15

13 GOOD FRIDAY

Afternoon:

**Celebration of the Passion
of the Lord** (#41)

Isaiah 52:13—53:12
Hebrews 4:14–16; 5:7–9
John 18:1—19:42

Crown of thorns

14 HOLY SATURDAY

Night:

The Easter Vigil (#42)

Genesis 1:1—2:2
Genesis 22:1–18
Exodus 14:15—15:1
Isaiah 54:5–14
Isaiah 55:1–11
Baruch 3:9–15, 32—4:4
Ezekiel 36:16–28
Romans 6:3–11
Matthew 28:1–10

Jewish seder is not to be compromised or given a Christian gloss. LTP publishes *The Passover Celebration* as well as the cassette, *Songs for the Seder Meal,* that are true to the Jewish traditions of this wonderful feast.

PASCHAL TRIDUUM

12–14 **The Paschal Triduum.** Please see the Triduum section of "The Seasons" in this book, beginning on page 65, where the principal liturgies of the Pasch are discussed. Here in "The Calendar" we deal with other aspects of the parish's keeping of the Triduum aside from these principal services.

◆ GATHERING THE PARISH: From Holy Thursday night through Easter Sunday, the whole church—the living and the dead, and even, in the words of Psalm 22, the "generations yet to be born"—gathers to keep *Pascha.* Perhaps that is why we begin the liturgy on Thursday night by ringing bells—it is a great summons. The liturgy of Thursday does not end with a dismissal; the liturgy of Good Friday neither begins with a greeting nor ends with a dismissal. What we begin to appreciate is that the movement from Holy Thursday night through Easter Sunday is one liturgy, a single gathering from which no one must leave.

Our task in preparing the Paschal Triduum becomes a task of gathering people for the entire Three Days, not merely for three liturgical events within those days. And there are many ways to keep people together: fasting meals; a teenager camp-out; a parish Easter breakfast after the Vigil; Morning, Midday, Evening and Night Prayer; nighttime observance of the Office of Readings; a continuous watch kept night and day.

There are practical questions to answer if we truly expect everyone to come together throughout these days: Is babysitting provided? What about transportation for the elderly or infirm? Will parish visitors be praying with shut-ins, inmates, the hospitalized? Is it made clear to folks that these Three Days are not a preparation for Easter, but that they *are* Easter? Is there a special invitation given to certain groups: youth, the parish schoolchildren (often noticeably and just about scandalously absent from the liturgies of the Triduum), the separated and divorced, single people, the families and friends of those to be baptized or received into the church? Maybe we need to provide something more than just an invitation. Maybe we need to give people opportunities for creative input to help "own" the worship of these days: dyeing Easter eggs to distribute after the Vigil, preparing the candles and containers of holy water to take home, spring cleaning parish property, and all the many preparations of the Easter decorations.

◆ A FOCUS FOR KEEPING WATCH: Some Central and Eastern European Roman Catholics have the tradition, borrowed from the Byzantine rite, of keeping watch near a shrine of the tomb of Christ during the time from the Celebration of the Lord's Passion until the Easter Vigil. This shrine is customarily set up in the center of the assembly, not in or near the sanctuary. The holy shroud, a massive winding sheet, often wrapped around an icon or statue of the dead Christ—or in some places the new (unlit) paschal candle—is laid on a bed of flowers, fragrant herbs and evergreens. The holy cross is kept nearby. This shroud is the object of veneration on Holy Saturday much the same way the cross is the object of veneration on Good Friday. In some parishes, the great winding shroud is unfurled down the aisles of the church, symbolically enshrouding the assembly. In Greece it is customary for people to place photos and names of all their beloved dead upon the tomb, for the resurrection of Christ is our hope for resurrection.

A simple focus of prayer throughout the Three Days might be the placing of an appropriate icon—perhaps of Gethsemane on Holy Thursday night, of the Crucifixion from Good Friday morning through the afternoon, and of the Burial of Christ from Good Friday night until the Easter Vigil—in a place of honor, perhaps right in the middle aisle of the church. Of course, the repository or tabernacle is a focus of prayer on Holy Thursday night, and the cross is a focus from Good Friday afternoon through Holy Saturday; perhaps the icon can simply be placed nearby.

◆ LITURGY OF THE HOURS: Thanksgiving hymn, psalms, brief reading, gospel canticle, intercessions, Lord's Prayer. Surely every parish deserves to have this simple order of prayer deep in their bones. Such prayer, most of it known by heart, without elaborate preparation, enables even worried parish ministers (who tend to fret the more elaborate services of the Triduum) to participate in lifting up minds and hearts to God.

The rubrics tell us that Evening Prayer is not observed on Holy Thursday or on Good Friday by those who participate in the Mass of the Lord's Supper and in the Celebration of the Lord's Passion. That's curious. Why do the rubrics even mention the possibility of not participating in these services? Why did the framers of the reformed liturgy feel a conflict between the time of Evening Prayer (around sunset) and the times of the liturgies of Holy Thursday (at night) and Good Friday (in the afternoon)? Since the liturgy of the hours presents beautiful formulas for Evening Prayer on Holy Thursday and Good Friday with little intention of anyone ever using them, some re-reformation of the liturgy is obviously in order.

According to rubrics, Evening Prayer takes place as usual on Holy Saturday. Does any parish celebrate this liturgy communally? Is it a fantasy imagining a parish—and its ministers—singing the psalms and offering prayer at this time rather than rushing around with last-minute preparations? And what a glorious fantasy this is: a parish that is so familiar with its Evening Prayer that it can be sung from memory as darkness descends and the holy night begins! The Easter Vigil itself starts with a lamp lighting that's oddly not in the context of Evening Prayer. Perhaps this suggests that on this one night of the year, the *lucernarium*—in this case the paschal fire—come at the conclusion to Vespers.

Many parishes find that the liturgies of Morning Prayer during the Triduum are the year's best attended celebrations of the liturgy of the hours. During these holy days, the year's responsorial-style psalmody can be recapitulated. The Office of Readings can precede Morning Prayer or follow Night Prayer. "Tenebrae" (Darkness) was a special paschal form of vigiling leading to Morning Prayer in which the gradual extinguishing of lights as morning came was interpreted as "the hour of darkness"—the holy days on which even the sun hides its light. Midday Prayer is also an important liturgy these days, and has a special place at noontime both on Good Friday and Holy Saturday. Holy Thursday Morning Prayer is *not* a Triduum liturgy; however, the daily Mass crowd would appreciate this liturgy, and then could be part of some before-the-fast brunch or maybe join in a trip to the cathedral for the Chrism Mass.

Night prayer is also an important liturgy during the Triduum. On Holy Thursday night it can conclude eucharistic adoration (but the paschal vigiling would continue through the night). On Good Friday night the holy cross can be placed so that people can continue to approach it for veneration before or after the prayer. On Holy Saturday night, of course, the Easter Vigil makes redundant both Night Prayer and the Office of Readings.

◆ FASTING MEALS ON GOOD FRIDAY AND HOLY SATURDAY: The spirit of the paschal fast calls for nothing to be eaten these two days. That is why, as in the Jewish all-day fast of Yom Kippur, it is essential to provide all-day prayer for the community that undertakes such a fast. We need each other's support to keep such a fast! That is why the liturgy of these days must ebb and flow, but never cease altogether. The purpose of the paschal fast is not to have us dwell on our empty stomachs but to free our time for unceasing prayer.

A fasting supper is a compromise, an alternative to not fasting at all, an important way to continue the communal vigiling and prayer. If the parish has the facilities to seat a goodly crowd, suppers and perhaps simple brunches can begin and end with "At Table during the Easter Triduum" from *Catholic Household Blessings and Prayers*. Songs and psalms and readings can be part of the meals, instead of conversation. Customary foods for the fast are made without animal products, low salt, low oil, and bland: potatoes, flatbreads, beans, rice, pasta, green salads. By all means prepare ethnic fasting dishes that are part of parishioners' heritages.

◆ SEDER SUPPERS: Some parishes enjoy keeping a Jewish Passover seder meal on Holy Thursday. While this custom may be done with the best of intentions, all too often it makes the rituals of the Jewish Passover subservient to the Christian Passover, something we do merely to spark up Holy Thursday. What we may be doing to honor "our Jewish roots" winds up as an injustice to the integrity of the Jewish seder. Keep in mind, the Christian Passover is not celebrated on Holy Thursday night alone: The *entire* Triduum is *Pascha*. The paschal fast from Holy Thursday night through the Easter Vigil and then the paschal feast beginning after the Vigil is the way we Christians keep our Passover.

If a Holy Thursday seder has become a beloved tradition in your parish, why not think in terms of *all* Three Days when preparing this meal? Begin by having a pre-fast supper, complete with blessings and psalms late in the afternoon on Holy Thursday well before the evening liturgy. Move to simple fasting meals on Good Friday and Holy Saturday: Traditional Christian paschal fasting soups are made from bitter and green spring herbs, such as the French and German "seven herb soup." Then break the fast after the Easter Vigil with a sharing of Easter treats—including such Passover fare as lamb, bitter herbs, eggs and honeyed *haroset*—along with the singing of the Hallel, Psalms 114–118, with their many shouts of "Hallelujah!"

◆ THE GREAT SABBATH: The middle day of the Three Days—from Good Friday sunset to Holy Saturday sunset—has traditionally been a day without any liturgy—liturgy means "work" and we do not work on the Sabbath. But without liturgy, the mystery of this day has remained largely undefined, unknown for many people. It is the mystery of rest, of silence, of death, of ultimate nothingness, of the chaos that preceded creation. The Eastern Christian rites for Good Friday night and Holy Saturday richly ponder this Sabbath mystery. The church gathers, not outside the tomb of Christ, but within, buried with Christ, dead with Christ. The people are anointed with myrrh, a fragrant resin also called chrism, in preparation for that rest we all shall enter. In the Roman rite strong references to this vigil within the tomb are made in the patristic reading from the Office of Readings for Holy Saturday, as well as to the brief rubrics for Holy Saturday in the sacramentary.

Again and again, the documents of the church call for both Friday and Saturday (through the Vigil itself) to be days of fasting from food *and work*. The RCIA provides for this also with special attention to the elect: "The elect are to be advised that on Holy Saturday they should refrain from their usual activities, spend their time in prayer and reflection, and, as far as they can, observe a fast." (185) Those are plain and direct words. They may be the most severe test of a parish's practice of the RCIA, for what they encourage should flow naturally from all that has gone before. If this is a day of frantic preparation for *anyone* in the parish, or a day of work and errands and shopping, then something has been very wrong. Parish staff and all responsible should set themselves to pondering the spirit and content of their initiation work. But "initiation" must be broadly understood: We are all being initiated yet, and this paschal season is to do that. Are we ourselves discovering, a little more each year, that we just cannot imagine any business-as-usual during these days? Not only the pattern of eating is suspended, but of sleeping, working, seeking out diversion. How can we help each other in this?

◆ HOLY SATURDAY ALSO HAS ITS OWN RITES IN PREPARATION FOR INITIATION. The elect can be gathered for reflection and prayer, and one or more of the following: presentation of the Lord's Prayer (if not done previously), the "return" of the Creed (RCIA, 193–196), the *ephphetha* rite (197–199), and the choosing of a baptismal name (200–202). See RCIA, 185–186 for an introduction to these rites. The invitation to these brief rites can go to the whole parish and the rites themselves can be scheduled in proximity to Morning Prayer or Midday Prayer on Holy Saturday.

◆ EASTER BREAKFAST: The eucharistic feast of the Easter Vigil breaks the paschal fast. Liturgical commentators delight in reminding us that in certain ancient traditions milk and honey were offered to the newly baptized at the time of their first communion. Is it more than coincidence that sweet dairy dishes are just about universal Easter fare? A sumptuous meal of customary Easter foods is not just a nice way to end the Vigil, and it's not just "the reception for the newly baptized"—a phrase that can make it sound like a polite social affair. The Easter breakfast is a flourishing of eucharist, our wedding banquet, our love feast.

If you truly expect the parish to join in this breakfast, then instead of dismissing everyone, an invitation can be made to process to the parish hall or other place for the meal. Psalm 136, the "Grand Hallel," with its concluding verse, "God gives food to all living things; to the God of heaven give thanks," would be a wonderful processional song. The meal begins with the blessing over Easter foods. (See the discussion on the next page about this blessing.) Parishes that do not have a suitable place for this meal might consider breaking the fast in the worship hall itself. The spirit of the breakfast involves something more than coffee and doughnuts; individuals and maybe a parish group can be responsible for its preparation. Parishioners can be asked to bring Easter dishes to share, and perhaps some foods can be ordered from a bakery and delicatessen.

15 EASTER SUNDAY
SOLEMNITY

Acts 10:34, 37–43
Colossians 3:1–4
  or I Corinthians 5:6–8
John 20:1–9
  or Matthew 28:1–10 (#42)
  or at an evening Mass
    Luke 24:13–35 (#47)

Orthodox Pascha

Saucer magnolia

15 **Easter Sunday.** For more information on Eastertime, see pages 95–111 in "The Seasons."

◆ THE EXSULTET SINGS: "May the Morning Star who never sets find this flame still burning." So let the flame of a lively faith and an exuberant celebration mark this happy morning. Take a cue from the Exsultet (and from a rubric in the Dominican ordo) that the paschal candle remains burning from the time it is lit, through the night, through the next day and up to Evening Prayer. No wonder we need such an enormous candle!

Perhaps dawn will see many (and over the years the numbers will grow) gathering at the front door of the church to intone Psalm 95 and kindle lights again from the paschal candle's flame for Morning Prayer. It's delightfully surprising how many folks, especially those who attend all the Triduum liturgies, are eager to meet near dawn on this morning—and Morning Prayer is our liturgical tradition's own "sunrise service," held every sunrise of the year!

◆ USING THE SACRAMENTARY: Triduum and Eastertime overlap today. It is the first of the Fifty Days and the last of the Three Days. The morning eucharist is more Eastertime than Triduum. In the alternative opening prayer "men" can be "those." Be sure to sing the sequence in one of its many possible guises. If Eucharistic Prayer I is used, there are proper inserts. Preface of Easter I is prescribed. Today has a proper solemn blessing. Someone should be sure to sing the traditional melody for the dismissal no matter how challenging those Alleluias are.

◆ THERE MAY BE INFANT BAPTISMS at the morning Masses, although any Sunday in Eastertime is fitting; there will certainly be a generous sprinkling of the faithful after baptismal vows are renewed. Fill the water bucket directly from the font and then pour what's left after the sprinkling back into the font, rather than filling it before Mass. Use a thick, bundled bunch of juniper or arborvitae as a sprinkler. The newly baptized and those received into the church during the Vigil should be invited to return in their white robes to the principal Easter Sunday morning Mass and to sit with godparents and family in a place of honor.

◆ THE INSERTION OF THE RENEWAL OF BAPTISMAL VOWS into this liturgy seems redundant to what happened last night; did the framers of the liturgy assume most of the parish would not be in attendance at the Easter Vigil? The wording of the suggested invitation to this rite, "Now that we have completed our lenten observance . . . ," seems oddly placed three days after Lent is past. Many liturgical scholars question the notion of renewing baptismal vows in this fashion. As Aidan Kavanagh reminds us: "I call the renewal of baptismal promises abnormal simply because the normal way we do this is to say Amen each time we receive holy communion. Baptism, after all, is the way eucharist begins, and eucharist is how baptism is sustained in the life of Christians."

◆ THE BLESSING OF FOODS: Blessing foods on Holy Saturday afternoon made sense 40 years ago when the Easter Vigil took place on Saturday morning and the paschal fast came to an end at noon. It makes no sense to bless foods before the Vigil, although many parishes continue to do this. Don't treat it as a quaint ethnic custom; it's a tradition for *all* Christians to bless the foods of Easter. Make it a real part of the parish's liturgical life: Throughout Lent remind people to bring baskets of food as well as children's Easter baskets to any Mass on Easter

Sunday—including the Vigil. (The notion here is that households can bring their "breakfast" foods to the Vigil, and then return for morning eucharist bearing the children's baskets.) Tables can be set up to receive the baskets. Ushers need to be cued in so they can direct folks to place their foods on the tables. The brief prayer of the Order of the Blessing of Food for the First Meal of Easter should be used from the *Book of Blessings,* and it can take place after the prayer after communion. *Catholic Household Blessings and Prayers* has a home prayer for the meal that breaks the Easter fast (which has been going on since Thursday evening).

◆ HOSPITALITY: If the pastoral staff and parish leaders make a solid commitment to celebrate the Triduum in its fullness from Holy Thursday evening to Easter Sunday evening, the entire parish will begin to see this time as a total consecration to the central mystery by which we are saved, delivered, reborn. Such total consecration—the word means a purposeful setting apart—is bound to have an effect on those whose commitment is minimal or simply cultural. A sensitive heart must welcome them home on this day of beginnings. Let their eyes be drawn immediately to the loveliness of what is central: ambo, altar, font, cross, candle. Let ears that rarely hear sacred stories be intrigued by today's message of reconciliation, forgiveness, peace, the invitation to believe. Model your homily after John Chrysostom's Easter words: "And you who did not fast, come and rejoice as well!" Let hearts that may be restless find some rest in the Risen Lord visible in the midst of the assembly by reason of his followers' loving welcome to the stranger.

Even parishes with frequent hospitality around coffee and doughnuts tend to postpone it on great feast days. The crowds, the rush, the demands of family all can become excuses to let hospitality slip. After-worship camaraderie today can take on several customary guises: hot cross buns and eggnog after Mass, an egghunt for adults and children alike, a visit from the Easter bunny in the parking lot as folks are leaving, a parish breakfast on this happy morning that breaks the paschal fast.

◆ EASTER EVENING PRAYER CLOSES THE TRIDUUM. This prayer is truly one of the principal Triduum liturgies—yet often it gets short shrift. Unfortunately, on Easter Sunday evening most worship personnel can hardly function. At the same time, many parishioners may be looking for something to do in the spirit of the holiday, an Easter outing, another opportunity to offer praise. As one parish family exclaimed as they gathered for Paschal Vespers: "We're here for another dose of Easter!" Perhaps a crew different from the folks who prepared the Vigil and Sunday morning can prepare Evening Prayer. See the order of Paschal Vespers found in LTP's *A Triduum Sourcebook.* Diocesan worship personnel should offer Evening Prayer at the cathedral along with a concert or Easter caroling—well-advertised in all diocesan parishes. And wouldn't Eastertime Vespers, this Sunday or next, make a glorious ecumenical service?

 **EASTERTIME**

15—22 **The Easter Octave.** Every day of this week is a solemnity, including next Sunday. If the Fifty Days of Easter are the "Great Sunday," this week is Sunday morning. Yes, parish ministers are pooped. To many it is a delicious exhaustion. Although all parish business should be put

16 MONDAY
Easter Monday
SOLEMNITY (#261)
Acts 2:14, 22–32
Matthew 28:8–15

17 TUESDAY
Easter Tuesday
SOLEMNITY (#262)
Acts 2:36–41
John 20:11–18

18 WEDNESDAY
Easter Wednesday
SOLEMNITY (#263)
Acts 3:1–10
Luke 24:13–35

19 THURSDAY
Easter Thursday
SOLEMNITY (#264)
Acts 3:11–26
Luke 24:35–48

20 FRIDAY
Easter Friday
SOLEMNITY (#265)
Acts 4:1–12
John 21:1–14

21 SATURDAY
Easter Saturday
SOLEMNITY (#266)
Acts 4:13–21
Mark 16:9–15

22 SUNDAY
Second Sunday of Easter
SOLEMNITY (#44)

Acts 2:42–47
1 Peter 1:3–9
John 20:19–31

Yom ha-Shoah,
Holocaust Memorial Day

off for this week of celebration, a gathering of ministers sometime this week is necessary to organize and put away all the paperwork of the Triduum for next year; this gathering should include discussion of the way things went, with copious notetaking. One of the most venerable of Easter week traditions is the daily gathering of the newly baptized (in their baptismal robes) and their godparents for mystagogical preaching and eucharist. And that implies the gathering of the entire parish each of these eight days.

Parishes that hold annual week-long missions could not choose a better week. The parish school especially, if they hold classes this week, must see to it that this is a festival period and not business-as-usual. Lent's momentum should be maintained. In Eastertime the lenten spirit of repentance and conversion must be transformed into evangelical energy. Like the disciples on the road to Emmaus, all of us are called to declare, "Were not our hearts burning inside us?" For texts and prayers for all the Fifty Days, see LTP's *An Easter Sourcebook*. It takes the days one by one and, in the back, has a simple form of Morning and Evening Prayer.

22 **Second Sunday of Easter.** This Sunday was called, in the former calendar, the *Dominica in albis,* literally, "in whites." The neophytes wore their baptismal garments for the whole of what the Eastern church calls "Bright Week," laying them aside after Vespers today. Certainly their privileged place at the eucharistic celebration and perhaps even their vesting in their baptismal garments should continue throughout the Fifty Days. One parish kept the neophytes' baptismal candles—stuck into a great clay pot of sand—burning brightly by the font throughout the season. We got the wrong impression by the old designation for this day, "Low Sunday." The words "high" and "low" meant beginning and end (of the octave), not big and little. What's most important about today is that everything of the exuberance and majesty of Easter Sunday is also part of this Eastertime Sunday—and of all the Easter days until Pentecost.

The eight Sundays of Eastertime—beginning on Easter Sunday itself and ending on Pentecost—are the Sundays of the Sunday of the year (the Fifty Days, one-seventh of the year, are the year's Sunday). There should be nothing like them all year long. Eastertime will not live in hearts and households unless we can count on the sustained exuberance of these Sunday liturgies. Like the Jewish Sabbath, they are a visitation of eternity in time, of paradise on earth.

♦ USING THE SACRAMENTARY: Either opening prayer fits well with the readings. The sequence or any of its metrical adaptations can be sung again today before the gospel procession, or perhaps at the conclusion of the proclamation of the gospel. The 1985 edition of the sacramentary permits any of the Easter prefaces to be used during the octave and the whole season following. To keep the unity of the first eight days, choose one and stick with it through today. (Psalm 118, "This is the day the Lord has made," might also be used only throughout the octave, although it is one of the two common seasonal psalms for all of Eastertime.) The Solemn Blessing of the Easter Vigil and Easter Sunday bears repeating today and perhaps throughout the season. Don't forget that dramatic double Alleluia at the dismissal—why can't it be part of all the dismissals of Eastertime?

♦ MYSTAGOGY: "The third step of initiation, the celebration of the sacraments, is followed by the final period of postbaptismal catechesis or mystagogy. This is a time for the community and the neophytes together to grow in deepening their grasp of the paschal mystery and in making it part of their lives through meditation on the gospel, sharing in the eucharist, and doing the works of charity. . . . Since the distinctive spirit and power of the period of postbaptismal catechesis or mystagogy derive from the new, personal experience of the sacraments and of the community, its main setting is the so-called Masses for neophytes, that is, the Sunday Masses of the Easter season." (RCIA, 244, 247)

Mystagogy is a mouthful of a word that means "learning the mystery." How does our community approach, enter into, and stay within a mystery that lasts 50 days—a symbol of eternity? The Spirit is the teacher of the language of mystery. "Our perspective on this season would profit much from recognizing that these 50 days *are Pentecost.* Pentecost Sunday (the fiftieth day) is but the glorious closing to this season of the Spirit." *(Saint Andrew Bible Missal)*

The Eastertime lectionary challenges us—those reborn in Christ and those of us who have renewed that baptismal grace—to enter upon the lifelong, timeless task of living—in community—the gospel of the Lord. This year's readings from the First Letter of Peter offer us perhaps the most ancient mystagogical texts of the church. This letter is an extended postbaptismal sermon, rich with practical advice in Christian living. It is a primer in the language of Christian mystery.

The choice of Acts as the community's public reading at all eucharistic liturgies for these 50 days is not arbitrary. As one European ordo notes: "This tradition is attested by John Chrysostom (Sermon 4,5) as well as Augustine (Sermon 315); into this climate of joyful celebration the church also introduces the proclamation of successive pages from the Gospel of John, for John is the theologian and catechist of the Lord's *Pascha,* and of the paschal sacraments."

◆ REMEMBER TO KEEP THE CHURCH LOOKING LIKE EASTER. Don't let the harvest of spring colors and flowery scents wilt and turn brown by the third Sunday. Many parishes with strong ethnic traditions observe this "second Easter Sunday" as a day for a parish potluck supper when folks bring ethnic specialties to share—a sort of parish-wide Easter breakfast. You might consider scheduling Sunday Evening Prayer a bit later than during Lent; surely the overwhelming beauty of springtime brings forth our praise—but it can also make it harder to drop our afternoon activities to come to prayer.

◆ TODAY IS EARTH DAY, the twentieth anniversary of the first Earth Day. As of this writing, celebrations are still in the planning stages. This day is meant to be a national consciousness-raiser for environmental issues. The work that needs to be done is enormous—a work for which many of the social teachings of the church can prepare us, for example, Pope John Paul's 1987 encyclical, "On the Social Concerns of the Church." For thoughts about how the concerns of Earth Day are part and parcel of our Eastertime, see the entries in this Calendar on April 25 and May 15.

◆ YOM HA-SHOAH, THE DAY OF THE DESTRUCTION (Holocaust Memorial Day). On the Jewish calendar this comes 12 days after Passover. This year the day is a Sunday. Just as the Jewish custom is to transfer days of sorrow and fasting that fall on the Sabbath to the next day, so Christians might transfer this Sunday observance to the next day, Monday, April 23. If the parish has made any efforts to restore ember days, then this might be one that is kept each year. What is suggested here is that there be a day on which both Jewish and Christian

23 MONDAY
Easter Weekday (#267)

George, martyr
OPTIONAL MEMORIAL

Acts 4:23–31
John 3:1–8

24 TUESDAY
Easter Weekday (#268)

Fidelis of Sigmaringen,
    priest and martyr
OPTIONAL MEMORIAL

Acts 4:32–37
John 3:7–15

25 WEDNESDAY
Mark, evangelist
FEAST (#555)

1 Peter 5:5–14
Mark 16:15–20

Rogation Day

26 THURSDAY
Easter Weekday (#270)

Acts 5:27–33
John 3:31–36

27 FRIDAY
Easter Weekday (#271)

Acts 5:34–42
John 6:1–15

28 SATURDAY
Easter Weekday (#272)

Peter Chanel, priest and martyr
OPTIONAL MEMORIAL

Louis Grignion de Montfort,
    priest
OPTIONAL MEMORIAL (Canada)

Acts 6:1–7
John 6:16–21

29 SUNDAY
Third Sunday of Easter (#47)

Acts 2:14, 22–28
1 Peter 1:17–21
Luke 24:13–35

communities observe a time of remembering (and, for Christians, also of repenting for what happened and for what was not done to stop it.) In the words of Rabbi Lawrence Hoffman: "For Jew and Christian alike, Yom ha-Shoah offers the opportunity for more than the expression of guilt. It calls for a ritual rehearsing of memory, appropriate confession before God, affirmation of the saved remnant, and dedication toward those tasks which our Holocaust memory demands."

This ember day falls within our most festive season, the Eastertime we have only begun to recover. This might be the right place. Within the Fifty Days of Eastertime there would be something broken—a fast day, a mourning day, a day for renunciations of evil. In the midst of Easter it would have to raise up every question the Holocaust itself raises.

23 **George, martyr, fourth century.** George the dragon fighter is an *alter Christus,* a new Christ slaying death's dragon. George weds the princess—a symbol of the church. He is patron of springtime, and his name appropriately means vinedresser or farmer—one of the Easter titles for Christ.

25 **Mark, evangelist,** traditionally considered the founder of the church at Alexandria in Egypt. *The Gospel According to Mark* (Collegeville: The Liturgical Press, 1983) summarizes the challenge of Mark's Gospel:

> When Christians choose to encounter Mark's Jesus, they meet with that side of Jesus that is simplest of the four [gospels]—and the most demanding! Mark's version of Jesus' life centers on his death and on the meaning of suffering. When they open themselves to involvement with Jesus as Mark presents him, they realize that they too are invited to give meaning to life (and to death) as he did, namely, by radical trust in God and by loving service to others' needs.

◆ MARK'S FEAST IS ONE OF THE TRADITIONAL ROGATION DAYS—days of asking questions, days of asking for blessings from God for our earth and its peoples. In the sacramentary, "Masses and Prayers for Various Needs and Occasions; For Productive Land" is in the spirit of a Rogation Day. Perhaps its opening prayer can be used as a collect for appropriate intercessions today or on the three Rogation Days that precede the Ascension. If you haven't already done so, find out if your diocese has a rural life office and discover its resources. The new *Book of Blessings* has a beautiful Order for the Blessing of Fields and Flocks and an Order of Blessing for the Seedtime. Throughout the spring, there is much to worry about and much to pray for as animals are born, crops emerge, orchards blossom and spring weather runs its often dangerous course.

29 **Third Sunday of Easter.** "The two recounted what had happened to them along the road, and how they had come to recognize him in the breaking of the bread." This text from Luke's Gospel, together with the readings from Peter's Pentecost sermon and the First Letter of Peter, combine to provide a rich and deeply moving liturgy of the word.

◆ USING THE SACRAMENTARY: Look carefully over the five Easter prefaces; perhaps one could be chosen and memorized, then heard Sunday after Sunday. (In Preface IV "man" can be "humanity.") What eucharistic prayer is being offered in the community's name? If one of the reconciliation prayers was used for Lent, and Eucharistic Prayer I for the Easter octave, then maybe Prayer III could be used from now till Pentecost (even on weekdays). There are also special Easter inserts in the Eucharistic Prayer for Masses with Children III. A few of the musical settings of the Eucharistic Prayer for Masses with Children II are so worthwhile that they deserve being used, at least at the principal parish Mass, during all of Eastertime.

◆ EASTERTIME FLOWERS: This is the Sunday that the lilies go brown. Have you budgeted for flowers throughout the season? Mums are boring and autumnal, although cheap and long-lasting. Daisy-type or anemone-type mums in pastel colors fit spring better than more commonly available mums. Cinerarias and calceolarias are generally also inexpensive and long-lasting, but they fit the springtime better than any variety of mums. A well-grown azalea will sometimes last a good four weeks. In the north, large cut branches of flowering trees brought indoors will go from bud to bloom in a week. They're attractive stuck into enormous pots of wet sand. Just make sure the sand is saltless. Perhaps, where you live, everything is flowering all around you. Ask parishioners to help out in keeping the worship environment at its flowery best. Giant, stable, waterproof pots or glass vessels make arranging branches much easier.

◆ CATHERINE OF SIENA, VIRGIN, MYSTIC, DOCTOR OF THE CHURCH, 1347–1380. Catherine wrote: "I know of no means of savoring the truth and living with it, without self-knowledge. It is this knowledge that makes us really understand that we are nothing, and that our being came from God when we were created in God's image and likeness." Catherine, whose name means "pure," like George and Athanasius, is one of our Eastertime patrons, an *alter Christus,* another Christ.

MAY

1 **May Day.** Eastertime is the church's Maytime. May is Mary's month. This custom is rooted in dedicating the fullness of springtime to Mother Mary. Perhaps we should think of Eastertime itself as "Mary's month," the season when we crown Mary—an image of the church itself—as *Regina caeli,* the Queen of heaven. If you pay special attention to the church's Marian shrine during May, consider giving the shrine this attention throughout *all* of Eastertime. Has Lent and Eastertime taken notice of the springtime passover occurring all around us? Are we sensitive to what goes on outside our windows, or do we cling to a puritanical attitude that creation somehow remains unredeemed, unworthy of becoming part of the way we worship?

2 **Saint Athanasius, bishop of Alexandria, doctor of the church, c.297–373.** Athanasius's name means "the deathless one," and it was Athanasius who first called these fifty days of Easter "The Great Sunday." Like George, Athanasius is an *alter Christus,* a new Christ whose very name tells us of Easter.

6 **Fourth Sunday of Easter.** Christ calls himself "the door of the sheep" in the gospel of this "Good Shepherd Sunday." Adrian Nocent looks at this passage, looks also to the call to conversion in the first two readings, and comments: "Anyone who wants to hear and understand and who believes that Christ, really present, is addressing his kindly but demanding message to us today cannot continue to live as before. The celebration of the liturgy requires that we examine our conscience and be converted." This call to rebirth in the Risen Christ must be the principal focus of the liturgy, despite everything else

30 MONDAY
Easter Weekday (#273)
Pius V, pope
OPTIONAL MEMORIAL
Acts 6:8–15
John 6:22–29

May 1990

1 TUESDAY
Easter Weekday
Joseph the Worker
OPTIONAL MEMORIAL
Acts 7:51—8:1 (#274)
John 6:30–35
or for memorial (#559)
Genesis 1:26—2:3 or Colossians
  3:14–15, 17, 23–24
Matthew 13:54–58
May Day

2 WEDNESDAY
Athanasius, bishop and doctor
MEMORIAL (#275)
Acts 8:1–8
John 6:35–40

3 THURSDAY
Philip and James, apostles
FEAST (#561)
1 Corinthians 15:1–8
John 14:6–14

4 FRIDAY
Easter Weekday (#277)
Acts 9:1–20
John 6:52–59

5 SATURDAY
Easter Weekday (#278)
Acts 9:31–42
John 6:60–69

6 SUNDAY
Fourth Sunday of Easter (#50)
Acts 2:14, 36–41
1 Peter 2:20–25
John 10:1–10

7 MONDAY
Easter Weekday (#279)

Acts 11, 1–18
John 10:11–18

8 TUESDAY
Easter Weekday (#280)

Acts 11:19–26
John 10:22–30

9 WEDNESDAY
Easter Weekday (#281)

Acts 12:24—13:5
John 12:44–50

10 THURSDAY
Easter Weekday (#282)

Acts 13:13–25
John 13:16–20

11 FRIDAY
Easter Weekday (#283)

Acts 13:26–33
John 14:1–6

12 SATURDAY
Easter Weekday (#284)

Nereus and Achilleus, martyrs
OPTIONAL MEMORIAL

Pancras, martyr
OPTIONAL MEMORIAL

Acts 13:44–52
John 14:7–14

13 SUNDAY
Fifth Sunday of Easter (#53)

Acts 6:1–7
1 Peter 2:4–9
John 14:1–12

Mothers Day

that happens this time of year: prayers for vocation to the priesthood and religious life, confirmations and first communions, weddings, Mothers Day, and maybe even the Bishops' Annual Appeal (or whatever they call it in your diocese).

◆ USING THE SACRAMENTARY: The alternative form of the opening prayer is a paraphrase of the psalm appointed for today, Psalm 23. There is no need to abandon the Easter seasonal responsorial psalm just as it is beginning to become a part of the community's collective consciousness. However, Psalm 23 should also be a part of Eastertime. It has many settings suitable for the communion procession, from metrical folk hymns like "My shepherd will supply my need" and "The living God my shepherd is" to responsorial-style arrangements (is there a lovelier version than Gelineau's?).

◆ THE RIPENING OF EASTER: The Byzantine rite divides Eastertime into early, middle and late periods. These are natural divisions that somewhat mirror the passage of spring into summer, a movement toward fruition and ripening occurring all around us. The early period is marked by the telling of resurrection appearances, corresponding every year in both Western and Eastern lectionaries to the First, Second and Third Sundays of Easter. The middle period in the Byzantine liturgy is marked by the great Johannine gospels that we in the West associate with the scrutinies—which means that in Eastern tradition, these gospels are *the* mystagogical readings. (Imagine that!) Late Eastertime is, of course, the ten-day period from Ascension until Pentecost.

Our own rite's "middle period" of Eastertime is characterized by the reading of the Last Discourse in John, also mystagogical in every sense. It would be just as well to maintain the same texts and music for the gathering song, introductory rites, psalm, communion and concluding rites throughout Eastertime, especially from Easter Sunday until the Sixth Sunday, but perhaps the gathering song and maybe the communion song can change these next few weeks to reflect something of the images of John's Gospel, especially the call to be faithful witnesses and the commandment to love one another. An example of such music (and there are many) is Chepponis's "You shall be my witnesses" (GIA, G-2543).

◆ CONFIRMATION AND FIRST COMMUNION: This Fourth Sunday of Easter would be fitting as the parish's annual first communion day. Both confirmation and first eucharist deserve Eastertime Sunday—and not just "the month of May"— celebrations right in the midst of a parish Sunday Mass. What is the ongoing parish practice for connecting the sacraments into the liturgical year? Are people sensitive to these connections? Are the sacramental preparation programs integrated into the parish's liturgical life and leadership—or do these programs function outside of the cooperation of parish liturgical ministers? And—the biggest question of the lot—what gradual steps are being taken to lead the parish toward a mature understanding of confirmation as a sacrament of initiation and away from the understanding of confirmation as merely a "graduation exercise" for the religious education program? A very helpful book to help begin the dialogue is *When Should We Confirm?* (LTP, 1989).

13 **Fifth Sunday of Easter.** The selection from Acts shows the diversification of ministries in the early community as adaptations are made. The First Letter of Peter reminds us that we are "living stones, built as an edifice of spirit into a holy priesthood." Jesus predicts that his followers will not only do the works that he himself does, they will do "greater far than these."

This Sunday's gospel contains the familiar phrase, "I am the way, the truth and the life." Would there be a finer song to sing (or hear sung) than Ralph Vaughan Williams's setting of George Herbert's poem, "Come, my way, my truth, my life"?

◆ USING THE SACRAMENTARY: The first of the opening prayers is particularly beautiful. This might be a good weekend to consider using Easter Preface III: "He is still our priest, our advocate who always pleads our cause. . . ." Several of the Easter prefaces seem to have been written with Jesus' "Final Discourse" in mind (chapters 14—17 of John's Gospel).

Many of the sacramentary's prayer texts address God as Father. This image is used to make clear to whom our prayers are addressed: to the Father, through the Son, in the Spirit (although prepositions here fall short of being precise). Even those who do not see a problem in these many masculine references to God often recognize the problem of limiting our imagery of God to only a few phrases. Is "God our Mother and Father" a good substitute, or does it merely remind us that this is not how these prayers are worded in our holy books?

◆ THIS IS ALSO MOTHERS DAY. An intercession can be included today for all people who are examples of a mother's love. A blessing of mothers may be found in the *Book of Blessings,* which might be prayed over all the people before the final blessing, as well as in *Catholic Household Blessings and Prayers* for use at home. But the focus of the day cannot be divided. Mothers Day must be an aside to the Lord's Day. Too many parish communities have exalted Mothers Day into an exercise in civil religion. Gimmicks such as "Mothers Day novenas" not only are in bad taste, they twist liturgy into moneymaking devices, or worse, into superstition. There is a practical consideration when choosing even an intercession or special blessing for this day: Weigh on the one hand the advantages of offering mothers public support and prayer for what is, to be sure, a holy calling, and on the other hand the disadvantages of isolating even further those adult women in the parish who do not have children.

15 **Isidore, patron of farmers.** A few years ago Bishop Michael Sheehan of Lubbock, Texas, spoke of the church and farmers:

> Those in crisis know that the church does not control the price of commodities, and they know that the churches don't have large sums of money available as loans. But they do know that we can provide on-site moral, emotional and spiritual support that hurting families need to endure the present pain and find some hope and meaning in their unfolding futures.

Such support might begin today in a small, sound way through the observance of the memorial of St. Isidore, patron of farmers. The Mass for productive land, in the sacramentary under "Masses and Prayers for Various Needs and Occasions," is a possible text for this day. The gospel might fittingly enough be John 20:1–2, 11–18 (#603 in the lectionary), the appearance of the Risen Lord who was mistaken as a gardener. In addition to or instead of the eucharist, the Order for the Blessing of Fields and Flocks from the *Book of Blessings* might be celebrated communally, or the Rogation Day blessing of fields and gardens from *Catholic Household Blessings and Prayers* might be celebrated in backyards.

20 **Sixth Sunday of Easter.** Ascension Day is this week—it could be the beginning of the community's novena of prayer and renewal. Ascension to Pentecost is the original novena, when in mystery we gather

---

14 MONDAY
Matthias, apostle
FEAST (#564)
Acts 1:15–17, 20–26
John 15:9–17

15 TUESDAY
Easter Weekday (#286)
Isidore, farmer
OPTIONAL MEMORIAL (U.S.A.)
Acts 14:19–28
John 14:27–31

16 WEDNESDAY
Easter Weekday (#287)
Acts 15:1–6
John 15:1–8

17 THURSDAY
Easter Weekday (#288)
Acts 15:7–21
John 15:9–11

18 FRIDAY
Easter Weekday (#289)
John I, pope and martyr
OPTIONAL MEMORIAL
Acts 15:22–31
John 15:12–17

19 SATURDAY
Easter Weekday (#290)
Acts 16:1–10
John 15:18–21

20 SUNDAY
Sixth Sunday of Easter (#56)
Acts 8:5–8, 14–17
I Peter 3:15–18
John 14:15–21

21 MONDAY
Easter Weekday (#291)

Acts 16:11–15
John 15:26—16:4

Victoria Day (Canada)

Rogation Day

22 TUESDAY
Easter Weekday (#292)

Acts 16:22–34
John 16:5–11

Rogation Day

23 WEDNESDAY
Easter Weekday (#293)

Acts 17:15, 22—18:1
John 16:12–15

Rogation Day

24 THURSDAY
Ascension of the Lord
SOLEMNITY (#59)

Acts 1:1–11
Ephesians 1:17–23
Matthew 28:16–20

*In Canada, the Ascension is
celebrated on May 27.*

Hepatica

together for nine days with Mary and the other disciples to await the outpouring of the promised gift of the Spirit. The canceling of business-as-usual (just like the priority given to Lent) could be a signal to all levels of parish life that these days will "bring the paschal mystery to its completion" (Pentecost Preface). This is a perfect opportunity to celebrate (or introduce) communal Evening Prayer.

◆ USING THE SACRAMENTARY: The first form of the opening prayer is straightforward; the alternative is clumsy. Again, Easter Prefaces III or V reflect something of the imagery of the "high priestly prayer" of John.

◆ PREACHING DURING THESE WEEKS OF EASTERTIME is sometimes difficult because the readings do not always offer concrete images or colorful stories. Yet the focus of a homily can be *any* of the prayer texts of liturgy. During this season of mystagogy, why couldn't homilies focus on introducing neophytes and reintroducing all of us to the ritual actions and attitudes of eucharist—of taking bread and cup, of offering thanks and praise, of breaking the bread, and of eating and drinking in unity? As a further recommendation regarding preaching, the late Orthodox liturgist Alexander Schmemann reminded us that the homily is not supposed to be *about* the Good News. The homily is supposed to *be* the Good News. We Christians are not dispensers of information but announcers of news, a news hot with the fire of the Spirit, the fire of true evangelization.

◆ LITURGICAL PARTIES: Festivities should be part of any community's life as Pentecost draws near. It might be a good idea to include in a special way all who helped with the Lent, Triduum and Eastertime liturgies. Such a parish party or picnic could become an annual tradition. "To close the period of postbaptismal catechesis, some sort of celebration should be held at the end of the Easter season near Pentecost; festivities in keeping with local custom may accompany the occasion." (RCIA, 249) That's probably the only rubric in the liturgy that prescribes a party (demonstrating that sometimes the church's business should be "monkey business"). Although the primary celebration should be diocesan, involving the bishop with the neophytes and their godparents, a parish celebration is also fitting.

◆ BE SURE TO ANNOUNCE ASCENSION DAY coming this Thursday, May 24. The Monday, Tuesday and Wednesday of this week are the traditional Rogation Days. See the entries in this calendar under April 25 and May 15 for a brief discussion of these seedtime celebrations.

24 **Ascension of the Lord.** "Ascension is a day that unfolds the promise that Jesus will return. . . . [On this day] we do not observe a departure. We celebrate a presence." *(Saint Andrew Bible Missal)* "A few days before Pentecost we send Christ on ahead into the heavenly land, so that in all fairness Christ might send back from heaven our sweetest desire. The full sweetness of earth is Christ's humanity, and the full sweetness of heaven—our desire—is the Spirit." (Aelred of Rievaulx)

◆ USING THE SACRAMENTARY: The first opening prayer is beautiful: ". . . his ascension is our glory and our hope." Notice how all the texts speak not of absence but of the mystery of *our* presence alongside Lord Jesus in the peaceable kingdom. The responsorial psalm proper to today is one of the most powerful in the psalter; also remember the special insert for Eucharistic Prayer I. The first of the Ascension prefaces is the richer and might well provide (the week before) a bulletin summary of what the feast is all about. Use the proper solemn blessing.

◆ THE PASCHAL CANDLE REMAINS IN THE PROMINENT PLACE it has had through-out Eastertime and continues to be lighted until and including Pentecost. In former times, a ritual associated with Ascension was the extinguishing of the paschal candle after the gospel. The diffusion of the smoke rising and dispersing from the smoldering wick was a subtle sign of Christ's life filling the universe. Yet in truth, the snuffing out of the Easter light could be interpreted in mostly negative ways. That's why the rubrics now insist that the paschal flame must continue to shine through Pentecost—both unifying the Fifty Days and imply-ing that the fire of the Spirit is one with the light of Christ. Why not mark Ascension Day by surrounding the candle in a "cloud" of black locust, oleander or rose blossoms? Setting a bowl of incense underneath the candle throughout the liturgy of the word today would be another tradition worth returning to year after year.

◆ A PLEA AGAINST GIMMICKRY: The releasing of balloons to symbolize the Ascension is one of the worst sorts of gimmicks. Littering a neighborhood with colored plastic may be pretty and loads of fun for some people, but it seems to signify that the Lord Jesus floated up, up and away into the wild blue yonder. Even the least mature among us can realize that such an image is laughable.

◆ A PASCHAL PROCESSION: Balloons notwithstanding, it's long been customary to celebrate Ascension outside under the open skies; one of the most ancient traditions of this day is called "beating the bounds," a procession that covers the boundaries of the parish, or at least parish property. Easter water is sprinkled along the route. It signifies that the presence of the Risen Christ has filled the world, the same triumphal spirit of Palm Sunday's procession. An Ascension Day procession would make a fitting introductory rite for Mass today. (See the discussion about processions on Palm Sunday, April 8. It's much more than coincidence that Psalms 24 and 47 are part of the liturgical mystery of both this day and the Palm Sunday procession.)

◆ MOST PARISHES WILL HAVE AN EVENING LITURGY. Why not let the Mass be one part of an evening's worth of festivity—a potluck supper, a concert, a parish dance? These weekday holy days are surprise Sundays, especially this holy day which falls in a season we call the "Great Sunday." We aren't merely obliged to keep the holy day by attending Mass. We are obliged to keep the entire day holy, with creative joy. If the parish school is responsible for preparing a Mass this day, see the recommendations for Ascension in the *Leader's Manual* for the *Hymnal for Catholic Students* (GIA/LTP).

27 Seventh Sunday of Easter. We are a community rejoicing in the exaltation of our Risen Lord, but at the same time, and in obedience to his command, waiting "in the city until we are clothed with power from on high." So everything should be moving toward next Sunday's culmina-tion of the paschal season in the glorious celebration of Pentecost.

A different gathering song and psalm (repeat Psalm 47 from Ascension) would probably be the only changes from the Eastertime music. The rich musical tradition of the Roman rite could provide some of the music for this Sunday and next. *Veni Creator Spiritus* is a hymn whose melody *was* Pentecost to a previous generation. This final blessing from the Episcopal *Book of Occasional Services* might be suitable:

28 MONDAY
Easter Weekday (#297)

Acts 19:1–8
John 16:29–33

Memorial Day (U.S.A.)

29 TUESDAY
Easter Weekday (#298)

Acts 20:17–27
John 17:1–11

Shavuot (Jewish Pentecost) begins at sundown.

30 WEDNESDAY
Easter Weekday (#299)

Acts 20:28–38
John 17:11–19

31 THURSDAY
Visitation
FEAST (#572)

Zephaniah 3:14–18
 or Romans 12:9–16
Luke 1:39–56

> May the Spirit of truth lead you into all truth,
> giving you grace to confess that Jesus Christ is Lord
> and to proclaim the wonderful works of God.
> And may the blessing of almighty God . . .

◆ USING THE SACRAMENTARY: The entrance antiphon is splendid: "Do not hide from me." That seems to echo the yearning of the lovers in Song of Songs and also our own yearning for the full presence of God in the Spirit. Perhaps the Preface of the Holy Spirit I, the former Pentecost Preface, could be used today; the two Ascension prefaces do not have this forward-looking orientation. The Solemn Blessing for Ascension doesn't quite fit today unless "on this day" reads "at this season." Interestingly, the Solemn Blessing for Advent is appropriate to these days before Pentecost. The phrase "as man" can be dropped.

◆ BE SURE TO ANNOUNCE NEXT SUNDAY'S SOLEMNITY, perhaps along with an announcement to come help decorate the church and share in any other preparations for parish celebrations.

28 **Memorial Day (U.S.A.).** In many places this national holiday has been turned into All Souls Day in spring. (In fact, this day often gets far more attention than All Souls as a day to remember the dead—and that's an enormous loss within our tradition.)

Memorial Day was born after the Civil War in a spirit that connected remembering those who died in war with the desperate need to forgive and to rebuild. If in the United States we no longer understand what it means to remember the horror of war and to dedicate ourselves to the work of reconciliation between nations and peoples, we really should not be observing this day at all, much less turning it into All Souls Day.

Sadly, there are many families in this country who have their war dead, families who need to forgive and who need to return to places to rebuild what war has destroyed. In our arrogance and confusion since Hiroshima, as a nation we seem to have forgotten so much of our history, including the origins—and the necessity—of an authentic celebration of Memorial Day.

If there is a Mass for Memorial Day, particularly appropriate readings from the Masses for the Dead are 2 Maccabees 12:43–46 (Judas took up a collection among the soldiers for the dead); Acts 10:34–36, 42–43 (Those of any nation are acceptable to God) or Philippians 3:20–21 (We have our citizenship in heaven); and John 12:23–26 (Unless a grain of wheat . . .). Coming as it does before Pentecost, the scriptures of the Jubilee (Leviticus 25, Isaiah 61)—the fiftieth year when debts were forgiven, prisoners set free, mourners comforted and lands restored—would certainly be appropriate today. The Mass for peace and justice (despite its noninclusive language) fits both this day and the Easter season.

31 **Visitation of Mary and Elizabeth.** This feast used to come on July 2. But now on its new date it can be celebrated as a prelude to the Midsummer birth of John the Baptist—a Sunday this year. Tonight is a perfect occasion for Marian prayer, remembering the holy greeting of two women awaiting the birth of God's reign as well as remembering the novena in the upper room when the disciples, women and men, gathered with Mary to await the fulfillment of God's reign in the outpouring of the Spirit. Chapter 2 of the Song of Songs just about begs to be proclaimed today, as Eastertime closes, as Mary's month closes, as everything of winter is forgotten, as the "beloved leaps across the mountains," like Mary going "in haste" to visit her kinswoman, like the unborn John in his mother's womb—in the "hill country" of Judah.

JUNE

2 **Pentecost Vigil.** Masses celebrated in the afternoon or evening use the Vigil of Pentecost texts (#63 in the lectionary). In Jewish tradition, Pentecost is observed with a vigil in remembrance of the nightwatch Israel kept at the foot of Mount Sinai before receiving the Law "in fire and wind." The tradition of the church is to keep vigil for Pentecost in the manner of the Easter Vigil, with a beautiful *lucernarium* (lamp lighting), a lengthy liturgy of the word (the heart of any vigil keeping), and the liturgy of the eucharist when the vigil is complete. Pentecost is also a customary day for initiation. See page 110 for a vigil service for Pentecost Eve.

In *Praise God in Song* (GIA), the section called "Resurrection Vigil of the Lord's Day" presents background information and a simple order of service. Surely this spirit should be part of the way we keep all Sundays, especially this concluding Lord's Day of our 50-day-long Great Sunday. A prerequisite for this vigil would be the raising of parish consciousness and enthusiasm for the importance of Pentecost, making sure the festival is kept not just at Mass but throughout the day, from Saturday vigiling to Sunday morning eucharist to an afternoon picnic and Sunday Evening Prayer.

◆ LEARNING TO LIVE COUNTERCULTURALLY: What is being written about here is not one more liturgical service added to the parish's docket of worship—with the high hopes that maybe a hundred people might show up. What a resurrection vigil is, what the observance of Pentecost is, involves a parish whose consciousness of the countercultural demands of its liturgical life has been raised mightily. And this is something that *can* happen over years, not just in extra-special parishes with extra-special people but in ordinary communities of ordinary people, especially where parish leadership has remained faithful to year-by-year tradition and where religious education, the parish school, the various ministries of the parish all regard the liturgy as the source and summit of their life together.

3 **Pentecost.** Culmination. Fulfillment. These are the key words to remember in preparing the Pentecost liturgy. The day, however, is not about endings. The culmination and fulfillment that characterize Pentecost signal a beginning. Some parishes make sure to schedule (and ask everyone to come to) their principal liturgy at nine in the morning—one of the few specific time references in the scriptures (Acts 2:15)—and then to reschedule the other liturgies of the day around that time. Because the day marks such a high point of the year (and has been known as the birthday of the church) for Christians and because it is about being many yet one, it is an ideal Sunday to cancel as many Masses as possible so that this one time a year the parish can come together, all together, at one Mass (or two or even three if the space just is not adequate). In some parishes this can mean a combining of ethnic and language communities,

June 1990

1 FRIDAY
Justin, martyr
MEMORIAL (#301)
Acts 25:13–21
John 21:15–19

2 SATURDAY
Morning:
Easter Weekday (#302)
Marcellinus and Peter, martyrs
OPTIONAL MEMORIAL
Acts 28:16–20, 30–31
John 21:20–25
Evening:
Pentecost Vigil (#63)
Genesis 11:1–9 *and/or* Exodus 19:3–8, 16–20 *and/or* Ezekiel 37:1–14 *and/or* Joel 3:1–5
Romans 8:22–27
John 7:37–39

3 SUNDAY
Pentecost (#64)
SOLEMNITY
Acts 2:1–11
1 Corinthians 12:3–7, 12–13
John 20:19–23

John XXIII died this day in 1963.

Iceland poppies

of "choir music" and "contemporary music" communities, of all sorts of communities. Choose neutral times and involve everybody. Friendly persuasion will be necessary. The liturgy must be done well with lots of good singing, and the homily carefully and sensitively prepared. But then this can be an annual event—and it can teach us a lot, by experience, about the advantages of liturgy in a full house.

◆ Do you need to be convinced of the splendor and importance of this day? Consider some of the titles, ancient and modern, for this solemnity: Feast of First Fruits, The Sealing of Passover, The Arrival at Sinai, Milk and Honey Day, Fire and Wind Day, New Wine Day, The Feast of Seven Weeks, The Fiftieth Day, The Completion of the Grain Harvest, The Revelation of the Trinity, Birth of the Church, Holy Spirit Day, White Sunday, Green Sunday, Red Sunday.

These three colors have a marvelous significance: "Red Sunday" obviously refers to the vestments, the color of fire and blood, since Pentecost was the only Sunday in the old calendar on which this color was worn (and now, quite wondrously, red vesture marks the two poles of Easter: Passion and Pentecost). "White (Whit) Sunday" refers to the color of the robes of the newly baptized, since the completion of Easter was also an occasion for initiation. "Green Sunday" refers to the just about universal custom in both synagogues and churches of decorating for Pentecost with leafy branches.

Why not employ these most traditional of Pentecost decorations for the church today by festooning the worship space with branches of foliage, even whole poplar trees cut and stood in water? (Christmas is not the only season when we decorate with greenery.) Bundles of green wheat, field flowers and freshly cut plumes of grasses are also customary. While that seems like a lot of trouble and mess, perhaps that's the whole point: It shows the abundance of our joy. This day is our welcome to summer, the completion of springtime's passover represented by all the signs of warmth and light and burgeoning life.

◆ Flowers and tongues of fire: Filling the church with fragrant flowers, all signs of the Spirit, could be made easier by requesting garden flowers from parishioners—a good practice throughout the year, especially Eastertime. Fragrant flowers are signs of the christening Spirit, the "aroma of Christ": In the North this is the season of roses, peonies and iris; in the South the bull bay magnolias are in bloom. Flowers can surround the paschal candle alongside many other candles and vigil lights: the light of Easter multiplied fifty-fold.

◆ First fruits: One of the biblical titles for Pentecost is *Yom ha-Bikkurim,* the day of first fruits. The after-worship hospitality can include some of these first fruits in the form of rhubarb pie, strawberry shortcake and cherry cobblers— part of the flavor of the feast. Celebrate the wind today with fluttering windsocks and streamers. For the ideal Pentecost decorations, simply take Easter's finery and "ripen" it: Pastels become vivid scarlets, flowers become fruits, eggs become birds, unleavened bread becomes yeast-raised loaves.

◆ Using the sacramentary and the lectionary: Applying the "interchangeability" provision found with the texts of so many feasts, perhaps the beautiful alternative opening prayer from the Vigil Mass could be used at all Masses, thus eliminating the need for too much explanation about the meaning of the day. (The alternative prayer for the Mass during the Day sounds like a pop song from the '60s: "horizons of our minds.") Today is a fitting occasion for infant baptisms as it is for the sprinkling rite. See the Eastertime section of "The Seasons" for additional notes on Pentecost.

Many parishes embellish the readings or the intercessions by having several lectors do them in different languages. The sequence should be sung: Reciting any song is deadly. Metrical versions can be found in any hymnal. There is a proper Preface today, inserts for Eucharistic Prayer I and a proper solemn blessing. Notice that the dismissal includes the double Alleluia, which implies continuing this song with a recessional rich in our Easter word of praise. One parish sings as the recessional song the setting of the Alleluia it sings as the gospel acclamation of the Easter Vigil, used only these two times in the year.

◆ "THE WHOLE OCCURENCE ASTONISHED THEM." (Acts 2:7) Something about today's worship—and this sounds terribly close to recommending a gimmick—should offer us a surprise, a startling windy noise that upsets our order and then sends us out of our comfortable enclosures to proclaim the "marvels God has accomplished." The natural place for this is the homily. The beginning and end of liturgy may also somehow be unique to this day—an avant-garde choral or instrumental piece, a grand procession out the doors as the paschal candle leads us into the world, a shower of rose petals (a medieval custom) cast upon the assembly, a great rush of brass and bells that crescendos at nine o'clock.

How does the completion of Easter rouse in us a renewed commitment to the universal mission of the church? Today's strong images of reconciliation and global unity make tonight (or Pentecost Eve) a good opportunity to gather with other churches in our area for ecumenical prayer. Evening Prayer this day concludes Eastertime and deserves attention. In the Byzantine rite, this Evening Prayer is marked by the command for everyone to kneel—the first kneeling since Easter Eve. Many parishes have the great custom of a Pentecost picnic—in fact, in many places in Europe, "to make a Pentecost" means eating *al fresco,* like the disciples spilling into the streets.

 **ORDINARY TIME**

 4 **Ordinary Time resumes.** This is the ninth week in Ordinary Time, Year II. At weekday Mass we complete Mark and read from 2 Peter and 2 Timothy.

10 **Trinity Sunday.** Today is the Tenth Sunday in Ordinary Time. The readings and prayers are for Trinity Sunday.

◆ THIS SUNDAY AND NEXT ARE SOMETIMES DIFFICULT TO LOCATE in the sacramentary and lectionary. Expressing these two rather cerebral solemnities is best done through some familiar trinitarian or eucharistic hymns. Do not make it seem to the assembly that Eastertime has been extended by two more weeks. Make sure the Easter-Pentecost decorations are down; that doesn't mean the church gets austere, just simplified. At the very least, choose white vestments that are noticeably different from Eastertime's vesture. The paschal season is a long and intense period as it is. It cannot bear extension in either direction and it would be pastorally counterproductive to do so.

◆ USING THE SACRAMENTARY AND LECTIONARY: Use a Gloria different from that of Eastertime (if your parish sings the Gloria during Ordinary Time). Even if you sing the same seasonal psalm throughout several-week blocks of Ordinary Time,

---

4 MONDAY
Weekday (#353)

2 Peter 1:2–7
Mark 12:1–12

Ninth Week in Ordinary Time

5 TUESDAY
Boniface, bishop and martyr
MEMORIAL (#354)

2 Peter 3:12–15, 17–18
Mark 12:13–17

6 WEDNESDAY
Weekday (#355)

Norbert, bishop
OPTIONAL MEMORIAL

2 Timothy 1:1–3, 6–12
Mark 12:18–27

7 THURSDAY
Weekday (#356)

2 Timothy 2:8–15
Mark 12:28–34

8 FRIDAY
Weekday (#357)

2 Timothy 3:10–17
Mark 12:35–37

9 SATURDAY
Weekday (#358)

Ephrem, deacon and doctor
OPTIONAL MEMORIAL

BVM
OPTIONAL MEMORIAL

2 Timothy 4:1–8
Mark 12:38–44

10 SUNDAY
Trinity Sunday
SOLEMNITY (#165)

Exodus 34:4–6, 8–9
2 Corinthians 13:11–13
John 3:16–18

11 MONDAY
Barnabas, apostle
MEMORIAL

Acts 11:21–26; 13:1–3 (#580)
Matthew 10:7–13
 or Matthew 5:1–12 (#359)

Tenth Week in Ordinary Time

12 TUESDAY
Weekday (#360)

1 Kings 17:7–16
Matthew 5:13–16

13 WEDNESDAY
Anthony of Padua,
 priest and doctor
MEMORIAL (#361)

1 Kings 18:20–39
Matthew 5:17–19

14 THURSDAY
Weekday (#362)

1 Kings 18:41–46
Matthew 5:20–26

15 FRIDAY
Weekday (#363)

1 Kings 19:9, 11–16
Matthew 5:27–32

16 SATURDAY
Weekday (#364)

BVM
OPTIONAL MEMORIAL

1 Kings 19:19–21
Matthew 5:33–37

17 SUNDAY
Body and Blood of Christ
SOLEMNITY (#168)

Deuteronomy 8:2–3, 14–16
1 Corinthians 10:16–17
John 6:51–58

Fathers Day

try defining the next three Sunday's solemnities with their own proper psalms. Today's "psalm" is the glorious canticle of the three youths in the fiery furnace, Daniel 3:52–56. Eucharistic Prayer III includes praise of the Trinity. Eucharistic Prayer for Children II also recounts the work of the Father, Son and Spirit.

The following are sample Mass texts by Peter Scagnelli:

> *Introduction:* Today's solemnity is a celebration of the mystery of God's self-revelation. Through the scriptures of Israel, in the person of Jesus, and through the unfolding centuries of the church's life, we have come to know the One who loves us as Father, Son and Holy Spirit.

> *Invitiation to the Penitential Rite:* My brothers and sisters: let us confess our sinfulness before the God of tenderness and compassion, the God who is slow to anger and rich in kindness, the God who sent his Son not to condemn the world but to save it.

> *Penitenital Rite (invocations):* Revealing the Father's love: Lord, have mercy. Giving yourself to us in word and sacrament: Christ, have mercy. Breathing your Spirit upon the church: Lord, have mercy.

> *Introduction to the Readings:* We return to Ordinary Time after Easter's Fifty Days. The scriptures present our extraordinary God, who so loved the world that God has revealed the divine nature as the relationship of a compassionate parent and child, who offers us their abiding Spirit on our journey to glory.

◆ TRAVELERS AND VACATIONS: This is a time of year when people begin to leave on vacations. The *Book of Blessings* contains a special order for the blessing of travelers. Such a gift of prayer could be offered weekly throughout the summer, with family and friends remaining behind after liturgy to pray with those who are leaving on trips and vacations.

11 **Weekday.** This is the tenth week in Ordinary Time, Year II. At the weekday Mass we begin to read through Matthew's Gospel and the stories from 1 Kings about Elijah.

13 **Anthony of Padua, priest, doctor of the church, 1195–1231.** "It is the Franciscan custom to give out 'St. Anthony's bread' on Tuesdays to honor his love for the poor. Families might bake their own St. Anthony's bread on his day [which this year, coincidentally, falls on a Tuesday] and make an offering to the poor in his honor." (*The Saint Book,* The Seabury Press, 1979)

17 **Body and Blood of Christ.** Today is the Eleventh Sunday in Ordinary Time. The readings are for the solemnity of the Body and Blood of Christ. (See the notes for Trinity Sunday about vesture and mood.)

◆ USING THE SACRAMENTARY: Beautiful Latin hymns such as "Pange lingua" and "Adoro te devote" have their place today, although they are metrically difficult for many people. Perhaps one can be sung by a soloist during the preparation? Incensation of the table could take place at the preparation time.

The following are sample Mass texts by Peter Scagnelli:

> *Introduction:* On this Lord's Day we celebrate the gift that makes us one body, one Spirit in Christ: the broken bread which is his flesh offered in sacrifice for us, the blessing-cup of his blood poured out for our redemption.

Invititation to the Penitential Rite: My brothers and sisters, let us acknowledge our sinfulness, by which we have offended the God of all goodness, and by which we have wounded the body of Christ, the church.

Penitential Rite (invocations): You are the bread of life come down from heaven: Lord, have mercy. You nourish us with your own body and blood: Christ, have mercy. You alone have the words of everlasting life: Lord, have mercy.

Introduction to the Readings: The Hebrew Scriptures recount the gift of manna, heavenly bread for the desert journey, while Paul celebrates our unity in and communion with the body and blood of Christ. Thus is fulfilled the imagery of ancient days and the promise of Jesus to be himself our living Bread.

◆ REFLECTIONS ON BREAD AND WINE: What kind of bread do we use and where do we get it? Has there been any attempt to use one of the approved recipes for unleavened eucharistic bread and to include the ministry of breadbaking in the parish's roster of liturgical roles? Is communion under both species the norm, the exception, or the "we're not ready for that" practice in the community? Is drinking from the cup encouraged with hospitality and enthusiasm, or is it spoken of legalistically, as an optional personal choice—as if the Lord's command to "take and drink" were appended with "if you feel like it"? Is there honest dialogue regarding people's fear of disease? See Gordon Lathrop's article "AIDS and the Cup" in the March 1988 issue of *Worship* magazine, reprinted in the July 1988 issue of *Liturgy 80*. See also a new LTP publication, *The Communion Rite at Sunday Mass* by Gabe Huck, for a practical and thorough discussion of how this rite can be done each Sunday.

◆ FATHERS DAY IS TODAY—a holiday of "civil religion." The day does not need too much attention from the church; advertisers will ensure its observance. The fathers of the community may be prayed for in the general intercessions, and the new American edition of the *Book of Blessings* has a simple blessing for this day. (Call people's attention to the blessing in *Catholic Household Blessings and Prayers* for use at home.) But, as with Mothers Day, pastoral sensitivity is needed. Consider how this day is more a celebration of a particular kind of love rather than a glorification of a particular sex or vocation.

◆ BE SURE TO ANNOUNCE NEXT SUNDAY'S FESTIVAL OF THE BIRTH OF JOHN THE BAPTIST—this should be a busy week for preparations, decorating, making ready the festivities.

18 **Weekday.** This is the eleventh week of Ordinary Time. The daily lectionary continues marvelous stories of Elijah, Ahab, Jezebel, Athaliah and Elisha from 1 and 2 Kings, 2 Chronicles and Sirach. A remarkable coincidence—or is it?—in these week before the Birth of John, the prophet who comes in the power and person of Elijah!

22 **Solemnity of the Sacred Heart.** This day is difficult to locate in the liturgical books. You will find it after the last two Sundays' solemnities, one of the three days curiously called "Solemnities of the Lord during the Season of the Year," or "during Ordinary Time." The opening prayer texts reveal this day as a model Friday, an occasion to renew after Eastertime the ways we keep every Friday with prayer, fasting and almsgiving in preparation for the Lord's Day. June is a good month to distribute LTP's little prayer cards *Prayer for Fridays*, sold in packs of 100.

18 MONDAY
Weekday (#365)
I Kings 21:1–16
Matthew 5:38–42
Eleventh Week in Ordinary Time

19 TUESDAY
Weekday (#366)
Romuald, abbot
OPTIONAL MEMORIAL
I Kings 21:17–29
Matthew 5:43–48

20 WEDNESDAY
Weekday (#367)
2 Kings 2:1, 6–14
Matthew 6:1–6, 16–18

21 THURSDAY
Aloysius Gonzaga, religious
MEMORIAL (#368)
Sirach 48:1–14
Matthew 6:7–15
Summer Solstice

22 FRIDAY
Sacred Heart
SOLEMNITY (#171)
Deuteronomy 7:6–11
I John 4:7–16
Matthew 11:25–30

23 SATURDAY
Weekday
Morning:
Immaculate Heart of Mary
OPTIONAL MEMORIAL
2 Chronicles 24:17–25 (#370)
Matthew 6:24–34 or for IHM
  Luke 2:41–51 (#573)

Evening:
Vigil of the Birth of John the Baptist (#586)
Jeremiah 1:4–10
I Peter 1:8–12
Luke 1:5–17
Midsummer Eve

*Daisies and
St. John's wort*

24 SUNDAY
Birth of John the Baptist (#587)
SOLEMNITY

Isaiah 49:1–6
Acts 13:22–26
Luke 1:57–66, 80

Midsummer Day

25 MONDAY
Weekday (#371)

2 Kings 17:5–8, 13–15, 18
Matthew 7:1–5

Twelfth Week in Ordinary Time

26 TUESDAY
Weekday (#372)

2 Kings 19:9–11, 14–21,
31–35, 36
Matthew 7:6, 12–14

27 WEDNESDAY
Weekday (#373)

Cyril of Alexandria,
bishop and doctor
OPTIONAL MEMORIAL

2 Kings 22:8–13; 23:1–3
Matthew 7:15–20

28 THURSDAY
Morning:
Irenaeus, bishop and martyr
MEMORIAL (#374)

2 Kings 24:8–17
Matthew 7:21–29

Evening:
**Vigil of Peter and Paul,
apostles**
(#590)

Acts 3:1–10
Galatians 1:11–20
John 21:15–19

29 FRIDAY
Peter and Paul, apostles (#591)
SOLEMNITY

Acts 12:1–11
2 Timothy 4:6–8, 17–18
Matthew 16:13–19

*Poppies, wheat and
cornflowers*

◆ NOTICE HOW THE MONTH OF JUNE IS "BUSTING OUT" with solemnities? There's a simple but compelling reason: the weather. Many of these special days were first popularized in central and northern Europe, where the weather finally settles down this month. In contrast, the principal festivals of our faith, founded so closely upon the Jewish festivals, have their most ancient roots among Mediterranean peoples who found it more to their liking (and their agrarian calendars) to celebrate any time but the blazing summer.

24 **Birth of John the Baptist.** John is the Lampstand of the Light, the Best Man of the Bridegroom, the Voice of the Word! (John 5:35; 3:29; 1:23) Today John is born in time, and his birth is heralded by the signs of the coming of God's reign. It is the summer solstice when our days have reached their longest. The barren are made fruitful, the tongue of the dumb shouts for joy.

If there is any question as to the magnitude of this day, it may be helpful to recognize an ancient festal dynamic perhaps not all that readily apparent in the bright summertime of the church: first the Visitation, May 31; then the Birth of John situated between the feasts of Elisha, June 14, and Elijah, July 20 (principal feasts on the Byzantine calendar); then Transfiguration, August 6 (Elijah again making an appearance: notice how this event employs the image of the shining sun and is connected to the identification of John the Baptist with Elijah—see Matthew 17 and Mark 9). Finally, the Beheading (the passover) of John is celebrated on August 29. One of John's (and Elijah's) primary symbols is the summer sun (the "flaming chariot"), an image drawn from the Benedictus (see Luke 1:78) and 2 Kings 2:1–14 and Sirach 48:1–14.

◆ THE BIRTH OF JOHN IS A GREAT FESTIVAL THAT DESERVES ANY EFFORT to bring people together in celebration throughout the eve and the day. It's the Midsummer nativity! The day is traditionally kept with all the gusto of Christmas, with carols, wreaths, flowers (the daisy—day's eye—is John's flower) and even a great bonfire to celebrate John's title as "Lamp of the Light." (Decorators, take note: Wreaths are splendid symbols of either solstice, and today's customary colors are red, white and green.)

◆ "JACK BE NIMBLE" who jumps over the candlestick is none other than John: We jump over the bonfire (or candle for the timid) to represent the turning of the sun now that the summer solstice is passing (old ritual books sometimes had a blessing for this fire). John said "I must decrease if Christ is to increase," and so this day marks the beginning of the decrease in the length of day. (Those among us who wax romantically about the imagery of the solstice during Advent and Christmastime need to be reminded that this imagery returns in reverse every June!) This solemnity is called "Midsummer Day" in Europe because it is the midpoint in the sun's journey from the spring to autumn equinoxes. In Scandinavia they raise enormous maypoles decked with wreaths to celebrate the day. Yet this day is not just observed by Europeans. It is a great festival in Quebec, in Puerto Rico, even among the Christian communities of Egypt—where legend has it that John the Baptist was buried. And why all this merriment? Read Luke 1:14 and 1:58; *twice* we are told to rejoice in John's birth. A parish night of Midsummer magic is in order, complete with Evening Prayer.

◆ NOTES FOR LITURGY: Make connections with this day and Christmas. Wear the same vestments. In *Praise God in Song* (GIA), the Canticle of Zachary is set in a metrical version that can be sung to any of the tunes for "O little town of

Bethlehem." "The great forerunner of the morn" is a song found in many hymnals which is more rollickingly sung to the tune "Puer nobis nascitur." (Save "On Jordan's banks" for Advent.)

◆ USING THE SACRAMENTARY: Saturday afternoon and evening Masses use the Vigil Mass. Observing a real vigil is possible by preceding/combining this Mass with Evening Prayer I for the solemnity, following the guidelines for this combination in the *General Instruction on the Liturgy of the Hours, 94–96*. Many of the sacramentary's texts—vigil or day—were not composed for the birth of the Baptist; rather, they mostly reflect a votive, "generic" feast of John. Perhaps altering one or two of the texts to read "birth" instead of "feast" would make better sense of them.

You might not want to use a sprinkling rite today if that was your pattern throughout Eastertime; water obviously is one of the elements that comes to mind today, but so is fire and a host of other holy signs. We are still so near to Pentecost that infant baptisms at Sunday Mass would have been more appropriate that day than today, although today's texts speak beautifully of infancy and entrance into God's reign. Overtly employing baptismal symbols today has the potential for appearing forced: "Baptist-baptism-water . . . do you get it?" Don't neglect to use the proper preface.

The following are sample Mass texts by Peter Scagnelli:

Introduction: Only three times each year does the Christian calendar mark the festival of a birth: the birth of Christ, the birth of Mary, and, on this solemnity, the birth of John the Baptist. Thus does the church establish John as one of the principal characters in the drama of salvation. As the words of the gospel ask us to do, let us rejoice today in John's birth: In life he is the herald and forerunner of the Lord, in death a martyr to the demands of righteousness and truth.

Invitation to the Penitential Rite: My brothers and sisters: let us heed John the Baptist's call to conversion and turn our repentant hearts toward the Lord in obedience and faith.

Penitential Rite (invocations): Lord Jesus, you are the Sun of justice and the Bridegroom of holy church: Lord, have mercy. Lord Jesus, you are the Lamb of God, who takes away the sins of the world: Christ, have mercy. Lord Jesus, you are the faithful witness, the first-born from the dead: Lord, have mercy.

Introduction to the Readings: Vigil: John stands in the prophetic line of Jeremiah, called from the womb to a mission that will require fidelity and courage. Peter's First Letter places us in that same tradition. Our baptismal anointing makes us prophets like John, heralds of Christ to a hostile world.

Day: John stands in the prophetic line of Isaiah, called from the womb to a mission that will require fidelity and courage. The Acts of the Apostles places the beginning of Christ's mission—and our salvation—in the preaching of John, whose very name means "God's gracious gift."

25 **Weekday.** This is the twelfth week in Ordinary Time. The daily lectionary continues our reading from 2 Kings.

29 **Peter, apostle; Paul, teacher of the gentiles.** The opening prayer of the Vigil Mass for the solemnity of Peter and Paul succinctly lauds their invaluable contribution to Christianity by referring to the two as "the apostles who strengthened the faith of the infant church." Since this day marks a

30 SATURDAY
Weekday (#376)
First Martyrs of the Church of Rome
OPTIONAL MEMORIAL
BVM
OPTIONAL MEMORIAL
Lamentations 2:2, 10–14, 18–19
Matthew 8:5–17

July 1990

1 SUNDAY
Thirteenth Sunday in Ordinary Time (#98)
2 Kings 4:8–11, 14–16
Romans 6:3–4, 8–11
Matthew 10:37–42
Canada Day (special proper Mass for Canada or Masses for peace and justice)

2 MONDAY
Weekday (#377)
Amos 2:6–10, 13–16
Matthew 8:18–22

3 TUESDAY
Thomas, apostle
FEAST (#593)
Ephesians 2:19–22
John 20:24–29

4 WEDNESDAY
Elizabeth of Portugal
OPTIONAL MEMORIAL (#379)
Amos 5:14–15, 21–24
Matthew 8:28–34
Independence Day (special proper Mass for U.S.A.)

5 THURSDAY
Weekday (#380)
Anthony Zaccaria, priest
OPTIONAL MEMORIAL
Amos 7:10–17
Matthew 9:1–8

6 FRIDAY
Weekday (#381)
Maria Goretti, virgin and martyr
OPTIONAL MEMORIAL (#381)
Amos 8:4–6, 9–12
Matthew 9:9–13

7 SATURDAY
Weekday (#382)
BVM
OPTIONAL MEMORIAL
Amos 9:11–15
Matthew 9:14–17

8 SUNDAY
Fourteenth Sunday in Ordinary Time (#101)
Zechariah 9:9–10
Romans 8:9, 11–13
Matthew 11:25–30

9 MONDAY
Weekday (#383)
Hosea 2:16, 17–18, 21–22
Matthew 9:18–26

10 TUESDAY
Weekday (#384)
Hosea 8:4–7, 11–13
Matthew 9:32–38

11 WEDNESDAY
Benedict, abbot
MEMORIAL (#385)
Hosea 10:1–3, 7–8, 12
Matthew 10:1–7

12 THURSDAY
Weekday (#386)
Hosea 11:1, 3–4, 8–9
Matthew 10:7–15

13 FRIDAY
Weekday (#387)
Henry
OPTIONAL MEMORIAL
Hosea 14:2–10
Matthew 10:16–23

14 SATURDAY
Kateri Tekakwitha, virgin
MEMORIAL (U.S.A.) (#388)
Camillus de Lellis, priest
OPTIONAL MEMORIAL (Canada)
Isaiah 6:1–8
Matthew 10:24–33

15 SUNDAY
Fifteenth Sunday in Ordinary Time (#104)
Isaiah 55:10–11
Romans 8:18–23
Matthew 13:1–23 or 13:1–9

customary day for the beginning of the grain harvest (Peter and Paul began the harvest of God's reign), a fine summertime decoration is a wheat or straw wreath, symbol of the harvest, festooned with the red poppies (Peter's flower), white daisies (John the Baptist's flower) and blue bachelor buttons (Paul's flower—who else?) called "cornflowers" because they color the edges of grain fields in June and July. This "red, white and blue" harvest would fit right in with the parables we will be hearing on the coming summertime Sundays.

JULY

1 **Thirteenth Sunday in Ordinary Time.** This Sunday and next prepare the community to hear the parables of Jesus, gospel selections that will culminate in his challenge to seek the real treasure (Seventeenth Sunday in Ordinary Time). It would be artificial to construct a theme, but the call is clearly to welcome the Lord who is gentle and humble of heart by welcoming his word. The scriptures of this month are rich in the imagery of plowing, seedtime and the grain harvest—perfect for July. All who prepare the liturgy, especially homilists, will want to look at Sundays 13 through 17 as a kind of unit.

Choose one set of penitential invocations for these five Sundays. Or combine short phrases from the passages that will be heard over the next weeks, for example:

Lord Jesus, gentle and humble of heart: Lord, have mercy.
Lord Jesus, sower of the good seed: Christ, have mercy.
Lord Jesus, our priceless treasure: Lord, have mercy.

◆ CHOOSE ONE RESPONSORIAL PSALM FOR THIS PERIOD: perhaps Psalm 19 with its refrain, "Lord, you have the words of everlasting life," or Psalm 95 with "If today you hear his voice, harden not your hearts." (See the other suggestions in the music section of Ordinary Time in "The Seasons" in this book.) Choose the same preface (Preface for Ordinary Time II and VI work well) and the same eucharistic prayer for this five-week block, with the introduction to the Lord's Prayer (maybe the old intro, "Taught by our Savior's command and formed by the word of God, we dare to pray") and the invitation to communion (perhaps, "This is the Lamb of God, whose words are spirit and life, whose flesh and blood are true food and drink. Happy are those . . ."). In these and similar simple ways, a kind of basic unity can be established, without forcing the Sundays into too strict a mold. A handout could also be prepared, tracing the journey through Matthew for the community.

◆ CANADA DAY: Prayers for the people of Canada are fitting in the general intercessions today.

3 **Thomas, apostle, martyr.** Thomas is known as the apostle who would not believe Jesus was risen until he could see Christ with his own eyes and even touch his wounds. His doubt is often considered something less than admirable, but St. Gregory the Great offers an interesting reflection on the incident: "What (Thomas) saw and what he believed were two different things. God cannot be seen by mortals. Thomas saw a human being, whom he acknowledged to be God, and said, 'My Lord and my God.' Seeing, he believed; looking at one who was human, he cried out that this was God, the God he could not see."

4 Independence Day. See the special votive Mass in the back of the sacramentary, Appendix X of the 1985 edition. Elements of the Fourth of July may make their way back into the previous weekend, and it may indeed be a time to pray in the general intercessions for the nation's people and leaders, for all of us as we struggle to honor our freedom through works of justice and solidarity.

We have several texts for use on this day. (Why do we have so many options? There are more choices for July 4 than for Easter!) Preface of Independence Day I is a hodgepodge of confused thoughts and noninclusive language. Preface II doesn't have anything to do with anything. Far better would be Eucharistic Prayer for Reconciliation II with its call to peace. Our world is small enough and the nightly news critical enough to keep us from a facile patriotism that is blind to the darkness in our past and in our world today. (And this comes through in a small way in the song "America the Beautiful" only if we sing all its verses.) We have motive for repentance as well as cause for thanks! In no way should nationalism or jingoism or easy slogans distort the fact that as Catholics we belong to a universal church. Baptismal water should be thicker than blood!

◆ QUESTIONS: What is the price of the freedoms outlined in our Declaration of Independence and Bill of Rights? Are those freedoms worth any and every cost? Are those freedoms always compatible with the freedom given us by the Creator in whose image we are created? What are we celebrating today?

8 Fourteenth Sunday in Ordinary Time. See the notes for July 1 for preparing this July Sunday. Read over the entrance antiphons for these five Sundays—the closest thing the liturgy has to "theme songs" that can help in the choice of an appropriate gathering song. The antiphons this July focus on the justice of God's holy house, how God "will give a home to the lonely." On each of these Sundays, the sample prayers found on pages 128–34 highlight the images of the first reading and gospel in a way that would make them appropriate for use at the conclusion of the general intercessions.

14 Kateri Tekakwitha, memorial. Robert Lentz of Bridge Building Icons (PO Box 1048, Burlington VT 05401; 802/864-8346) has done a beautiful icon of this American Indian. If the community is accustomed to the display and veneration of seasonal icons, this image could be given a place of honor in the community this week. This would be a fitting opportunity to sensitize the parish to the situations of many Native American peoples. Dwellers in this land for centuries before the immigrants arrived, they have been mistreated to one degree or another by national and local governments.

"Tekakwitha" means "she who feels her way along." Kateri was blinded and disfigured with smallpox, one of the "European" diseases that ravaged Native Americans during the last century. This exporting of diseases to which the indigenous population has little resistance is continuing today among the Amazon peoples of Brazil in a government-sponsored program of relocation of native peoples and the destruction of natural habitats, not unlike what Americans did a hundred years ago in this country.

16 MONDAY
Weekday (#389)
Our Lady of Mount Carmel
OPTIONAL MEMORIAL
Isaiah 1:10–17
Matthew 10:34—11:1

17 TUESDAY
Weekday (#390)
Isaiah 7:1–9
Matthew 11:20–24

18 WEDNESDAY
Weekday (#391)
Isaiah 10:5–7, 13–16
Matthew 11:25–27

19 THURSDAY
Weekday (#392)
Isaiah 26:7–9, 12, 16–19
Matthew 11:28–30

20 FRIDAY
Weekday (#393)
Isaiah 38:1–6, 21–22, 7–8
Matthew 12:1–8

21 SATURDAY
Weekday (#394)
Lawrence of Brindisi, priest and doctor
OPTIONAL MEMORIAL
BVM
OPTIONAL MEMORIAL
Micah 2:1–5
Matthew 12:14–21

22 SUNDAY
Sixteenth Sunday in Ordinary Time (#107)
Wisdom 12:13, 16–19
Romans 8:26–27
Matthew 13:24–43 or 13:24–30
St. Mary Magdalene's Day

23 MONDAY
Weekday (#395)
Bridget, religious
OPTIONAL MEMORIAL
Micah 6:1–4, 6–8
Matthew 12:38–42

24 TUESDAY
Weekday (#396)

Micah 7:14–15, 18–20
Matthew 12:46–50

In many nations, Muslim New Year begins tonight.

25 WEDNESDAY
James, apostle
FEAST (#605)

2 Corinthians 4:7–15
Matthew 20:20–28

26 THURSDAY
Joachim and Ann, parents of Mary
MEMORIAL (#398)

Jeremiah 2:1–3, 7–8, 12–13
Matthew 13:10–17

27 FRIDAY
Weekday (#399)

Jeremiah 3:14–17
Matthew 13:18–23

28 SATURDAY
Weekday (#400)

BVM
OPTIONAL MEMORIAL

Jeremiah 7:1–11
Matthew 13:24–30

29 SUNDAY
Seventeenth Sunday in Ordinary Time (#110)

1 Kings 3:5, 7–12
Romans 8:28–30
Matthew 13:44–52 *or* 13:44–46

St. Martha's Day

30 MONDAY
Weekday (#401)

Peter Chrysologus, bishop and doctor
OPTIONAL MEMORIAL

Jeremiah 13:1–11
Matthew 13:31–35

31 TUESDAY
Ignatius of Loyola, priest
MEMORIAL (#402)

Jeremiah 14:17–22
Matthew 13:35–43

Tisha B'Av, the Jewish fast day for the destruction of the Temple.

Today also is an invitation and opportunity to become more familiar with Native American spirituality with its often profound respect for creation. Did you know that the dried fronds of the common white cedar tree have been used by Native Americans as a sweet incense? The *Meditation* series (New Mexico: Bear and Company, Inc., 1984) ponders different Native American traditions through poems and reflections from the Hopi, Navajo and Lakota spiritualities.

15 **Fifteenth Sunday in Ordinary Time.** See the notes for July 1 for preparing this Sunday. It might be appropriate this week to take a moment before the readings to invite a careful listening to the word. This does not have to become a catechetical lesson, but could be as simple as asking all but the hearing-impaired to put aside missalettes (if these are still around to stifle your community's worship) and really listen to the scriptures. Then let the silences be generous and the psalm prayerfully rendered.

22 **Sixteenth Sunday in Ordinary Time.** See the notes for July 1 for preparing this Sunday. The patient justice of our God, the justice of a God who wants all to be saved and come to the knowledge of the truth, is the good news this weekend. The call to repentance at the beginning of the liturgy might invite us to see ourselves as a community of fellow sinners. The Eucharistic Prayer for Reconciliation II speaks of people from "every race and language and way of life" sharing in one eternal banquet. Is that reflected in this community's eucharistic assembly here and now?

◆ MARY MAGDALENE: Today is her feast day, eclipsed by the Lord's Day this year. The Eastern Church honors her as "Equal to the Apostles." Mary Magdalene was one of the holy women, who stood faithfully by the cross, to whom Jesus entrusted the news of the resurrection (John 20:1–10). The icon of Mary Magdalene shows her holding a vessel of myrrh and a red Easter egg—heralding the victory of Christ.

25 **James, apostle, martyr.** Pilgrims to the shrine of St. James wear a scallop shell—a symbol that traditionally guarantees them the hospitality of any village through which they pass. (The seashell, with its baptismal allusions, thus is a symbol for both John the Baptist and James—and for anyone coming home from a summertime trip to a beach!) This is a grand day to review parish hospitality and to consider hospitality to a new breed of "pilgrims"—folks on vacation. The *Book of Blessings* offers an order of blessing that can be used throughout the summer when folks leave on vacation or other trips. This blessing may be prayed immediately after Mass.

29 **Seventeenth Sunday in Ordinary Time.** See the notes for July 1 for preparing this Sunday. Both opening prayers today are beautiful. The parable readings conclude this weekend with the challenge to give all and risk all for the buried treasure and the pearl of great price—another seashell image that pops up in June and July. During these weeks, Solemn Blessings (if used) #11 and #14 are appropriate.

AUGUST

✸ **5 Eighteenth Sunday in Ordinary Time.** Again, without imposing an artificial "theme" where no such theme is to be found, those who prepare the liturgy could look at the next few Sundays (the Eighteenth through Twenty-fourth Sundays in Ordinary Time, August 5 through September 16) as one unit:

A quick look at the gospel of the first four of these Sundays shows a God who:

feeds the people (Sunday 18, August 5)

calls us to come in faith, despite all obstacles (Sunday 19, August 12)

establishes a place of prayer and community for all people (Sunday 20, August 19)

builds this community on the rock of a living profession of faith and ministry of service (Sunday 21, August 26)

This seven-week block continues on Sundays 22–24 with the prediction of the Passion and the "community sermon" of Matthew's Gospel. See the entry on September 2 for a discussion of these three weeks. See also the Introduction and Outline of the Gospel of Matthew in Ordinary Time on pages 135–36 of this *Sourcebook*.

For this seven-week block of Sundays, excerpt phrases from the scriptures and form them into a series of penitential invocations that can be memorized and made familiar by repetition; for example:

> You feed your people with word and eucharist: Lord, have mercy. You call your people to walk in faith and live in courage: Christ, have mercy. You establish your church on rock to be a safe home in which all are welcomed: Lord, have mercy.

For the liturgy of the word, consider using throughout the next seven weeks either Psalm 27, one of the common responsorial psalms for Ordinary Time, with its refrain, "The Lord is my light and my salvation," or Psalm 63 with "My soul is thirsting for you, O Lord my God." (Other suggestions for the psalm are found in the music section of Ordinary Time in "The Seasons" in this *Sourcebook*.) Let the general intercessions be standard over these next weeks, including petitions composed from ideas that run through all of the scriptures. Eucharistic Prayer III with one of the prefaces for Ordinary Time (Preface V is good) or Eucharistic Prayer II with its own preface would be appropriate.

6 Transfiguration of the Lord. It's customary to celebrate this feast, held at the height of summer, with signs of the fullness of August bounty. Transfiguration is a celebration of all that we are meant to be for each other, and all that we are meant to become in the Lord.

◆ THE AUGUST FAST: In so many ways, this feast employs the same images as Assumption—they are sister feasts. August 6 falls within the ancient 14-day fast that preceded August 15, a "festive fast" in celebration of the bounty of August gardens. Meals had to be sparse because the entire community needed to pitch in to gather and preserve this bounty if the community was to survive— and such joint effort to enable the community to stay alive is the sacramental

August 1990

1 WEDNESDAY
Alphonsus Liguori, bishop and doctor
MEMORIAL (#403)
Jeremiah 15:10, 16–21
Matthew 13:44–46

2 THURSDAY
Weekday (#404)
Eusebius of Vercelli, bishop
OPTIONAL MEMORIAL
Jeremiah 18:1–6
Matthew 13:47–53

3 FRIDAY
Weekday (#405)
Jeremiah 26:1–9
Matthew 13:54–58

4 SATURDAY
John Vianney, priest
MEMORIAL (#406)
Jeremiah 26:11–16, 24
Matthew 14:1–12

5 SUNDAY
Eighteenth Sunday in Ordinary Time (#113)
Isaiah 55:1–3
Romans 8:35, 37–39
Matthew 14:13–21

6 MONDAY
Transfiguration of the Lord
FEAST (#615)
Daniel 7:9–10, 13–14
2 Peter 1:16–19
Matthew 17:1–9
Hiroshima Memorial Day

7 TUESDAY
Weekday (#408)
Sixtus II, pope and martyr, and companions, martyrs
OPTIONAL MEMORIAL
Cajetan, priest
OPTIONAL MEMORIAL
Jeremiah 30:1–2, 12–15, 18–22
Matthew 12:22–36 or 15:1–2, 10–14

8 WEDNESDAY
Dominic, priest
MEMORIAL (#409)
Jeremiah 31:1–7
Matthew 15:21–28

9 THURSDAY
Weekday (#410)

Jeremiah 31:31–34
Matthew 16:13–23

Nagasaki Memorial Day

10 FRIDAY
Lawrence, deacon and martyr
FEAST (#618)

2 Corinthians 9:6–10
John 12:24–26

11 SATURDAY
Clare, virgin
MEMORIAL (#412)

Habakkuk 1:12—2:4
Matthew 17:14–20

12 SUNDAY
Nineteenth Sunday in Ordinary Time (#116)

1 Kings 19:9, 11–13
Romans 9:1–5
Matthew 14:22–23

13 MONDAY
Weekday (#413)

Pontian, pope and martyr
OPTIONAL MEMORIAL

Hippolytus, priest and martyr
OPTIONAL MEMORIAL

Ezekiel 1:2–5, 24–28
Matthew 17:22–27

Florence Nightingale

14 TUESDAY

Morning:
Maximilian Mary Kolbe,
   priest and martyr
MEMORIAL (#414)

Ezekiel 2:8—3:4
Matthew 18:1–5, 10, 12–14

Evening:
Vigil of the Assumption (#621)

1 Chronicles 15:3–4, 15, 16;
   16:1–2
1 Corinthians 15:54–57
Luke 11:27–28

root of seasons of fasting. Surely the two contemporary memorials of Hiroshima and Nagasaki offer a new way to interpret this traditional fasting period.

◆ AN EMBER DAY: The shadowy history of ember days reveals that in origin these were very much "popular" rites, springing from the needs and lives of the people. By fifth-century Rome, the days were being handed on with overtones of thanksgiving for the seasons and their produce. (The summer, autumn and winter ember days corresponded to the times in the Mediterranean lands of the harvesting of grain, of fruits and of olives, respectively.) They were also penitential days: Fasting was both a token of special thanksgiving and something that was expected in a Christian's life with the regular rhythm of year and week and season. But the days and the people lost touch somewhere. After Vatican II, the ember days disappeared from the reformed calendar.

Even though the days are gone from the universal calendar, they are far from being forgotten. *The General Norms for the Liturgical Year and the Calendar* speak of the restoration of the days (#45–47), and in a commentary published by the Worship Congregation at the same time as the *Norms,* we read: "In our own day, when all are concerned with the problems of peace, justice and hunger, the ember days should be restored to their former importance as days devoted to penance and prayer."

◆ TWO EMBER DAYS THAT DESERVE TO BE PART THE RHYTHM OF THE YEAR are August 6 and August 9, the anniversaries of the atomic bombing of Hiroshima and Nagasaki. In their pastoral letter, *The Challenge of Peace,* the U.S. bishops make a very strong statement about the significance of the bombing of those two cities to us as Americans:

> We speak here in a specific way to the Catholic community. After the passage of nearly four decades and a concomitant growth in our understanding of the ever-growing horror of nuclear war, we must shape the climate of opinion which will make it possible for our country to express profound sorrow over the atomic bombing of 1945. Without that sorrow, there is no possibility of finding a way to repudiate future use of nuclear weapons or of conventional weapons in such military actions as would not fulfill just-war criteria.

Could this summons to remember, to express sorrow, to find strength in that expression, take the form of a diocese or a large part of the church observing August 6 and August 9 as ember days? *Catholic Household Blessings and Prayers* contains a prayer appropriate for today that would make a fitting conclusion to the general intercessions, especially if these were oriented to the ember days. Parish households could make use of this prayer at home in their observance of these days with fasting and special prayer.

◆ THE OBSERVANCE OF FEASTS AS STRICT FASTS MAY BE UNUSUAL FOR US, but as suggested above, this has often been a traditional part of the keeping of several of the holy days that come in late summer: the Transfiguration, today; the beheading of John the Baptist, August 29; and the Triumph of the Cross, September 14—for who can bear to eat in the presence of such mysteries? These ancient days of fasting are in the tradition of the Jewish calendar with its great fast of *Tisha b'Av* (July 31 this year), the day of the destruction of both the First and Second Temples, a day preceded by weeks of gradually intensifying fasting. Something about late summer evokes memories of destruction, of wars, of plagues, of sorrows that must be ritualized to be remembered.

10 **Lawrence, deacon, martyr, died 248.** Tradition has it that when asked to hand over the riches of the church, Lawrence gathered all the cripples, orphans, widows and outcasts, and then presented them to the Emperor as the real treasure of the church.

Today is an opportunity to thank any deacons who may be at the service of the local church in this parish. An act of real hospitality, as well as thanksgiving, would be for the parish to invite all the permanent (and transitional) deacons of the area to a celebration of Evening Prayer in honor of St. Lawrence—with refreshments to follow, perhaps even a barbecue! (Lawrence died on a gridiron.)

◆ St. Lawrence's Tears, the Perseid meteor shower, is one of the finest of the year and the only shower so readily viewable because of summer's weather (about one meteor can be seen each minute if the night is clear). It reaches its peak before dawn on the mornings of August 11 and 12.

12 **Nineteenth Sunday in Ordinary Time.** See the notes for August 5 for preparing this late-summer Sunday. In the alternative opening prayer, "celebrate our sonship" might be "celebrate our being your sons and daughters"; "men" can be "people."

The figure of Peter should certainly be for us an image of hope and comfort. If such an ordinary person—alternately enthusiastic and doubtful, self-confident and self-defeating—could become by God's grace a rock of faith, then there's hope for us. (And today we have another story about Elijah; he's getting to be quite a familiar fellow this summer.) Hymns in celebration of faith, centered on Jesus, would be appropriate thoughout this seven-week block of Sundays, for instance, "The church's one foundation." Peter will appear again on the 21st and 22nd Sundays; the musical choices might extend through those weeks to achieve some kind of general unity.

15 **Assumption of Mary.** Today is the greatest of Mary's festivals, her passover, set in this month of greatest fruitfulness.

◆ Using the sacramentary: Tuesday evening Masses use the Vigil Mass. Wednesday Masses use the Mass during the Day. All four opening prayers are beautiful, although in neither of the Vigil texts is it clear which feast we are celebrating. The preface of today's Mass provides good material for the homilist's interaction with the readings. And remember the Solemn Blessing (#15) for the Blessed Virgin Mary.

Some of Easter's vesture and vessels could be used today; if there is a special "Eastertime only" set of acclamations (or scent of incense), these should be used to honor Mary's sharing in the risen glory of her child. The summertime sun receives another mention this summer in the reading from Revelation—the colors for today should shine with "gold from Ophir." An appropriately oriental-sounding arrangement (very beautiful, as well) of today's Psalm 45 is "Assumption Psalm" by Howard Hughes, sm (GIA, G-2028).

◆ Today is a harvest festival, a celebration of the blessing of fruitfulness in the presence of Mary: ". . . and blessed is the fruit of your womb." It is a day to fill the church with the abundance of our August gardens: Request that people bring in baskets of produce, herbs and flowers for the special blessing of the day. See the chapter on the Assumption in Gertrud Mueller Nelson's *To Dance with God*

15 WEDNESDAY
Assumption of Mary (#622)
SOLEMNITY

Revelation 11:19; 12:1–6, 10
I Corinthians 15:20–26
Luke 1:39–56

blessing of produce

*Sunflower
and lunaria*

16 THURSDAY
Weekday (#416)

Stephen of Hungary
OPTIONAL MEMORIAL

Ezekiel 12:1–2
Matthew 18:21—19:1

17 FRIDAY
Weekday (#417)

Ezekiel 16:1–15, 60, 63
 or 16:59–63
Matthew 19:3–12

18 SATURDAY
Weekday (#418)

Jane Frances de Chantal
OPTIONAL MEMORIAL (U.S.A.)
BVM
OPTIONAL MEMORIAL

Ezekiel 18:1–10, 13, 30–32
Matthew 19:13–15

19 SUNDAY
**Twentieth Sunday in
 Ordinary Time** (#119)

Isaiah 56:1, 6–7
Romans 11:13–15, 29–32
Matthew 15:21–28

20 MONDAY
Bernard, abbot and doctor
MEMORIAL (#419)

Ezekiel 24:15–24
Matthew 19:16–22

21 TUESDAY
Pius X, pope
MEMORIAL (#420)

Ezekiel 28:1–10
Matthew 19:23–30

22 WEDNESDAY
Queenship of Mary
MEMORIAL (#421)

Ezekiel 34:1–11
Matthew 20:1–16

23 THURSDAY
Weekday (#422)

Rose of Lima, virgin
OPTIONAL MEMORIAL

Ezekiel 36:23–28
Matthew 22:1–14

24 FRIDAY
Bartholomew, apostle
FEAST (#629)

Revelation 21:9–14
John 1:45–51

25 SATURDAY
Weekday (#424)

Louis
OPTIONAL MEMORIAL

Joseph Calasanz, priest
OPTIONAL MEMORIAL

BVM
OPTIONAL MEMORIAL

Ezekiel 43:1–7
Matthew 23:1–12

26 SUNDAY
**Twenty-first Sunday in
Ordinary Time** (#122)

Isaiah 22:15, 19–23
Romans 11:33–36
Matthew 16:13–20

27 MONDAY
Monica
MEMORIAL (#425)

2 Thessalonians 1:1–5, 11–12
Matthew 23:13–22

28 TUESDAY
Augustine, bishop and doctor
MEMORIAL (#426)

2 Thessalonians 2:1–3, 14–16
Matthew 23:23–26

29 WEDNESDAY
Beheading of John the Baptist
MEMORIAL (#634)

Jeremiah 1:17–19
Mark 6:17–29

(Paulist Press, 1987) for a fine reflection and useful suggestions. The *Book of Blessings* has an Order for a Blessing on the Occasion of Thanksgiving for the Harvest that might be celebrated communally today or this weekend. *Catholic Household Blessings and Prayers* also has a blessing of garden produce for Assumption Day, and although this is meant primarily for home use, it is very useful for communal celebration.

19 **Twentieth Sunday in Ordinary Time.** See the notes for August 5 for preparing this late-summer Sunday. The alternative opening prayer today might be copied and used on occasions of racial tension or in interracial meetings.

How does your community define who belongs and who doesn't? All are welcome on the mountain of the Lord and in God's house—even those whom some people would harshly call "dogs" or treat as animals. The Preface for Sundays in Ordinary Time VIII reminds us that all have been gathered—in some way—into the family of the church.

26 **Twenty-first Sunday in Ordinary Time.** Again, see the notes for August 5 for preparing this Sunday. The alternative opening prayer is very strange: "May all the attractions of a changing world serve only to bring us the peace of your kingdom."

The general intercessions might conclude with one of the collects from the "Masses and Prayers for Various Needs and Occasions: For the Church," in the back of the sacramentary. If another preface is not being used for a block of Sundays, then the Preface of Christian Unity would certainly be fitting. An excerpt:

> How wonderful are the works of the Spirit,
> revealed in so many gifts!
> Yet how marvelous is the unity
> the Spirit creates from their diversity,
> as [the Spirit] dwells in the hearts of your children,
> filling the whole church with [God's] presence
> and guiding it with wisdom.

SEPTEMBER

2 **Twenty-second Sunday in Ordinary Time.** This Sunday, and the two that follow it, might be thought of as a capsule summary of that section of Matthew's Gospel that has been referred to as the "charter of the church's life and order." These are three Sundays where Adrian Nocent (*The Liturgical Year,* The Liturgical Press, 1977) sees a connection among the three readings under these general headings and specific points:

Sunday 22: The suffering required of the disciple.

Jeremiah 20:7–9	I am insulted and mocked.
Romans 12:1–2	Offer one's person and life in sacrifice.
Matthew 16:21–27	Renounce self and follow the Lord.

Sunday 23: Fraternal correction.

Ezekiel 33:7–9	Warn the wicked.
Romans 13:8–10	Love fulfills the law.
Matthew 18:15–20	Win your neighbor over.

Sunday 24: Forgiveness.

Sirach 27:30—28:7	Forgiveness of neighbor and of sins.
Romans 14:7–9	We live and die for the Lord. Do not judge.
Matthew 18:21–35	Forgive seventy times seven times.

This is, of course, somewhat artificial as the second readings are merely where we happen to be in our reading of Romans. Refer back to the suggestions on August 5 about a standard set of prayer texts for these weeks. The eucharistic prayers for reconciliation would be appropriate the next three weeks. The common responsorial psalm might change to Psalm 100 with the refrain, "We are his people, the sheep of his flock."

◆ LABOR DAY WEEKEND: Sometimes too little of the church's developing teaching about social issues makes its way into the homily. While Labor Day may seem to be kept primarily as a last fling with summer, the holiday retains some of what gave it impetus: the rights and dignity of working people. Pope John Paul's early encyclical *Laborem exercens* (On Human Work) and his 1988 encyclical *Sollicitudo rei socialis* (*The Social Concern of the Church*) would be two sources, but the U.S. bishops' pastoral letter *Economic Justice for All* has much to say also.

Only so much can or should be done on a given Sunday, but preachers have a responsibility to know and use these teachings year round. The Sunday scriptures need to be in dialogue with this sort of biblically based teaching— otherwise homilies can easily become mushy with platitudes. Today's homilist should ponder *Economic Justice for All* in one hand and today's gospel from Matthew in the other: "What profit would people show if they gain the whole world only to ruin themselves in the process?"

The Pastorals on Sundays is an LTP annual publication that lists each Sunday's scripture readings, then places beside them several quotes from the church's teaching on peace and justice. These texts are drawn from the pastoral letters of the U.S. bishops, from Vatican II and from papal documents.

◆ WITH THE FALL SEASON UPON US, what is the status of the work of those who prepare the parish liturgy and its ministers? Has a calendar for the coming year been circulated, studied and made firm? Does that calendar center on the Triduum (March 28–31 in 1991) and move from there to fill in the times of training and preparation? Have the materials that will be needed for the year ahead been ordered? What is the status of the RCIA in the parish? Who are being presented for acceptance into the order of catechumens?

3 **Labor Day.** As a national holiday, Labor Day for most of us has few associations with our own work or with working people in general. It is the holiday at the end of summer, the beginning of the new school year. It could perhaps be argued that whatever its origins, it does have something to do with human work by the very fact of its position at the end of the leisurely summer and the return to business-as-usual, to work, to studies.

---

30 THURSDAY
Weekday (#428)

I Corinthians 1:1–9
Matthew 24:42–51

31 FRIDAY
Weekday (#429)

I Corinthians 1:17–25
Matthew 25:1–13

September 1990

I SATURDAY
Weekday (#430)

BVM
OPTIONAL MEMORIAL

I Corinthians 1:26–31
Matthew 25:14–30

2 SUNDAY
Twenty-second Sunday in Ordinary Time (#125)

Jeremiah 20:7–9
Romans 12:1–2
Matthew 16:21–27

3 MONDAY
Gregory the Great,
  pope and doctor
MEMORIAL (#431)

I Corinthians 2:1–5
Luke 4:16–30

Labor Day (Canada and U.S.A.)

4 TUESDAY
Weekday (#432)

I Corinthians 2:10–16
Luke 4:31–37

5 WEDNESDAY
Weekday (#433)

I Corinthians 3:1–9
Luke 4:38–44

6 THURSDAY
Weekday (#434)

I Corinthians 3:18–23
Luke 5:1–11

7 FRIDAY
Weekday (#435)

I Corinthians 4:1–5
Luke 5:33–39

8 SATURDAY
Birth of Mary
FEAST (#636)

Micah 5:1–4 *or* Romans 8:28–30
Matthew 1:1–16, 18–23
   or 1:18–23

9 SUNDAY
Twenty-third Sunday in Ordinary Time (#128)

Ezekiel 33:7–9
Romans 13:8–10
Matthew 18:15–20

10 MONDAY
Weekday (#437)

1 Corinthians 5:1–8
Luke 6:6–11

11 TUESDAY
Weekday (#438)

1 Corinthians 6:1–11
Luke 6:12–19

12 WEDNESDAY
Weekday (#439)

1 Corinthians 7:25–31
Luke 6:20–26

13 THURSDAY
John Chrysostom,
   bishop and doctor
MEMORIAL (#440)

1 Corinthians 8:1–7, 11–13
Luke 6:27–38

14 FRIDAY
Triumph of the Cross
FEAST (#638)

Numbers 21:4–9
Philippians 2:6–11
John 3:13–17

15 SATURDAY
Our Lady of Sorrows
MEMORIAL (#639)

Hebrews 5:7–9
John 19:25–27 *or* Luke 2:33–35

16 SUNDAY
Twenty-fourth Sunday in Ordinary Time (#131)

Sirach 27:30—28:7
Romans 14:7–9
Matthew 18:21–35

We won't make any argument for letting the "Labor Day weekend" change the character of the church's Sunday liturgy. Yet a heedless passing of Labor Day should pose a problem. Whenever does the church pray and reflect and preach about that which fills so much of human life, our work? John Paul II wrote an encyclical on labor, *Laborem exercens,* which stands worthily in the line started by Leo XIII with *Rerum novarum* (Of New Things). Have you read it?

In a talk published in *Origins* (July 29, 1982), Ed Marciniak, president of the Institute of Urban Life, raised a number of excellent questions about *Laborem exercens* and the contemporary attitude of the church "establishment" toward people's work. He echoes Bishop Mark Hurley's call for the church to renew its practice of a Labor Day Mass. The point of that would not be to patronize workers but to join with John Paul in recognizing that it is in our work that we spend our lives. He challenges our own system (and not just the other guy's) to be one in which all considerations of labor begin with this: that the one who labors is a person. In the encyclical, John Paul is eloquent on that. He is consistent in challenging systems East and West.

What then to do with Labor Day and its weekend? Some possibilities:

1. Make and keep a resolution that on this weekend you will do no more than read and ponder *Laborem exercens* (available from religious bookstores, from the U.S. Catholic Conference, and from Paulist Press in a book entitled *The Priority of Labor,* which includes a commentary by Gregory Baum).

2. Read the scriptures of that Sunday in light of the encyclical and the work that is done by people of your parish. If you are the preacher, preach accordingly.

3. Invite people to celebrate the eucharist or a vesper service on Labor Day. See the votive Mass in the sacramentary under "Masses and Prayers for Various Needs and Occasions: For the Blessing of Human Labor." All the possible opening prayers need to be emended to make them more inclusive. (The rubrics also permit the observance of Joseph the Worker.) For scripture readings, the lectionary provides a number of possibilities in #846–50.

4. Ponder a few of the quotes with which Marciniak filled his article. From Cardinal Bernardin: "The laity's specific role is not to serve the church in an institutional sense, but the world." And this from Dorothy Sayers, decades ago: "The church's approach to an intelligent carpenter is usually confined to exhorting him not to be drunk and disorderly in his leisure hours, to come to church on Sundays. What the church should be telling him is this: that the very first demand that his religion makes upon him is that he should make good tables. Church, by all means, and decent forms of amusement, certainly—but what use is all of that if in the very center of his life and occupation he is insulting God with bad carpentry?" And from Marciniak himself in speaking of the encyclical:

> John Paul does not seem to be proposing some new socioeconomic order as a third way or a third alternative to existing systems. He has no blueprint. Instead he is offering a way of looking at and evaluating an economic arrangement however primitive or technological, to determine how it can enhance the dignity of the worker. Consequently, the civilization he foresees is not based on that leisure that relies upon escapist entertainment or the commercial and advertising vices associated with the mass media. . . . Allow me to paraphrase what John Paul II is saying to us in my own vernacular: Don't ask me for a blueprint. I don't have

one. Don't ask me to spell it out for you. That's your job. Mine is to be provocative, to be challenging, to remind you about the dignity of the work and how human rights are being violated. For God's sake and your own, use your imagination. Exploit your ingenuity. Puzzle out what in the workaday world needs changing—and then do it.

 9 Twenty-third Sunday in Ordinary Time. See the notes on August 5 and September 2 for preparing this late-summer Sunday.

Firm but loving correction, forgiveness, God's scandalous generosity, repentance—images of the next few Sundays suggest using the powerful Eucharistic Prayer for Reconciliation II which calls Jesus "the word that brings salvation, the hand you stretch out to sinners, the path that leads to your peace."

◆ EVERY SEPTEMBER BRINGS IMAGERY OF RECONCILIATION AND FORGIVENESS to our liturgy; see the entrance antiphons for these Sundays. September is also a good time to schedule communal reconciliation, something that could become an annual event on September 14, the feast of the Triumph of the Cross. There should also be plans for a Friday Mass or Evening Prayer and Stations of the Cross at a convenient time so that today everyone could be invited to come and celebrate this great feast.

14 Triumph of the Cross. This feast commemorates the dedication of the church erected by Emperor Constantine over the site of Christ's crucifixion, Calvary. The Byzantine celebration of Evening Prayer on this night concludes with the assembly coming forward to kiss the cross which rests in a bed of September herbs and flowers; the day is a fast day—Good Friday celebrated near the other equinox of the year. Graced coincidence places this feast on a Friday this year (and tomorrow's observance on a Saturday, always dedicated to our Lady). The Triumph of the Cross is an occasion to renew the parish's Friday discipline. Today and Michaelmas, September 29, are the days we welcome the autumn. We raise the holy cross in the face of the growing darkness as a sign of protection and a promise of eternal light. The parish worship environment should begin expressing autumn this weekend.

◆ SCHOOL IS BACK IN SESSION, and the *Leader's Manual* for the *Hymnal for Catholic Students* (GIA/LTP) contains suggestions for this day, celebrated as the opening eucharist of the school year. There are other suggestions for this time of year, including prayer for the beginning of the academic year and for the observance of Michael, Gabriel and Raphael on September 29 and Saint Francis of Assisi on October 4.

15 Our Lady of Sorrows. Today is a continuation of yesterday's feast. A Marian celebration tonight could feature the praying of the sorrowful mysteries of the rosary, or even the "Rosary of Our Lady's Sorrows," outlined in *Celebrating the Marian Year* (USCC), a resource that continues to be valuable.

16 Twenty-fourth Sunday in Ordinary Time. See the notes on August 5 and September 2 for preparing this last Sunday in summer. Today's alternative opening prayer is particularly beautiful.

Since the Triumph of the Cross is the customary beginning of the church's autumn (most monastic orders begin now their winter regimen in clothing,

17 MONDAY
Weekday (#443)
Robert Bellarmine,
  bishop and doctor
OPTIONAL MEMORIAL
1 Corinthians 11:17–26, 33
Luke 7:1–10

18 TUESDAY
Weekday (#444)
1 Corinthians 12:12–14, 27–31
Luke 7:11–17

19 WEDNESDAY
Weekday (#445)
Januarius, bishop and martyr
OPTIONAL MEMORIAL
1 Corinthians 12:31—13:13
Luke 7:31–35
*Rosh ha-Shanah (the Jewish
  New Year) begins at sundown.*

20 THURSDAY
Andrew Kim Taegon, priest and
  martyr; Paul Chong Hasang, and
  companions, martyrs
MEMORIAL (#446)
1 Corinthians 15:1–11
Luke 7:36–50

21 FRIDAY
**Matthew, apostle and
  evangelist**
FEAST (#643)
Ephesians 4:1–7, 11–13
Matthew 9:9–13

22 SATURDAY
Weekday (#448)
BVM
OPTIONAL MEMORIAL
1 Corinthians 15:35–37, 42–49
Luke 8:4–15

23 SUNDAY
**Twenty-fifth Sunday in
  Ordinary Time** (#134)
Isaiah 55:6–9
Philippians 1:20–24, 27
Matthew 20:1–16
Autumn Equinox

24 MONDAY
Weekday (#449)
Proverbs 3:27–34
Luke 8:16–18

25 TUESDAY
Weekday (#450)

Proverbs 21:1–6, 10–13
Luke 8:19–21

26 WEDNESDAY
Weekday (#451)

Cosmas and Damian, martyrs
OPTIONAL MEMORIAL

Proverbs 30:5–9
Luke 9:1–6

27 THURSDAY
Vincent de Paul, priest
MEMORIAL (#452)

Ecclesiastes 1:2–11
Luke 9:7–9

28 FRIDAY
Weekday (#453)

Wenceslas, martyr
OPTIONAL MEMORIAL

Lawrence Ruiz and companions,
 martyrs
OPTIONAL MEMORIAL

Ecclesiastes 3:1–11
Luke 9:18–22

*Yom Kippur (the Jewish Day
 of Atonement) begins at sundown.*

29 SATURDAY
**Michael, Gabriel, and
 Raphael, archangels**
FEAST (#647)

Daniel 7:9–10, 13–14
 or Revelation 12:7–12
John 1:47–51

Michaelmas

*Goldenrod and
Michaelmas daisies*

30 SUNDAY
**Twenty-sixth Sunday in
 Ordinary Time** (#137)

Ezekiel 18:25–28
Philippians 2:1–11 or 2:1–5
Matthew 21:28–32

fasting, scheduling), the worship environment might shift this Sunday or the next toward autumn with a change of vesture to darker greens with earth tones—browns, oranges and golds. While it seems best to reserve for November the full glories of an autumnal worship environment, this could slowly build the next six weeks as we approach All Saints and All Souls.

19 **Tonight *Rosh Ha-Shanah* begins.** Although this is commonly called "Jewish New Year," it is also the beginning of the "ten days of awe," a period of intense reflection and repentance, and an anticipation of the day of judgment. The sending of greetings at this time of year includes the wish *L'Shanah tovah tikatevu:* "May you be inscribed (in the Book of Life) for a good year."

20 **Andrew Kim Taegon, priest and martyr, Paul Chong Hasang, and companions, martyrs.** There is a new supplement from Catholic Book Publishing Company with the proper office (and a very nice reading for the Office of Readings), and only the 1985 edition of the sacramentary has the proper prayers. Surely prayers for the strife-torn nation of Korea are in order as its people struggle for the personal and political freedoms so long denied them.

21 **Matthew, apostle and evangelist.** Our evangelist this year. *The Gospel According to Matthew* (Collegeville: The Liturgical Press, 1983) introduces this gospel by way of its most unique characteristic:

> Matthew's Gospel has a strongly Jewish flavor. Its special concerns are to place Jesus within the traditions of God's chosen people. From beginning to end, there is a tension between tradition and newness. Neither pole of the tension is rejected. The interplay between the two generates life and fresh insights.

 23 **Twenty-fifth Sunday in Ordinary Time.** In today's alternative opening prayer, "mankind" can be "humankind."

The six Sundays from late September through October present selections from a portion of Matthew's Gospel that one scholar entitles: "Jesus leads his disciples to the cross, as he confounds his enemies" (John P. Meier, *Matthew*, Michael Glazier, 1980). Look at the general images with which Adrian Nocent summarizes these Sundays and, without pushing the matter too much, try to prepare the liturgies in a way that will give some unity and coherence to this block of Ordinary Time. For example, in the penitential rite:

> Called to the feast of the kingdom, let us acknowledge our failures in love toward God and neighbor, turn from our sins, and embrace the Lord's gospel.

> You call us to sincere love of God and self-sacrificing love of neighbor: Lord, have mercy. You challenge us to give ourselves completely to your kingdom: Christ, have mercy. You strengthen us for persevering work in your vineyard: Lord, have mercy.

Psalm 145 is appropriate throughout this block of Sundays, from the common psalms of the lectionary, with the response: "I will praise your name for ever, my king and my God." (See the discussion of music for this block of Sundays in the Ordinary Time section of "The Seasons" in this *Sourcebook*.) "Sundays in Ordinary Time I" would be a good preface. This, with Eucharistic Prayer II or III could be used on all the Sundays of this block. For the concluding rite, choose a solemn blessing carefully, perhaps #11.

◆ GRAPES AND VINES are mentioned several times in the scriptures over the next few weeks (although, to be sure, the context is harsh; blood flows freely in these vineyards). Grapevines make splendid autumnal decorations, spiraling up and around the ambo, woven into wreaths for doors and elsewhere. They can be embellished with bittersweet. Don't make the common mistake of using too small or too little of a decoration; generally speaking, use something like a grapevine in a single place in a large quantity. The best place for decoration is almost always in the assembly's space, not near the altar. This decoration should remain through the autumn and not be used as a "theme" for a particular Sunday or two.

◆ FRIDAY IS A GREAT FESTIVAL: Michael, Gabriel, Raphael. Michaelmas—the feast of the angels and a day that has marked the year's turning toward autumn. Could a Mass or Evening Prayer be scheduled, perhaps with a social event? You might also announce the Jewish Day of Atonement, Yom Kippur, and include prayer for the Jewish people in the intercessions.

27 **Vincent de Paul, priest, 1581–1660.** Founded the Congregation of the Missions (Vincentians). Also founded the Congregation of the Daughters of Charity. Patron of charitable organizations. What is our community's commitment to charity? How are the organizations this community supports chosen? How is the parish made aware of its commitments? Are new groups added to our outreach? Many parishes pledge a certain percentage of their total collection to charity, which is in keeping with John Paul's plea: "You must give not from your surplus, but from your want."

28 **Wenceslas, martyr; Lawrence Ruiz and companions, martyrs.** Yes, this Wenceslas (a Bohemian prince) is the "Good king" who says in the carol, "Ye who now will bless the poor, shall yourselves find blessing." Lawrence Ruiz and companions is a new memorial in the church's calendar, and a new "patronal day" for Christians of Japan, the Philippines and Taiwan. The day commemorates 16 native missionaries, women and men, nonordained and ordained, all martyred in Nagasaki in the seventeenth century. Lawrence Ruiz was a "husband and father."

◆ TODAY BRINGS TOGETHER CELEBRATIONS for people of Czech, Chinese, Filipino, Japanese and a number of other ancestries. What is parish practice on such national "patronal" festivals? Sometimes these days are found on the Roman Calendar, but sometimes a bit of searching is required to locate saints' days that may be significant to the parish's nationalities. Throughout the year, use the bulletin to teach the parish about its "patrons" and get the ball rolling to help celebrate the cultural diversity within your community.

◆ TONIGHT *YOM KIPPUR,* THE JEWISH DAY OF ATONEMENT, BEGINS. This is the holiest day in the Jewish calendar, a day of complete fast, a day of prayer. The liturgy is rich and complex, including the reading of the book of Jonah. At Mass, announce Yom Kippur and include prayer for the Jewish people in the general intercessions.

29 **Michael, Gabriel and Raphael, archangels.** This is the church's "welcome" to autumn. Michael defends us in the battle against evil. Raphael gathers up the wounded. Gabriel announces the victory. Assumption

October 1990

1 MONDAY
Theresa of the Child Jesus
  (of Lisieux), virgin
MEMORIAL (#455)

Job 1:6–22
Luke 9:46–50

2 TUESDAY
Guardian Angels
MEMORIAL (#650)

Exodus 23:20–23
Matthew 18:1–5, 10

3 WEDNESDAY
Weekday (#457)

Job 9:1–12, 14–16
Luke 9:57–62

*Sukkot (the Jewish festival
  of harvest homes) begins
  at sundown.*

4 THURSDAY
Francis of Assisi
MEMORIAL (#458)

Job 19:21–27
Luke 10:1–12

blessing of animals

Mushrooms

5 FRIDAY
Weekday (#459)

Job 38:1, 12–21; 40:3–5
Luke 10:13–16

6 SATURDAY
Weekday (#460)

Bruno, priest
OPTIONAL MEMORIAL

Marie-Rose Durocher, virgin
OPTIONAL MEMORIAL

BVM
OPTIONAL MEMORIAL

Job 42:1–3, 5–6, 12–16
Luke 10:17–24

7 SUNDAY
Twenty-seventh Sunday in Ordinary Time (#140)

Isaiah 5:1–7
Philippians 4:6–9
Matthew 21:33–43

8 MONDAY
Weekday (#461)

Galatians 1:6–12
Luke 10:25–37

Thanksgiving Day (Canada)

Columbus Day (U.S.A.)

9 TUESDAY
Weekday (#462)

Denis, bishop and martyr, and
  companions, martyrs
OPTIONAL MEMORIAL

John Leonardi, priest
OPTIONAL MEMORIAL

Galatians 1:13–24
Luke 10:38–42

10 WEDNESDAY
Weekday (#463)

Galatians 2:1–2, 7–14
Luke 11:1–4

*Sh'mini Atzeret (the conclusion
  of the Jewish Sukkot festival)
  begins at sundown.*

11 THURSDAY
Weekday (#464)

Galatians 3:1–5
Luke 11:5–13

*Simhat Torah (the Jewish "Rejoicing
  in the Torah") begins at sundown.*

12 FRIDAY
Weekday (#465)

Galatians 3:7–14
Luke 11:15–26

13 SATURDAY
Weekday (#466)

BVM
OPTIONAL MEMORIAL

Galatians 3:22–29
Luke 11:27–28

Day, today, All Saints Day and Martinmas are four of the several harvest thanksgivings of the church. Throughout the autumn we continue to enjoy these ingathering and homecoming thematics until Epiphany. (In today's opening prayer, "men" can be "humans." Notice how the texts are really about "All Angels" rather than any particular ones.)

30 **Twenty-sixth Sunday in Ordinary Time.** See the notes for September 23 for preparing this autumn Sunday. Today's first opening prayer is particularly beautiful—a strong early breath of Advent!

The idea of tax collectors and prostitutes entering the kingdom of heaven ahead of the finance board and the altar-rosary society ought to be just as shocking to folks at liturgy this week as it was back then. How can today's liturgy challenge this assembly to match words with deeds?

◆ THE BLESSING OF ANIMALS AND PETS is a custom for St. Francis Day (also for St. Anthony's Day on January 17) kept on this Sunday afternoon in many parishes. A fine service for this blessing can be found in *Catholic Household Blessings and Prayers*. Invite people to come for liturgy on St. Francis' Day and plan Mass or Evening Prayer at a convenient time.

OCTOBER

3 *Sukkot,* **the eight-day Jewish festival of harvest homes,** begins tonight. Why not visit a synagogue or Jewish center to experience the joy of standing within a *sukkah* (plural: *sukkot*), a harvest home (the huts that harvesters build in the fields so they can work uninterruptedly). This could be an inspiration for the parish or for families to build their own *sukkot* to keep this splendid biblical festival, also called the feast of tabernacles or booths, and "the season of our joy." The moon will be full tonight, as at Passover. The harvest moon is just about universal in its appeal; besides the romantic associations, it affords the practical opportunity to spend the night continuing the harvest.

4 **Francis of Assisi, 1181–1226.** He founded the Friars Minor (Franciscans) and, with Saint Clare, the Poor Clares. Dedicated to a life of simplicity and "Lady Poverty." Francis wrote, "Our friends, then, are all those who unjustly afflict upon us trials and ordeals, shame and injustice, sorrow and torments, martyrdom and death; we must love them greatly for we will possess eternal life because of what they bring upon us." See the notes for this day in the *Leader's Manual* for the *Hymnal for Catholic Students* (GIA/LTP).

 7 **Twenty-seventh Sunday in Ordinary Time.** See the notes for September 23 for preparing this Sunday. Today's alternative opening prayer is somewhat trite, "your strength is more than the mind can bear."

◆ THE "BOOK OF THE DEAD": Throughout the month of October put out (near the baptismal font, perhaps) the parish's "Book of the Dead" for people to sign the names of the dead to honor in November. Why not keep the paschal candle nearby and light it during the Masses of November beginning on All Saints Day? If you don't have a "Book of the Dead," you can make one by asking someone skilled with a needle and thread to cover a three-ring binder with some handsome fabric, maybe adding a thick dacron padding underneath to give the cover body. Upholstery fabrics in autumnal colors are good, perhaps employing a trim or design from the vestments the parish uses in autumn. Add three-hole punched paper to the binder and keep a pen on a ribbon attached to it. From year to year, let pages be added, keeping the old ones. Invite people to sign the names of all their dead.

◆ OUR LADY OF THE ROSARY: Every Catholic parish has several parishioners who are devoted to praying the rosary. Today is their feast day, of sorts, and they deserve recognition today. When parishioners gather to pray the rosary communally, in the name of the parish, often they do so immediately before or after Mass. How can the parish best support this prayer? Is it possible to occasionally add psalms and Marian songs to the communal rosary?

14 **Twenty-eighth Sunday in Ordinary Time.** See the notes for September 23 for preparing this early autumn Sunday. The wedding feast is open to all—but not everyone is willing or ready to come. Today's scriptures might prompt a reflection on how this community is reaching out to the unchurched or disaffiliated.

◆ AND SPEAKING OF WEDDINGS: The parish may have elaborate procedures to help a couple prepare for their life together, but when is the last time the community's policies concerning worship at weddings was publicized? That's right; the parish itself should put together policies on everything from wedding flowers, selecting the readings, appropriate music, lists of cantors and musicians. The parish should then take this opportunity to discuss the problem of ostentatious overspending or such questionable practices as "giving away" a bride. LTP's resources are many on this subject; now would be a good time to get things in readiness as preparation classes for spring weddings get underway.

21 **Twenty-ninth Sunday in Ordinary Time.** See the notes for September 23 for preparing this autumn Sunday. "The church proclaims the gospel against the prevailing ideologies, i.e., those structures of thought which are self-absolutizing. . . . The church's eschatological preaching is that everything is to be placed underneath the reign of God and that there within the kingdom, genuine humanity can be achieved." (Richard McBrien)

28 **Thirtieth Sunday in Ordinary Time.** See the notes for September 23 for preparing this Sunday.

◆ WE ARE ENTERING INTO THE MONTH OF NOVEMBER with, at least in the northern part of the world, its universal emphasis on death, the dead, the questions about whether the circle will be unbroken. This Sunday's liturgy, preaching and bulletin must be part of a transition into the last phase of Ordinary Time. All Saints is more than a holy day of obligation that must be announced today. It is one of the great festivals of the church and should live in every parish as far more than a day to try to get to Mass. Granted, the holy days are not well observed in most places, even among Catholics who would not think of missing Sunday Mass. That in itself tells us that our approach to the holy days is a failure; attendance will not result from a legalistic approach, and that's about all we've really offered the past few generations. Reinvigorating All Saints

14 SUNDAY
Twenty-eighth Sunday in Ordinary Time (#143)
Isaiah 25:6–10
Philippians 4:12–14, 19–20
Matthew 22:1–14 or 22:1–10

15 MONDAY
Teresa of Jesus (of Avila), virgin and doctor
MEMORIAL (#467)
Galatians 4:22–24, 26–27, 31—5:1
Luke 11:29–32

16 TUESDAY
Weekday (#468)
Hedwig, religious
OPTIONAL MEMORIAL
Margaret Mary Alacoque, virgin
OPTIONAL MEMORIAL
Blessed Marguerite d'Youville
OPTIONAL MEMORIAL (Canada)
Galatians 5:1–6
Luke 11:37–41

17 WEDNESDAY
Ignatius of Antioch, bishop and martyr
MEMORIAL (#469)
Galatians 5:18–25
Luke 11:42–46

18 THURSDAY
Luke, evangelist
FEAST (#661)
2 Timothy 4:9–17
Luke 10:1–9

19 FRIDAY
Isaac Jogues and John de Brébeuf, priests and martyrs, and companions, martyrs
MEMORIAL (#471)
Ephesians 1:11–14
Luke 12:1–7

20 SATURDAY
Weekday (#472)
BVM
OPTIONAL MEMORIAL
Ephesians 1:15–23
Luke 12:8–12

21 SUNDAY
**Twenty-ninth Sunday in
Ordinary Time** (#146)

Isaiah 45:1, 4–6
1 Thessalonians 1:1–5
Matthew 22:15–21

22 MONDAY
Weekday (#473)

Ephesians 2:1–10
Luke 12:13–21

23 TUESDAY
Weekday (#474)

John of Capistrano, priest
OPTIONAL MEMORIAL

Ephesians 2:12 -22
Luke 12:35–38

24 WEDNESDAY
Weekday (#475)

Anthony Claret, bishop
OPTIONAL MEMORIAL

Ephesians 3:2–12
Luke 12:39–48

25 THURSDAY
Weekday (#476)

Ephesians 3:14–21
Luke 12:49–53

26 FRIDAY
Weekday (#477)

Ephesians 4:1–6
Luke 12:54–59

27 SATURDAY
Weekday (#478)

BVM
OPTIONAL MEMORIAL

Ephesians 4:7–16
Luke 13:1–9

28 SUNDAY
**Thirtieth Sunday in
Ordinary Time** (#149)

Exodus 22:20–26
1 Thessalonians 1:5–10
Matthew 22:34–40

Sts. Simon and Jude's Day

Reformation Sunday

Daylight Savings Time ends.

and All Souls begins by putting aside the "obligation" and beginning to speak of the scripture stories and foods and folklore and music—and all the other splendors of these days that are so richly filled with good reasons to get off one's duff and to gather in celebration.

Parishes might take All Saints and All Souls and the month of November for what they are: the way this church grapples with death—all the way from calling out to Sister Death (as St. Francis did) to the way we are summoned to struggle against the ways of death in our world. It means helping people write their wills and decide about cremation or burial or donation to medical science. It means confronting the ways in which death is prolonged by technology and the ways it is covered over by our funeral practices. It means confronting some of the hard ethical questions that government and business and science face about the value of a human life. All of this and more is really part of the work of a parish, people engaging each other in these matters and making sure we come back to it every year, learning little by little how to die.

◆ TODAY IS REFORMATION SUNDAY in many Protestant churches. Greetings are in order to neighboring Christian denominations. Ecumenical prayer this day or this week can make the fitting connection between the circle of the saints in heaven and the constant need for reformation and reconciliation of the church on earth.

31 **Halloween.** Secular culture has turned All Saints Eve into a mess, as if the "theme" for the day was everything that is wicked, rotten and superstitious about humans. Perhaps this is the church's own fault. Here for All Saints and All Souls we have a hundred wonderful customs, folktales and images derived from the best of Christian tradition: trick or treat (door-to-door hospitality), jack o'lanterns (a welcoming lamp to guide us home), apple-bobbing and nut-crack games (a foretaste of the harvest of God's reign). Even the costumes are a holy sign of a kingdom where nothing will be as it seems to be, where our world will be turned upside-down. These are All Saints customs; Halloween is simply the eve we begin the festivities—with storytelling by firelight as at any Christian vigil.

A playful vigiling service for this night, found in *The Book of Occasional Services* (an Episcopalian church book published by the Church Hymnal Corporation), shows what can be done on this eve of "Hallowmas," All Saints Day. Parish schools and religious education programs take note: See the extensive suggestions for Halloween, All Saints and All Souls in the *Leader's Manual* for the *Hymnal for Catholic Students* (GIA/LTP).

NOVEMBER

1 **All Saints Day.** Today is the harvest homecoming of the church. Through the image of autumn's ingathering we celebrate the saints. Read carefully today's preface, one of the loveliest in the sacramentary: "Today we keep the festival of your holy city, the heavenly Jerusalem, our mother. . . ." These words bring to mind the wealth of early American hymnody with their melodies that sound so right at this season of the year: "Jerusalem, my happy home," "There is a happy land," "Jerusalem the golden," "Come away to the skies."

"Come, ye thankful people, come" (the "harvest home" song) is another fine selection; notice how its words are not so much oriented to thanksgiving in the harvest as the consummation of the world. Certainly we can dust off and sing today, tomorrow and on all the Sundays of November our great litany of the saints (another echo of Easter in the November liturgy), either with the more familiar melody or in a contemporary setting. Remember, it is a litany and needs to flow with a good back-and-forth.

◆ ABOUT THE MASS: (See the discussion below on November 4 for a general overview of the liturgy in November.) White/gold vesture or the parish's November vesture, festive entrance (perhaps to the accompaniment of the litany of the saints), incense, candles and fall flowers as well as November's harvest bounty (the full flowering of all of autumn's worship decor), a proper preface that leads into the Roman Canon (Eucharistic Prayer I with its long list of saints). Another option is Eucharistic Prayer II or III with the following insert from France and Germany.

> Lord, you are holy indeed,
> the fountain of all holiness:
> Therefore we come before your presence,
> and, in communion with the whole church,
> we celebrate this day consecrated to the memory of all the saints
> who followed Christ in this life
> and received from him in death the crown of glory.
> Through him who is the origin of faith
> and who brings it to completion, we pray:
> let your Spirit come upon these gifts to make them holy. . . .

◆ HELP THE PARISH KEEP THE DAY, not just an hour of the day. Halloween parties are just the beginning of our celebration; surely the day itself deserves much more merrymaking. The costumes and customs and certainly the decorations of Halloween are in celebration of All Saints: They speak of the reign of God where even ragtag children, warty old crones, mouldering skeletons and rough-and-tumble bums will be raised into glory.

◆ CLIMBING TO HEAVEN: One parish sets up a great wooden ladder, over 20-feet tall, decorating it with cornstalks and autumn flowers, and then sets lighted jack o'lanterns ascending the steps. You might call this a gimmick but the parish has been doing this for All Hallows for at least a dozen years now. The "tradition" seems to have "stuck," perhaps because the image of a ladder is richly scriptural, perhaps because so many people in the parish have to contribute their carved pumpkins. Eventually everyone learned the folk song "As Jacob with travel was weary one day" (*Worship II*, GIA) with its refrain: "Alleluia to Jesus who died on the tree and has raised up a ladder of mercy for me!"

2 **All Souls Day.** The customs associated with the day reveal the fullness of Christian attitudes towards death. At one extreme, death is the enemy conquered by Christ. At the other, death is a sister and a brother to us all, leading us into the heavenly reign.

29 MONDAY
Weekday (#479)
Ephesians 4:32—5:8
Luke 13:10–17

30 TUESDAY
Weekday (#480)
Ephesians 5:21–33
Luke 13:18–21

31 WEDNESDAY
Weekday (#481)
Ephesians 6:1–9
Luke 13:22–30
Hallowe'en

November 1990
1 THURSDAY
All Saints Day
SOLEMNITY (#667)
Revelation 7:2–4, 9–14
1 John 3:1–3
Matthew 5:1–12
Hallowmas

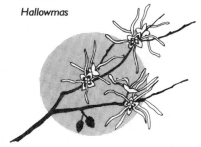
Witch hazel

2 FRIDAY
All Souls Day (#668)
Readings taken from Masses for the Dead, numbers 789–793

3 SATURDAY
Weekday (#484)

Martin de Porres, religious
OPTIONAL MEMORIAL

BVM
OPTIONAL MEMORIAL

Philippians 1:18–26
Luke 14:1, 7–11

4 SUNDAY
Thirty-first Sunday in Ordinary Time (#152)

Malachi 1:14—2:2, 8–10
1 Thessalonians 2:7–9, 13
Matthew 23:1–12

The rich Mexican traditions of *El Día de los Muertos* include graveside picnics, sweet candy skulls, scathing satire showing politicians and movie idols as the playmates of Death itself. There is hardly a culture without equally profound (or outright enjoyable) customs for celebrating the dead. The parish has a responsibility in keeping such ethnic traditions alive and well and in bringing to the American consciousness a Christian response to death—a death being sung by the very month of November, in the falling leaves and lengthening nights, in frost-ruined gardens and the music of the migrating birds.

◆ ABOUT THE MASS: White, black or violet vestments can be worn, or better still, the parish's November vesture. The paschal candle should be prominent, with the Book of the Dead in front of it. Although any readings from the section "Masses for the Dead" may be used, Daniel 12:1–3; the "November" Psalm 122; Revelation 21:1–5, 6–7; and Luke 12: 35–40 are particularly appropriate. Prefaces for Christian Death IV or V with Eucharistic Prayer III (and its beautiful extended intercession for the departed) are appropriate. Use the Solemn Blessing for Masses for the Dead. The Sanctus and the Agnus Dei can be used from the old funeral chants (Chant Mass XVIII).

◆ IF THE CEMETERY IS NEARBY, consider a procession with the singing of appropriate psalms, concluding in the cemetery with intercessions from the office of the dead and the sprinkling/incensing of the graves, then the solemn blessing and dismissal. Even if the cemetery is some distance, go to great pains to celebrate this day in a graveyard, near the holy earth that is our common tomb.

◆ AGAIN, IT'S IMPORTANT TO KEEP THE WHOLE DAY HOLY: How will you help the parish gather to keep this day? Are both All Saints and All Souls kept free from religious education and other parish organizations' meetings? Are the families who have celebrated a funeral in the church within the past year given a special invitation to today's liturgy? This means more than a general announcement at the end of a Sunday Mass or an article in the bulletin. A number of the people concerned might not be from the parish or might not even be regular church-goers. A mailed invitation to the immediate families of all who have had a funeral service within the church the past year or so would show ongoing concern for the bereaved and comfort many who may feel very alone in their grief. If the parish has a ministry for those who wish to work with the bereaved, this would be part of their service. The mailing list for each All Souls Day would be built up as names are entered after each funeral.

4 Thirty-first Sunday in Ordinary Time. Today's alternative opening prayer is rather dense. We begin reading from First Thessalonians, one of the epistles that gives these weeks their advental character.

◆ FOR THE REMAINING SUNDAYS OF ORDINARY TIME, special attention should go to some small changes in the order of the Sunday liturgy. These will not make November into a season in itself, but will allow for the changing tone of the liturgy as we approach the end of the cycle of readings and the coming of Advent. See the suggestions for November music in "The Seasons" beginning on page 125. See also the previous few and the next few pages of this Calendar for ideas for the entire month of November. Here are some other possibilities:

Introductory rites. You might echo Eastertime, as the month of November so often does, by using the Rite of Blessing and Sprinkling Holy Water in place of the penitential rite if this was done in Eastertime; Form B is good. In this time of growing darkness and cold, it is appropriate that texts make reference to many of the images that are part of the church's Night Prayer: protection from evil, refuge in the Lord, longing for the reign of God. Form C5 of the penitential rite is also fitting.

Psalm. The lectionary (#175, under "Season of the Year") has only one seasonal responsorial psalm and it is a good one: Psalm 122 with the refrain, "Let us go rejoicing to the house of the Lord." Find and learn and keep from year to year a good setting of this psalm. Psalm 126, "When the Lord delivered Zion from bondage," is also an important and beautiful psalm for this time of year.

Gospel acclamation. The melody could change to something special these last weeks—or it could repeat the Eastertime Alleluia. See #164 in the lectionary for the verse for these last weeks (these are numbers 14 through 16, but pick one and stick with it).

Preface and eucharistic prayer. Preface VI for Ordinary Time celebrates the Spirit's gift as "foretaste and promise of the paschal feast of heaven." The memorial acclamation would be one place where words and a melody appropriate to the Advent season could be used now and kept through Advent (but not used at other times). A setting of "Dying you destroyed our death . . ." would be most in keeping with the liturgies of the next two months.

Blessing and dismissal. This text from 1 Thessalonians would be good from now through Christ the King: "The God of peace make you perfect in holiness, keep you whole and entire, spirit, soul and body, free from fault at the coming of our Lord Jesus Christ. . . ."

Visuals. The "summer" green should be gone now, and a deeper, richer green with brown or orange accents might replace it. Flowers and candles placed near the statue of the Virgin and near other mosaics or statues or windows (if any of these are representations of our saints) could signal not only All Saints Day, but the whole of November. The Book of the Dead (mentioned with the notes on the first Sunday in October) will also be part of the environment. It should not contribute to clutter but should have its very approachable space; flowers and the lit paschal candle nearby would be fitting.

As discussed before, Thanksgiving is not the only day this month that pumpkins and cornstalks and other harvest bounty can be used in decoration. These are a common denominator in all the days of November. It might not at first be apparent what the connection is between a bunch of Indian corn and All Saints or Christ the King. However, the relationship becomes much more evident when we do not fixate on a single word, such as "saint" or "king." We must open our imaginations to the life and death activity of harvest and all it represents for those who live off the land—and that includes ourselves.

9 **The Dedication of Saint John Lateran,** the feast of the dedication of the cathedral church of the bishop of Rome. This is a feast of the Lord, as all feasts of dedication are. It is very much a part of November, and any of the songs for All Saints Day fit well today. Choose texts from the common of dedications which emphasize the eschatological nature of this time of year. For presidential prayers, Section 2 (anniversary), Texts B (outside the dedicated church) are

5 MONDAY
Weekday (#485)
Philippians 2:1–4
Luke 14:12–14

6 TUESDAY
Weekday (#486)
Philippians 2:5–11
Luke 14:15–24
Election Day (U.S.A.)

7 WEDNESDAY
Weekday (#487)
Philippians 2:12–18
Luke 14:25–33

8 THURSDAY
Weekday (#488)
Philippians 3:3–8
Luke 15:1–10

9 FRIDAY
Dedication of St. John Lateran, Cathedral of Rome
FEAST (#671)
Readings taken from the Common of the Dedication of a Church, numbers 701–706

10 SATURDAY
Leo the Great, pope and doctor
MEMORIAL (#490)
Philippians 4:10–19
Luke 16:9–15

11 SUNDAY
Thirty-second Sunday in Ordinary Time (#155)
Wisdom 6:12–16
I Thessalonians 4:13–18
  or 4:13–14
Matthew 25:1–13
Martinmas
Veterans Day (U.S.A.)
Remembrance Day (Canada)

12 MONDAY
Josaphat, bishop and martyr
MEMORIAL (#491)

Titus 1:1–9
Luke 17:1–6

13 TUESDAY
Frances Xavier Cabrini, virgin
MEMORIAL (#492)

Titus 2:1–8, 11–14
Luke 17:7–10

14 WEDNESDAY
Weekday (#493)

Titus 3:1–7
Luke 17:11–19

15 THURSDAY
Weekday (#494)

Albert the Great,
 bishop and doctor
OPTIONAL MEMORIAL

Philemon 7–20
Luke 17:20–25

16 FRIDAY
Weekday (#495)

Margaret of Scotland
OPTIONAL MEMORIAL

Gertrude, virgin
OPTIONAL MEMORIAL

2 John 4–9
Luke 17:26–37

17 SATURDAY
Elizabeth of Hungary, religious
MEMORIAL (#496)

3 John 5–8
Luke 18:1–8

18 SUNDAY
**Thirty-third Sunday in
 Ordinary Time** (#158)

Proverbs 31:10–13, 19–20, 30–31
1 Thessalonians 5:1–6
Matthew 25:14–30
 or 25:14–15, 19–20

used. Do we know the feast of dedication of our community's place of worship? How is it celebrated? See page 127 for suggestions.

11 Thirty-second Sunday in Ordinary Time. See the notes on November 4 for an overview of some of the possibilities for this November Sunday.

> Vigil, night, door—these are paschal themes, connected with liberation and entry into the kingdom. In today's parable the door is closed against the virgins who did not trim their lamps properly. Their cries are useless; the hour for the feast has come, and they are excluded. The moral admits of no exceptions: "Watch, therefore, for you know neither the day nor the hour."
>
> During vigils, and especially during the Paschal Vigil, the church thinks unceasingly of Christ, her spouse, who will come to lead her into his kingdom. The chief concern of the church, therefore, is that the faithful should keep their lamps lit and never be caught by surprise at Christ's coming to them. The chief concern of the faithful should be to seek the wisdom and light of Christ and to keep ever alight the lamp they received at baptism so that with Christ they may enter the banquet hall of the kingdom. (Adrian Nocent, *The Liturgical Year*)

◆ ADVENT IS FAST APPROACHING: This week's texts, together with next week's summons to persevering work for the coming of the kingdom, should provide homilists with ample material for kindling the enthusiasm of the community for the Advent season that lies just ahead. November is the time for some of the Advent music to begin to be heard—perhaps before liturgy as a prelude or after communion. Special prayer gatherings (Evening Prayer, the Lord's Day vigil) that are especially "Advent" in spirit should receive their publicity now, well before the season is upon us. Commercially, the Christmas shopping crunch is already in full gear. Give Advent the same kind of running start! Any parish-wide discussion of how to keep Advent as Advent—instead of jumping the gun on Christmas—needs to take place now; it's way too late if you wait until after Thanksgiving, at which time the advertisers will expect every household in America to have its Christmas tree in place.

◆ MARTIN OF TOURS, BISHOP, 316–397. It's more than a coincidence that today is also Veterans Day in the United States, or in Canada and much of Europe a remembrance day for those killed in war. Saint Martin left military service because of his commitment to Christ. He is praised (together with Saints Justin and Cyprian) in the United States bishops' pastoral letter on peace for his nonviolent witness. The letter quotes Martin's decision to leave the military for Christianity: "Hitherto I have served you as a soldier. Allow me now to become a soldier of God. . . . I am a soldier of Christ. It is not lawful for me to fight."

18 Thirty-third Sunday in Ordinary Time. See the notes on November 4 for an overview of some of the possibilities for this November Sunday.

Matthew gives this Sunday its keynote: The "last days" are upon all who dwell in this time between the Lord's first coming and his glorious return. A lot is at stake—our share in the master's joy depends on our persevering work with the gifts he has seen fit to entrust to each of us.

"From the beginning of time," says the alternative opening prayer, "you promised [humanity] salvation through the future coming of your Son, our Lord Jesus

Christ." This Sunday and next should blend gracefully into the beginning of Advent as testimony that his "worthy wife" even now considers her Lord to be close at hand. With unmistakable clarity the call should be sounded this weekend: "Take time out for Advent!" The "Book of the Dead," and all the symbols and signs of the end that is also the beginning should remain in place through next week's celebration of the reign of Christ.

19–21 The days before Thanksgiving.

In recent years the civic holiday of Thanksgiving has been marked by an increased recognition that somehow this bounty must remind us of all those to whom this day is a stinging reminder of their own poverty, nakedness and hunger—or the dispossession of their ancient lands. The parish could set aside one or all three of the weekdays preceding Thanksgiving as parish "ember days" with a focus on the world's hunger, the care of its lands, and our great responsibilities. A quote from St. Leo says what is needed: "Our fast must be turned into a banquet for the poor." That is indeed what would motivate our fasting during these days.

22 Thanksgiving Day (U.S.A.).

More and more communities are sensing that this day (or its eve) is *the* premier time for an interfaith service. Allow the assembly to sing its heart out, *not* with patriotic songs but with all the splendid American hymn tunes that seem so right to November and to this day: "All people that on earth do dwell," "My shepherd will supply my need," "How firm a foundation," or any of the wonderful spirituals. What today could use is probably akin to a rousing Presbyterian hymn-sing. (See November 1 for other hymn suggestions for this day.) LTP has published *Thank God: Prayers for Jews and Christians Together* that is a treasury of interfaith texts for Thanksgiving Day and for other occasions of worship that bring Jews and Christians together. If you have eucharist today, see the special votive Mass in the middle of the sacramentary under the Proper of the Saints. Try the Preface for Weekdays in Ordinary Time IV, "our desire to thank you is itself your gift," or the Preface for Sundays in Ordinary Time V, "you made [us] the steward of creation" ("man" and "him" can be "us"), and *not* the preface designated "Thanksgiving Day," a mixed-up version of messianic nationalism. Readings can be any from the lectionary, #881–885, or the readings for the votive Mass for Thanksgiving Day in the Appendix. Particularly appropriate for this harvest festival are Deuteronomy 8:7–18, Psalm 67, Colossians 3:12–17 and Luke 12:15–21, the story of the rich fool. These fit well with the points made by the bishops in their pastoral on economic justice. Christian liturgy has never been solely congratulations on a job well done, but a call to conversion and a celebration of God's bounty.

◆ TODAY IS ALSO SAINT CECILIA'S DAY, the virgin martyr who is patron of music and musicians. Cecilia, Lucy, Holy Mary, Agnes and Agatha are the "five wise virgins" (see Matthew 25:1–13) who surround the Christmastime coming of the Bridegroom.

 # 25 Christ the King.

See the notes on November 4 for an overview of some of the possibilities for this Sunday.

The notes in the *Saint Andrew Bible Missal* are too beautiful not to repeat in trying to capture the feeling of this last Sunday of November:

> Today's gospel draws our attention to the relationship between the endtime and our life. Christ the King will preside over the judgment, whose outcome will be

---

19 MONDAY
Weekday (#497)
Revelation 1:1–4; 2:1–5
Luke 18:35–43

20 TUESDAY
Weekday (#498)
Revelation 3:1–6, 14–22
Luke 19:1–10

21 WEDNESDAY
Presentation of Mary
MEMORIAL (#499)
Revelation 4:1–11
Luke 19:11–28

22 THURSDAY
Cecilia, virgin and martyr
MEMORIAL (#500)
Revelation 5:1–10
Luke 19:41–44

Thanksgiving Day (U.S.A.)
(special proper Mass:)
Sirach 50:22–24
I Corinthians 1:3–9
Luke 17:11–19 *or any readings*
from Appendix

23 FRIDAY
Weekday (#501)
Clement I, pope and martyr
OPTIONAL MEMORIAL
Columban, abbot
OPTIONAL MEMORIAL
Revelation 10:8–11
Luke 19:45–48

24 SATURDAY
Weekday (#502)
BVM
OPTIONAL MEMORIAL
Revelation 11:4–12
Luke 20:27–40

25 SUNDAY
Last Sunday in Ordinary Time
Christ the King
SOLEMNITY
Ezekiel 34:11–12, 15–17
I Corinthians 15:20–26, 28
Matthew 25:31–46

26 MONDAY
Weekday (#503)

Revelation 14:1–3, 4–5
Luke 21:1–4

27 TUESDAY
Weekday (#504)

Revelation 14:14–19
Luke 21:5–11

28 WEDNESDAY
Weekday (#505)

Revelation 15:1–4
Luke 21:12–19

29 THURSDAY
Weekday (#506)

Revelation 18:1–2, 21–23;
    19:1–3, 9
Luke 21:20–28

*Dorothy Day died this day
   in 1980.*

30 FRIDAY
Andrew, apostle
FEAST (#684)

Romans 10:9–18
Matthew 4:18–22

December 1990

1 SATURDAY
Weekday (#508)

BVM
OPTIONAL MEMORIAL

Revelation 22:1–7
Luke 21:34–36

Advent Eve

determined by our care for one another. We should not dream about heaven as an escape from present responsibility.

We already live in the presence of the Son of Man. His special dwelling is among the needy. Our attention to him there opens us to his full revelation as the ruler and judge of the endtime.

This leads us to a more authentic understanding of Christ as king. To proclaim him king is not to demand a state religion. Jesus will claim his full title as king only at the hour of his coming in glory. But he lives now no less as king in a hidden way in the poor and the little ones. He is the defender of their rights and their appointed protector. In serving the poor, we serve him.

◆ EVEN MORE IMPORTANT THAN THE FACT THAT IT IS "CHRIST THE KING," today is the "Last Sunday in Ordinary Time," the last Sunday in November (the reading from Matthew is simply a continuation, and conclusion, of the course of readings from this gospel). Today's solemnity echoes Ascension Day, Epiphany, Palm Sunday—any of the truly ancient celebrations of Christ's royal rule. However, the "newfangled" solemnity today does fit in with the rest of the month and affords a loud heralding of Advent. Maintain the November look in vesture and environment. Also continue a November-long commitment to local food banks and clothing drives—it's time for the Catholic overseas collection of clothing and financial gifts for the Campaign for Human Development. Volunteer requests for help with the homeless and the battered and troubled teens should be given due prominence this month.

The preface of Christ the King is beautiful and needs to be proclaimed or sung with great reverence and feeling. It could lead into Eucharistic Prayer I with its majestic images of Christ the priest interceding for the community before God. The solemn blessing that has been used for these late Ordinary Time Sundays ought to be sung once more today, and perhaps the lectionary (suitably decorated with a symbol of Matthew) could be carried out with some solemnity, since a new lectionary cycle begins next week. Evening Prayer might conclude the day's observance. It would not be inappropriate after such an evening service for those on the planning and presiding "team" to gather for a moment of thanksgiving and (well-earned) celebration of their own.

> Christ yesterday and today,
> the beginning and the end,
> Alpha and Omega!
>
> All time belongs to Christ
> and all ages.
>
> To Christ be glory and power
> through every age for ever.
>
> Amen.